Science and Engineering in Preschool Through Elementary Grades

THE BRILLIANCE OF CHILDREN AND THE STRENGTHS OF EDUCATORS

Committee on Enhancing Science and Engineering in Prekindergarten Through Fifth Grades

Board on Science Education

Division of Behavioral and Social Sciences and Education

A Consensus Study Report of

The National Academies of
SCIENCES · ENGINEERING · MEDICINE

THE NATIONAL ACADEMIES PRESS
Washington, DC
www.nap.edu

THE NATIONAL ACADEMIES PRESS   500 Fifth Street, NW   Washington, DC 20001

This activity was supported by contracts between the National Academy of Sciences and Carnegie Corporation of New York (G-19-57002) and Robin Hood Learning + Technology Fund (a1n5A0000025i9MQAQ). Any opinions, findings, conclusions, or recommendations expressed in this publication do not necessarily reflect the views of any organization or agency that provided support for the project.

International Standard Book Number-13: 978-0-309-68417-0
International Standard Book Number-10: 0-309-68417-X
Digital Object Identifier: https://doi.org/10.17226/26215
Library of Congress Control Number: 2022932768

Additional copies of this publication are available from the National Academies Press, 500 Fifth Street, NW, Keck 360, Washington, DC 20001; (800) 624-6242 or (202) 334-3313; http://www.nap.edu.

Copyright 2022 by the National Academy of Sciences. All rights reserved.

Printed in the United States of America

Suggested citation: National Academies of Sciences, Engineering, and Medicine. (2022). *Science and Engineering in Preschool Through Elementary Grades: The Brilliance of Children and the Strengths of Educators*. Washington, DC: The National Academies Press. https://doi.org/10.17226/26215.

The National Academies of
SCIENCES • ENGINEERING • MEDICINE

The **National Academy of Sciences** was established in 1863 by an Act of Congress, signed by President Lincoln, as a private, nongovernmental institution to advise the nation on issues related to science and technology. Members are elected by their peers for outstanding contributions to research. Dr. Marcia McNutt is president.

The **National Academy of Engineering** was established in 1964 under the charter of the National Academy of Sciences to bring the practices of engineering to advising the nation. Members are elected by their peers for extraordinary contributions to engineering. Dr. John L. Anderson is president.

The **National Academy of Medicine** (formerly the Institute of Medicine) was established in 1970 under the charter of the National Academy of Sciences to advise the nation on medical and health issues. Members are elected by their peers for distinguished contributions to medicine and health. Dr. Victor J. Dzau is president.

The three Academies work together as the **National Academies of Sciences, Engineering, and Medicine** to provide independent, objective analysis and advice to the nation and conduct other activities to solve complex problems and inform public policy decisions. The National Academies also encourage education and research, recognize outstanding contributions to knowledge, and increase public understanding in matters of science, engineering, and medicine.

Learn more about the National Academies of Sciences, Engineering, and Medicine at **www.nationalacademies.org**.

The National Academies of SCIENCES · ENGINEERING · MEDICINE

Consensus Study Reports published by the National Academies of Sciences, Engineering, and Medicine document the evidence-based consensus on the study's statement of task by an authoring committee of experts. Reports typically include findings, conclusions, and recommendations based on information gathered by the committee and the committee's deliberations. Each report has been subjected to a rigorous and independent peer-review process and it represents the position of the National Academies on the statement of task.

Proceedings published by the National Academies of Sciences, Engineering, and Medicine chronicle the presentations and discussions at a workshop, symposium, or other event convened by the National Academies. The statements and opinions contained in proceedings are those of the participants and are not endorsed by other participants, the planning committee, or the National Academies.

For information about other products and activities of the National Academies, please visit www.nationalacademies.org/about/whatwedo.

COMMITTEE ON ENHANCING SCIENCE AND ENGINEERING IN PREKINDERGARTEN THROUGH FIFTH GRADES

Elizabeth A. Davis (*Chair*), University of Michigan
Heidi Carlone, Vanderbilt University
Jeanane Charara, SOLID Start, Michigan State University
Douglas Clements, University of Denver
Katie Mcmillan Culp, New York Hall of Science, New York, NY
Ximena Domînguez, Digital Promise, Washington, DC
Daryl Greenfield, University of Miami
Megan Hopkins, University of California, San Diego
Eve Manz, Boston University
Tiffany Neill, Oklahoma State Board of Education
K. Renae Pullen, Caddo Parish Public Schools, Shreveport, LA
William Sandoval, University of California, Los Angeles
Enrique Suárez, University of Massachusetts, Amherst
Carrie Tzou, University of Washington
Peter Winzer (NAE), Nubis Communications, Holmdel, NJ
Carla Zembal-Saul, Pennsylvania State University

Amy Stephens, *Study Director,* Board on Science Education
Tiffany Taylor, *Program Officer,* Board on Science Education
Margaret Kelly, *Senior Program Assistant,* Board on Science Education
Heidi Schweingruber, *Director,* Board on Science Education

BOARD ON SCIENCE EDUCATION

Susan Rundell Singer (*Chair*), Vice President for Academic Affairs, Provost, Rollins College
Sue Allen, Senior Research Scientist, Maine Mathematics and Science Alliance
Megan Bang, Learning Sciences, Northwestern University, Senior Vice President, Spencer Foundation
Vicki L. Chandler, Dean of Faculty, Minerva Schools at Keck Graduate Institute
Sunita V. Cooke, Superintendent/President, MiraCosta College
Maya Garcia, Science Content Specialist, Colorado Department of Education
Rush Holt, former Chief Executive Officer, American Association for the Advancement of Science
Tonya Matthews, Chief Executive Officer, International African American Museum, Charleston, SC
William Penuel, School of Education, University of Colorado Boulder
Stephen L. Pruitt, President, Southern Regional Education Board
K. Renae Pullen, K-5 Science Curriculum-Instructional Specialist, Caddo Parish Schools, LA
K. Ann Renninger, Social Theory and Social Action, Swarthmore College
Marcy H. Towns, Department of Chemistry, Purdue University
Darryl N. Williams, Senior Vice President, Science and Education, The Franklin Institute

Heidi Schweingruber, *Director*

Preface

Every child deserves to experience the wonder of science and the satisfaction of engineering. Children, even at very young ages, are deeply curious about the world around them and eager to investigate the many questions they have about their environment. Engaging them in learning science and engineering takes advantage of this interest and helps them to answer their own authentic questions and solve real-world problems that are important to them. Doing so helps children develop into people who can be informed decision makers about issues that will matter to them as adults—issues related to their health or the environment, for example, and that deeply affect them and their communities.

From the start, this committee was dedicated to two key principles: first, the importance of recognizing and building on the assets of children, families, communities, and educators, and second, the imperative of working toward equity and justice in society through science and engineering in the early years.

Even very young children—from infancy, and certainly from around age 3, when this report's scope begins—can make sense of their world in sophisticated ways. From preschool through fifth grade, the older end of the report's scope, children are connecting ideas, building concepts, and engaging in meaningful science and engineering practices. Their proficiencies, as this report shows, are amazing. Such proficiencies are nurtured when educators design opportunities to learn that meet children's needs; when educators engage responsively with children's ideas and interests; and when they can hear children's ideas and see their successes. This report aims to support educators in this work by reviewing and elaborating on what the literature says about how to support children's engagement and growth.

Yet, at the same time as we are recognizing children's strengths, we must also recognize our country's struggles. Although a group of academics and educators who support and study how young children make sense of and engage in science and engineering is unlikely to end systemic injustice, such a group *can* use their expertise to try to work toward justice, locally and societally. This report takes seriously the charge of considering who the children are who have been historically marginalized from engaging in science and engineering—through assumptions about their cultural backgrounds, their prior knowledge or experiences, their linguistic resources, their gender, or any other dimension of potential oppression—and exploring what the literature says about how these children *can and do* engage in meaningful science and engineering, when supported. This report, then, also aims to help educators recognize and foster the brilliance of every child.

The educational system is often set up to work against children developing and demonstrating proficiencies in science and engineering. Teachers may feel underprepared for the work of teaching these subject areas. They may lack curriculum materials or other resources to support them in doing so. School leaders may not know what to look for in children's science and engineering and may not recognize the value of the seeming chaos that can precede children's insights. Community organizations may lack connections to schools, leading to further incoherence in the system. Children themselves may start to lose enthusiasm for sensemaking about the natural and designed worlds if they are not supported. All of this can be discouraging. Yet, all of it is rectifiable, and this report shows many examples of ways in which the system and its elements *are* functioning. This report aims to give guidance for improving each element of the system to help enhance the teaching and learning of science and engineering with children.

The committee did remarkable work in preparing this report. The committee's first introductory call took place on March 27, 2020—2 weeks after schools across the country closed their doors due to the COVID-19 pandemic. Every meeting of the committee was conducted virtually, via Zoom. The committee developed ways of collaborating and communicating across time zones and distance as well as across expertise and academic emphasis. We laughed that we had all of the work of serving on a committee like this without any of the perks of being together in community. Furthermore, across the families of the committee and the National Academies staff, there are roughly 20 kids in school or college. Those with young children were navigating supporting them in virtual school and scrambling for childcare, and those with older kids were nervously moving them into college dorm rooms and hoping they would be able to stay for a whole semester and would stay healthy. Unexpected new duties and suboptimal working conditions brought on by the pandemic further exacerbated the challenges. There were COVID scares and worse. Yet, the committee members and staff, to a one, dove in wholeheartedly to this work. I feel enormous gratitude to these individuals for the work they have done in helping to enhance science and engineering for children. I would be remiss if I did not also express my gratitude to these folks' families writ large (including partners and kids but also parents, in-laws, siblings, friends, and other support systems) for the material and emotional support that they provided during the extraordinary year of this committee's work.

This report, we hope, will support the next generation of young learners in being able to experience the wonder of science and the satisfaction of engineering and, in so doing, will work toward justice.

Elizabeth A. Davis, *Chair*

Acknowledgments

This report would not have been possible without the many individuals who provided their expertise, including those who served on the committee as well as those who participated in discussions with the committee. We recognize their invaluable contributions to our work. The first thanks are to the committee members, for their passion, deep knowledge, and contributions to the study.

This report was made possible by the important contributions of the Carnegie Corporation of New York and the Robin Hood Learning + Technology Fund; in particular Jim Short (program director, Learning and Teaching to Advance Learning) at the Carnegie Corporation of New York, Steven Azeka (program officer, Computational Thinking), and Amber Oliver (managing director) at the Robin Hood Learning + Technology Fund.

Members of the committee benefited from discussion and presentation by many individuals who participated in our fact-finding meetings.

- At the first meeting, we had the opportunity to talk with our study sponsors, Jim Short (Carnegie Corporation of New York) and Steven Azeka (Robin Hood Learning + Technology Fund), to get further clarity on the statement of task. The committee also explored the following topics:

    o **Elementary Science Education: A Look at the Numbers.** P. Sean Smith (Horizon Research Inc.) provided an overview of the state of elementary science education.

- Revisiting the Report *Science and Engineering for Grades 6-12: Investigation and Design at the Center.* The committee engaged in conversations with committee members Brett Moulding (Utah Partnership for Effective Science Teaching and Learning), Nancy Songer (University of Utah), Erin Furtak (University of Colorado Boulder), and study director Kerry Brenner (National Academies of Sciences, Engineering, and Medicine) about the report findings and recommendations and implications for prekindergarten and elementary school.
  - **Computational Thinking in Prekindergarten Through Fifth Grades: Defining Computational Thinking, State of the Evidence, and Promising Practices.** Presenters included Karen Brennan (Harvard Graduate School of Education), Maya Israel (University of Florida), Hilah Barbot (formerly at KIPP Foundation), and Aankit Patel (City University of New York).
- At the second meeting, the committee held a public comment and discussion with committee session to hear input from the elementary science and engineering education community and to answer questions. The committee also held three panel discussions and the following topics were explored:
  - **Equity, Justice, and Antiracism in Elementary Science and Engineering.** Panel members included Felicia Moore Mensah (Teachers College, Columbia University), Christopher Wright (Drexel University), and Ananda Marin (University of California, Los Angeles).
  - **Integrating Science and Literacy in Elementary Education.** Panel members included Nell K. Duke (University of Michigan), Amelia Gotwals (Michigan State University), Okhee Lee (NYU Steinhardt), and Tanya S. Wright (Michigan State University).
  - **Moderated Discussion of District Policies and Leadership in Elementary Schools.** Participants included Vanessa Lujan (University of California, Berkeley, Lawrence Hall of Science), Donald J. Peurach (University of Michigan), and Andrea Kane (Queen Anne's County Public Schools, Maryland).
- As part of the third meeting, the committee heard from three panels across the 2 days:
  - **Panel 1: Examining Science and Engineering in Preschools.** Panelists included Andres Bustamante (University of California, Irvine), Alissa Lange (East Tennessee State University),

Jessica Whittaker (University of Virginia), and Karen Worth (Education Development Center, Inc.).
- Panel 2: Integrating Science with other Content Areas. Panelists included Monica E. Cardella (Purdue University) discussing links to engineering education; Miranda Fitzgerald (University of North Carolina at Charlotte) discussing integration of literacy, science, and engineering; Diane Jass Ketelhut and Lautaro Cabrera (University of Maryland, College Park) describing computational thinking; and Anne Leftwich (Indiana University Bloomington) and Tamara Moore (Purdue University) discussing integration of computational thinking and computer science.
- Panel 3: Moderated Discussion with Science Specialists. Participants included Renee Belisle (Denver Public Schools), Amanda Buice (Georgia Department of Education), Amy L. Reese (Howard County Public School System, Maryland), and Claudia Walker (Murphey Traditional Academy, Greensboro, North Carolina).

The committee is very grateful for additional discussions with experts on antiracist pedagogies, including Angela Calabrese Barton (University of Michigan), Natalie Davis (Georgia State University), Tia Madkins (University of Texas at Austin), Daniel Morales-Doyle (University of Illinois Chicago), and Sepehr Vakil (Northwestern University). In addition, the committee is grateful to Jennifer Frey (Cincinnati Children's Hospital Medical Center, University of Cincinnati College of Medicine), who consulted with us on issues of learning differences and learning disabilities.

This Consensus Study Report has been reviewed in draft form by individuals chosen for their diverse perspectives and technical expertise. The purpose of this independent review is to provide candid and critical comments that will assist the National Academies of Sciences, Engineering, and Medicine in making its published report as sound as possible and to ensure that it meets the institutional standards for quality, objectivity, evidence, and responsiveness to the study charge. The review comments and draft manuscript remain confidential to protect the integrity of the deliberative process.

We thank the following individuals for their review of this report: Andres S. Bustamante, School of Education, University of California Irvine; Pauline W.U. Chinn, Curriculum Studies, College of Education, University of Hawai'i at Mānoa; Maya M. Garcia, Office of Standards and Instructional Support, Colorado Department of Education; Amelia Wenk Gotwals, Department of Teacher Education, Michigan State University; Jacqueline Jones, Office of President and CEO, Foundation for Child Development; Okhee Lee, Department of Teaching and Learning, Steinhardt School of Culture, Education, and Human Development, New York University; Ananda M. Marin, Graduate School of Education and Information Studies, University of California, Los Angeles; Felicia Moore Mensah, Science Education, Teachers College, Columbia University; Helen R. Quinn, Particle Physics and Astrophysics, SLAC National Accelerator Laboratory; Brian J. Reiser, Learning Sciences, Northwestern University; Maria Varelas, Science Education, Department of Curriculum and Instruction, University of Illinois Chicago; Mark Windschitl, Science Education, University of Washington; and Christopher G. Wright, Department of Teaching, Learning, and Curriculum, Drexel University.

Although the reviewers listed above provided many constructive comments and suggestions, they were not asked to endorse the conclusions or recommendations of this report nor did they see the final draft of the report before its release. The review of this report was overseen by Melanie M. Cooper, Department of Chemistry, Michigan State University, and Greg J. Duncan, School of Education, University of California, Irvine. They were responsible for making certain that an independent examination of this report was carried out in accordance with the standards of the National Academies and that all review comments were carefully considered. Responsibility for the final content rests entirely with the authoring committee and the National Academies.

Thanks are also due to the project staff. Amy Stephens, senior program officer for the Board on Science Education (BOSE), directed the study and played a key role in the development of the report and ushering it through review. Tiffany Taylor, program officer for BOSE, provided critical assistance throughout the project. Margaret Kelly, senior program assistant with BOSE, managed the study's logistical and administrative needs. Heidi Schweingruber, director of BOSE, provided thoughtful advice and many helpful suggestions throughout the entire study.

Staff of the Division of Behavioral and Social Sciences and Education also provided help: Laura Yoder substantially improved the readability of the report; Kirsten Sampson Snyder expertly guided the report through the report review process; and Yvonne Wise masterfully guided the report through production. The committee also wishes to express their sincere appreciation to Rebecca Morgan in the National Academies Research Center for her assistance with helping to identify potential committee members and conducting literature searches.

Contents

SUMMARY   1

1   INTRODUCTION   11
    About This Report, 12
    Working Toward Equity and Justice, 20
    Report Organization, 29

2   PRESCHOOL AND ELEMENTARY SYSTEMS
    AND STRUCTURES   31
    Components of the U.S. K–12 Education System, 32
    How Federal and State Policies Influence Instructional Time,
        Testing, and (In)Equities in Science and Engineering
        Education, 40
    Systems Within Historical Contexts, 49
    Policy and System Implications for Working Toward Equity, 50
    Summary, 51

3   THE CONTEXTUAL NATURE OF CHILDREN'S LEARNING   53
    Learning Is a Cultural Process, 55
    Learning Science and Engineering Is a Process of
        Identity Formation, 61
    Science and Engineering Learning Occurs Across Contexts, 63
    Learning Is Not Neutral, 68
    Equity and Learning Across Contexts, 69
    Summary, 70

4 DEVELOPING CHILDREN'S PROFICIENCY IN AND
 THROUGH INVESTIGATION AND DESIGN 73
 Instruction Centered on Investigation and Design in Preschool
   Through Elementary School, 75
 Features of Investigation and Design, 76
 Developing Conceptual Understanding Through Investigation
   and Design, 78
 Developing Proficiency in Investigation and Design, 83
 Considering Children's Proficiencies and Working
   Toward Equity, 95
 Summary, 96

5 LEARNING ENVIRONMENTS AND INSTRUCTIONAL
 PRACTICES THAT CENTER CHILDREN, INVESTIGATION,
 AND DESIGN 99
 Moving Beyond Dichotomies, 100
 Key Features of the Learning Environment, 101
 Equity and the Design of Learning Environments, 126
 Summary, 127

6 THE POTENTIALS AND PITFALLS OF INTEGRATING
 ACROSS DOMAINS 129
 Approaches to Content Integration, 131
 Approaches to Integrating with Specific Domains, 134
 Working Toward Equity and Integrating Across Domains, 154
 Summary, 155

7 THE ROLE OF CURRICULUM MATERIALS AND
 INSTRUCTIONAL RESOURCES 157
 Preschool Curriculum and Instructional Resources, 162
 Elementary Grades Curriculum and Standards Efforts, 164
 Teachers' Use of and Learning with Curriculum Materials, 172
 Working Toward Equity with Curriculum Materials, 178
 Summary, 180

8 SUPPORTING EDUCATORS TO CENTER CHILDREN,
 INVESTIGATION, AND DESIGN 183
 Teacher Learning, 185
 Preschool and Elementary Science and Engineering
   Educators, 190
 Supporting Educator Learning, 194
 Supporting Educators in Working Toward Equity, 212
 Summary, 213

9	**TRANSFORMATIVE LEADERSHIP** A Framework for Transformative Leadership, 216 Transformative Leadership and Equity, 232 Summary, 233	215
10	**PROGRESSING TOWARD A VISION FOR SCIENCE AND ENGINEERING IN PRESCHOOL THROUGH ELEMENTARY GRADES** Conclusions, 236 Recommendations, 244 Areas for Future Research, 249 Final Reflection, 259	235

REFERENCES	261
APPENDIX Biosketches of Committee Members and Staff	309

Summary

From a very young age, children are interested in exploring the world. They eagerly ask questions about their environment and have intuitive and imaginative ways of finding out about it. This curiosity and enthusiasm for learning can set the stage as children enter into formal schooling. In fact, recent transformations in science education, sparked by the National Academies of Sciences, Engineering, and Medicine's report *A Framework for K–12 Science Education* (hereafter referred to as the *Framework*; National Research Council [NRC], 2012), call for robust science and engineering learning experiences for children. However, a host of challenges remain as educators work to implement the vision of the *Framework* in the elementary grades and realize a consistent vision in preschool.

First, research on science and engineering education has focused largely on middle and high school, with less attention to preschool through elementary-age children, as well as less attention to engineering than science. Thus, educators may not know what children's meaningful engagement in science and engineering could look like. Second, educators focused on enhancing preschool through elementary science and engineering instruction have to navigate multiple demands placed on teachers and administrators, including an emphasis on English language arts (ELA) and mathematics; educators and school leaders who often do not have backgrounds in science and engineering; limited professional learning opportunities; and lack of time, space, and resources.

As a result, many preschool and elementary classrooms provide only limited opportunities to engage in science and engineering learning. This is a concern because foundational science and engineering experiences in preschool through elementary school are essential for success in later learning. Leveraging their curiosity about the natural and designed world allows children to answer questions and solve problems of interest to them while engaging in authentic science and engineering practices.

Given the importance of early opportunities to engage in science and engineering learning, as well as these complex challenges, the Carnegie Corporation of New York and the Robin Hood Learning + Technology Fund commissioned the National Academies of Sciences, Engineering, and Medicine to examine the research on effective approaches to science and engineering instruction in preschool through fifth grade.[1] The committee explored the kinds of learning experiences prior to entering school that help to provide a strong foundation for science and engineering learning; how children's learning can be supported in schools to include promising instructional approaches and integration of content; the design and use of curriculum and instructional materials; and how to support teachers through professional learning opportunities and policies, practices, and leadership at the national, state, and local levels.

This report was developed during a pivotal moment in history. Systemic racial inequities and injustices that have shaped this country's path for centuries have increasingly moved into the forefront of the national conversation. These inequities and injustices need to be addressed, in part, through children's educational experiences. Furthermore, the work on the report took place during a global pandemic. Although the effects of the pandemic on children's learning of science and engineering are still to be determined, it is clear that they will be substantial, and that due to existing inequities these effects will not be distributed evenly across communities.

For these reasons, the committee focused on equity across the report. The committee uses the term "equity" to address ways—through changing policies and practices—of removing barriers to participation in science and engineering and increasing achievement, representation, and identification, whereas the term "justice" refers to addressing systemic oppressions that cause those barriers, thus seeking fair treatment of all people and supporting opportunities for self-determination and thriving. The committee names four approaches to equity—(1) increasing opportunity and access to high-quality science and engineering learning and instruction; (2) emphasizing increased achievement, representation, and identification with science and engineering; (3) expanding what constitutes science and engineering; and (4) seeing science and engineering as part of justice movements—that reflect a spectrum of ways that educators can work toward equity and justice in preschool and elementary science and engineering.

---

[1] The full statement of task appears in Box 1-1 in Chapter 1.

Educators and leaders at local, state, and district levels can adopt one or more of these approaches to help them move their efforts toward equity and justice, even with young children learning science and engineering. Building toward the vision of the *Framework* while deepening attention to equity and justice is a significant, but crucial, challenge. The report provides starting points for engaging in this work and points to the gaps in research to fully realize an evidence-based, synthesized approach.

CORE FINDINGS

The committee's core findings are summarized below. The findings cover fundamental insights about children's learning, how to design instruction and curriculum, supports for educators, and the importance of administrative leadership and policy.

Prioritizing Science and Engineering in Preschool Through Elementary Grades

Starting from infancy, children begin to investigate the world and develop explanations; construct representations; scope problems and develop and refine solutions; communicate their reasoning and learn from others; and consider actions based on fairness, impact, or justice. All of these can be developed into scientific and engineering practice, with support, and leveraged as children come to understand the natural and designed world. However, national survey data have shown that science and engineering instruction is not prioritized in preschool through elementary schools, with engineering receiving the least attention. This lack of priority is exacerbated in under-resourced schools. In particular, science and engineering are often not attended to in preschool through elementary state policies, due in part to high-stakes accountability policies, which emphasize ELA and mathematics. Children are also pulled out from content areas like science and social studies to receive support services. Additionally, there is not clear alignment or coherence of the policies, standards, and teaching practices from preschool through elementary grades for science and engineering. Aligning these systems could support the enhancement of the teaching and learning of science and engineering across preschool through elementary schools.

Supporting Children's Learning, Engagement, and Proficiency in Science and Engineering

Designing effective, inspiring, and equitable science and engineering education pathways requires attention to the potential that all children bring with them; the unique identities and strengths of each individual child; and the systemic and contextual influences that shape patterns of difference in children's experiences of the world. Four big ideas help to conceptualize learning: it (1) is a social and cultural process that (2) involves identity formation, (3) occurs across contexts, and (4) occurs within historical and political contexts. These four big ideas are central to understanding both the core commonalities and the broad variations in how children learn science and engineering in preschool through elementary grades.

Children build proficiencies in science and engineering throughout their childhoods, including through their family relationships and experiences with play. For example, after splashing in puddles outside, preschoolers might come together at a water table to explore and learn core ideas related to flow and motion, as well as crosscutting concepts such as cause and effect (e.g., how pouring from different heights affects the size of a splash) and systems thinking (e.g., how increasing water flow through one portion of the water table relates to water volume available in another portion). They might engage in forms of activity such as making predictions and observations, explaining relationships, and communicating their ideas. Preschoolers might also have conversations about where storm water in their school's neighborhood goes and the importance of access to clean water.

Adults—including family members, community members, teachers, and many others—play a crucial role in supporting children's engagement in science and engineering experiences. Across the many contexts of children's science and engineering activity, children's development of ideas and practices is supported by long-term, sustained experiences, rich materials and settings, and engagement with peers and knowledgeable others. Teachers' use of instructional practices aimed at children's engagement in investigation and design helps to support the enactment of these environments. Teachers and other adults need to be able to notice, name, and build on children's ideas and experiences to help them continue to make sense of the natural and designed world. Moreover, engaging in science and engineering is a social endeavor—one where children develop relationships and engage in collective meaning-making and scientific and engineering discourse. Learning environments in science and engineering for preschool and elementary ages emphasize caring and respect, meaningful and rich contexts, iterative refinement of ideas and sensemaking, collaboration and collective thinking, meaningful assessment, and work to undo systemic oppression. By developing learning environments that support both development and demonstration of children's proficiencies, including making connections across contexts of learning, educators help children see their ideas, interests and identities, and practices as meaningful for school science and engineering as well as seeing how science and engineering can be useful in their lives.

Curriculum and Content Integration

Scientists and engineers work on problems that require interdisciplinary approaches to solutions. Children's work in science and engineering is interdisciplinary in similar ways. Science and engineering can be integrated with other subject areas, such as language arts, mathematics, and computational thinking. Integration, if done well, effectively adds time to the day for science and engineering. It contributes to building meaningful bridges across content areas. Orienting instruction toward rich phenomena and design problems provides opportunities to motivate, use, and develop skills and ideas in other content domains. Instructional designs incorporating integration need to respect the unique content and practices of each domain included, make meaningful connections among the domains, and be developmentally, culturally, and linguistically appropriate.

Preschool through elementary teachers benefit from access to high-quality curriculum materials. Rather than providing a script for teachers to blindly follow, such materials support teachers in being responsive to children's thinking and ideas. High-quality curriculum materials provide an important starting point for instruction: teachers adapt even high-quality materials to their own teaching context and students. Ideally, these adaptations are in keeping with the developers' vision of the materials as well as with the teacher's priorities, principles, and context. How teachers use and adapt curriculum materials depends upon the teachers' knowledge, beliefs, and attitudes as well as the characteristics of the curriculum materials and the teaching contexts.

Supporting Educators

Preschool through elementary school teachers typically teach all subject areas, including all areas of science and engineering. They also support children's social, emotional, and physical well-being and formally or informally attend to other areas important for children's growth, such as art and music. While these teachers may not have extensive preparation in (or affinity for) science and engineering, they bring many assets to the work, including care for children, capacity in building relationships with children and families, and inquisitiveness about the world. To build on those assets toward the vision of science and engineering teaching described in this report, teachers benefit from a constellation of supports across their preservice and professional career. Several factors can contribute to the development of teachers' beliefs, identities, knowledge, and practice with regard to teaching science and engineering. These include preservice teacher education that involves experiences with science and engineering practices and experiences with supporting children in engaging in those practices, as well as professional learning experiences that involve, for example, collaboratively analyzing teaching practice and children's thinking. Beyond preservice teacher education and ongoing professional learning opportunities, teachers also benefit from having adequate physical and digital resources, educative curriculum materials, and supportive school leadership. Curricular and physical and digital resources are often in short supply in under-resourced schools, which typically serve larger proportions of minoritized children.

Because the demographics of the preschool through elementary teacher workforce, which includes mainly white women, are different from the demographics of the children being taught, there may be differences between how teachers and learners relate to science and engineering. Furthermore, teachers may need support in being responsive to and supportive of the cultural and linguistic backgrounds of the children in their classrooms.

District and School Leadership

Organizational culture, policy and management, and educator capability interact to shape instructional reform efforts in school districts. These three related pieces allow researchers to analyze local leadership practices that enable equitable preschool and elementary science and engineering instruction.

School leaders play an important role in providing guidance for teachers, particularly in the area of science and engineering education. When leaders emphasize the importance of science and engineering and foster shared responsibility for science and engineering instruction, that instruction is strengthened in schools. Moreover, policy and management structures that matter for preschool and elementary science and engineering instruction include structures around instructional time, resources, and staffing. Staffing structures sometimes include the use of science specialists, departmentalization, or team teaching. When leaders are involved in science and engineering education and when there is value placed on science and engineering education in the system, specialists appear to have greater impact, in comparison to when leaders are not involved or when value is not placed on science and engineering. Lastly, professional learning experiences for leaders that align across the levels of district, school, and teacher leaders shape principals' supervision of teachers and thus teachers' opportunities to learn. Partnerships with science and engineering organizations and universities contribute to supporting such professional learning opportunities.

RECOMMENDATIONS

Following analysis of the available evidence, the committee reached consensus on a set of conclusions and recommendations. The conclusions and recommendations, as well as future directions for research that attend to the identified gaps in the current research, are discussed in depth in Chapter 10. The recommendations presented below are grouped and correspond with the themes highlighted in the core findings. Issues related to equity and justice are threaded throughout, illustrating the pervasiveness of these issues.

Prioritizing Science and Engineering in Preschool Through Elementary Grades

RECOMMENDATION 1: State policy makers should establish policies that ensure science and engineering are comprehensively, frequently, and consistently taught in all preschool through elementary settings. The policies should also ensure that children are not being pulled out of science and engineering instruction for remediation in other subjects.

RECOMMENDATION 2: District and school leaders in elementary and preschool settings should examine the amount of time and resources allocated to science and engineering instruction and then (a) develop schedules that allow a comprehensive, frequent, and consistent focus on science and engineering, (b) create coherence from preschool through elementary, and (c) allocate the necessary resources (fiscal, material, and human) to support equitable science and engineering learning opportunities.

RECOMMENDATION 3: Preschool and elementary school leaders should evaluate the characteristics of classroom instruction, the qualifications of teachers hired and whether the hiring practices serve to promote educator diversity, and the professional learning opportunities offered to teachers so that adjustments can be made as needed to support and enhance teachers' capacities for teaching science and engineering well.

RECOMMENDATION 4: State leaders, district leaders, and researchers should work together to build connections across preschool and elementary school and to conduct research to investigate how alignment and coherence across preschool through elementary supports children's learning of science and engineering.

Supporting Children's Learning, Engagement, and Proficiency in Science and Engineering

RECOMMENDATION 5: To draw on and further develop children's science and engineering proficiencies and identities, teachers should arrange their instruction around interesting and relevant phenomena and design problems that leverage children's natural curiosity and give children opportunities for decision making, sensemaking, and problem solving.

RECOMMENDATION 6: Teachers should enact science and engineering learning experiences that establish norms for a caring, collective culture and position children as active thinkers and doers while also providing opportunities to support collaboration and collective thinking.

RECOMMENDATION 7: Teachers should include formative assessment processes that gather multiple forms of evidence at multiple timepoints, with the goal of informing instruction.

RECOMMENDATION 8: Teachers should seek out opportunities to continue to build their expertise in working toward equity and justice in their science and engineering teaching.

RECOMMENDATION 9: Preschool and elementary school leaders and teachers should engage and collaborate with families and local community leaders to mutually support children's opportunities for engaging in science and engineering. Such collaboration allows for leaders and teachers to design learning experiences that are meaningful and relevant to children and helps families to better support their children's learning outside of the school.

Curriculum and Content Integration

RECOMMENDATION 10: Curriculum developers should work in partnership with researchers, teachers, school or district leaders, and families and community leaders to develop preschool through elementary science and engineering curriculum materials that are coherent and equitable, that build toward the vision of *A Framework for K–12 Science Education*, and that

- provide opportunities for children's sensemaking around investigation and design;
- build on children's interests and repertoires of practice;
- provide educative supports for teachers;
- provide opportunities for teachers to make productive adaptations to meet contextual needs;
- provide supports for teachers to make meaningful connections to communities and families;

- explore integrating science and engineering with other domains in ways that benefit children's learning and use instructional time effectively;
- are manageable for use in preschool and elementary settings;
- align preschool and elementary instruction; and
- show evidence of effectiveness.

RECOMMENDATION 11: State and district leaders should rely on a robust evidence-based review, selection, and implementation process when making decisions about preschool through elementary curricular programs to adopt to ensure that the science and engineering units build toward the vision of *A Framework for K–12 Science Education* and are grounded in investigation and design, coherent, flexible, adaptable, and equitable.

RECOMMENDATION 12: State and district leaders should provide teachers with sustained professional learning opportunities for using and adapting curriculum materials, and should ensure that they have adequate access to materials, equipment, and other physical and digital resources needed for children to engage in investigation and design.

RECOMMENDATION 13: As materials become available, state and district leaders should ensure that every school has the curriculum materials and instructional resources needed for engaging in science and engineering teaching that works toward equity and justice.

Supporting Educators

RECOMMENDATION 14: Teacher educators (in and outside of schools of education), facilitators of professional learning experiences, and school and district leaders should

- help preschool through elementary teachers to recognize the importance and value of teaching science and engineering;
- understand and address the needs and goals of classroom teachers;
- support teachers in connecting their professional learning with their classroom practice;
- foreground authentic and equitable science and engineering content and disciplinary practice;
- allow for meaningful integration of science and/or engineering with other subjects; and
- support teachers' effective use and adaptation of science and engineering curriculum materials.

RECOMMENDATION 15: Designers and facilitators of professional learning opportunities should ensure that sustained opportunities to work on science and engineering teaching that works toward equity and justice, in conjunction with supportive curriculum materials, are offered. These experiences should support teachers in developing the ability to recognize and value their learners' conceptual, linguistic, and cultural resources, such as funds of knowledge stemming from their families and communities and their sensemaking repertoires.

RECOMMENDATION 16: Schools of education should provide professional learning opportunities for science teacher education faculty on how to work toward equity and justice in teacher education.

RECOMMENDATION 17: Federal agencies should reassess how funds are allocated for research and development efforts to enhance teaching and learning of science and engineering within preschool through elementary classrooms and prioritize efforts that

- diversify the preschool through elementary teacher workforce;
- recognize the unique character of preschool through elementary teachers and teaching;
- develop teachers as leaders;
- support research and development that works across content areas to support teacher educators, teachers, and children in making meaningful connections; and
- elevate the study of equitable curricular resources and initial and ongoing teacher professional learning experiences that support teachers in working toward equity and justice in preschool and elementary science and engineering.

District and School Leadership

RECOMMENDATION 18: District leaders should provide professional learning opportunities for principals, center directors, and other school leaders to enhance leaders' capacity for providing instructional leadership for science and engineering. These professional learning opportunities should focus on science and engineering practices and support leaders in seeing multiple ways science and engineering are valuable for children.

1

Introduction

Every child deserves to experience the wonder of science and the satisfaction of engineering. Children, even at very young ages, are deeply curious about the world around them and eager to investigate the many questions they have about their environment. Decades of research suggest that children are capable of learning sophisticated disciplinary concepts and can engage in scientific and engineering practices (National Research Council [NRC], 2007, 2012). Engaging them in learning science and engineering takes advantage of this interest and helps them to answer their own authentic questions and solve real-world problems that are important to them. High-quality instruction builds toward the vision of *A Framework for K–12 Science Education* (hereafter referred to as the *Framework*; NRC, 2012) and this report unpacks what that instruction can look like, and what can happen when children are supported in meaningful opportunities to learn.

Building a solid foundation in science and engineering in preschool through the elementary grades sets the stage for later success—both by sustaining and enhancing children's natural enthusiasm for learning about the world around them and by establishing the knowledge and skills they need to approach the more challenging science and engineering topics introduced in later grades. Yet across the United States, children in elementary classrooms receive instruction in science an average of just 20 or so minutes a day, a few days a week, and engineering instruction far less frequently (Banilower et al., 2018). Furthermore, this instructional time for science and engineering is not evenly distributed. Schools with extensive resources, which tend to serve mostly white children, tend to have more science instruction, while schools that are under-resourced, which tend to serve mostly Black, Brown, and Indigenous children, tend to have less (Banilower et al., 2018).

These disparities lead to a number of concerns. Most common in the national parlance is concern about the "STEM pipeline," and Black, Brown, and Indigenous children certainly do deserve access to higher-paying STEM-related jobs. However, access to jobs is not the only goal; it is important that science and engineering be made epistemologically accessible and coherent (with a range of entrance points in terms of ways of knowing) for children of all backgrounds, not just those who come from backgrounds aligned with the white, middle-class perspectives that have typically been privileged in these disciplines. In addition, the converse is also true: science and engineering benefit, as disciplines, from the involvement of participants from a broader range of identities and backgrounds.

Additionally, as the committee writes these words, in 2021, the United States is currently reeling from a global pandemic (which has disproportionately affected communities of color) and bracing itself for ongoing and long-term environmental crises. Supporting young children to deeply understand authentic science and to solve real-world engineering and design problems will support them in becoming informed decision makers—perhaps helping to mitigate some of these health and environmental concerns that will continue to be faced in local communities and as a nation.

A final argument for the importance of providing children with a strong foundation in science and engineering is, simply, that each child has a right to experience the wonders of the natural and designed worlds. Children bring joy to their explorations, and they deserve to have that joy nurtured. For each of these reasons, and others, a focus on science and engineering with all young learners in preschool through fifth grade is crucially important.

ABOUT THIS REPORT

Sponsored by the Carnegie Corporation of New York and the Robin Hood Learning + Technology Fund, the Board on Science Education of the National Academies of Sciences, Engineering, and Medicine convened an expert committee to gather information and explore the range of issues associated with opportunities to engage with science and engineering learning in preschool through the elementary grades (see Box 1-1). The 16-member expert committee included individuals with expertise in early childhood education and development, elementary science and engineering learning and pedagogy, preservice and in-service teacher professional learning, as well as assessment, curriculum materials, and content integration. Committee members also had expertise with respect to educational systems and policies and links to informal settings.

> **BOX 1-1**
> **Statement of Task**
>
> The committee will conduct a consensus study to provide guidance on effective approaches to science and engineering instruction in prekindergarten through 5th grade that support the success of all students regardless of race, SES, home language, learning ability and needs, or the community in which they live. The committee will address the following questions:
>
> - What kinds of learning experiences prior to entering school (e.g., formal and informal, including play-based experiences, informal interactions at home and in the community) will help to prepare children with a strong foundation for science and engineering learning in the elementary grades?
> - What are promising instructional approaches for enhancing science and engineering (including computational thinking) in early childhood and grades pre-K through 5? What is necessary in order to implement these approaches? How do these need to be adapted to meet the disparate needs of students (e.g., high poverty, English learners, students with learning differences, students two or more years behind grade level)?
> - How can science and engineering be connected to, or integrated with, other subject areas such as mathematics, computer science, and English Language Arts?
> - What is the role of curriculum and instructional materials (including formative and summative classroom assessment) in advancing science and engineering in pre-K through 5?
> - What professional learning opportunities (both preservice and in-service) are needed to best support teachers to implement effective instruction in science and engineering?
> - How do policies and practices at the national, state, and local level constrain or facilitate efforts to enhance science and engineering in pre-K through fifth grade? What are examples of the best policies and practices on the state and local level that foster high quality education in science and engineering in pre-K through fifth grade? How might policies and practices across the pre-K–12 education system need to be changed to enhance science and engineering for all students in early childhood and the elementary grades including students from low SES backgrounds, English learners, students with learning differences, and struggling and striving students?
> - What are the gaps in the current research base and what are the key directions for research, both short-term and long-term?

The committee met six times over a 1-year period in 2020 and 2021. During this time, the committee reviewed the published literature pertaining to its charge and had opportunities to engage with many experts. Evidence was gathered from presentations and a review of the existing literature that included peer-reviewed materials, book chapters, reports, working papers, government documents, white papers and evaluations, editorials, and previous reports by the National Academies. The committee searched for information on the teaching and learning of science and engineering in preschool and elementary grades, with a focus on student engagement in doing science and engineering. In their work, the committee also drew from the broader literature on professional learning, curriculum, assessment, leadership, community connections, education policy, and school reform and improvement efforts. For each of these areas, careful consideration was given to the strength of the evidence (described below) as well as across the various grade bands (preschool, K–2, and 3–5) as appropriate.

Report Scope

The committee discussed the charge in detail at multiple points throughout the consensus process. In early meetings, discussions focused on getting clarity on what was intended by the charge and also identifying areas of potential focus and making decisions about whether they were in or out of scope. As time went on, the discussions became richer and fuller as committee members came to understand one another's perspectives and develop a shared vision. Through those conversations, the committee made a set of decisions that helped shape both the substance and the scope of the work.

One decision was—to maintain a reasonable scope and based on the charge—the committee would focus attention on the preschool or prekindergarten contexts rather than giving a full treatment to the time period between infancy and preschool. As the committee made this decision, a related conversation about how to describe this setting occurred. In the broader literature, several different terms can be used such as early learning, early childhood, preschool, and prekindergarten. "Early learning" is often used to encompass children from birth to age 8 (third grade); "prekindergarten" is the term often associated with public prekindergarten programs, which often serve children age 5; whereas "preschool" is often associated with programs serving children ages 3–5. Moreover, in states and programs where Head Start funds and state prekindergarten funds are combined to serve children and families to expand reach, preschool is used as a more encompassing term. Given this, the committee has decided to use the word "preschool" to describe this early stage, including prekindergarten. Given the complexity of this landscape, a limitation is that the committee was unable to do full treatment of the different settings (i.e., public versus private preschools, Head Start programs, prekindergarten) in which children may have opportunities to engage in science and engineering. To further conversations around alignment between preschool and elementary educational systems, the committee has chosen to use the phrase "preschool through elementary" to signal this continuity.

Similarly, fruitful discussions focused on ideas about and language for content integration (Chapter 6), engineering and computational thinking (addressed throughout the report), and assessment (see Chapter 5). For example, the committee grappled with the meanings of terms like integration, interdisciplinary, multidisciplinary, and transdisciplinary, as well as content area and domain, and eventually developed a common perspective of how these ideas can inform and enhance science and engineering teaching and learning in preschool through elementary. The committee also recognizes that there have been a number of initiatives pushing for computational thinking to be embedded within K–12 (National Academies of Sciences, Engineering, and Medicine [NASEM], 2021). To the extent possible, the committee explored how computational thinking is defined in the *Framework* (NRC, 2012), how it can meaningfully be connected to science and engineering, and at what ages children may engage in it and how (see Chapter 6); the committee felt that it is beyond their scope and expertise to make recommendations beyond those parameters, particularly given the limited research in that area.

Finally, through these discussions of the charge, the committee also identified areas that were important for inclusion in the report, despite not being named explicitly in the charge. Some of these included learning and learning processes (Chapters 3 and 4), the role of standards (Chapter 2 and throughout), and the role of educational leaders and leadership (Chapter 9). In addition, because some children do not have opportunities to attend preschool (or prekindergarten) and because the committee recognizes that families and communities serve as a context for learning science and engineering, the role of families and communities is discussed throughout the report (particularly in Chapter 3).

Study Approach

Over the course of this study, members of the committee benefited from discussion and presentations by the many individuals who participated in the three fact-finding meetings.[1] At the first meeting, the committee heard

---

[1] Links to recordings of the presentations and the public sessions can be found at the project page at https://www.nationalacademies.org/our-work/enhancing-science-in-prekindergarten-through-fifth-grade.

a presentation on the state of elementary science education and engaged in a discussion with leading experts on computational thinking.

During the second and third meetings, the committee had several discussions pertaining to the charge, including issues related to equity, content integration, as well as the role of district policies and leadership in elementary education. In particular, at the second meeting, the committee engaged with scholars with respect to the evidence on equity, justice, and antiracism in elementary science and engineering. Also at the second meeting, the committee heard presentations and had in-depth conversations around science and literacy integration. At the third meeting, the content integration discussion was expanded to include other content areas such as engineering, computer science, and computational thinking. The committee also engaged with scholars who could help unpack the evidence on what is happening in preschools with respect to science and engineering learning.

The committee commissioned four papers to provide more in-depth analysis on the integration of science and engineering with other content areas.[2] Monica E. Cardella (Purdue University), Gina Navoa Svarovksy (University of Notre Dame), and Scott Pattison (TERC) authored a paper that provided an overview of what is known about engineering education in prekindergarten through fifth grade. Diane Jass Ketelhut and Lautaro Cabrera (University of Maryland College Park) described the state of the evidence on the integration of computational thinking in early childhood and elementary science and engineering education. Tamara J. Moore (Purdue University) and Anne T. Ottenbreit-Leftwich (Indiana University) authored a paper that also examined issues of computational thinking but focused more on computational thinking through the lens of computer science. Annemarie Sullivan Palincsar (University of Michigan), Miranda S. Fitzgerald (University of North Carolina at Charlotte), Gabriel P. DellaVecchia (University of Michigan), and Kathleen M. Easley (University of Michigan) provided a comprehensive overview of the integration of literacy, science, and engineering in prekindergarten through fifth grade. The committee also commissioned a consultant, Jennifer Frey (University of Cincinnati), to ensure that the language and text throughout the report was inclusive of children with learning disabilities and/or learning differences.

Finally, the committee also had a series of conversations with scholars who are expert in the intersections of justice, antiracism, and science and engineering education: Angela Calabrese Barton, Natalie Davis, Tia Madkins, Daniel Morales-Doyle, and Sepehr Vakil. These conversations guided the committee in threading issues of justice through the report.

---

[2] Commissioned papers can be found on the project page at https://www.nationalacademies.org/our-work/enhancing-science-in-prekindergarten-through-fifth-grade.

Standards of Evidence

The committee takes an expansive view of evidence in this report and draws on and privileges a diversity of methods. Many types of studies were included: meta-analyses and reviews, qualitative case studies, ethnographic and field studies, interview studies, randomized controlled trials, quasi-experimental comparison studies, and large-scale surveys of educators. That said, the committee recognized that the literature consisted predominantly of studies that were more descriptive in nature with few studies that could demonstrate causal effects. As appropriate, throughout the report, the committee articulates the type of research being reviewed and its strength. The committee is also careful to qualify the conclusions and subsequent recommendations that can be made based on the type and strength of evidence.

Like other previous National Academies reports (e.g., NASEM, 2015; NRC, 2012), the committee draws on a foundational NRC report (2002) to adopt the stance that "a wide variety of legitimate scientific designs are available for education research" (p. 6). From that standpoint, to be considered scientific,

> . . . the design must allow direct, empirical investigation of an important question, [use methods that permit direct investigation of the question], account for the context in which the study is carried out, align with a conceptual framework, reflect careful and thorough reasoning, and disclose results to encourage debate in the scientific community. (NASEM, 2015, p. 21)

In making decisions about what evidence to include or exclude, again building on earlier committees' work, the committee "examined the appropriateness of the design to the questions posed, whether the research methods were sufficiently explicated, and whether conclusions were warranted based on the design and available evidence" (NASEM, 2015, p. 21).

The committee relied heavily on studies that had gone through a rigorous peer-review process to help to ensure quality of design, methods, and conclusions. The report's conclusions rely most substantially on research published in peer-reviewed journals and books. (The committee notes, however, that systemic biases mean that minoritized scholars are less likely to receive funding and have their work published in some top journals [e.g., see Li et al., 2020; Taffe and Gilpin, 2021], and thus the scholarship that is published may reflect similar systemic biases.) The committee also relied on technical reports containing information that would be hard to find in other venues (e.g., the results of a large-scale teacher survey).

In addition to peer-reviewed scholarship and technical reports, the committee also turned at times to descriptive work published in practitioner journals to round out descriptions of instructional approaches, when empirical scholarship suggested the work's efficacy or likely efficacy. Furthermore, the committee values and prioritizes the voices of practitioners, and thus at times turned to the wisdom of practice. When possible, these perspectives are complemented by peer-reviewed scholarship, but there are situations that reflect a gap in the literature (e.g., in some aspects of the education policy world) when wisdom of practice stands on its own.

Finally, the committee relied on theory to make logical conclusions where appropriate empirical evidence was lacking. The committee is careful to acknowledge when theory is the grounding for claims.

Given the charge, the committee focused most of its attention on scholarship in preschool through elementary science and engineering education. In some areas, though, studies were scarce. For example, the field of engineering education, in general, is relatively small (with somewhat more work in elementary grades than in preschool), and there is also little research connecting computational thinking with science teaching at the elementary level. As another example, there is not much research at the intersection of initial preschool teacher preparation and the teaching of science or engineering. Lastly, there is nascent research on asset-based, justice-oriented research in preschool through fifth grade science and engineering.

Because of gaps like these, the committee also drew on (a) studies in other subject areas (e.g., mathematics) and (b) studies involving older students (e.g., middle schoolers) or teachers of older students (e.g., high school biology teachers). The committee also needed at times to extrapolate beyond specific intersections. For example, some of what has been found about preparing elementary teachers of science likely also applies to preparing elementary teachers of engineering or to preparing preschool teachers of science. In those instances, though, the committee takes care to clarify where the evidence base is sparse and notes where such extrapolations seem unwarranted.

The committee's stance is that converging lines of evidence strengthen claims. Furthermore, the committee seeks to understand social phenomena from multiple perspectives. For these reasons, the committee looked at the convergence of evidence across studies, seeking—ideally—multiple studies reflecting converging and mutually informing orientations. In addition, the committee works throughout the report to provide a fair representation of the evidence related to a topic, rather than selecting only evidence that presents a particular perspective. When evidence is sparse but the focus seems important to highlight (e.g., as is the case with regard to what is known about preparing preschool through elementary teachers for justice-oriented science and engineering instruction), the committee signals this using language such as "nascent" or "emergent" evidence, or as being "suggestive" findings.

The committee takes care to describe studies and what can be known from them with consideration of how strongly to word claims and how to word conclusions and recommendations based on the evidence base. When possible, the committee describes key features of the contexts of studies. For example, the committee delineates when studies focus on preschool-age children or elementary children, because the committee recognizes the important differences across these groups. The field lacks strong methods for attending carefully to contextual variability (a point taken up in Chapter 10).

The committee notes that education in preschool through elementary science and engineering is unique in several important ways, and that those unique characteristics shape the kinds of research that can be done and is done (see Chapter 10). As this report establishes, science is rarely taught in these grades, and engineering is taught even less frequently. This idiosyncrasy and infrequency of instruction can make data collection a challenge. The low priority of science (and especially engineering) in schools can make it difficult to obtain administrators' buy-in for studies, particularly large-scale studies. Assessment can be tricky, because young children's talk, writing, drawings, and gestures can be a challenge to interpret (Greenfield, 2015). At the same time, the relative lack of large-scale standardized tests (in comparison to their prominence in English language arts (ELA) and mathematics at this age) can make it hard to obtain comparative baseline data about learners' performance. Children's primary learning context is their family, meaning learning is often situated within multiage or multigenerational groups. Changes in the populations of participants can lead to dynamic internal validity threats to studies that need to be accounted for. The vagaries of and inequities in the funding systems lead to skew, at best, and, at worst, to bias in what is and is not studied and who is involved as participants in the studies. All of these issues and more pose both conceptual and empirical challenges in conducting research in the scope of the committee's charge, and therefore, these issues lead to challenges in synthesizing this research and making sense of it. The committee notes where these issues appear to be in play in constituting the available evidence base for exploration.

Committee's Commitments

The committee's concerns about language in the charge (e.g., "struggling students," "striving students," "students 2 or more years behind grade level") led to important unearthing of commitments and the development of shared perspectives that would shape much of the committee's work. Rather than a deficit framing of children, the committee instead prioritized recognizing the assets of children, as well as educators and communities, while recognizing their needs and struggles; the report provides evidence that challenges deficit framings and puts forward other, more appropriate interpretations. Committee members further discussed how particular children are often *removed* from science or engineering learning opportunities, and that this seems often to be the case for emergent multilingual learners, children with learning disabilities and/or learning differences, and children who are perceived to be engaging in challenging behaviors (most frequently identified with Black, Indigenous, Latinx, or other children of color). Throughout the report, the committee draws on literature to show that all children can experience success in science and engineering when provided with supportive opportunities to learn.

The committee identified three categories of commitments that provided the lens through which evidence for this report was evaluated; in part, these are informed by the committee's understanding of learning, as discussed in Chapter 3, though these commitments are intentionally broader in scope than the big ideas about learning discussed there.

Commitment 1 acknowledges that science and engineering are not neutral and are situated within a complex historicized system that ultimately shapes the work of the teaching and learning of science and engineering in preschool through fifth grade. Therefore, the committee views antiracism and justice as central elements of an educational system that works to redress societal inequities, oppressions, and the education debt that exist across the United States. This leads to the committee contextualizing the strengths of children and adults within these systems and identifies systems themselves as an important unit of analysis. This committee also puts forth a vision for equitable and just science and engineering education in preschool through elementary grades, discussed below.

Commitment 2 recognizes the strengths of children, communities, and the range of educators involved with the teaching of science and engineering. Therefore, the committee uses sociocultural approaches and asset-based language in describing these different actors and explores ways that settings for learning science and engineering can draw on, build, and attend to their strengths and needs.

Commitment 3 centers on how the committee characterizes the design of science and engineering learning and teaching. The committee builds upon the multidimensional stance of science and engineering learning that intentionally combines science and engineering practices, disciplinary core ideas, crosscutting concepts, identities, and interest, as appropriate, within particular contexts and with particular children. Moreover, this form of learning would also connect to learners' goals, resources, and interests, and consider how those elements inform learners' language, literacy, mathematics, computational thinking, and social skills and knowledge. This perspective is informed by and builds toward the *Framework's* (NRC, 2012) vision for science and engineering teaching and learning.

WORKING TOWARD EQUITY AND JUSTICE

Science and engineering education can be conceptualized not just as a component of a school curriculum, but as a critical human and civil right for children (Larimore, 2020; Tate, 2001). Yet, many children are marginalized in science and in engineering. Historically marginalized learners in science and engineering, including Black, Brown, and Indigenous children and other children of color, children with learning disabilities and/or learning differences, emergent multilingual learners,[3] and children marginalized on the basis of gender, all deserve the opportunity to engage with science and engineering to make sense of the natural and designed world. The literature is replete with examples of challenges, but literature on ways to address those challenges is more recent and is advancing quickly. In this section, the committee presents a vision for how teaching science and engineering in preschool through elementary can also be work toward equity and justice. In doing so, the committee outlines issues of inequity and then lays out possible definitions of "equity."

Issues of Inequity in Preschool Through Elementary Science and Engineering Learning

This is a pivotal moment in history. As noted above, since the start of 2020, the country has been facing a convergence of both new and longstanding crises—the COVID-19 pandemic, ongoing systemic racism and societal unrest in response to it, and accelerating climate perils. All of these have implications for the teaching and learning taking place in and out of schools.

Science and engineering disciplines have historical connections to racism and other forms of oppression. In the United States, both science and engineering have come to be considered to be work best done by white men. Society at large has approached science and engineering from a Eurocentric perspective, valued mainly the science and engineering done by white men, and marginalized science and engineering as practiced by other groups, including Black and Indigenous peoples. Many groups, including though not limited to people of color and women, have been excluded from doing science, had their contributions stolen or misrepresented, or been ignored (Bang et al., 2012; Calabrese Barton and Tan, 2020). Western or Eurocentric science and engineering have also been, and continue to be, used as tools to subjugate people of color (Bang et al., 2012; Gould, 1996; Warren et al., 2020). While some people of color may have science- and engineering-related experiences within their communities based on trust and thriving, collectively many experiences and realities have also led to mistrust of Eurocentric science and a disconnect between science and the communities of children of color.

---

[3] Throughout the report, the committee uses phrases like "emergent multilingual learners" in keeping with the orientation of recognizing children's assets but uses "English learners" where referring to federal classifications or when it is the term used by the authors of a study being referenced.

In addition, funding for schools in the United States has historically been tied to property taxes, which are tied to property values (Baker and Corcoran, 2012; Morgan and Amerikaner, 2018). Because of redlining and other efforts to keep people of color out of certain neighborhoods, some schools have been inadequately funded for generations (NASEM, 2019a). This limits funding for science and engineering curriculum materials, instructional resources, and professional learning experiences for teachers. Furthermore, because of state accountability and other factors, these schools often have outsized focus on test scores, leading to emphasis on ELA and mathematics.

Finally, the preschool and elementary teaching force is predominantly white women (see Chapter 8), which is markedly different than the demographics of the current student population (NASEM, 2020). Children need opportunities to see their own ways of knowing (epistemologies) reflected in the work (Bang and Medin, 2010). That is: although representation is important—children need to see people who *look like them* doing the work of science and engineering—it is not enough. Children also need to discover that their ways of thinking about the world are valid and familiar to others, including teachers, scientists, and engineers (Sepehr Vakil, personal communication, November 18, 2020). Educators need to work to minimize this *epistemological dissonance* that children may experience in science and engineering learning. Educators can begin this effort by recognizing how their own identities shape their thinking about science and engineering teaching and learning in classrooms. Furthermore, teachers need to be supported in designing science and engineering learning environments and engaging in practices and pedagogies that support the full range of learners in their classrooms (NASEM, 2020).

School reform that works toward justice cannot involve simply tweaking the current status quo; educators must do meaningful work at the center of the enterprise (Daniel Morales-Doyle, personal communication, November 19, 2020). Recognizing and addressing these histories requires a reframing and reorganization of the purposes of learning, how children come to develop and demonstrate proficiencies for investigation and design, the pedagogies for supporting learning and development, the forms of science and engineering that are prioritized in the curriculum, how educators are supported in their learning and development, and the leadership in schools and districts. This report aims to work toward these goals. The approaches described next offer four levers for working toward change.

Approaches to Equity and Justice

"Equity," "justice," and related terms are used in the research literature in numerous ways; defining these ideas is not straightforward. The committee found that, across the literature in science and engineering education reviewed for the report, there were both implicit and explicit ways of using the terms "equity" and "justice." For example, the *Framework* (NRC, 2012) presented multiple definitions of equity, including "equity as an expression of socially enlightened self-interest," "equity as an expression of social justice," and equity based on "the commonsense idea of fairness" (p. 278). The committee benefited from discussions to gain clarity on definitions of equity that are present in the literature on preschool through elementary science and engineering education (e.g., Bell, 2019; Calabrese Barton and Tan, 2019; Haverly et al., 2020; Philip and Azevedo, 2017). Philip and Azevedo (2017) argue that "implicit and explicit values and goals...are intertwined with conceptions of equity" (p. 527), and that when definitions of equity and justice are left implicit, it opens the door to perpetuating historicized power and racial dynamics in learning settings.

The committee recognizes, though, that there is still much work to be done to advance and achieve equity and justice in science and engineering learning, including describing and accounting for consequences of intersecting identities in this work. Where possible, the report addresses research findings from multiple dimensions of identity (including based on race, [dis]ability or learning difference, language background, or gender) in science and engineering education in preschool through elementary.

Four approaches to equity were utilized throughout the report (noting that there are strengths and potential pitfalls for each): (1) increasing opportunity and access to high-quality science and engineering learning and instruction; (2) emphasizing increased achievement, representation, and identification with science and engineering; (3) expanding what constitutes science and engineering; and (4) seeing science and engineering as part of justice movements. Table 1-1 defines these approaches, adapted from Philip and Azevedo (2017) and Rodriguez (2015), and Table 1-2 shows examples of each from different aspects of teaching and learning science and engineering that this report covers.

The committee found it productive to consider approaches to equity within a spectrum—from increasing access to using science and engineering to redress injustices and disrupt systemic oppressions—that the field can work toward equity and justice in preschool and elementary science and engineering. This report uses the term "equity" to address ways—through changing policies and practices—to remove barriers to participation in science and engineering and increase achievement, representation, and identification (mainly the first two approaches, though all four approaches work toward equity). Equity thus strives for comparable levels of attainment and/or participation. The report uses the term "justice" to refer specifically to addressing systemic oppressions that cause those barriers (mainly the third

TABLE 1-1 Four Approaches to Equity and Their Possible Pitfalls

Description	Possible Pitfalls
*Approach #1: Increasing **opportunity** and **access** to high-quality science and engineering learning and instruction.*	
<ul><li>Shift forms of instruction and classroom norms to improve learning.</li><li>Provide supplemental experiences for historically under-represented communities.</li><li>Increase presence and distribution of high-quality science and engineering curriculum.</li><li>Increase presence of well-prepared teachers.</li></ul>	<ul><li>Leaves dominant forms of science and engineering untouched.</li><li>Leaves historicized ways that Eurocentric science and engineering have been used as tools of oppression invisible.</li></ul>
*Approach #2: Emphasizing increased **achievement, representation, and identification** with science and engineering.*	
<ul><li>Improve learners' achievement in school science by generating interest and fostering connections to classroom disciplines.</li><li>Attend to affective aspects of learning to promote personal relevance and invite learners' identities into the learning environment.</li></ul>	<ul><li>Leaves dominant forms of science and engineering untouched.</li><li>Leaves historicized ways that Eurocentric science and engineering have been used as tools of oppression invisible.</li><li>Can lead to static notions of "culture" or "cultural essentialization."</li><li>Leaves the door open for deficit-based perspectives that try to remediate learners and/or their communities.</li><li>Strategies might privilege only achievement or only identity, rather than both.</li></ul>
*Approach #3: **Expanding what constitutes science and engineering**.*	
<ul><li>Seeks to examine and reframe who does science, what counts as science, and in what contexts—and how they might be productively leveraged in science and engineering learning environments.</li><li>Curriculum and instruction allow for, invite, and build on learners' and families' diverse sensemaking and cultural and linguistic resources.</li><li>Accounting for heterogenous understandings of the natural and designed world can expand what constitutes science and engineering. Bringing this broader view supports more children, and also bolsters science and engineering as disciplines.</li></ul>	<ul><li>Not necessarily connected to larger social movement to upend systemic oppression.</li><li>Unlikely to change larger structures of science and engineering professional practices.</li><li>If not adopted as part of a larger structural change, can allow a mismatch with how children are evaluated and assessed, which may leave minoritized children at a disadvantage.</li></ul>

TABLE 1-1 Continued

Description	Possible Pitfalls
*Approach #4: **Seeing science and engineering as part of justice movements.***	
• Offers new possibilities for understanding the relationship between science, equity, and justice. Starts with prioritizing social movements that address the communities' needs and goals, and then finds ways for science and engineering to support the progress toward those projects. • Examining power and historicity can support learning about relationships between human communities and more-than-human communities across time periods.	• More proximal learning goals of approaches to equity 1-3 might be eclipsed. • Justice movements may not intersect with classroom activities. • Current assessment tools and practices may not take into account systemic barriers or historicized relationships with assessments.

SOURCE: Based on Philip and Azevedo (2017); Rodriguez (2015).

TABLE 1-2 Four Approaches to Equity and Nonexhaustive Examples of Each

Forms of Learning Activity and Design	The Roles of Teachers, Teacher Education, and Professional Learning	The Roles of Curricular Materials
*Approach #1: **Increasing opportunity and access** to high-quality science and engineering learning and instruction.*		
Barriers to participation are removed (technology access, accommodations for learning disabilities and/or learning differences, differentiation, etc.).	Teachers • see science "achievement gaps" as "opportunity gaps." • work to increase opportunities especially for children of color to engage with science and engineering.	Curricular materials • are translated into multiple languages. • use multiple modalities (text, audio, etc.) for children to access information. • use phenomena and design challenges to motivate children to engage in science and engineering practices.

continued

TABLE 1-2 Continued

Forms of Learning Activity and Design	The Roles of Teachers, Teacher Education, and Professional Learning	The Roles of Curricular Materials
*Approach #2: Emphasize increased **achievement, representation, and identification** with science and engineering.*		
Children apply science and engineering concepts to their everyday lives. Children have choices for conducting investigations and designs.	Teachers learn ways • to increase representation of "who does science and engineering" to include a range of historically marginalized groups, across gender, learning disabilities and/or learning differences, and linguistic and cultural background. • to connect science and engineering learning with children's interests and identities.	Curricular materials • include representations of scientists and engineers of color and children of color doing science and engineering. • encourage children to tie their cultural and linguistic backgrounds to science and engineering concepts.
*Approach #3: **Expanding what constitutes science and engineering.***		
Family knowledge and practices are regularly invited and incorporated into emerging classroom knowledge. Children conduct investigations that include data collection from both the natural or designed world and community interviews with elders. The learning environment accepts multiple forms of expressing sensemaking—from quantitative measurements to embodied descriptions.	Teachers • learn to see and respond to the richness in children's sensemaking, even if it does not reflect fully formed canonical science ideas, or "look and sound" like Eurocentric (and white, middle class) science and engineering norms or language. • recognize and build on the values and ways of knowing and being of their children and their communities, and integrate them into their teaching.	Curricular materials • make Eurocentric science and engineering norms and practices explicit; space is made for multiple ways of knowing, being, and valuing. • are designed to be flexible so that educators can adapt them to address local socioecological phenomena and the needs and goals of their children's communities. • support students and their families in examining their relationships with the natural world.

TABLE 1-2 Continued

Forms of Learning Activity and Design	The Roles of Teachers, Teacher Education, and Professional Learning	The Roles of Curricular Materials
Approach #4: Seeing science and engineering as part of justice movements.		
Children learn about the connection between the natural world and human actions and decision making. Children investigate how Black, Indigenous, and other communities of color experience disproportionate effects of food deserts, natural hazards, and environmental pollution.	Teachers • recognize the connection between their own power and positionality, Western or Eurocentric science and engineering, and children's and families' engagement in science and engineering. • learn about the connections among a science phenomenon or engineering design, local or global instances of the phenomenon or design, and implications for communities.	Curricular materials invite • children to ask and answer their own questions about community-relevant issues and make decisions for ethical futures. • children, families, and teachers to examine issues from historicized lenses, and understand how contemporary scientific practices or concepts may have deep roots in racist or other oppressive histories.

SOURCE: Based on Philip and Azevedo (2017); Rodriguez (2015).

and fourth approaches),[4] seeking fair treatment of all people and supporting opportunities for self-determination and thriving. When the committee says "working toward equity and justice," it refers to all four approaches, working synergistically.

To genuinely and fully work toward disrupting systemic oppression, all four approaches are necessary. That said, it is important to recognize a few key assumptions. First, systems, institutions, and individuals differ in their starting points for approaching this work, and thus may reasonably employ different approaches. Second, work is needed on multiple scales: from individual, to classroom, school, and institutional or systemic levels. Third, context matters; some contexts are more ready to engage in some approaches compared to others. This does not mean that working toward justice is not important in all settings—just that starting points may differ across contexts. Finally, it seems that progress toward equity may start with the first and second approaches, and more substantive steps toward justice

---

[4] "Justice" here refers to educational justice; social justice is a broader term.

may focus on the third and fourth approaches. Analyses at the end of each chapter of the report summarize research related to each approach to equity and illustrate how these steps may be taken. Fully connecting the vision of the *Framework* with the full range of approaches to promoting equity and justice will be challenging and require long-term investments. The end-of-chapter analyses provide starting points for engaging in this crucial work.

Each approach to equity listed in Tables 1-1 and 1-2 can be tied to specific equity projects, in particular antiracist education. For example, in Approach 1, *increasing opportunity and access*, a district could recognize that schools that serve predominantly Black, Indigenous, and other children of color are underserved in their science and engineering resources and intentionally provide more access to resources to those schools, children, and families (Spillane et al., 2001). In Approach 2, *emphasizing achievement, representation, and identification with science*, professional learning experiences could intentionally address culturally responsive pedagogies that support teachers in connecting school science and engineering to the cultural and familial practices of children. For example, teachers learn how techniques like photo-elicitation or self-documentation (Tzou and Bell, 2010) may allow children and families to document examples from their everyday lives that connect to specific science and engineering concepts taught in the classroom. In Approach 3, *expanding what constitutes science and engineering*, curriculum materials could support teachers and children in making space for multiple ways of knowing and doing science and engineering. For example, children could be encouraged to express their sensemaking using words in everyday language (including languages other than English) or embodied movements, rather than only using scientific vocabulary (e.g., Kotler, 2020). In Approach 4, *seeing science and engineering as part of justice movements,* curriculum materials could intentionally connect scientific concepts to larger societal institutions, thus supporting a kind of critical literacy in science (Davis and Schaeffer, 2019). For example, when taking a walk outdoors, preschool teachers could point out how much the neighborhood has changed over the years and ask about who is making those decisions, and how those decisions might be affecting the trees and animals that live there. As another example, curriculum materials could support children to explore the transportation needs of their community, design possible solutions that would make motorized transportation safer and more efficient, and build on their insights to advocate for better and safer transit infrastructure. Although these approaches can be used separately, finding synergies will be most productive for achieving equity and justice.

The approaches to equity and, potentially, justice outlined above do not necessarily lead to antiracist education. For example, in Approach 1, accommodations could be made for children with neurological differences but do nothing to address historicized differences in access to science and engineering resources that fall along racial lines, or in Approach 3, multiple ways of knowing and doing science and engineering could be invited into the learning space, but some could still be valued over others along racialized dynamics. The committee also recognizes the importance of teachers interrogating their own positionalities and identities in working toward equity and justice, as explored in Chapter 5.

To guide readers in considering how educators can work toward equity and justice in preschool through elementary science and engineering, each chapter ends with a synthesis of the evidence for each approach (numbered 1–4). The analyses at the end of the chapters of the report suggest that, overall, there has been substantial effort made in the first two approaches, some significant pockets of progress in the third, and relatively little with regard to the fourth.

REPORT ORGANIZATION

Overall, the report argues that preschool through elementary children bring many strengths to engaging with science and engineering—including interest, wonder, experiences with the natural and designed worlds, and early proficiencies with investigation and design—that can all be nurtured with support. Educators, as well, bring many strengths and can support children when provided with support themselves. Although there is a gap between the current status quo and the vision put forward in this report, equitably recognizing and leveraging all of these strengths—individually, collectively, and systemically—will help the educational endeavor move closer to the vision.

To help move toward this vision, this report examines the research on opportunities to engage with science and engineering learning in preschool through elementary grades. Chapters 2–4 provide the foundation upon which the subsequent chapters build. In Chapter 2, the committee provides a landscape of the preschool and elementary educational systems and outlines the different actors and factors that shape what is happening in the classroom. The chapter discusses the impact of accountability, standards, and time, and furthers the case for orienting toward equity and justice. Chapter 3 describes the contexts where children learn, including but not limited to the classroom, and puts forward an understanding of learning as situated in relationships and histories that shape the ways individuals engage with science and engineering. Chapter 4 turns to the development of children's proficiencies related to investigation and design, describing forms of activity in which children engage.

The next set of chapters (5–9) turns to designing and supporting instructional environments that build on children's proficiencies in investigation and design. Chapter 5 examines the evidence related to the design of learning environments. Chapter 6 describes the potential of integrating across domains, as this has been offered to be a solution to having more instructional time in a day to engage with science and engineering as well as reflecting more authentic scientific and engineering practice. Building on the previous chapters, Chapter 7 explores the role of curriculum materials and instructional resources. Chapter 8 turns to the educator and the opportunities that they need to ensure that children are engaged in robust, high-quality science and engineering. It examines what is known about preservice teacher education and the types of ongoing professional learning experiences in-service teachers need. Chapter 9 describes how policies and leadership can facilitate high-quality science and engineering learning in preschool through elementary grades. Finally, Chapter 10 presents the conclusions and recommendations and identifies key areas that warrant future research.

2

Preschool and Elementary Systems and Structures

Main Messages

- Science and engineering instruction is under-resourced and not highly prioritized in preschool through elementary schools, with engineering receiving even less attention. These concerns are exacerbated in under-resourced schools.
- On average, there is substantially less instructional time devoted to science compared to English language arts and mathematics.
- Science and engineering instructional policies, standards, and teaching practices from preschool to elementary grades lack alignment and coherence.
- Children receiving academic supports are often excluded or pulled out from key science and engineering learning experiences, limiting not just the research base but children's opportunities to learn.

Understanding the opportunities that children have to engage with science and engineering in preschool through elementary grades requires recognizing that schools are situated within policy and system contexts that shape when, how, and how often children have these opportunities. How teachers and leaders interpret these policies and systems shapes how they notice and value children's ideas and behaviors and what goals and expectations they set for children. Substantial variability exists in the policies for science and engineering across states and districts as well as across preschool and elementary systems. In this chapter, the committee provides an overview of the K–12 education system and highlights some of the key components at the national, state, and local levels that influence the degree to which science and engineering takes place in preschool through elementary grades. The discussion of the education system is followed by an examination of how federal and state policies have influenced instructional time, testing, and inequities in science and engineering education. The chapter concludes by recognizing that these systems are embedded within a historical context that has implications for equity and justice for preschool through elementary science and engineering.

COMPONENTS OF THE U.S. K–12 EDUCATION SYSTEM

Ensuring that science and engineering instruction in preschool through elementary grades supports equitable and inspiring learning opportunities for all children requires attention to multiple interacting components of the U.S. public education system. These components exist at the national, state, and local levels, and they influence the work and decision making of state and local education agencies as well as school principals and other instructional leaders and ultimately impact classroom instruction for millions of children in the United States. Figure 2-1 represents the committee's views of how different components of the K–12 U.S. education system interact to influence teachers' and learners' experiences in preschool and elementary science and engineering classrooms. The preschool context is different from elementary in important ways, and there have been few efforts to create alignment and coherence from preschool through elementary school for science and engineering.

In this chapter, the committee first describes the components and how they interact within and between levels of the system. Specifically, the committee discusses how national policies drive accountability and standards; then the committee details the impact of state standards, accountability, funding, and policies on critical factors like instructional time and instructional materials that impact children's access to meaningful science and engineering learning experiences. Throughout the chapter, the emphasis is primarily on the elementary system, which is where the majority of evidence exists with respect to systems and policies related to science and engineering education. The committee highlights distinctions related to the preschool context where appropriate and as evidence allows.

Influences of National Policy

Policies centered on accountability and academic standards in the U.S. education system drive funding and instruction—which in turn shape equi-

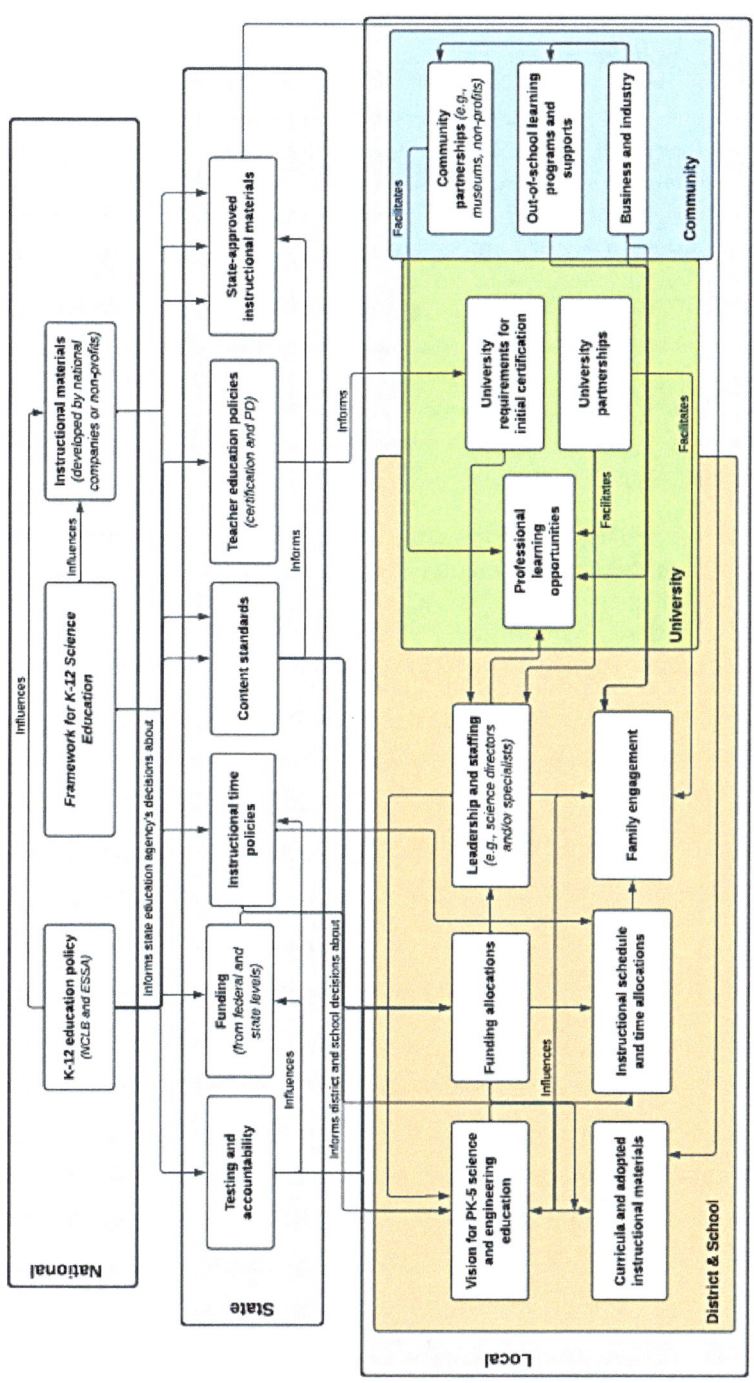

FIGURE 2-1 Components of the K–12 education system and their interactions.

table or inequitable learning opportunities for children. At the national level, K–12 education policies, most principally the Elementary and Secondary Education Act of 1965, reauthorized via No Child Left Behind (NCLB) in 2001,[1] and then the Every Student Succeeds Act (ESSA) in 2015,[2] mandate the use of test-based accountability systems at the state and local levels to monitor the academic performance of children across racial, socioeconomic, and linguistic subgroups. (NCLB and ESSA are taken up in more depth below, in consideration of their impacts on instructional time and testing.) Although these requirements were meant to ensure that all children had access to the same rigorous academic standards, in grades K–5 the policies primarily emphasized results in reading and mathematics (Penfield and Lee, 2010). Under NCLB, districts and schools were expected to demonstrate adequate yearly progress (AYP) on assessments administered in literacy and mathematics to all student subgroups each year in grades 3–8. State science assessments were required starting in 2007 at least once in grades 3–5; however, results were not required to be reported as part of AYP (Judson, 2013). The testing provisions are the same under ESSA, yet states have more authority to design their own accountability systems, and at least 19 states chose to make science part of their school rating systems (Klein, 2018). These policies are described in more detail below.

Federal education policy also requires states to adopt challenging academic standards in reading, mathematics, and science. In 2012, the National Academies published *A Framework for K–12 Science Education* (hereafter referred to as the *Framework*; National Research Council [NRC], 2012) that outlines a broad set of expectations for children in science and engineering in grades K–12, not preschool, to inform the development of new standards and, subsequently, revisions to curriculum, instruction, assessment, and professional development for educators. The vision for science and engineering education reflected in the *Framework* promotes learning experiences that engage children in the activities of scientists and engineers as they develop and use understanding. The *Framework* was informed by past research and national recommendations for science education which were then reflected in many state science standards (see Box 2-1). These documents include *Science for All Americans* (American Association for the Advancement of Science [AAAS], 1989) and the *Benchmarks for Science Literacy* (AAAS Project 2061, 1993), and the *National Science Education Standards* (NRC, 1996).

Although the *Framework* does not include preschool, work is currently under way to create alignment between what is known about teaching and learning in preschool and the vision of the *Framework*. Preschool programs include both state prekindergarten programs and national preschool programs such as Head Start. Although there is substantial variability in early

---

[1] See No Child Left Behind Act of 2001, Pub. L. 107–110.
[2] See Every Student Succeeds Act of 2015, Pub. L. 114–95.

BOX 2-1
Shifts in Science and Engineering Learning

The *Framework* put new expectations in place for the elementary grades with a vision that is ambitious yet simple: Children participate in science and engineering learning by making sense of phenomena and designing solutions through exploration, reflection, and discussion, in a process that involves the interaction of three dimensions: scientific and engineering practices, crosscutting concepts, and disciplinary core ideas.

The first dimension, scientific and engineering practices, includes the following:

1. Ask questions (for science) and define problems (for engineering)
2. Develop and use models
3. Plan and carry out investigations
4. Analyze and interpret data
5. Use mathematics and computational thinking
6. Construct explanations (for science) and design solutions (for engineering)
7. Engage in argument from evidence
8. Obtain, evaluate, and communicate information

The second dimension of crosscutting concepts includes patterns; cause and effect; scale, proportion, and quantity; systems and system models; energy and matter; structure and function; and stability and change. These serve as unifying concepts that have explanatory power across disciplines and domains of science and engineering. The third dimension includes disciplinary core ideas in four areas: physical sciences; life sciences; earth and space sciences; and engineering, technology, and applications of science. The Next Generation Science Standards, which is based on the *Framework,* is written as performance expectations that blend these three dimensions to express what children should know and be able to do at the end of a grade band or grade level.

This "three-dimensional learning" model moves children away from learning discrete facts and puts central value on children, starting at the earliest grades, engaging authentically in science and engineering to describe and explain phenomena or solve problems in the natural and designed world. The *Framework* places attention on the need for children to experience science and engineering to deepen knowledge, engage in sensemaking, increase engagement, and provide meaningful learning experiences for every learner that center on their interest and identities.

The *Framework* outlines goals for what children should know and be able to do at particular grade bands and showcases progressions in learning, illustrating possible development over time. To work toward the ideals of the *Framework*, science and engineering educators need to work to address systemic oppression at all levels—for Black, Brown, and Indigenous children and other children of color; children with learning disabilities and/or learning differences; emergent multilingual children; and children marginalized on the basis of gender.

SOURCE: Adapted from National Research Council (2012) and National Academies of Sciences, Engineering, and Medicine (2018a, 2019b).

learning standards across states, most state programs currently address science to some degree (Greenfield et al., 2009), as does the Head Start Early Learning Outcomes Framework.[3] These standards and frameworks of these individual programs are not yet fully formally aligned to the vision of the K–12 *Framework*. However, the science-as-practice approach highlighted in the *Framework* does align with the combination of holistic understanding and developmentally appropriate practice—that is, understanding children's thinking and learning and using teaching practices to provide experiences that are challenging and achievable—typical in early childhood education (Larimore, 2020); for example, preschool instruction typically connects to children's own interests, resources, and goals, as emphasized in the *Framework*. Thus, throughout the report, when the committee discusses "building toward the vision of the *Framework*," it intends to suggest a connection to the *Framework* for preschool *through* elementary and a role for preschool in building *toward* that vision, while recognizing that the *Framework* begins at kindergarten and while resisting the push of academic content down into preschool.

The Next Generation Science Standards (NGSS; NGSS Lead States, 2013) for K–12 were subsequently developed in 2013 based on the *Framework* (NRC, 2012), and have been adopted by 20 states and the District of Columbia. Another 24 states have developed their own standards based around the recommendations in the *Framework*. As of the time of this report, only six states have science standards that show little influence of the *Framework* or NGSS: Florida, North Carolina, Ohio, Pennsylvania, Texas, and Virginia. Several national publishers have designed science instructional materials addressing the NGSS. Commercially published textbooks or modules are designated for use in two-thirds of elementary teachers' classrooms nationally (Banilower et al., 2018). Chapter 7 explores the role of curriculum materials, how well published materials reflect the current research-informed vision for science and engineering education, and how districts may make decisions about their use.

Standards in preschool have called attention to science and engineering to varying degrees. The national Head Start's Learning Outcomes Framework conceptualizes scientific reasoning as including scientific inquiry (i.e., observing and describing phenomena, engaging in scientific talk, and comparing/categorizing observable phenomena) and reasoning and problem solving (i.e., asking questions/gathering information/making predictions, planning and conducting investigations, and analyzing data/drawing conclusions/communicating findings). Many of these practices are similar or aligned to those in the K–12 *Framework*. State-funded preschool programs rely on state

---

[3] For more information, see https://eclkc.ohs.acf.hhs.gov/school-readiness/article/head-start-early-learning-outcomes-framework.

standards, which vary widely.[4] For instance, California's preschool learning foundations do not list science as one of their four domains or areas of emphasis, whereas other states such as Massachusetts provide guidance and have worked toward alignment with the *Framework* and NGSS.[5]

Influences of States

Just as federal components of the education system depicted in Figure 2-1 influence state policies and priorities, components of the education system under the authority of state legislatures and state education agencies (SEAs) have a great deal of influence over what is taught, and how it is taught, at the local level in districts, schools, and community organizations (broadly defined, including, e.g., museums, community centers), local businesses and industry (e.g., local technology or pharmaceutical companies, science, technology, engineering, and mathematics (STEM) ecosystems partnerships), as well as universities (including a range of partnerships for a variety of purposes, including research projects, teacher education field partnerships, research-practice partnerships, etc.). SEAs and state legislatures direct test-based accountability policies, academic standards, teacher accountability measures, funding allocations, and their allowable expenses. Although districts are provided substantial decision-making power through local control, in many ways SEAs and state legislatures indicate the priorities through policy decisions by which districts, schools and classroom teachers operate. These policies influence decisions about several aspects of preschool through elementary science and engineering education and shape the learning experiences of children. How state legislatures and SEAs shape instructional time and testing is taken up in more depth in a later section.

State-funded preschool programs are an increasingly important part of public education. These programs have been developed to support early learning and development, better prepare children to succeed in primary grades, and reduce achievement gaps that emerge well before kindergarten (Friedman-Krauss and Barnett, 2020). However, state-funded programs have limits in enrollment and face challenges in ensuring program quality and that enrollment is equitable.

As depicted in Figure 2-1, beyond being responsible for establishing their own accountability systems, states are also responsible for adopting statewide academic standards that shape decisions about curriculum,

---

[4] For more information regarding the variability across states, see https://nieer.org/wp-content/uploads/2021/08/YB2020_Full_Report_080521.pdf.

[5] See https://www.cde.ca.gov/sp/cd/re/psfoundationsvol1intro.asp for more information on California's preschool standards. Information for Massachusetts can be found at https://www.doe.mass.edu/frameworks/scitech/2016-04.pdf.

instruction, assessment, and professional development by school districts (also known as local education agencies [LEAs]). Many states offer lists of approved instructional materials that align with state standards for adoption by LEAs, as described further in Chapter 7. State policies and priorities inform and regulate the use of federal funding and state education funding to support standards implementation at the state and local levels. Some states have policies in place that mandate minimum instructional minutes to be dedicated to particular subject areas at the elementary level. Finally, teacher credentialing policies at the state level articulate certification requirements for preservice teachers and professional development mandates for in-service teachers.

Influences of Districts and Schools

School districts (i.e., LEAs) are the primary arbiters of education policy in the United States and serve as key intermediaries between the state and schools (Gamson and Hodge, 2016). Subsequently, district and school leaders are central agents in crafting coherence among factors within education systems and have long determined the extent to which there is more or less coherence (Honig and Hatch, 2004). When a lack of alignment among components of the education system exists, it exacerbates the need to craft coherence at the local level. For example, if standards and state assessments are not well aligned, districts and schools receive mixed messages for the learning goals. If the instructional materials and benchmark or classroom assessments are not well aligned to learning goals associated with state standards, districts and schools face the arduous challenge of modifying them to create stronger horizontal coherence (Cherbow et al., 2020; NRC, 2015a).

Nationwide, school districts have launched efforts to fundamentally change their central offices to support improved teaching and learning for all children (Honig, Venkateswaran, and McNeil, 2017). Influenced by these efforts—which include state standards, funding, accountability, and instructional time policies (i.e., the middle level of Figure 2-1)—school districts shape the vision for preschool through elementary science and engineering education in schools; central office leaders have the authority to align resources and support to enact this vision through many of the elements depicted in the lowest level of Figure 2-1. Resources include fiscal resources for the adoption of high-quality instructional materials and associated professional development, as well as human resources to appoint instructional support staff (e.g., content specialists or coaches). Other support entails the designation of specific instructional time to science and engineering and the engagement of families in robust science and engineering learning opportunities. Districts and schools can also engage university and community partners to support their instructional vision via collaborations focused on teacher professional learning as well as on providing out-of-school experiences for children that augment in-school science and engineering learning.

Though school districts have the autonomy to develop instructional policies and make determinations about funding allocations, they must attend to the pressures of national and state policies and rely on instructional materials and resources produced by national companies and nonprofits to support equitable and inspiring science and engineering instruction in preschool through fifth grade. Enactment of the ideas presented in the *Framework* requires substantial changes to teaching and learning, and these changes will depend on building toward a common vision for preschool and elementary science and engineering education held by teachers, leaders and other education stakeholders (vertical coherence), and alignment of all components in the system to that vision (horizontal coherence).

School-Level Factors

Figure 2-1 depicts school-level factors that may be driven by the district (e.g., the choice of instructional materials is typically a district-level decision) or may be specific to a given school. For example, schools have unique staffs of teacher-leaders and unique levels and types of family engagement—both of which can shape how science and engineering are taught in elementary settings.

Much is expected of elementary and preschool teachers. They typically teach all content areas, as well as being responsible for children's emotional and physical well-being (see Chapter 8). Yet, as discussed in subsequent chapters, they may have inadequate curriculum materials, instructional resources, preparation, and/or administrative support for science and engineering instruction. Even when there is observed alignment among state standards, curriculum, and professional development, teachers may not use curriculum materials in ways that align with the vision of the designers, and teachers' perceptions of the suitability of materials may diverge. School-level goals for science and time allocated for teachers to prepare to implement the curriculum are strong influences in the use of materials (Penuel et al., 2008). Teachers in schools facing accountability pressure were actually more likely to implement the curriculum, perhaps because they had fewer other options and felt obligated to comply with the state. Thus, there is a need to tailor implementation support and professional development to local level needs (Penuel et al., 2008).

In some schools or districts, mainly in the upper grades, elementary teachers may specialize such that one teacher for the grade level teaches all of the science units for the grade, while another teacher teaches all of the social studies units—or any number of permutations of this setup. Chapter 9 explores the research related to science specialists.

HOW FEDERAL AND STATE POLICIES INFLUENCE INSTRUCTIONAL TIME, TESTING, AND (IN)EQUITIES IN SCIENCE AND ENGINEERING EDUCATION

This section takes up one factor that has outsize influence on the teaching and learning of science and engineering in preschool through elementary school: *instructional time*. As shown in Figure 2-1, national policies (including NCLB and ESSA) shape (among other things) state policies on instructional time. Those state policies, in turn, shape district instructional schedules and time allocations, which, in turn, either dictate or at least inform the day-to-day classroom schedule. As this section shows, the amount of time allocated to science and engineering tends to be low compared to the time spent on other subjects.

The typical length of a school day in the elementary grades is 6–7 hours. How that time is used is informed by organizations that make recommendations about "best practices." For example, the American Association of Pediatrics and the Centers for Disease Control and Prevention recommend that children of this age get at least one hour of physical activity each day, including physical education (PE) and/or recess. Children typically get about 25 minutes for lunch. They often have a 90-minute English language arts (ELA) block,[6] a 60-minute block for mathematics, one or two specials (such as PE, library, art, or music) for 45 minutes plus transition time, some dedicated time for social-emotional learning and community building within the classroom, as well as transition times throughout the day. In addition, children may need some additional support in language or in academic content areas; based on studies across elementary and secondary education, these learners may be pulled out during times that are not seen as core content areas (NASEM, 2018a; in particular, see Table 7.1 in Smith, 2020). Schools not meeting state-level accountability measures receiving Title 1 federal funds and schools with large populations of children coming from low-income families often incorporate double blocks for reading and mathematics in their elementary school schedules (Au, 2007) or narrow the curriculum (Bacon and Ferri, 2013). These accountability measures may thus limit the amount of time afforded to children for subject area learning outside of reading and mathematics; Anderson (2012) provides a review of test-based accountability policies and implications for K–12 science teaching and learning with some studies focusing on elementary settings and a subset examining effects with historically marginalized populations.

In elementary school, instructional time for science is not usually *mandated* at the state level but is left up to districts, school leaders, or individual teachers (Blank, 2013). In most districts, science is seen as a core content

---

[6] Children in K–3 traditionally have a 90-minute reading block with additional time devoted for writing and spelling whereas in grades 4 and 5 they have the 90-minute ELA block which includes reading and writing.

area, though some districts treat science as a special. Engineering is less often included as an academic content area, either as part of science or on its own, though in some contexts, engineering may be addressed in a makerspace or STEM specials time block. It has been suggested that the emphasis on ELA and mathematics, often to the exclusion of science and engineering, is due in part to the demands of high-stakes testing in ELA and mathematics at the elementary grades (Amrein and Berliner, 2002; Anderson, 2012; Bacon and Ferri, 2013; Christenson et al., 2007) (as discussed below; the integration of science and engineering with ELA and mathematics is explored in depth in Chapter 6). Therefore, the elementary grades—particularly the lower elementary grades, often called the primary grades—often include little instructional time for science (or social studies, or informational text of any kind) (Anderson, 2012; Duke, 2000; Fitchett and Heafner, 2010; Jeong, Gaffney, and Choi, 2010; McGuire, 2007; Pace, 2011; VanFossen, 2005; Vogler et al., 2007). The same is true of science and engineering instructional time in preschool (Early et al., 2010; Piasta, Pelatti, and Miller, 2014; Tu, 2006). In fact, preschool children spend substantially less time (roughly half the proportion of learning time) on science than other disciplines such as literacy (Early et al., 2010).

In an effort to ensure that learners perform well on high-stakes testing in elementary school, some states have adopted policies about language instruction, like third-grade reading laws,[7] which has implications for emergent multilingual learners. As described in a previous National Academies report (NASEM, 2018a), "a majority of districts and schools, especially in states that do not require or offer support for bilingual programming, implement pull-out [English as a Second Language] ESL programs at the elementary level" (p. 258). Some states have English-only policies. These policies require emergent multilingual learners to participate in extended daily English Language Development instruction (i.e., 4 hours), sometimes at the expense of inclusion in content instruction (Gándara and Hopkins, 2010).

There has been a shift away from pulling out learners from regular classroom instruction. In 2016, 63 percent of learners identified as needing special services received 80 percent or more of their instruction in regular classrooms. However, one-half of children categorized with multiple disabilities or intellectual disabilities received their education inside a regular classroom less than 40 percent of the time (Clements et al., 2021; Office of Special Education and Rehabilitative Services, 2018).[8] Overall, policies aimed at providing additional supports for children often lead to them missing core instruction in science and engineering and not having the same opportunities as their

---

[7] For more information, see http://ceelo.org/wp-content/uploads/2019/09/CCSSO_CEELO_third_grade_reading.pdf.

[8] These data reflect children and youth ages 3–21 receiving special education services (or roughly 6 million learners). The data are not disaggregated by elementary grades and do not speak to which subject areas learners are being pulled out for additional instruction.

peers to gain foundational skills and content knowledge that allow them to excel in these disciplines from elementary through middle and high school.

The sections that follow first unpack how policies at the federal and state levels have contributed to the comparatively low amount of instructional time allocated to elementary science and engineering and depict in more detail the realities of instructional time in those subjects. Then, the impacts of these policies (and resulting instructional time) on testing and on inequities across groups of children are explored.

Impact of NCLB and ESSA on Instructional Time

The Every Student Succeeds Act (ESSA) of 2015 is the eighth reauthorization of the *Elementary and Secondary Education Act* (ESEA), which was first passed in 1965 and which aimed to improve educational equity for children from lower-income families by providing federal funds to school districts serving them. In return, federal funds allocated to states and districts were tied to federal accountability requirements outlined in the law; this continues in the present with $19.4 billion to be allocated to states through federal block grants in FY21 alone (U.S. Department of Education, 2020). This represents the single largest source of federal funding for elementary and secondary education for states and districts in the United States. Since funding to states, then passed through to school districts, is contingent on states and school districts meeting the requirements outlined in the law, it is a significant driver in the public education system, driving state and local policies and directly influencing priorities for classroom instruction.

NCLB (passed in 2001), the previous form of ESEA, served as the education law of the land for approximately 15 years. Under NCLB, as with ESSA, priority was given to mathematics and reading as districts and schools were expected to demonstrate AYP on assessments administered in reading and mathematics to all student subgroups each year in grades 3–8. Although NCLB required states to adopt science standards at all grade levels, state science assessments were not required until 2007; policies only required states to assess science once in grades 3–5 and did not require them to incorporate science assessment results as part of accountability measures determined by AYP (Judson, 2013).

The federal requirements created a strong incentive for state policies and programs to focus on reading and mathematics in preschool and elementary and for schools and classroom teachers to prioritize instructional time for these two subjects over other subjects like science and engineering. Although time allocated to instruction of different subjects is often made at the local level and sometimes by individual teachers (McMurrer, 2008; Murnane and Raizen, 1988), a few states, like Florida, enacted policies requiring that all elementary schools teach reading in a dedicated, uninterrupted block of time of at least 90 minutes duration daily to all children (Florida State Board Rule 6A-6.053). Florida also requires that children who do not meet reading proficiency benchmarks through assessments given at the beginning of the school year be provided additional instructional time for reading intervention services and require that the 300 lowest-performing elementary schools in reading achievement provide an additional hour per day of intensive reading instruction to all children. Other states do not set forth specific amounts of time for reading instruction daily but do recommend it.

Data from the Schools and Staffing Survey of teachers conducted from 1987 through 2008 provide insights into the amount of instructional time allocated for science and other core academic subjects in elementary grades before and after NCLB were enacted (Blank, 2013; Snyder, Dillow, and Hoffman, 2009). Figure 2-2 shows that time for science instruction in grades 1–4 declined from an average of 3.0 hours per week in 1993–1994 (180 minutes) to 2.6 hours (156 minutes) in 2000 (when NCLB was initiated) and to 2.3 hours (138 minutes) in 2004 and 2008 (Blank, 2013). English language arts instructional time increased concomitantly.

The Center on Education Policy (Kober and Usher, 2012) reported that

> ... seventy-one percent of the school districts [they] surveyed reported that they reduced elementary school instructional time in at least one other subject to make more time for reading and mathematics—the subjects tested for NCLB. In some case study districts, struggling students receive double periods of reading or math or both—sometimes missing certain subjects altogether. (p. 2)

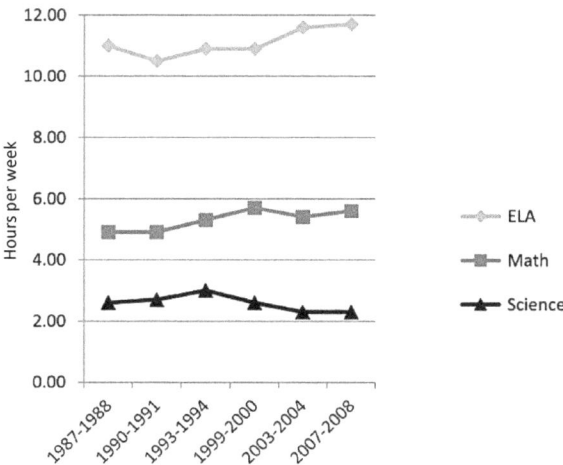

FIGURE 2-2 Instructional time for science in grades 1–4.
SOURCE: Blank (2013).

Though science has long been considered an "undervalued school subject" in elementary schools (see Spillane et al., 2001), accountability measures and policies have pushed science off the daily school schedule altogether (Marx and Harris, 2006). Post-NCLB studies describe how teachers emphasized language arts and mathematics over science (Diamond and Spillane, 2004) and principals told teachers not to teach nontested subjects, especially in the few months prior to the testing window (Lee and Luykx, 2005; Milner et al., 2012).

Furthermore, the more recent National Survey of Science and Mathematics Education (NSSME+) (Banilower et al., 2018) collected data on elementary science instruction. The survey examined time spent on different subjects in the elementary grades, looking at connections to the composition of the classes (such as gender or race/ethnicity of children and their prior achievement levels). The survey asked elementary teachers in self-contained classrooms how often they taught science. Table 21 in the NSSME+ report (reproduced in Table 2-1 here) shows that 18 percent of teachers in K–2 and 26 percent of teachers in grades 3–5 reported teaching science most or all days every week of the school year. On the other hand, about 40 percent of the teachers reported teaching science 3 or fewer days each week, and another 40 percent reported teaching science some weeks but not every week. In terms of instructional time, teachers reported teaching science about 20 minutes per day on average, with fewer instructional minutes (17) at the primary (K–2) level and slightly more instructional minutes (23) at the upper elementary level (3–5).

When survey data from Blank (2013) and NSSME+ (2018) are combined, it shows that average time for elementary science instruction has steadily declined from 3.0 hours per week in 1994 to 1.8 hours per week in 2012, representing a 40 percent reduction in time (on average) for elementary science instruction since the enactment of policies and accountability measures under NCLB in 2000. Table 2-2 summarizes these findings.

Although many teachers reported less time for science instruction under NCLB, the frequency of teachers reporting spending at least 4 hours of

TABLE 2-1 Frequency with Which Self-Contained Elementary Teachers Teach Science

	Percentage of Classes		
	All Elementary	K–2	3–5
All/most days, every week	21% (1.5)	18% (1.7)	26% (2.1)
Three or fewer days, every week	39% (1.6)	41% (2.0)	8% (2.3)
Some weeks, but not every week	39% (1.8)	42% (2.3)	36% (2.1)

NOTE: Standard errors are listed in parentheses.
SOURCE: Banilower et al. (2018).

TABLE 2-2 Instructional Time for Science in Elementary Classrooms, 1994 to 2018

Year	1994	2000	2004	2008	2012	2018
Hours per/week	3.0	2.6	2.3	2.3	1.8	1.9

SOURCE: Drawing on Blank (2013) and Banilower et al. (2018).

weekly instructional time on science was significantly higher in states that integrated fourth grade science achievement into accountability formulas versus states where science did not figure in high-stakes accountability (Judson, 2013).

Elementary teachers who participated in the NSSME+ indicated that engineering concepts and skills received the least attention in the instructional time devoted for science instruction, indicating that children are provided less time for engineering education in elementary. However, elementary teachers and schools are not often asked to report set-aside time for engineering education in makerspaces or other time blocks devoted to engineering or STEM specials that might incorporate engineering concepts and skills.

Impact of NCLB and ESSA on Student Achievement and Testing

Instructional time is typically a reflection of a school's priorities, which are often driven by accountability and testing. However, preschools and other early childhood spaces are less constrained by high-stakes testing and accountability, and thus could serve as a model for older grades. What impact have these reform efforts had in terms of ELA, mathematics, and science testing in elementary settings? ESEA aimed to improve educational equity for children. However, the relative performance of low-income districts only climbed by about 0.1 standard deviation (SD) on the National Assessment Educational Progress after a decade of reform efforts under NCLB (Hansen et al., 2018). The white-Black gap in eighth-grade reading has stayed more consistent over the past two decades, with each measurement between 0.7 and 0.8 SD. Although more time and resources have been afforded to literacy under NCLB at the federal, state, and local levels and instructional time for science has declined, little gains have been made in literacy proficiencies or science proficiencies and the racial/ethnic achievement gaps have been marginally reduced between Black and Hispanic children and their white peers (Snyder, de Brey, and Dillow, 2019).[9]

---

[9] Some scholars have suggested that achievement gaps have provided a limited understanding of educational injustices and that "gap gazing" may be counterproductive (Gutiérrez, 2008). Looking at these gaps as "education debt" may be a more productive orientation (Ladson-Billings, 2006), and is in keeping with this report's use of the system as a unit of analysis.

Although the testing provisions are the same under ESSA, as compared to NCLB, states were given more authority to design their own accountability systems. Both NCLB and ESSA require state testing in *reading and mathematics* annually in grades 3–8 and once in high school. Both also require state testing once in *science* annually in each grade span including 3–5, 6–8, and 10–12. NCLB required that 100 percent of children be proficient in reading and mathematics by the end of school year 2013–2014. ESSA, on the other hand, has extensive requirements for state-developed accountability systems, including that they (a) include performance goals for each subgroup; (b) annually measure student performance based on state assessments; (c) for high schools—annually measure graduation rates; (d) for elementary and middle schools—annually measure student growth (or another valid and reliable statewide academic indicator); (e) include one other indicator of school quality or student success that allows for meaningful differentiation, such as student or educator engagement, or school climate and safety; (f) for all students classified by districts as English learners—measure English language proficiency annually in grades 3–8 and once in high school; (g) annually identify and differentiate schools based on all indicators; and (h) differentiate schools in which any subgroup is consistently underperforming. ESSA allows states to decide how much weight to give tests in their accountability systems and determine what consequences, if any, should attach to poor performance. ESSA also requires states to give more weight to academic factors than other factors (ASCD, 2015).

At least 19 states made science part of their school rating systems (Klein, 2018). However, states are not setting goals around science the way they are for English language arts and mathematics (Achieve, 2017).

Impact of NCLB and ESSA on Equity and Opportunities for Improvement

In many ways, rather than redressing inequities, these policies have exacerbated inequities in elementary science and engineering. Marginalized children are disproportionately affected (Tate, 2001), with inequities in science learning found by third grade (Quinn and Cooc, 2015). Even only a few years into the NCLB era, scholars were concerned about its inequitable effects in science. For example, Marx and Harris (2006) wrote:

> We worry that standards-based science instruction, with its emphasis on scientific thinking and reasoning skills in the context of meaningful real-world investigations, will become a kind of "upper-class science" available primarily to students in high-performing schools and districts and less common in schools that serve poor and minority students. (p. 471)

More recently, scholars are concerned about whether some children are less likely to be provided science and engineering instruction (e.g., Berg and Mensah, 2014; Blank, 2013; Carrier, Tugurian, and Thomson, 2013; Judson, 2013). This concern is certainly borne out in the NSSME+ (2018) (see Trygstad et al., 2020), which shows that teachers in schools serving larger numbers of children who receive free and reduced-price meals perceive instructional time, access to resources, and other related factors to be more limiting, in terms of their engaging in effective science instruction, than do teachers in schools serving children from families with more resources. Concerns also focus on whether the nature of those experiences is likely to be poorer—for example, less authentic. Merely "including" all children in science and closing the achievement gap are not enough (Calabrese Barton and Tan, 2020; see also Gutiérrez, 2008).

As indicated by the *Framework*, science and engineering skills and concepts build from early elementary, through late elementary, middle school, and high school. Table 2-3 showcases recommendations from the *Framework* for how children build understanding toward the disciplinary core idea of *Chemical Reactions* across the grade bands of K–12.

As indicated in the table, learning of science and engineering relies on children experiencing and understanding concepts that build upon one another across the grade levels, in ways similar to how foundational literacy knowledge and skills develop toward reading comprehension and secondary literacy proficiency. This makes foundational science and engineering essential for success in later grade levels and postsecondary settings, and requires that all children have access to these foundational learning experiences starting in preschool and continuing throughout all elementary grades. Yet the instructional time data presented above make clear that this is not currently the case.

Opportunities exist under ESSA to address some of the inequities in elementary science and engineering. These opportunities are sometimes underutilized in state plans. ESSA, for example, allows states to use a single annual summative assessment or multiple statewide interim assessments throughout the year that result in one summative score (ASCD, 2015). This means that states can work alongside school districts to offer a series of authentic assessment tasks through the school year that engage children in explaining scientific phenomena and solving problems through investigations conducted on site in schools. ESSA also requires state-developed accountability systems that include performance goals for each subgroup. As a result, states can ensure that children who have been historically marginalized are afforded the supports needed, even if a school district has a lower population of children from certain subgroups. ESSA allows states to decide how much weight to give tests in their accountability systems and determine what consequences,

TABLE 2-3 Recommended Progression for Building Understanding

By the End of Grade 2	By the End of Grade 5	By the End of Grade 8	By the End of Grade 12
Heating or cooling a substance may cause changes that can be observed. Sometimes these changes are reversible (e.g., melting and freezing), and sometimes they are not (e.g., baking a cake, burning fuel).	When two or more different substances are mixed, a new substance with different properties may be formed; such occurrences depend on the substances and the temperature. No matter what reaction or change in properties occurs, the total weight of the substances does not change.	Substances react chemically in characteristic ways. In a chemical process, the atoms that make up the original substances are regrouped into different molecules, and these new substances have different properties from those of the reactants. The total number of each type of atom is conserved, and thus the mass does not change. Some chemical reactions release energy, others store energy.	Chemical processes, their rates, and whether or not energy is stored or released can be understood in terms of the collisions of molecules and the rearrangements of atoms into new molecules, with consequent changes in total binding energy (i.e., the sum of all bond energies in the set of molecules) that are matched by changes in kinetic energy. In many situations, a dynamic and condition-dependent balance between a reaction and the reverse reaction determines the numbers of all types of molecules present. The fact that atoms are conserved, together with knowledge of the chemical properties of the elements involved, can be used to describe and predict chemical reactions. Chemical processes and properties of materials underlie many important biological and geophysical phenomena.

SOURCE: Based on the *Framework* (NRC, 2012).

if any, should attach to poor performance. It also requires states to give more weight to academic factors than other factors—although ESSA, like NCLB, continues to prioritize ELA and mathematics for preK–12 education. Therefore, there are opportunities to address accountability in novel ways that expand rather than narrow the curriculum to which elementary children have access. As noted above, preschool settings do not have these same pressures from high-stakes testing and could serve as a model.

Finally, ESSA allows 100 percent transferability between Title II (educator supports) and Title IV, and also from Titles II and IV into Title I. As a result of this funding flexibility, schools have fewer restrictions on how they might utilize federal funds to achieve school improvement efforts or support subgroup populations of children. Although the flexibility offers the possibility for schools to utilize funds for the purpose of improving elementary science and engineering education, if schools continue to feel the pressure to prioritize ELA and mathematics, the flexibilities could further reduce the amount of funding schools allocate to elementary science and engineering education.

SYSTEMS WITHIN HISTORICAL CONTEXTS

Preschool and elementary science and engineering are situated within policy and system contexts that shape when, how, and how often these subjects are taught. Schools and systems are also shaped by longstanding expectations that in schools, children acquire basic skills; comply with rules; learn how to get along with others; be self-directed enough to carry out tasks independently; and complete their work carefully and accurately.

Schooling practices can reinforce notions that intelligence is fixed and natural, rather than a cultural construct that can differ across contexts and timepoints (Hatt, 2012; Oakes, 2005). These practices, on the surface, could be interpreted as well intentioned, ensuring all children get equal access to a good education; however, decades of research on these kinds of practices have suggested that they have the potential to harm youth (Nieto and Bode, 2007; Schissel, 2019; Tyack and Cuban, 1997). They can perpetuate deficit-based assumptions about minoritized youths' intelligence and academic potential, which follow them through their schooling (Knoester and Au, 2017).

Change is needed; however, practices or institutional policies that fall too far afield from these historical practices would be difficult to sustain (Carlone, Kimmel, and Tschida, 2010; Penuel, 2019; Tyack and Cuban, 1997). Penuel (2019) suggests approaching school reform through the work of infrastructuring, which focuses on supporting educators in redesigning existing routines of schools and school districts, rather than overhauling the entire system.

These analyses of systems and policies show the complexities of the educational endeavor. They also show the effects of systemic injustices that have been in play in the education system for decades. Thus, beyond the instructional vision of three-dimensional learning put forward by the *Framework* and the resulting changes in instructional materials, assessments, and professional learning opportunities, there is an imperative to address issues of equity and justice at all levels of the system. The next section addresses some of the implications of the evidence base for conceptualizing policies and systems.

POLICY AND SYSTEM IMPLICATIONS FOR WORKING TOWARD EQUITY

Beginning with the first approach to equity outlined in Chapter 1, the biggest issue in terms of children's *increasing opportunities for and access to high-quality science and engineering* (Approach #1) in preschool through elementary is the instructional time devoted to these areas, and the accompanying provision of resources. Without time devoted to science and engineering, children do not have access. The chapter shows how instructional time for science has steadily dropped over recent decades, with concomitant increases in the instructional time for mathematics and, especially, for English language arts. One specific issue relates to children being pulled out of their few opportunities for science and engineering learning to receive remedial reading help or Individualized Education Program services.

With regard to *increased achievement, representation, and identification with science and engineering* (Approach #2), systems and policies have the biggest focus on achievement. The chapter shows how education policies that have aimed to increase student achievement—in mathematics and reading—have had the perhaps unintended effect of decreasing children's opportunities to learn science, as discussed above. Districts are working to redress these issues through providing fiscal resources and setting instructional time expectations.

The *Framework* itself attempted to *expand what constitutes science and engineering* (Approach #3), in that it emphasizes that science entails much more than memorizing facts. The turn toward practice reflects the idea of engaging children in the work of science and engineering to help them understand and appreciate the natural and designed world. And yet, as the chapter emphasizes, systems can serve to reify the status quo, making change toward *any* expansion of "what counts" as science or engineering to be a challenge.

The committee did not find literature focused on how systems or policies do or could support a move toward recognizing *science and engineering as a part of justice movements* (Approach #4). This would be an area for future research.

SUMMARY

A new vision for science and engineering education calls for all children to be afforded the opportunity to engage in meaningful, interesting, and compelling science and engineering learning experiences that engage them in describing and explaining phenomena and solving problems as scientists and engineers do. However, policies and components within preschool and elementary systems must align and be supportive of that vision if children are to benefit from it. With time for science instruction declining steadily over the past 20 years under the accountability pressures associated with other subjects like English language arts and mathematics, it will be challenging for teachers to provide the science and engineering learning experiences preschool and elementary children deserve and need to be proficient in later grades and postsecondary science and engineering courses and fields. For children with learning disabilities and/or learning differences, emergent multilingual learners, or those not meeting benchmark proficiencies for reading, writing, and mathematics, time for science and engineering instruction is further limited or absent completely as they are pulled for remediation or additional support services. Without intentional efforts to develop local, state, and federal policies that prioritize foundational science and engineering, children in preschool and elementary will continue to receive limited instructional time for science and engineering and the system will perpetuate inequitable access to quality science and engineering learning experiences that many children in the United States currently experience.

3

The Contextual Nature of Children's Learning

Main Messages

- Four big ideas guide this report's perspective on learning: (1) learning is a social and cultural process; (2) learning is a process of identity development; (3) children move through a range of cultural contexts where they learn science and engineering, and variations in these contexts shape what and how children learn; and (4) learning in these disciplines is not neutral because the disciplines themselves are not neutral.

- Science and engineering learning experiences provide unique opportunities for children to identify as people who do and value science and engineering. When children are provided opportunities to explore questions that matter to them and are recognized as knowledge-producers and problem solvers, increases in motivation and disciplinary affiliation are observed.

- The broadly defined family context is a child's primary learning community; therefore, families are essential partners in the learning of science and engineering in preschool through elementary grades.

During the preschool and elementary years, children's worlds expand and grow in complexity in ways that steadily broaden their approaches to posing scientific questions, pursuing investigations, and designing solutions to self-defined engineering problems. Children's learning in general is connected to and interdependent with both the human communities where they live and the natural ecosystems where those communities exist. This chapter looks at how both natural and social systems shape children's science and engineering experiences.

As children make their initial ideas and understanding visible, consider disagreements and gaps in their knowledge, and evaluate how new data and experiences relate to and help refine their ideas, they engage in *sensemaking* (Schwarz, Passmore, and Reiser, 2017; Warren et al., 2001). Schwarz and colleagues write:

> Sense-making... is the conceptual process in which a learner actively engages with the natural or designed world; wonders about it; and develops, tests, and refines ideas with peers and the teacher. Sense-making is the proactive engagement in understanding the world by generating, using, and extending scientific knowledge in communities. Sense-making is about actively trying to figure out how the world works and exploring how to create or alter things to achieve design goals. (p. 6)

Children's sensemaking is shaped by their social, cultural, historical, and even political contexts and the norms and practices, implicit social goals, relationships, and material and semiotic resources available in those contexts (including materials that may be inherently biased). Learning to see the value in children's sensemaking, or taking a *sensemaking stance* (Bang et al., 2017; Warren et al., 2001), is an important task of educators and others who support children's learning, as subsequent chapters address.

This chapter explores how children engage in sensemaking and the many contexts in which they learn about disciplinary approaches to and explanations of the natural and the designed world, about themselves as thinkers and actors, and about scientific investigation and engineering design as distinctive approaches to understanding the world (Bricker and Bell, 2014). It does not address how children come to be proficient in investigation and design (addressed in Chapter 4) nor how to support children's learning (addressed in Chapter 5). And in keeping with the rest of the report, the focus of this chapter is on preschool through fifth grade, though foundations for science and engineering learning begin from the start of children's lives.

This chapter is organized around four big ideas. First, learning is a social and cultural process, where culture is understood as shared behaviors, practices, and orientations of socially distinguishable groups passed down from one generation to the next (Eisenhart, 2001). Second, learning is a process of identity development. As children engage in scientific and engineering practices, they position themselves and get positioned by others as particular kinds of people (e.g., as people who competently do science or engineering). Third, children move through a range of cultural contexts where they learn science and engineering, and variations in these contexts shape what and how children learn. Fourth, how teachers teach and children learn science and engineering are shaped by social and political forces—learning in these disciplines is not neutral because the disciplines themselves are not neutral. Box 3-1 provides an example of how these big ideas play an important role in children's learning and sensemaking. The box is followed by sections that elaborate further on each of the four big ideas.

LEARNING IS A CULTURAL PROCESS

Learning is not merely *influenced by* culture, it *is* a cultural process (Nasir et al., 2014), by which it is meant that people learn in interaction with others, through participation in cultural activity, and with material and conceptual tools. Culture is dynamic and constitutes a repertoire of practices rather than a set of traits or characteristics attributable to a group of people (Gutiérrez and Rogoff, 2003). On one hand, there is some stability to culture and cultural practices, as culture is generational, defined by "patterns in the collective behaviors and central orientations of socially distinguishable groups" (Eisenhart, 2001, p. 201). On the other hand, cultural groups and their behaviors are adaptable as social, political, and geographic realities change. In response to changing conditions, cultural groups improvise and adapt existing cultural practices, such as uses of time, rituals, norms, discourse patterns, tools, beliefs, design of physical spaces, and values. Additionally, individuals are not defined by any one cultural group, nor are cultural groups homogenous. Thus, it is a mistake to make assumptions about learners based on one or two cultural groups to which they belong.

That said, children are always shaped and directed in their learning by the cultural groups in which they *participate*, and they build their own, rapidly developing internalized understanding about how those groups work, how to participate in them, and the ways of doing and being they value and marginalize (Legare, 2019). And as children participate in multiple cultural groups, they develop competency within a broad range of practices that, in turn, promote *variation* in how they participate in and make meaning of their communities' activities (Gutiérrez and Rogoff, 2003).

Viewing learning as a cultural process does not negate the role of biological processes (Lee, Meltzoff, and Kuhl, 2020). Neuroscientists have a growing interest in learning, investigating how experiences shape genetic expression. Biology and cultural experiences cannot be viewed as separate aspects of learning, nor should they be considered fixed or deterministic

BOX 3-1
Learning in Places Vignette

Ms. Poppy's second-grade class is on an outdoor learning walk as part of the Learning in Places project. Their school is in a large city in the Pacific Northwest and is connected to a city park. The class has a regular practice of walking the main path in the park throughout the year. This "wondering walk" supports children in noticing and wondering about seasonal phenomena, histories of places, humans' relationships to the natural world, and ethical decision making. In this particular wondering walk, they were asked to notice and wonder about seasonal phenomena as they walked. Ms. Rivers, a white teacher who is the school librarian, accompanies Nick's group on a walk-along with a researcher.

Nick, a Black boy, is wearing a Go-Pro camera to capture what he notices and wonders on the walk. Nick excitedly points out various aspects of the place: a young tree, commenting that he has never seen that before. He calls out repeatedly to his group-mates, "Baby tree! Baby tree! Sandy! Ella!" He goes on to exclaim, "It's a pine tree! I think it's an evergreen, actually. I've never seen a baby tree like that!" He starts walking again and approaches another part of the group that is exploring a shell they found. They talk about when they found a shell, and how long they think it might have been there. Nick says, "I think it was over a year ago."

Nick then comes upon a computer charger on the ground. He says, "What? How did a charger? Look at this. There's even a charger here!" Nick has his hands full of tools for investigation and starts to move the charger around with his feet and kick it to move it closer to where his group is standing. Meanwhile, Ms. Rivers and Ms. Dalia, another teacher, are speaking to the other children in the group. Nick again cries out, "Who would pu... And look there's even a charger!"

At this point, Carly, a white child, says, "Nick, please stop kicking that. You're kicking that there and making dust go everywhere." Ms. Rivers walks over to Nick and says, "Can I make a suggestion? She just asked you to stop doing something. Did you stop? Listen, did you stop?" Nick shakes his head. Ms. Rivers asks, "Why?"

Nick: Because it looks so weird.
Ms. Rivers: Okay. But does that-- is... She said the dirt was going in their eyes. Is that okay?
Nick: They never said-- She never said they were going...
Ms. Rivers: She said it's kicking up dirt. So come here, friend. Turn off the camera a second. Come here. We need to talk.

Ms. Rivers turns the camera off. Another child's Go-Pro camera picks up Ms. Rivers admonishing Nick for using his body and voice inappropriately outdoors.

In the above interactions with place, Nick excitedly notices trees, the kinds of trees, and the age of trees. Nick also comments about time, with regard to the shell. When he notices the charger, he rightly points out how "weird" it is to see this charger on the path in the park, especially given his familiarity with the park. Because the class makes regular visits to this park, these noticings and comments are made in the context of the other visits that Nick and his class have made throughout the year. The camera he wears captures his excitement and his repeated bids for attention from Ms. Rivers and his group-mates. When he is finally noticed, he is noticed by the teacher for a disciplinary action, thus negating the interesting sensemaking he was doing around place. More specifically, his behavior was interpreted by Ms. Rivers as directly harming Carly ("She said the dirt was going in their eyes"), despite Carly never claiming that harm.

Both Nick and Carly likely learn something from this interaction. Carly may learn that, through her words, she can mobilize the authority of a powerful figure (Ms. Rivers) to take action against a Black boy. Nick may learn that his actions can be interpreted as harmful against a white girl, rather than as curiosity and sensemaking. By turning off the camera, Ms. Rivers also communicates to Nick that their interaction is to be kept off the record. While Nick and Carly are physically in the same location, opportunities for what and how they learn are vastly different.

The lesson in this vignette was designed to engage children directly with the *cultural* and the *contextual* dimensions of science learning by inviting them to bring a scientific lens to an environment they knew well through everyday experience, and by creating space for children's personal experiences and observations of that environment to be surfaced and shared. As the lesson unfolded, two children moved through different experiences of *identity formation*. One child was told (through talk, body language, actions like the camera being turned off, and physical movement in place) that his observations were not recognizable in the way that he expressed them—his noticings were penalized, not taken up. Another was told that her ability to work and think scientifically was important enough to not be disrupted by the actions of others. Finally, the vignette suggests that both the objects of scientific study and the process of science teaching and learning are not *neutral*—that what is seen, heard, recognized, and validated may be dependent on histories and patterns of interaction that operate without regard to classically scientific ideas of objectivity or empirical analysis.

SOURCE: Based on research from the Learning in Places project (Learning in Places Collaborative, 2020). For more information about the Learning in Places project and sample storylines, see http://learninginplaces.org.

variables of the learning process (Lee, Meltzoff, and Kuhl, 2020). Variability in learning and development points to the need to organize learning settings to be adaptive and responsive to learners. Encouragement and guidance from the adults in their lives shape children's understanding of what kinds of expressions of their curiosity are valued and appropriate to their identity and the settings where they live. Participation in social and cultural practices affects an individual's development at the same time that individuals push on, innovate, and ultimately "hand down" cultural practices to the next generation of descendants (Rogoff, 2003).

The inherently social and cultural nature of learning and development is well established (National Academies of Sciences, Engineering, and Medicine [NASEM], 2018b). Here, in discussing the chapter's first big idea, that learning is a cultural process, the focus is on how symbolic resources, made available through talk and text, and material resources (i.e., physical objects and tools) mediate children's opportunities to learn science and engineering. This section first considers how children's interactions with these resources are constituted through relationships, then turns to the roles of discourses and material resources—all important dimensions of learning when construed as cultural.

Relationships and Culture

Humans primarily learn "from, with, and in relationships with social others" (Lee, Meltzoff, and Kuhl, 2020, p. 25), and these relationships occur within the multiple cultural groups to which children belong. Children imitate and get feedback from others in their immediate environment as they learn to talk, think, act, and use tools to engage in sensemaking and problem solving. These social others include family members, caregivers, siblings, friends, teachers, and other people with whom children might interact. Across all the settings in which they participate, children's healthy development depends upon sensitive, attuned, trustworthy, consistent relationships with adults (Darling-Hammond et al., 2020; Osher et al., 2020).

Children also learn from, and with, the natural world, and these relationships between humans and the more-than-human world are, like children's relationships with other people, also shaped by cultural beliefs and practices (Barajas-López and Bang, 2018). In contrast, perpetuating a nature-culture divide separates and elevates humans from the "natural world" such that places are seen as existing in the service of humans (Tuck and Yang, 2012).

Learning from and with others, including the natural and designed world, is a complex endeavor that involves (a) understanding unwritten rules of behavior that shape what and who gets counted as competent; (b) interpreting and adapting to new experiences; (c) managing emotions; (d) a psychological need for belonging; and (e) judgments about the relevance, safety, or threat of the learning setting to one's goals, self-efficacy, or identities (Lee, Meltzoff, and Kuhl, 2020). In the vignette given in Box 3-1, Nick's behaviors were punished, while Carly's actions reinforced school's norms of compliance and bodily control rather than scientific norms of careful observation and curiosity.

Understanding the central role of relationship building and supportive environments in which children learn with one another in creating equitable science and engineering learning environments means that learners are recognized and supported in risk taking, managing uncertainty, and developing joint understanding with others (Jordan and McDaniel, 2014; Manz, 2018). Strong relationships in a learning setting make it more likely that youth will develop competence with important tools and semiotic resources in the setting (Nasir et al., 2020).

Discourse and Culture

Everyday life is accomplished through discourse. Discourse is commonly defined as language-in-use, including talk, nonverbal language, text, signs and symbols, and other semiotic resources such as gesture, eye gaze, prosody, and lexicon (Kelly and Green, 2019). Since Vygotsky (1962), developmental researchers have been interested in how learning includes the appropriation of, and can be seen in, patterns of communication and action. Discourse structures how people interact with each other, and a central way that children learn to act appropriately in various cultural settings is by learning the valued forms of communication in those settings. Discourse is cultural; it cannot be understood separately from the contexts in which it occurs.

Kelly (2017) describes science learning as developing a "repertoire of discursive practices" (p. 224). Discursive practices (or discourse) include language use, symbolic resources, values, beliefs, attitudes, and ways of being in the world. Discursive practices are central to defining, evaluating, and legitimizing knowledge in science and engineering. Indeed, framing science and engineering as practice, as envisioned in *A Framework for K–12 Science Education* (NRC, 2012), means that there are disciplinary discourse practices that are a part of the knowledge-building work.

Children's access to and identification with science and engineering is accomplished, in part, through their increased engagement in the fields' specialized discourse practices. Equitable science and engineering learning settings provide children opportunities for deepening participation in the fields' specialized discourse practices, while not negating the productivity of other practices that are productive and familiar to them. For instance, argumentation is a central discourse practice of science, but too narrowly defining what counts as productive argumentation can thwart youths' productive participation and affiliation in the learning community (Bricker and Bell, 2008). Revisiting Box 3-1, Nick astutely and excitedly shared his observations with peers, listened to and contributed to peers' inferences about geologic time, and joyfully wondered about the curious presence of the computer charger along the trail—his contributions were on point with the stated goals of the lesson. Yet, the historical culture of schooling set parameters for what counted as productive engagement in science and what constituted appropriate discourse.

Research on discourse in education highlights how language use affects learning, but also how language use reproduces and creates social groups (Wortham, Kim, and May, 2017). Discourse practices of schooling, science, and engineering are intimately connected to culture and power. The more rigidly learning settings define acceptable science or engineering discourse, the less likely youth will affiliate with those fields of study (Brown and Spang, 2008; Varelas et al., 2008). For example, the restricted space of traditional school science discourse, with its emphasis on abstract vocabulary, makes it difficult for minoritized learners "who do not command middle-class language practices to participate or be understood" (Rosebery et al., 2010, p. 326) to fully participate or have their contributions be fully understood. Varelas and colleagues (2014) provide another example of how minoritized learners—in this case, Latinx third graders—make sense across informational text and empirical inquiries, using language as they engage in sophisticated sensemaking.

Exploration of the Material World

Sustained and diverse exploration of material resources (physical objects and tools, both natural and made by humans) is central to the development of children's scientific and engineering reasoning (Kelly and Cunningham, 2019; Legare, 2014), their ideas about how the world works (Wertsch, 1985), and their understanding of themselves as competent actors who can effect change in their immediate environment (Schlegel et al., 2019). Investigating the material world—from observing a caterpillar over time to measuring the length of a shadow at different times of day to testing how well a structure can keep ice cream cold—builds critical banks of experiential knowledge that support future learning, not only within science and engineering (Gelman and Brenneman, 2004; Shapiro and Nager, 2000) but also in other domains such as literacy (Lesaux, 2012).

Experiential knowledge of materials forms a central resource that can support learners as they encounter canonical explanations of scientific phenomena or engage in engineering design activities (Duckworth, 1972; National Research Council [NRC], 2007; Worth, 2010). Exploration of materials can also become central to the development of model- and simulation-based reasoning across the elementary grades (Lehrer et al., 2001). Hands-on exploration and design work can also be thought of as a form of learning-through-doing (Keune and Peppler, 2019; Papert, 1980). In contrast, Nick's "kicking dust" in Box 3-1 was not recognized as a mechanism for sensemaking. The use of his foot (while his hands were full) was not recognized as a tool for exploration or as evidence of his attempting to share his finding with his peers. As a result, the sanctioned tools for investigation in his hands were overlooked as resources for continued sensemaking.

LEARNING SCIENCE AND ENGINEERING IS A PROCESS OF IDENTITY FORMATION

What counts as successful learning? Histories of assessment, evaluation, and research predict most people's lists would include children's understanding of science and engineering *knowledge* at the top of the list. Yet, researchers have questioned the reliance on narrow measurement of knowledge and skills as primary indicators of science learning (Luke, Green, and Kelly, 2010). The move toward understanding learning as competent participation in practices is a step toward broadening what counts as learning (Lave and Wenger, 1991; NRC, 2012). An additional step is to understand learning as a process of identity formation (Big Idea 2). How and what children learn is related to the kinds of people children see themselves as, the kinds of people they want to become, and the people they are able to be in a learning context (Hand and Gresalfi, 2015).

Recognizing the centrality of identity calls attention to the individual knower, the kinds of social and cultural practices that enable learning, the opportunities one has to participate legitimately in the social practices that are important to a community of practice, and the meanings one makes of those opportunities (Lave and Wenger, 1991). As learners gain access to the knowledge-generating practices of a community (i.e., scientist or engineers) and get positioned in particular ways by members of a group, they begin to see themselves in relation to the norms and values of that community, as an aspect of identity formation that develops over time (Nasir and Cooks, 2009).

Cultural studies of science learning reveal that learners who succeed in school forms of science may not have positive attitudes about it (Kanter and Konstantopoulos, 2010), may comply with classroom norms without being intellectually engaged (Aikenhead, 2006), may make distinctions between "doing" science and "being" a scientist (Archer et al., 2010), or may not see themselves as being "science people" (Carlone, Haun-Frank, and Webb, 2011).

Viewing learning as identity formation means that science and engineering educators' work is to nurture *humans*, not only to nurture humans' minds. Science and engineering identity development have been documented among elementary-aged youth (Kane, 2012; Tai et al., 2006) and even among younger children in their play choices (Rowe and Neitzel, 2010) and in the kinds of science or engineering engagement families provide (Pattison et al., 2020). In a study of 58 amateur adult astronomers and 49 birders, Jones and colleagues (2017) found that many hobbyists' lifelong science interests began in childhood, shaped by family members and the social capital they provided through science-related leisure activities. Lifelong learning in these hobbies is an indicator of sustained science identity work (Bell et al., 2012).

Many researchers see identity development as situated in the interactional contexts in which people participate rather than a stable set of personality characteristics (Falk, 2009; Gee, 2000; Penuel and Wertsch, 1995). Pattison and colleagues' (2018) identity-frame model demonstrates the processes involved in science and engineering identity work. The model highlights youths' *performance* and *definition work* coupled with others' *recognition* and *positioning work*. Children engage in *performance work* when they make bids to be recognized as a certain kind of person. Identity performances can come in the form of asking lots of questions, holding the floor to explain why one fiddler crab's claw is bigger than another, authoring oneself as the class expert about the solar system, or making a passionate argument for the logic of using a unique material in a small-group's engineering design. *Definition work* comes in the form of youth actively claiming identities ("I'm a tinkerer"), roles they can play in the activity ("I'll be the scribe"), and how they define or frame the activity ("This is a fun puzzle!"). In *recognition work*, bids to get recognized as a certain kind of person can be taken up or rejected by others (Gee, 2000). Others may also *position* youth in ways that support or threaten youths' identity bids, for example, by nurturing or squelching particular actions or statements.

For instance, identity work is visible in the vignette (Box 3-1) as Nick *performs himself* as a curious, enthusiastic investigator, he makes *bids to be recognized* for his sensemaking, and is *framing the activity* as an opportunity to notice, wonder, share discoveries with peers, and make connections. Ms. Rivers *does not recognize his identity bid* and, instead, ascribes an unwanted identity of "troublemaker endangering peers" to his performances. Compliance and control were valued over sensemaking. In another context, Nick may have been celebrated for his enthusiastic, embodied sensemaking, which would bolster his ongoing science identity work.

There is a racialized storyline here, too (Nasir et al., 2012), that factors into how youth and adults define what and who counts as being scientific and what is labeled legitimate scientific practice (Bell, Van Horne, and Cheng, 2017). Nick's behavior gets interpreted as deviant, defiant, and unkind to peers, and he is bodily removed from the activity. This is an all-too familiar story in science and engineering learning settings. Black children are punished more often and more severely than white peers engaging in similar behavior (Basile, 2021; Joseph, Hailu, and Matthews, 2019; Milner, 2020), and may proscribe their own opportunities to learn in order to avoid being labeled as troublemakers (Wright, Wendell, and Paugh, 2018).

A growing body of literature demonstrates that educators overlook children of color's brilliance in early childhood settings (Salazar Pérez and Saavedra, 2017), elementary school science (King and Pringle, 2019; Varelas et al., 2012), and elementary engineering (Pattison et al., 2018; Wright, 2019). In a study of 25 African-American first through third graders' identity work relative to science, Varelas and colleagues (2012) found that "doing school" was a cultural narrative tightly intertwined with "doing science." This construction of "science person" emphasized the accumulation of knowledge and complying with school's behavioral norms and regulations, which can squelch sensemaking, problem solving, risk taking, and expressions of emotional investment, which are all part of developing science and engineering identities (Varelas, Kane, and Wylie, 2011). Nick's experience reflects much of what the research shows is a common experience for many Black children.

SCIENCE AND ENGINEERING LEARNING OCCURS ACROSS CONTEXTS

Children's science and engineering learning develops in multiple settings, in and out of school, and over time (Big Idea 3). These settings differ in the specific forms of engagement with other people, places, and materials that support children's learning.

The available evidence base about children's science and engineering learning is shaped by the settings in which that learning happens and the opportunities involved in conducting research in those settings. Research on children's science learning is often conducted in formal education settings with similarly aged peers (preschool, elementary schools), or in laboratory-based settings involving individual children or child–caregiver dyads. Research in these settings sets aside the complexity of the social contexts in which much of children's learning actually occurs—including multigenerational family groups, and in self-selected social groupings that are often of mixed age—which are all contexts that are relevant to how and where children spend their time. Informal learning environments provide important opportunities to study how learning unfolds in these more complex social groupings (Callanan, 2012). To understand what science and engineering education might look like in formal preschool and elementary school settings, it is crucial to recognize that children bring with them a wide repertoire of knowledge and strategies developed within and across the multiple sites of their activity; from children's perspectives none of these sites are "prior to" the others (Vossoughi and Gutiérrez, 2014).

The Role of Families in Children's Learning

For children, the family unit is a critical social context in which learners both build and make use of their "funds of knowledge" (Moll et al., 1992) and begin to develop the cultural frames that they will use to organize their understanding of themselves as learners and as teachers. The family unit also brings individual learners into contact with a range of more and less formal learning environments in which children can develop generalizable knowledge and understanding of science and engineering. These experiences also contribute to a child's corpus of experiences, observations, and ways of relating that they will draw upon in future, more formal science and engineering learning. For example, in their study of Indigenous families engaging in robotics and storytelling, Tzou et al. (2019) found that parents use family and cultural stories, or *storywork* (Archibald, 2008), to teach their children about ways of knowing and reading the land, as well as their familial and communal responsibilities, both now and in the future. As families built their family stories through robotics, they navigated across their knowledge of robotics, place, family stories, and language. The stories themselves seemed to motivate families to exercise considerable agency over the robotics materials to accurately re-create scenes in their stories. In this way, the act of programming through robotics became a way to build toward cultural thriving and Indigenous futures.

As another example, Bustamante (personal communication, October, 28, 2020) and his colleagues worked with a group of families and caregivers in a predominantly Latinx community. Family elders told stories about going to the grocery store with children; many of these stories involved culturally situated science practices like using one's senses to make observations (e.g., of produce) and crosscutting concepts like structure–function relationships (e.g., of when an avocado may be useful for making guacamole). The group co-designed signs that encouraged families to involve children in selecting produce through making careful observations, and to share their cultural knowledge linking observations with produce selection. Both of these examples, in addition to illustrating the role of families in children's learning, also illustrate the multiple ways of knowing that can add value within children's science and engineering learning, above and beyond a purely Eurocentric perspective.

The portrait of the social nature of learning that children often encounter first with and within family units points to the importance of organizing for social engagement in formal school settings in the preschool and elementary years, not only among age-alike peers but among families and schools (Ishimaru, 2019). Recent research has reframed the family as an intergenerational group in which learning and teaching are distributed in flexible and varying ways (Bang, Montaño Nolan, and McDaid-Morgan,

2018). Within the familial learning community, members can work together to coordinate cultural ways of knowing with formal scientific and engineering ideas and practices that are valued in formal educational and professional settings. Within these settings, every generation brings expertise and knowledge into the group from their experiences in other contexts and sources of expertise.

The role of the family as a resource to support children's learning alongside formal education (e.g., as part of school–family partnerships) is well documented. For example, in Bryk's (2010) study including hundreds of elementary schools in the Chicago Public School system, he found five major factors that influence school improvement, with *strong family–community ties* among them. Mapp and Kuttner (2013) found that effective school–family partnerships involve school staff that can recognize, honor, and connect family funds of knowledge to school learning and families in multiple roles, including as supporters, advocates, and decision makers. Family engagement has been found to be a powerful antiracist tool in pushing schools to de-center whiteness in the literacy curriculum (Delgado-Gaitan, 1990; Reyes and Torres, 2007). Finally, research is increasingly showing that family engagement can have a positive impact on specific disciplinary learning in mathematics (Epstein and Sheldon, 2016), and that young children within family contexts can jointly engage in scientific inquiry around everyday phenomena of interest (Keifert and Stevens, 2019).

Informal Settings Designed for STEM Learning

Science centers, zoos, botanical gardens, and natural history museums are all examples of designed, curated institutional settings that work both to elevate and celebrate various forms of scientific achievement and domination (Harraway, 1984), and to invite and support the public to explore science and engineering in self-directed ways (Falk and Storcksdeick, 2005). These institutions provide spaces where families can explore and explain phenomena together (Gutwill and Allen, 2017; Willard et al., 2019) and discover or pursue topics they are passionate about through programs, camps, and exhibits (Hassinger-Das et al., 2018; Honey and Kanter, 2013; Pattison and Dierking, 2018). There are a variety of pedagogical traditions that guide the design of different informal learning environments, and they can influence children's science and engineering learning in multiple ways (NRC, 2009).

Informal settings can have their drawbacks. Learning in informal environments has been described as "free-choice learning" (Falk and Dierking, 2002), but critical studies have also shown that many learners feel excluded, uncomfortable, or unsure about how to engage with the types of learning experiences these institutions provide (Dawson, 2014). Engagement with traditional sites of science and engineering learning (such as science centers, natural history museums and zoos, as well as scouting programs and outdoor camps) has long been inequitably distributed and dominated by upper-income and white families (Wonch Hill et al., 2020).

They also, of course, have unique affordances. Physical and material forms of play, exploration, and discourse that can be difficult or impossible to support in formal school settings can be encouraged and supported in environments that are spacious, often outdoors, and rich in materials to manipulate and novel settings to explore, and where opportunities and time frames for discussion are more flexible than in most school settings (Bennett and Monahan, 2013; Wohlwend et al., 2017). These environments can provide powerful opportunities for sensemaking (Callanan, Martin, and Luce, 2015), even in contexts that may sometimes initially appear to be "free-wheeling nonsense" (Wohlwend et al., 2017, p. 447).

These opportunities are also highly influenced by the kind of invitations that are extended to visitors. For example, working with 4- to 6-year-olds, Willard and colleagues (2019) examined the talk of parent–child dyads as they explored an exhibit about gears. Signage that prompted caregivers to "explore" with their child produced substantively different conversations, and different patterns of interaction with the gear system, compared to prompts to "explain" the exhibit. Peppler, Keune, and Dahn (2020) have demonstrated that including details about the specific end users whose needs are the subject of engineering design challenges can provoke learners' empathy for the end user, which then supports more diverse and elaborated engagement with the stages of the engineering design process, as compared to design challenges that do not specify their end user. Both of these examples (as well as the example from Bustamante, discussed above) suggest the distinctive opportunities that well-designed informal STEM learning environments can provide for learners and their families as sites for sensemaking and intellectual risk taking (Bencze et al., 2020; Pedretti and Iannini, 2020), which can contribute to children's positive identity formation as science learners among older youth (Lin and Schunn, 2016).

Place-Based Learning

All children learn in places: whether at home, at playgrounds, in neighborhoods, or at school, *places* are ever present. In science education, place-based education (Semken and Freeman, 2008; Sobel, 2004) can have many meanings: from place as a context for connecting local issues to science concepts (Semken and Freeman, 2008) to land-based education that deeply investigates the relationships between humans and the more-than-human world within complex systems (Barajas-López and Bang, 2018; Malone,

2018; Nxumalo, 2019) and considers multiple timescales, including Indigenous people's time (Learning in Places Collaborative, 2020).

Place-based education refers to both geographical locations as well as lived experiences in communities and the natural environment (Gruenewald, 2003). Humans' understanding of place is shaped by family and cultural knowledges and practices and consists of interdependent relationships across local and global scales. Therefore, place-based learning can happen across a full range of settings—places such as parks, forests, or recreation areas; in alleyways, parking lots, and other urban settings; or in rural areas such as farms or creeks.

Place-based science learning often emphasizes the connection between ecological and social systems. It provides a way for children to encounter phenomena in the natural world, wonder and notice, engage in investigations in their communities, and possibly design solutions and work toward local collective action (Lim and Calabrese Barton, 2006). The place-based observation that Nick engages in, as illustrated in Box 3-1, is an example of the opportunities for learning and sensemaking that places afford. Nick notices and wonders about trees, their age, and evidence of human presence in the place.

Places can also provide children with a sense of belonging within both ecological and human communities (Malone, 2018). For example, for children from Indigenous communities that are deeply connected to the land, learning science with place and land (Cajete and Bear, 2000; Kawagley, Norris-Tull, and Norris-Tull, 1998) is a deep way of knowing and being in the world. Therefore, in the places where outdoor learning occurs, those places embody environmental and social narratives and norms that are racialized, historicized, contested, and powered (Gruenewald, 2003; Lim and Calabrese Barton, 2010; Nxumalo, 2019). From this perspective, people and their actions within outdoor learning settings are not neutral or random; they are, instead, situated within historical and spatial contexts that invite or prohibit opportunities for learning (Tzou and Bell, 2012).

Digital Media and Online Learning

Another context for children's learning involves their use of technology; this was true even before the global COVID-19 pandemic that interrupted many children's face-to-face schooling. Most children spend significant portions of their time online and engaging with digital resources. An enormous array of digital media devoted to science and engineering are available and can play constructive roles in expanding young people's understanding of science and engineering phenomena, environments, and ways of working. When integrated with other modes of exploration and discussion, narrative digital media can support young children's science talk and understanding (Penuel et al., 2010). Emergent work with young children suggests the scalable promise of conversational agents in supporting children's sensemaking when viewing public television science programming (Xu and Warschauer, 2020). This is important in part because of the high frequency with which children engage with science-related media such as educational television shows (Silander et al., 2018).

Digital simulations can also be used effectively to support preschool and elementary grade children's learning, with appropriate scaffolding and support from teachers (Smetana and Bell, 2012), though relatively few classroom-based (i.e., not laboratory-based) studies have focused on the use of digital simulations in early science (Falloon, 2019). Digital science journals and other tools for capturing and visualizing photo and video data have also been found to uniquely support science investigation in preschool (Presser et al., 2017, 2019). This work with digital science journals showed how the tools could help children to observe, document, review, and make sense of phenomena that occur across a range of time scales (e.g., plant growth, movement down a ramp; Presser et al., 2019). Finally, emergent findings looking at digital game-based learning in elementary science are suggestive of these games' potential in supporting learning; the systematic review of the (limited) literature also, however, identified possible barriers, including the attitudes of parents and teachers (Hussein et al., 2019).

Electronics can also play an important part in children's informal explorations of engineering. Well-established robotics and programming initiatives and resources for preschool and elementary grade learners have demonstrated young children's ability to design and solve engineering problems using computational strategies (Bers, González-González, and Armas-Torres, 2019), and a range of programs and materials designed to support young learners' exploration of robotics and programming have been studied in classrooms (Pila et al., 2019; Strawhacker and Bers, 2019). Horn (2018), Peppler and colleagues (2019), and others (Kumpulainen, Burke, and Ntelioglou, 2020) have also explored how electronics and computational tools can be integrated into other domains of engineering and making with young learners, including through textiles and visual art. Through making and engineering experiences, children can build their fluency with both electronics and analog materials and ways to integrate them to create artifacts that express their ideas or solve problems that matter to them (Peppler, Halverson, and Kafai, 2016).

LEARNING IS NOT NEUTRAL

Learning is not neutral (Big Idea 4). What is learned, how it is learned, and what counts as competence in learning is continuously shaped by the values, practices, norms, and opportunities in a given setting. These settings themselves exist in relationship to historical and social structures of power. Consequently, learning has moral and ethical dimensions.

Historically, white, middle class, heteronormative, and monolingual discourse practices and values define what is "normal" and expected learning and development (Spencer et al., 2020). This functions to (a) restrict the content and form of science valued and communicated through science education and (b) locate children, particularly minoritized youth, in positions that undermine their engagement in meaningful science learning (Bang et al., 2012)—as illustrated in Box 3-1, with Nick's contributions being dismissed and punished. Children from nondominant communities are asked to give up who they are and how they know to engage in school science, and the result can be that family and community knowledge is positioned as "less rigorous" or "less scientific" than Eurocentric scientific knowledge impacting who is seen as a science learner (Warren et al., 2020). In this way, children who express their learning in language and behaviors that fall outside of those norms get labeled, implicitly and explicitly, as deficit (Brown, Mistry, and Yip, 2019).

EQUITY AND LEARNING ACROSS CONTEXTS

The three key elements considered in the discussion of the first big idea (learning is cultural)—the roles of relationships, discourse, and materials—each have a substantial impact on the design of learning environments and thus children's *increasing opportunities for access to high-quality science and engineering* (Approach #1). For example, when teachers build relationships with children, it can make it more likely that children will take up the tools and resources of a setting (Nasir et al., 2020).

Learning inherently connects to children's *increased achievement, representation, and identification with science and engineering* (Approach #2). Children engage in performance and definition work and this is coupled with others' recognition and positioning work (Pattison et al., 2018). Inequitable disciplinary practices impede children of color from developing positive identification with science and engineering (Basile, 2021; Joseph, Hailu, and Matthews, 2019; Milner, 2020; Wright, Wendell, and Paugh, 2018).

These big ideas have important implications for an *expansive perspective on what constitutes science and engineering* (Approach #3). Because learning is cultural (Big Idea 1) and because learning science and engineering is not neutral (Big Idea 4), the discourses used for science and engineering learning matter. Expanding how science and engineering discourses are defined can bring more children into the work; alternatively, defining these as needing to match white, middle class ways of speaking and expressing ideas leaves children out (Rosebery et al., 2010; see also Bang et al., 2012; Spencer et al.,

2020; Varelas et al., 2014; Warren et al., 2020). Furthermore, science and engineering learning occurs across contexts (Big Idea 3). Taking advantage of and connecting to families and places can also help to develop this more expansive perspective—as shown, for example, when families told stories of the land while engaging with robotics (Tzou et al., 2019).

The scenario of Nick presented in Box 3-1—and the larger research project within which it is situated (Learning in Places Collaborative, 2020)—provides one example of how instruction can support children to *see science and engineering as part of justice movements* (Approach #4). In the project's efforts to make Indigenous people's and future time visible, and to broaden children's perspectives on time and place, the project pushes children to work toward more just futures. Participating children see Indigenous people in the curriculum (thus refusing their invisibility, as is much more typical in school settings). Further research on learning in contexts within projects aimed at seeing science and engineering as a part of justice movements is warranted.

SUMMARY

This chapter explored the rich and varied ways that children make sense of their worlds, learn to connect their increasingly sophisticated sensemaking to their emerging identities as scientific knowers and doers, and engage in learning across settings within and across ever-expanding and overlapping communities. Children engage with multiple cultural groups and develop skills with a broad range of dynamic practices, or repertoires of practice. Yet, learning science and engineering is not only about accumulation of knowledge and skills. Rather, learning science and engineering is a process of identity formation that is ongoing throughout a person's life and can start in productive ways during childhood. When children have opportunities to engage in meaningful scientific work within communities that position them as competent knowers and doers of science, and with the support of adults and peers who know the learner and can recognize and respond to their expressions of their ideas, children can form identities that reinforce connections to being scientists and engineers. Families, other learning partners, out-of-school settings, and digital media can all serve to expand children's opportunities for sensemaking. However, learning settings and learning science and engineering are not neutral. All learning occurs in places that involve powered and racialized relationships that affect what and how children learn.

Across contexts and modalities, children's science and engineering learning is powerfully shaped and potentially supported by both their relationships with others and their opportunities to express and make sense of their own experiences of the world. Subsequent chapters take up how children engage in investigation and design (Chapter 4), how learning environments and instructional design can support them in doing so (Chapters 5 and 6), and how different levers can support the development and enactment of those learning environments (Chapters 7, 8, and 9).

4

Developing Children's Proficiency in and Through Investigation and Design

> **Main Messages**
> - Children engage in meaningful science and engineering from a very young age, across multiple contexts and settings.
> - Forms of activity for investigation and design in preschool through elementary include orienting to phenomena and design challenges, gathering and analyzing data and information, constructing explanations and design solutions, communicating reasoning to self and others, and connecting learning across content areas and across contexts.
> - Children's engagement in investigation and design involves the full range of science and engineering practices. The practices and the forms of activity can be undertaken in any order and combination and this engagement looks different across preschool through fifth grade.
> - The development and expression of children's proficiencies in science and engineering is related to their knowledge, experiences, their cultural and linguistic backgrounds, and the characteristics of the instructional environment and pedagogical approaches.
> - Children's development of ideas and practices is supported by their own intuitive and imaginative ways of investigating and designing.

From infancy, children build on their interactions with both the material world and with the people around them to discover how the world works—physically, socially, and linguistically (National Academies of Sciences, Engineering, and Medicine [NASEM], 2018b). As noted in *Science and Engineering for Grades 6–12* (NASEM, 2019b), "the centerpiece of the vision of the *Framework* is engaging students in making sense of phenomena and designing solutions to meet human needs" (p. 12), and this report builds on that in making science investigation and engineering design central. Science and engineering can be understood as ways of knowing that children can deploy to address questions and issues that matter to them. These investigations can be playful, creative, and sources of joy. They can also be challenging and even troubling as children seek to understand the sources of difficulties and dangers in their lives. Regardless of the direction in which children point their curiosity, young children are developmentally and cognitively capable of making robust, recognizable, and meaningful use of the practices, tools, and big ideas of science and engineering on their own terms and for their own purposes across the contexts of their activity.

This chapter highlights how children's proficiencies, interests, and identities are drawn on and developed through science investigation and engineering design and provides a picture of what this might look like in preschool through elementary school settings. First, the chapter defines investigation and design, describing some key features of these activities. Next, the chapter explores how children develop conceptual understanding through investigation and design, showing the sophistication of children's ideas. Then, the chapter turns to the proficiencies children bring to investigation and design, unpacking how children orient to phenomena and design challenges, collect and analyze data and information, develop explanations and design solutions, communicate reasoning, and connect learning across both content areas and sites of activity. Throughout, the chapter looks at how children can engage in sophisticated scientific and engineering work that is meaningful to them, even from young ages.

This chapter presents research that examines what children do in specific contexts, at specific ages of their cognitive and physical development. Most of this research cannot untangle maturational change from learning and from the context in which the learning occurred (e.g., school experiences, informal spaces, home); this could be achieved through longitudinal studies or cross-sectional developmental research explicitly designed for this purpose, but such research is currently limited. Thus, the discussion in this chapter hangs on a somewhat limited evidentiary base, and the committee does not attempt to untangle learning, maturation, and context.

INSTRUCTION CENTERED ON INVESTIGATION AND DESIGN IN PRESCHOOL THROUGH ELEMENTARY SCHOOL[1]

Centering investigation and design in children's classroom experiences from the earliest years helps them demonstrate and develop their proficiency in science and engineering. This approach emphasizes introducing children to the purposes of science and engineering, and it creates opportunities for learners to develop and use ideas, practices, and tools in the context of meaningful activity (Lehrer and Schauble, 2015; NASEM, 2019b; National Research Council [NRC], 2012; Schwarz et al., 2017). This, in turn, invites exploration of practices, contexts, and questions of their everyday lived experiences (Bang et al., 2012; Davis and Schaeffer, 2019; Rosebery et al., 2010). In learning environments that put investigation and design at the center, children extend their understanding and learn science concepts as they observe and seek to explain puzzling phenomena or work to propose, evaluate, and refine solutions to design problems. Careful design of the learning environment, strategically chosen activities, and teacher guidance support children's learning about and through science and engineering practice (Hmelo-Silver, Duncan, and Chinn, 2007; NRC, 2007).

Defining Investigation and Design

Following *Science and Engineering for Grades 6–12* (NASEM, 2019b), the committee uses the term *investigation* in a broader sense than the science and engineering practice of "planning and carrying out investigations" described in the *Framework* (NRC, 2012) and the Next Generation Science Standards (NGSS; NGSS Lead States, 2013). Investigation highlights the ways that people develop knowledge by puzzling, posing questions, gathering information from a variety of sources—including designing empirical tests and collecting observational data—and revising their ideas in light of that information. The committee uses *investigation* to encompass the full range of science practices children and guiding adults might engage as they seek to understand their world (NASEM, 2019b). This approach is quite different from the so-called "scientific method," in that practices are engaged iteratively, as needed, rather than in lockstep order, and are applied in different combinations across science disciplines (NASEM, 2019b; NRC, 2012).

A focus on *design* recognizes that the overarching enterprise of engineering differs from that of science and that engineering design provides a

---

[1] Portions of this section include content from a paper commissioned by the committee titled "Engineering Education in Pre-Kindergarten through Fifth Grade: An Overview" (Cardella, Svarovsky, and Pattison, 2020).

useful context for allowing children to pose problems, draw on and refine science understanding, and develop their understanding of how the world works. Engineering design is an intentional, iterative activity to develop an object, system, or process that addresses a particular need, solves a particular problem, or accomplishes a particular goal. This activity involves defining and designing optimal solutions to complex problems, testing and refining designs in light of goals for their use, and balancing numerous tradeoffs. Although engineering has often been approached as a process focused on achieving technical quality or innovation, both the profession and K–12 engineering education increasingly recognize the critical role that end users or recipients play in shaping the implementation and sustainability of engineering solutions (Gunckel and Tolbert, 2018; Walther, Miller, and Sochacka, 2017). Cultivating empathetic social perspective-taking is well aligned with engineering practice and with a broader range of goals for science and engineering education (Mouw et al., 2020) and connects to social studies or social sciences, writ large, as well. Here, too, the committee includes the full range of engineering practices when conceptualizing "design."

Thus, investigation and design, together, draw on all of the science and engineering practices named in the *Framework*: asking questions (for science) and defining problems (for engineering); developing and using models; planning and carrying out investigations; analyzing and interpreting data; using mathematics and computational thinking; constructing explanations (for science) and designing solutions (for engineering); engaging in argument from evidence; and obtaining, evaluating, and communicating information. The next section depicts how the science and engineering practices—with disciplinary core ideas and crosscutting concepts—are in play in the forms of activity of investigation and design.

FEATURES OF INVESTIGATION AND DESIGN

The evidence presented throughout this chapter shows that preschool through elementary aged children can engage productively with investigation and design, and through investigation and design can engage in meaningful and robust learning. Children's engagement in investigation and design can be organized into five forms of activity (described in the 6–12 report, NASEM, 2019b) that resemble (but are not identical to) the work of scientists and engineers: children (1) engage with phenomena and design challenges, (2) collect and analyze data and information, (3) construct explanations and design solutions, (4) communicate their reasoning to self and others, and (5) connect learning across content areas and contexts (NASEM, 2019b). Table 4-1 describes the connections between these forms of activity and the science and engineering practices laid out in the *Framework* and NGSS. The forms of activity, and the science and engineering practices encompassed in them, interact throughout the work of investigation and design (Bell et al., 2012; NASEM, 2019b; NRC, 2012), and can be undertaken in any order and in any combination.

TABLE 4-1 Examples of Children's Experiences Within Forms of Activity of Investigation and Design

Orient to Phenomena and Design Challenges	Gather and Analyze Data and Information	Construct Explanations and Design Solutions	Communicate Reasoning to Self and Others	Connect Learning Across Content Areas and Across Contexts
Develop and ask questions about the causes of phenomena.	Plan and conduct investigations or tests of explanations and solutions.	Develop models of the relationships among components within and between systems.	Develop models and artifacts to communicate reasoning.	Use three-dimensional learning to make sense of phenomena across content areas, grades, and contexts such as home and school.
Define engineering challenges by identifying stakeholders, goals, constraints, and criteria for evaluating solutions.	Collect and organize data and seek patterns.	Develop arguments for how the evidence supports an explanation for how and why phenomena occur.	Engage in productive and respectful discourse and argumentation.	Apply learning to make sense of phenomena beyond the classroom.
	Analyze data and evaluate information for evidence.	Design and evaluate solutions based on evidence.	Reflect on learning.	Draw on practices and ideas from mathematics, literacy, social studies, etc.
	Obtain and evaluate information from other sources.			

SOURCE: Adapted from NASEM (2019b, Table 4-2).

DEVELOPING CONCEPTUAL UNDERSTANDING THROUGH INVESTIGATION AND DESIGN

The focus on investigation and design is consistent with the *Framework's* emphasis on the connections between "knowing" and "doing" in science and engineering, underpinning a commitment to integrating science and engineering practices, disciplinary core ideas, and crosscutting concepts in instruction. Cognitive accounts of learning and knowledge development emphasize that expertise involves not only the accumulation of facts and explanations, but the development of networks of concepts, categories, and heuristics for making sense of the world and for problem solving. These networks influence what people notice in new situations, how they organize and interpret information, and how they construct and evaluate explanations (NASEM, 2018b; NRC, 1999). Learning involves integrating information across experiences and contexts, "putting together different sorts of information and experiences, identifying and establishing relationships and expanding frameworks for connecting them" (NASEM, 2018b, p. 90). In addition, the development of a sense of the application and use of knowledge and the ability to extend knowledge beyond the context in which it is learned are essential components of deep and flexible learning (NRC, 1999).

Taking Science to School (NRC, 2007) describes the research base regarding how children understand concepts in physical, biological, and astronomical science and how they develop their conceptual thinking. For example, with instruction, children can come to recognize the importance of internal organs in the human body and elaborate their ideas about how those organs function, combining ideas about structure and (physical) function. They see the heart as a pump and that the body has a system of interconnected tubes for transport of materials. In terms of digestion, children may recognize that food is broken down into pieces—but often miss the idea that digestion involves chemical breakdown as well as physical breakdown.

As described in Chapter 3, practices and ideas are conceptual tools used to navigate activity (NASEM, 2018b; Vygotsky, 1980; Wertsch, 1998) and to understand the natural and designed world. Participating in communities involves learning about and taking up concepts and ideas that shape that community's work (Hall and Jurow, 2015). Disciplinary learning involves learning to use tools developed over the history of disciplines or communities for particular purposes; for example, children learn how to meaningfully use a ruler, conduct a controlled experiment, engage in sampling procedures, and apply the laws of motion.

The *Framework* therefore recommends that from kindergarten, children be supported to use, connect, represent, and refine understanding through science and engineering practices, with the idea that such activity can support children to develop deeper, more connected, and more flexible understanding.[2] Necessarily, the phenomena and design challenges, associated conceptual understanding, complexity of the activity, and needed support will differ from middle and high school grades and across the preschool through elementary years.

Table 4-2 provides a snapshot of what investigation and design might look like in preschool, the primary grades, and later elementary school, each focusing on the study of water, while exploring different disciplinary core ideas and crosscutting concepts. The examples in the table draw from portions of instructional units, selected to help to illustrate some of the forms of activity for investigation and design. At the preschool level, children are exploring how to move water at a water table, using a range of tools and materials. In the second grade example, children are discussing why a town flooded after a dam was built, collecting data on how water moves through different substances; they are making progress on disciplinary core ideas in Earth Sciences and are supported to attend to scale and cause and effect. In the fifth grade example, children explore issues of water contamination and water access through the context of the Flint water crisis. Throughout the rest of the chapter, these three examples are drawn on consistently to illustrate the forms of activity and what they may look like at different ages, with different purposes, and in different contexts.

Box 4-1 describes the unfolding of the fourth and fifth grade unit described in Table 4-2 as one example of a sequence that situates science investigation in grappling with the sociopolitical context of science content—specifically, a context of water use, water access, and health. (As noted later in the chapter, children are able to engage with justice issues across the preschool through elementary ages.) Although this example takes up *in*justice—the poisoning of water within a community and larger issues of access to clean water—the authors of the study in which this example appears note the importance of not focusing solely on identifying community problems but also engaging children with "examples of liberation, imagination, and healing" and "community innovation and ingenuity" (Davis and Schaeffer, 2019, p. 386). Kotler (2020) took up related issues, also using the Flint water crisis to explore issues of sustainability and justice. The author found that the participating Latinx fifth graders could engage in perspective-taking, including through embodied performance, and that they constructed scientific knowledge at the same time as developing critical consciousness and agentic identities.

---

[2] The *Framework* does not explicitly address preschool. However, emerging evidence indicates that preschool children can and do engage productively in science and engineering in ways that are playful, build on their interests, and are consequential for learning (Larimore, 2020).

TABLE 4-2 Examples of Developing Understanding Through Investigation and Design in Preschool, Primary, and Upper Elementary Grades

	Preschool
Disciplinary Core Ideas	Water flows from higher points to lower points. The flow of water can be changed by changing the size of the opening where it flows, the amount of water flowing, and the steepness of the surface it flows on.
Crosscutting Concepts	Cause and Effect Systems and Systems Thinking
Phenomenon or Design Challenge	Children explore how to move water at a water table with a pegboard, tubes, sieves, cups, and bottles, and a funnel.
Data and Information	Children gather information from posing and trying out challenges (e.g., moving the water out of a container faster or slower). Teacher provides bottles with holes of different sizes. Children predict and observe.
Construct Explanations and Solutions	Children explain relationships between actions or materials and water flow within challenges.
Communicating	Children share observations and experiments with teacher and each other at the water table. Children use collage materials (e.g., yarn) to show water movement, describing their work to their teacher, who records their thinking.
Connecting	Children go on a walk to examine sources of flowing water in their community. Children solve related design challenges (e.g., figuring out how to fill a bucket far from a source of water).

SOURCES: Chalufour and Worth (2004); Davis and Schaeffer (2019); Salgado and Salgado (2019); Shim et al. (2018).

Grade 2	Grade 5
ESS1.C: Some events happen very quickly; others occur very slowly, over a time period much longer than one can observe. ESS2.A: Wind and water can change the shape of the land.	PS1.A: Matter of any type can be divided into sub-particles that are too small to see. ESS3.C: Human activities in agriculture, industry, and everyday life have had major effects on the land, vegetation, streams, ocean, air, and even outer space.
Cause and Effect Scale, Proportion, Quantity	Cause and Effect Systems and Systems Thinking
Children discuss why they think the town of Moncton flooded a year after a dam was placed on the other side of a mountain.	Children read about the Flint water crisis, asking questions about water contamination, water access, and water as a human need.
Children collect data on how fast water moves through sand, soil, clay, and rocks.	Children identify and study local bodies of water.
Children examine maps showing glaciers and glacial retreat.	Children collect and analyze water samples from a local river.
Children explain how the dam caused water to pool and move through the mountain, which is a glacial moraine.	Children choose a stance on the question of whether water is a human right and support their stance with evidence.
Children construct models showing a cross section of the moraine and how water moves through the sand and pebbles that make it up.	Children develop posters and, later, a video about their local river.
Children examine the movement of water in their communities and explore a map of their watershed.	Children make informational posters, drawing on literacy practices, and connect science to issues in their local communities and in other communities.
Children consider the history of the land and people interacting with land and water.	Children interview activists, understanding how science knowledge can be drawn on for social change.

BOX 4-1
Developing and Demonstrating Proficiencies: Debating Water as a Human Right

In Ms. Janelle's fourth and fifth grade classroom, a guiding question for the year was "How does water support life?" (Davis and Schaeffer, 2019). Ms. Janelle was a white teacher who taught in a place-based school referred to as Mission City in a city called Riverview, which had a majority Black student population. The school was within 100 miles from the city of Flint, MI. During the yearlong unit, children explored questions such as "Is water a human right?" and "What is water justice, and why would it benefit society?"

In Module 1, children first read a news article outlining the dangers of lead poisoning and the Flint water crisis. Children expressed outrage over having to pay for water that was "poison," but also raised ethical questions about why the water was called *Flint water*, in effect questioning the ethics of water *belonging* to a place. They discussed the issue of water shut-offs in Flint and how water was only shut off for Black residents and not white residents. During this first module, children made posters to summarize their understanding of lead poisoning and the water crisis, but expressed that Flint was distal to them in Riverview, that they were disconnected both geographically and ethically from Flint.

In Module 2, children learned about the body's need for water, the properties of water, bodies of water, and local waterways and water scarcity. They were also introduced to the issue of widespread water shut-offs in Riverview and connected that with their own families' experiences with shut-off water. This led them into a debate around the statement, "water is a human right." Children started to reason that clean water sustains life and thus that people who cannot afford water fees should not have to pay for water. Children began to make connections between communities through their concern about access to clean water for all.

In the final part of the year, children traveled to a nearby river and took water samples. They continued engaging with questions around water rights by watching documentaries and engaging with a panel of activists. Finally, they made a video on water in their community. At the end of the year, children spoke increasingly about water as a collective human right, recognized the sociopolitical and racialized dimensions of water access, and experienced their community as connected to the Flint community through the lived and affective dimensions of inequities stemming from treating water as a commodity. Further, they took up the science data they had gathered and the models they had studied (water samples, the particulate nature of water and of mixtures) in service of communicating their understanding and desire for change.

SOURCE: Adapted from Davis and Schaeffer (2019).

Further, children develop understanding through investigation and design across contexts, as described in Chapter 3. They bring this learning into classroom contexts. As described in *Taking Science to School* (NRC, 2007), children continually build on their prior knowledge, work to develop more detailed mechanistic explanations (e.g., understanding biological processes like blood flow and digestion or physical ones like gear action), and put together concepts to create new, more sophisticated ones. The 4-year-olds (preschoolers in Table 4-2) likely knew that water can move through holes in containers; instruction supported them in testing what affected that movement. The 8-year-olds (second graders in Table 4-2) likely knew that water has force, can move through materials and move materials, and can be frozen or melted; in turn, instruction helped them see these ideas as useful for a new phenomenon and engaged them in connecting and extending their ideas (diSessa and Wagner, 2005; Hammer et al., 2005; see also Kuhl et al., 2019, for an example of preschoolers taking up similar ideas). Similarly, the 10-year-olds in Box 4-1 and Table 4-2 likely knew that humans need clean water for survival, and instruction supported them in extending their knowledge to the ethical implications of access to clean water and how race relates to environmental justice, as well as to develop more sophisticated understanding about mixtures and solutions, water quality, and the environmental impact of humans (Davis and Schaeffer, 2019).

DEVELOPING PROFICIENCY IN INVESTIGATION AND DESIGN

Although children of different ages might engage in similar forms of activity, with those becoming generally more sophisticated for older children (see Table 4-2), it is impossible to specify a precise set of activities and learning supports that will be most appropriate for a particular age or grade band given developmental variability within ages and grade bands as well as diversity of previous experiences and knowledge. Proficiency must be taken into consideration along with children's neurodevelopment, cognitive skills, prior knowledge, cultural variation, and—as discussed in Chapter 5—the instructional context.

How People Learn II (NASEM, 2018b) described how the brain develops throughout an individual's life. This development is "broadly consistent for humans but is also individualized by every learner's environment and experiences" (p. 68). Thus, development—including brain development—shapes what children will do and show in their activity. At the same time, children's knowledge shapes how they engage in and demonstrate their engagement in practice (Metz, 2011; NRC, 2007; Schauble, 1996). Children's cultural repertoires of practice include dimensions such as their language use, question asking, observation, and collaboration (Gutiérrez and Rogoff, 2003) (see Chapter 3). Cultural repertoires of practice are consequential for how children's proficiencies get recognized and positioned in science and engineering learning settings. At the same time, children's cultural repertoires of practice must not be viewed as individual traits or as static over time, and nondominant groups especially must not be viewed through homogenous or essentialized lenses, as if every member of a group shares every cultural practice. (See Chapter 5 for a discussion of *how* learning environments and teachers' instructional practices can help such proficiencies to blossom, and Chapters 7 and 8 for ways of supporting teachers in engaging in this challenging work.)

Based on research on learning through investigation and design (e.g., NASEM, 2019b) and the description of children's developing proficiencies above, the committee reviewed literature pertinent to the forms of activity of investigation and design. The research is not even across the forms of activity, meaning the treatment here varies in depth. Furthermore, connecting across content and across sites of activity is not taken up in depth here (see Chapter 6).

Children Orient to Phenomena and Design Challenges

Science and engineering activity typically begin not with fully formed questions, but with puzzling phenomena, challenges, and unmet needs (NRC, 2012). Before preschool and continuing through elementary school, children ask *how* and *why* questions, seek patterns, and develop and engage with design challenges as they go about their everyday activity (Bagiati and Evangelou, 2011; Bairaktarova et al., 2011; Brophy and Evangelou, 2007; Fusaro and Smith, 2018).

Posing genuine, investigable questions in new contexts can be challenging for children and adults alike (Kuhn and Dean, 2004, 2005; Samarapungavan, Manzicopolous, and Patrick, 2008). If children are asked to pose questions about phenomena without further support, they are likely to pose a wide array of questions, including many that are less fruitful for exploring the desired content or less investigable (Chin, Brown, and Bruce, 2002; Manz, 2012) (for more discussion, see Chapter 5). Likewise, children (and adults) might not immediately recognize gaps in their understanding or ways that they disagree with one another about ideas (McNeill and Berland, 2017; Mills and Keil, 2004).

The examples in Box 4-2 and Table 4-2 illustrate how orienting around phenomena and design challenges set the stage for other forms of activity that are entailed in investigation and design. Box 4-2 presents two engineering design challenges and shows how they support opportunities for children to engage in collecting data and information, posing and evaluating design solutions, communicating their ideas, and making connections. The water-related phenomena in Table 4-2 similarly open up opportunities for scientific questioning, investigation, and the development of ideas. In the preschool example, children explore how to use different tools (e.g., cups, funnels, tubes) to move water at a water table (a staple of many preschool environments), whereas in the second grade example, children are oriented around the puzzling flooding of a town as an opportunity to ask and explore questions about land and water (e.g., how water interacts with different materials such as soil, sand, and clay), and in the fifth grade example, children explore water contamination and access, reconceptualizing a phenomenon that at first seems distant as something that they and others could seek to change.

Berland and colleagues (2016) argue that science learning should be meaningful to the scientific community and meaningful to the classroom community. Careful attention to the kinds of phenomena and design challenges to which children orient themselves may require a shift from privileging what matters to science or engineering as disciplinary fields, to privileging what matters to the thriving of all humans and the natural world. Children can engage with "should we" questions (Learning in Places Collaborative, 2020), exploring issues of ethics, power, and history. Chil-

---

BOX 4-2
Orienting to Engineering Design Challenges

Engaging with the Wee Engineer materials, preschoolers can engage in a design challenge of building a basket through using a set of materials that provides an initial frame for the design work. Children explore materials at will during open play before sharing ideas for different designs. Finally, children build their design ideas, test them, and continue to play, build, and iterate (Cunningham, Lachapelle, and Davis, 2018).

Similarly, kindergartners engaging with the SOLID Start curriculum materials (Wright and Gotwals, 2017) can develop understanding of what makes objects move, move faster, and turn as they work to design a boxcar (Edwards, Gotwals, and Wright, 2020). While watching a video that shows children competing in homemade boxcars, they can engage in noticing and posing questions, such as how the type of initial push or position affects the boxcar (e.g., does a harder push make the boxcar go faster? does starting on a higher ramp make the boxcar go faster?). Working on the design challenge of "How to make a boxcar move fast, far, and around an obstacle," children can use model cars to test their ideas, then design a solution for making their car travel (e.g., by using a ramp, pushing harder, or using washers for weight).

SOURCE: Adapted from Cunningham, Lachapelle, and Davis (2018); Edwards, Gotwals, and Wright (2020); Wright and Gotwals (2017).

dren's readiness to explore justice-linked topics extends across the ages of childhood (e.g., Davis and Schaeffer, 2019; Verwayne, 2018). Children may benefit from engaging with phenomena and design challenges that connect to equity and justice issues as well as ethical issues as they are presented with opportunities to consider the potential societal, cultural, and ethical implications of their designs (Gunckel and Tolbert, 2018; Rodriguez and Shim, 2020); this is a central aspect of engaging in engineering design (Paugh, Wendell, and Wright, 2018).

Children Collect and Analyze Data and Information

Developing empirical systems and gathering and analyzing data are central to science and engineering activity, including making decisions about what data to collect and about how to organize it to identify patterns. From infancy, children observe the world around them and draw conclusions about how it works. They consider the frequency of events, use their bodies to act out "what if" questions (Keifert and Stevens, 2019), and draw interpretations about the reasons for adults' actions to inform their own strategies (Gergely, Bekkering, and Kiraly, 2002). They build and manipulate structures purposefully, developing and testing ideas about balance (Karmiloff-Smith and Inhelder, 1974; Metz, 1993) and force and motion (Counsell et al., 2015). In contexts that are meaningful to them, children can also interpret evidence and recognize the difference between informative and uninformative evidence (Bullock, Sodian, and Koerber, 2009; Köksal, Sodian, and Legare, 2021; Sandoval et al., 2014). Further, children spontaneously engage in more exploratory play, and extend such play, when engaging with toys and devices characterized by confounded evidence or inconsistent outcomes (Legare, 2012; Schulz and Bonawitz, 2007). In situations where there is information to be gained, children are more likely to engage in play that is informative to distinguish between potential mechanisms for how a toy works; that is, they spontaneously select or design actions that isolate relevant variables (Cook, Goodman, and Schulz, 2011).

With opportunities and support, preschool and elementary school children can reason through processes of constructing, representing, and critiquing data and methods (Gerde, Schachter, and Wasik, 2013; Lehrer and Schauble, 2015; Manz, 2016; NRC, 2007; Piekny, Grube, and Maehler, 2014; Sandoval et al., 2019). This involves, for example, making decisions about what data are needed, what sorts of methods are appropriate, how data can be represented, and how to make sense of representations. By kindergarten, children can plan comparisons to test competing hypotheses (Sandoval et al., 2014); identify sources of uncertainty in data and propose reasonable improvements to data collection and instrumentation (Kanari and Millar, 2004; Metz, 2004, 2011). Elementary aged children can engage in sophisticated thinking about "empirical systems" and how they inscribe relations between phenomena, data, and claims (Manz, Lehrer, and Schauble, 2020). Whereas very young children tend to draw inferences from single instances, over the course of the elementary years, they increasingly attend to sample size and variability when drawing inferences (Sandoval et al., 2014).

Table 4-2 describes different experiences children might have with data. In preschool, the teacher supports children to manipulate materials as they pose new questions, uses carefully selected materials (bottles with different size holes) and directs children's attention to where the water goes to deepen their play toward explanation. Second graders engage with an empirical system (different materials in a filter/funnel apparatus) to understand how water might move through a glacial moraine and discuss how to time the water movement to draw comparisons. Fifth grade children collect data on water quality but also use second-hand data from research and newspaper articles to draw conclusions about water quality and access to clean water.

Cultural knowledge and family experiences shape children's engagement with data and data analysis. Ethnographic studies demonstrate that Indigenous children's communities may put more emphasis on learning through observation and relationship with the land and the more-than-human world, supporting their science observation skills (Mejía-Arauz, Rogoff, and Paradise, 2005). Marin and Bang (2018) provide an expanded vision of observation grounded in Indigenous ways of knowing that disrupts Eurocentric science's orientation toward obtaining "objective" data. They illustrate how "walking, reading, and storying the land" while in an urban forest is a way of "learning about the natural world and coming to know one's place in the world" (p. 89). Taking up such perspectives of children and their families, especially when learning in and moving through place, develops a broader range of knowledge on which the class can build and positions children as knowers. For example, when children's focus extends broadly rather than narrowly, and when they draw on observations across time and place, they are able to "see" (and therefore value) relationships across an entire ecosystem, rather than focusing only on a single organism at a time; this supports, ultimately, complex systems thinking and socio-ecological decision making.

Although children demonstrate many strengths as scientific thinkers, there is also evidence that some aspects of investigative work are challenging for children, due to both their developing scientific reasoning skills and understanding, including

- *Developing informative comparisons:* Although young children can produce informative contrasts when testing hypotheses, they often struggle to produce controlled tests themselves (Bullock, Sodian, and Koerber, 2009). Children, but also adults, commonly distort or ignore evidence that does not fit prior beliefs and can struggle to test hypotheses systematically (Bullock, Sodian, and Koerber, 2009; Koerber et al., 2015).

- *Attending to data as evidence:* Children tend not to privilege, or sometimes even perceive, the forms of evidence that an expert in the domain would (Eberbach and Crowley, 2009). For example, they might not pay attention to features of birds that allow them to draw conclusions about feeding patterns (Trumbull, Bonney, and Grudens-Schuck, 2005), differentiate between geologically important and irrelevant features when producing observations of rocks (Ford, 2005), or attend to characteristics of surfaces when examining how objects move when pushed down ramps (Presser et al., 2019).

- *Understanding assumptions inherent in phenomena represented in classrooms:* Children may not accept assumptions about how an investigation represents, and thus has implications for, events in the wider world. For example, sixth graders rejected experiments intended to help them understand relationships between the volume of model boats and their carrying capacity because of the lack of verisimilitude between the aluminum foil models and real boats (Schauble et al., 1995).

Children Construct Explanations and Design Solutions

As children orient to phenomena and design challenges, they work toward developing explanations and design solutions. Explanations and design solutions serve as both products and processes within science and engineering. The emphasis here is on the process of *developing* explanations and design solutions; learning involves the development of tentative explanations and design solutions throughout investigation and design. It is important for educators to consider cultural variation as they interpret children's explanations and design solutions. Research has suggested that educators may privilege forms of expression that align with middle-class, European American adults' language (Brown, Mistry, and Yip, 2019), invoke narrow ideas about "proper" scientific explanations (Warren et al., 2001), or place higher value on the technical aspects of engineering design work over the relational work (Turpen et al., 2019). This privileging may make it more challenging to see the strengths of children's many ways of communicating (e.g., using everyday language, gesture, drawing), yet when a broader perspective is taken, those strengths can be visible. For example, in a comparative study of 4-year-olds' play with a forest diorama, Washinawatok and colleagues (2017) found that rural and urban Native American children were more than twice as likely as non-Native American peers to take on the perspective of an animal in their play, and that the diorama was an effective way to elicit relational thinking. As educators recognize the richness in youths' cultural repertoires of practice, they come to appreciate the high-level, cognitive complexity in relational ways of thinking (Bang, Medin, and Altran, 2007), the use of everyday language as a means to communicate scientific understanding (Warren et al., 2001), and the use of cultural linguistic word play as a semiotic resource in scientific critique (Wright, 2019).

Developing Explanations

An explanation can be defined as a set of connected claims about how something happens or functions, whether a natural phenomenon or an engineered artifact. Scientific explanations strive to articulate causal mechanisms, to explain *how* or *why* something happens, and often support predictions about what might happen under specified conditions (Russ et al., 2008). Models are related to explanations in that they articulate sets of relationships between entities in some system to characterize how that system works, or how it is structured. Models and explanations can take many forms, including theories, mathematical equations, diagrams, and physical instantiations (Giere, 1990; Lehrer and Schauble, 2006; Schwarz et al., 2009; Windschitl, Thompson, and Braaten, 2008).

Young children typically display a range of competence in developing explanations. By preschool, children seek plausible causal mechanisms to explain events and take alternative explanations into account, and by second grade, they can distinguish conclusive from inconclusive tests of hypotheses (Bullock, Sodian and Koerber, 2009; Sandoval et al., 2014). Furthermore, elementary-age children express a preference for data as a justification for claims, when data are consistent (Bullock, Sodian, and Koerber, 2009; Sandoval and Çam, 2011). Elementary children can develop robust practices of explanation, including developing norms for evidentiary justification (Manz, 2016; Ryu and Sandoval, 2012), identifying gaps in explanations and seeking coherence (Phillips, Watkins, and Hammer, 2018); and coordinating the behavior of molecular entities to explain observable changes in materials (Kenyon, Schwarz, and Hug, 2008; Schwarz et al., 2009).

Returning to Table 4-2, preschool children primarily described relationships between actions and outcomes; cause and effect produced through actions and observation of outcomes is a crosscutting concept that seems to start early, and is relatively straightforward for adults to recognize. For example, children showed that they could hold a tube of water up higher to make the water travel faster and that larger holes in containers led to a wider, faster flow of water. Second grade children constructed an explanation of how a dam caused the water from a river to first pool and then to move through the glacial moraine—moving through the sand and rocks that made it up—whereas the water did not move through the mountain range on the other side of the valley, which was made of solid rock. Fifth grade children constructed an explanation that went beyond cause and effect and involved taking a stance on water as a human right, supporting their claims with evidence from their investigations, text, and engagement with community activists. Further, fifth grade students might use molecular-level understanding to explain contaminated water as a mixture and to describe the mechanisms used in water purification systems (Kenyon, Schwarz, and Hug, 2008).

The research on children's strengths, struggles, and needs for support highlights the cultural, situated, and knowledge-based nature of explanatory work. Children might be cued into different forms of explanatory work depending on their audience, task, and knowledge base. For example, Louca and colleagues (2004) documented how third grade children discussing why leaves changed in the fall first provided nonmechanistic descriptions ("In the winter I don't think the tree needs the leaves"). However, when the teacher asked, "What's going on inside of the leaf?" and pointed out that that this question called for different forms of reasoning, children drew on new resources, such as their understanding of cells, veins, and pigments, and engaged in mechanistic reasoning to explain what made the leaves change color. McNeill (2011) demonstrated fluctuations in third grade children's written explanations as they encountered new content. Across ages, there is evidence that youth's explanatory strategies are flexible and situationally dependent, and that forms of explanation (i.e., teleological and anthropomorphic thinking) that are often discouraged can serve as productive reasoning tools and building blocks for more sophisticated understanding (diSessa, 2014; Gouvea and Simon, 2018).

There is not yet consensus about the appropriate targets of explanatory work for children in preschool through elementary grades. For example, although the standards for first and second grades focus on children observing generalizable changes between liquids and solids, some scholarship shows children sometimes—with support—reason with ideas about particles and molecules (DeLiema, Enyedy, and Danish, 2019; Samarapungavan, Bryan, and Wills, 2017) and about gases in addition to solids and liquids (Varelas et al., 2008). Furthermore, there is little research that focuses on children's socioscientific explanations, particularly at younger ages, as well as around issues of equity and justice (see Box 4-1).

Children are likely to require support as they develop their explanations. Areas that need support include

- *Forms of explanation*: When reasoning about a phenomenon, many forms of explanation are possible, including generalization, probabilistic, teleological (an explanation for something as a function of its purpose), relational, and mechanistic (Braaten and Windschitl, 2011; Russ et al., 2008). Children may use forms of explanation other than those that teachers expect or that scientists might use to explain specific phenomena (Kelemen, 2004; Louca et al., 2004).
- *Invisible entities/scale:* Many mechanisms undergirding scientific explanations occur at scales of time and space to which children do not have experiential access. Children can struggle to coordinate the actions of unseen entities with observable changes to phenomena (Grotzer, 2003; Schwarz et al., 2009).
- *Correctness:* Children may display productive questions and tools for explanation well before they have developed, or even before it is productive for them to develop, an understanding of the mechanisms for a "correct" or canonical explanation (Gallas, 1995; Russ et al., 2008; Suárez, 2020).
- *Explanation products*: Numerous studies have documented the difficulties learners of all ages experience in developing written explanations that include a how/why explanation, evidence, and connections to canonical understanding (Berland and Reiser, 2009; McNeill, 2011; Schwarz et al., 2009; Zembal-Saul, McNeill, and Hershberger, 2013). Children may demonstrate proficiencies in each of these aspects of explanatory work when co-constructing ideas with teachers or in conversation with peers, but might struggle to put them together independently, in writing, and for an imagined audience (Berland and Forte, 2010; Berland and Reiser, 2009).

Developing Design Solutions

A design solution in an engineering context can be defined as one of many possible ways to solve a given problem. Once a set of design solutions has been identified, further restrictions may be imposed to identify the best-suited design solution for a given context. For example, the problem of "lifting a heavy object" may be solved using, among other aids, a lever, an inclined plane, or a set of pulleys as a design solution for the problem. Which of these design solutions works best will depend on the nature of the object and the ability to place machinery in its surroundings. For example, an object that is hard to pull on the floor may not be suitable for lifting using an inclined plane; an object that does not have sufficient structural integrity within may not lend itself to lifting using a pulley system. Iterative experimentation and collaboration are generally needed to identify the best possible design solution in any given design context.

Preschool-age children use many of the reasoning skills underlying engineering design, such as identifying relational and causal patterns, categorization, deductive and inductive reasoning, generating questions, foundational modeling skills such as the appreciation of representational qualities of objects and images, use of problem-solving heuristics, experimentation, and reasoning about evidence (Bjorklund and Causey, 2018; Klahr, Zimmerman, and Jirout, 2011; NRC, 2007; Shwe Hadani and Rood, 2018; Zimmerman and Klahr, 2018). By this age, children are also increasingly sophisticated problem solvers. For example, by the age of 2 children can develop questions, maintain focus on a goal, monitor their progress, make corrections, and evaluate results (Bjorklund and Causey, 2018; Zimmerman and Klahr, 2018). Elementary children continue to build on these strengths. For example, children can develop design solutions that center around humans and their problems (rather than just "the thing" being designed) (Hynes and Swenson, 2013; National Academy of Engineering [NAE], 2008; Zoltowski, Oakes, and Cardella, 2012). They can also come to see failure as a constructive part of the design process (Lottero-Perdue and Parry, 2017; Martin, 2015). Cunningham and colleagues (2018) articulated a framework for thinking about engineering design across ages 3–8, and note that by the upper age band, design solutions can include designs that are entirely new to children. One main area for support in terms of children's design solutions is consideration of the role of failure; however, further research is needed to more fully explore areas in which children may need support in developing design solutions.

Children Communicate Reasoning

Science and engineering rely on a range of communication modalities, practices, and even languages to support sensemaking and problem-solving efforts (Gee, 2000; Grapin, 2019; Paugh, Wendell, and Wright, 2018; Warren et al., 2001). "Communication," here, is more than simply sharing one's thinking with another; it is the mechanism through which much of the work of science and engineering practice and sensemaking takes place.

Discourse and artifacts are fundamental mediational tools through which children can externalize and develop their observations and reasoning (Keifert and Stevens, 2019; Michaels, O'Connor, and Resnick, 2008; Rosebery et al., 2010; Suárez, 2020; Varelas et al., 2008). Learners often make progress through externalizing ideas and revising artifacts (see Chapter 5). Moreover, opportunities to communicate one's observations and reasoning invite learners to engage with their peers' ideas, which in turn creates opportunities for them to check their own understanding and see if they (dis)agree and help them refine their and their peers' thinking through a process of collaborative knowledge co-construction (Berland and Hammer, 2012).

One main way children communicate their reasoning is through generating, testing, and revising models and representing their ideas. (This chapter focuses on this dimension; Chapter 6 takes up other ways of representing ideas, through writing and other literacy practices.) Modeling principally involves representation: selecting features and relationships to focus on, using analogies, and inscribing entities and relationships in objects or drawings (Hesse, 1966; Nersessian, 2005, 2008). Children bring substantial representational proficiencies to the work of scientific modeling. In play, they use objects to stand in for other objects and maintain complex "act as if" stories. They produce and interpret pictures, and by preschool, they can recognize and interpret representational intent and representational choices (Callaghan and Corbit, 2015; DeLoache, 2004).

Useful entrees into modeling for young children include models such as physical microcosms that rely on correspondence and developing drawn observations in which children make choices about what to show and how to show it (Lehrer and Schauble, 2015). Over time, they can iterate these, moving from making models that look like objects to models that represent processes and functions (Penner et al., 1997). Working collectively with models by comparing representational choices and implications can support both the proficiency with modeling purposes and practices and development of conceptual understanding (Georgen and Manz, 2021; Schwarz et al., 2009). Children can be supported to work with a wide range of representations and to coordinate across representations, discussing what different representations show and hide in regard to the same phenomenon (Tytler et al., 2013). Forms of modeling that depart further from physical resemblance (e.g., molecular models of phase change; mathematical models) may require further support for children to understand what the model is meant to represent and to construct or use it flexibly (Danish, 2014; Dickes et al., 2016; Lehrer and Schauble, 2015).

Attending to cultural variation in children's reasoning about and representing ideas means offering them multiple ways to represent their ideas, such as diagrams, photographs, drawings, gestures, dramatic play, and journaling. This diversity of representations is even more important for multilingual children (Siry and Gorges, 2020; Suárez, 2020; Varelas et al., 2010). Poza (2016), for example, found that fifth grade emergent bilingual children's language and science learning deepened when they were encouraged to use their full linguistic repertoire—such as coordinating and flexibly using Spanish and English across speech, text, and digital imagery.

Models and modeling represent an opportunity for children to expand modes of engagement and engage with two- and three-dimensional representations of science concepts (Varelas et al., 2010), but attention to multiple modalities is important. Varelas and colleagues (2010) demonstrated how molecule- and food-web drama activities were forms of modeling where primary grade, mostly Latinx and Black children (grades 1–3) thought about how concepts related to one another, brought in their own funds of knowledge, recruited emotion as a resource in learning science, and moved back and forth between imaginary and actual worlds. Modeling scientific ideas through dramatic play became a way for children to explore scientific ideas in sophisticated ways and to author their own understanding even as they were shaped by others' ideas.

Table 4-2 illustrates how children across preschool through elementary can communicate their ideas. Preschoolers' communication was highly supported by the teacher; they shared their observations with the teacher and with one another, and they built a physical record of their ideas and dictated their thinking to their teacher, who recorded their ideas. Second graders constructed models to show the mechanism of water movement through the glacial moraine, and fifth graders made a video and posters. These examples all use different media and illustrate the range of options for children's communication of their thinking and reasoning.

Children's communication of their reasoning with models thus requires support, to include

- recognizing correspondences and differences between a model and the phenomenon (or design solution) it represents, and moving from literal depiction to representation of attributes and causal factors (Carey and Smith, 1993; Penner et al., 1997; Schwarz et al., 2009; Varelas et al., 2010);
- understanding how models show and hide different aspects of a phenomenon depending on their purpose, and identifying the limitations of particular models or representations (Schwarz et al., 2009; Tytler et al., 2013); and
- seeing models as a way of strengthening sensemaking and not just for representing current thinking or as a correct explanation (Schwarz et al., 2009).

Children Connect Learning Across Content Areas and Across Sites of Activity

Learning about the natural and designed worlds entails learning across an individual's lifespan, learning across the various contexts that individuals navigate and move between, and learning by making meaning of natural phenomena and design challenges through the lenses of personal and cultural value systems (Bell et al., 2012; Bricker and Bell, 2014). Productive science and engineering learning environments in preschool through elementary can nurture and build upon the multifaceted nature of who children are, have been, and will become.

Children come to school with an inclination to identify patterns and integrate ideas across the many contexts of their activity (see Chapter 3). Children engaging in the forms of activity described above are consistently and constantly engaging with literacy and mathematics practices and using ideas from those domains, and others (French, 2004; Gelman et al., 2009; Nayfeld, Brenneman, and Gelman, 2011) (Chapter 6 discusses connections across content areas). Chapter 5 addresses how teachers and designers can develop instructional contexts where children see their ideas, concerns, and practices as meaningful for school science and engineering and, conversely, see school science and engineering as useful for their lives.

Table 4-2 shows how children can make progress toward these ends through making connections to their local environments. Preschool children can solve design challenges that are related to the phenomena and/or disciplinary core ideas under consideration, such as how water can flow from one place to another; connections often involve children engaging with a series of interrelated experiences that build coherently upon each other. Similarly, in an attempt to connect to what they were learning about the relationships among waters, lands, and humans, the second grade children made a connection to the role water played in shaping the history of the land, and fifth graders brought together content areas (e.g., drawing on literacy practices to make informational posters) and used their interviews with activists to see connections between science knowledge (e.g., water quality) and social change (e.g., water as a right).

CONSIDERING CHILDREN'S PROFICIENCIES AND WORKING TOWARD EQUITY

Drawing on each child's resources—including their cultural repertoires of practice, their linguistic resources, and their funds of knowledge—can give a broader range of children *increasing opportunity and access to high-quality science and engineering* (Approach #1). For example, drawing on children's relational ways of thinking can allow children to demonstrate their proficiencies with regard to developing explanations and design solutions (Bang, Medin, and Altran, 2007), which supports their access to meaningful opportunities to learn.

With respect to *increased achievement, representation, and identification with science and engineering* (Approach #2), helping children to orient to phenomena and design challenges that are of interest to them and connect to the needs and goals of their communities may help them to engage more fully in sensemaking, and children can engage with such issues from a young age (Davis and Schaeffer, 2019; Verwayne, 2018). Moreover, incorporating this kind of learning experience can help children develop their identities as people who do science and engineering.

An ***expanded vision of what constitutes science and engineering practices*** (Approach #3), such as observation, helps demonstrate the strengths Indigenous children bring to science (Marin and Bang, 2018; Mejía-Arauz, Rogoff, and Paradise, 2005) but at the same time, extends (all) children's perspectives about what constitutes science. Similarly, allowing children's ways of expressing their ideas (in explanation and design solutions and in communicating their reasoning) that go beyond standard Eurocentric discourse practices (e.g., taking on a perspective of an animal, Washinawatok et al., 2017; using their full linguistic repertoire, Poza, 2016; Siry and Gorges, 2020; Suárez, 2020) supports a similar expansion. Children's cultural practices of explanation and communication may privilege cooperation, respect for authority, or an emphasis on social and emotional support. An accurate default position, then, is to assume that all children are engaged in sensemaking. Indeed, in *How People Learn II* (NASEM, 2018b), a central assumption is that learning is a process of incrementally building on whatever resources learners bring to the situation. By failing to recognize the science and engineering in what children say and do—because they use everyday language rather than scientific language, for example, or because they use strategies or perspectives different from Eurocentric science—educators may fail to capitalize on rich, meaningful opportunities for children's learning.

Children engage with ***science and engineering as a part of justice movements*** with support (Approach #4). For example, Box 4-1 illustrated how at first, children saw the water issues in Flint as problematic, but as distant from their own home 100 miles away. By the end of the year of exploration, they recognized water justice as an issue that connected to them, too—at the same time as developing central understanding of ideas about matter, cause and effect, and systems thinking (Davis and Schaeffer, 2019). Kotler (2020), also exploring the Flint water crisis with fifth graders, found benefits for children's science knowledge, critical consciousness, and agentic identities. Both examples, though taking on the same specific issue, illustrate the broader point of helping children see how science and engineering can be a part of justice movements.

SUMMARY

This chapter explores how children's development, knowledge, cultural background, and the instructional context itself all interplay to shape how children demonstrate and develop their proficiencies related to investigation and design. From a young age, children can engage in the five forms of activity used to organize this chapter: (1) orienting to phenomena and design challenges; (2) collecting and analyzing data and information; (3) constructing explanations and design solutions; (4) communicating their reasoning; and (5) connecting learning across content areas and contexts.

Their engagement in these forms of activity is deeply tied to the purposes, knowledge, and cultural practices they bring to investigation and design. Their engagement draws upon the eight science and engineering practices named in the *Framework*, the crosscutting concepts, and the disciplinary core ideas. Thus, engaging in investigation and design work toward the vision of the *Framework* by engaging children in three-dimensional learning (NRC, 2012).

Children bring strengths to these forms of activity that provide the basis for much of what can happen inside (and outside) classrooms. For example, they can think about what data they need to collect to answer a question or solve a problem, how they can bring those data to bear as evidence in support of explanations or design solutions, consider mechanistic accounts, reason about what representations of a phenomenon show or do not show, and build connections across many dimensions of their work. Children's engagement in investigation and design not only looks different from adults, or even from middle or high school learners, but changes across the preschool through elementary ages. This means that children's work with investigation and design needs to be carefully orchestrated to support their developing proficiency, as discussed in Chapter 5.

5

Learning Environments and Instructional Practices That Center Children, Investigation, and Design

> **Main Messages**
> - Children's development of ideas and practices is supported by long-term, sustained experiences, rich materials and settings, and engagement with peers and knowledgeable others.
> - Children can share, use, connect, and develop their understanding of big conceptual ideas in science and engineering when instruction (1) is anchored in design problems and phenomena that are conceptually rich, accessible, and meaningful to children and (2) provides supports for children to iteratively refine their explanations and solutions.
> - Science and engineering learning are social endeavors. Instructional and curricular supports are needed to promote relationships, collective meaning making, and discourse across children's development and learning contexts.
> - When teachers are able to elicit, notice, value, and build on the many ideas, experiences, and communicative resources that children bring to the classroom, they can organize connections between children's existing knowledge and curiosity and the environment around them, supporting children to continue to make sense of the natural and designed world.
> - A robust formative assessment approach provides appropriate supports for children to show their understanding and skill, includes ways for children to show their understanding in multiple modalities, and specifies a way of making inferences about children's understanding.

This chapter summarizes what research suggests are the key features of learning environments and instructional practices that support children's participation in forms of science and engineering activity. It illustrates how these features support investigation and design, including how they may productively vary to support children of different ages or experience. The review of research is guided by findings described in Chapters 3 and 4: children come to school with orientations toward, as well as proficiencies and interest in, investigation and design. Whether and how children show their competence depends on contextual factors; furthermore, it is important to draw from and provide support for children's developing interests, identities, and the contexts in which they engage in science and engineering.

How to design high-quality and equitable learning environments for preschool through elementary science and engineering is the focus of this chapter. Thus, the identification of key features of learning environments and instructional practices is guided by a commitment to equity (see Chapter 1). Instructional practices aligned with this commitment elicit, honor, and leverage the diverse repertoires of talking, being, and sensemaking that children bring to instruction, and it is important for teachers to recognize their own orientations to this work. This stance considers how the repertoires of minoritized children (or other children who are potentially marginalized on the basis of gender, [dis]ability, or learning difference) can be, and are likely to be, silenced by the content and valued practices of classrooms that are not intentionally designed with equity and justice at the foreground.

MOVING BEYOND DICHOTOMIES

Preschool and elementary learning environments have sometimes been dominated by discourse emphasizing dichotomous distinctions. These dichotomies include (1) calls for early childhood learning environments to center free play versus calls to center school readiness and academic learning (Clements and Sarama, 2004; Sarama et al., 2017; Weisberg et al., 2016); (2) recommendations that children discover ideas by themselves versus those that highlight the need for explicit instruction (Furtak et al., 2012; Kirschner, Sweller, and Clark, 2006); and (3) framing children as natural scientists versus claims that children can engage only in a subset of science practices (Metz, 1995, 2004). These dichotomous framings pit educational approaches against each other in ways that are often not evidence based or productive for instructional design.

Instead, the committee was guided by the following perspectives. First, the committee views children's play and learning as mutually supportive. Free play and open-ended exploration play key roles in young children's learning (e.g., Charara, Miller, and Krajcik, 2021; Golinkoff and Hirsch-Pasek, 2008); they make children's interests visible and provide opportunities for children to learn social-emotional skills crucial to learning more broadly (e.g., Veiga, Neto, and Rieffe, 2016). During free play, children also naturally engage in mathematics (Seo and Ginsburg, 2004) and science (Bulunuz, 2013; Gross, 2012). Adults support play and strengthen the learning of these skills by purposefully designing the environment and facilitating interactions that draw on and extend children's activity (Bustamante, White, and Greenfield, 2017; Weisberg et al., 2015). Intentional and sequenced instruction leads not only to improvements in learning (e.g., Whittaker et al., 2020) but also enriched play (Sarama et al., 2017).

Second, the committee recognizes that children's science and engineering practice activity can be supported, rather than usurped, by purposeful instruction, and that adults and children can share responsibility for posing questions and problems, designing investigations, and developing explanations (Furtak et al., 2012; Hmelo-Silver, Duncan, and Chinn, 2007; Reiser, 2004). Dichotomous notions of teachers "telling vs. not telling students" are likely to be unhelpful; instead, guidance on what forms of support teachers can provide, when, and for what purposes are more useful (Furtak and Alonzo, 2010; Manz and Suárez, 2018). Finally, as discussed in Chapter 4, children are capable of and benefit from engagement in a wide spectrum of science and engineering practices; however, the form of their engagement and the contexts they experience as productive and meaningful will differ, both from secondary students and across the preschool through elementary trajectory (Metz, 2011; National Research Council [NRC], 2012).

KEY FEATURES OF THE LEARNING ENVIRONMENT

Science and engineering educators, especially at the middle and high school levels, have generated an evidence base of key features of learning environments, formal and informal, that support and develop learners' science and engineering learning (National Academies of Sciences, Engineering, and Medicine [NASEM], 2019b; Schwarz, Passmore, and Reiser, 2017). Although research in preschool through elementary science and engineering is less extensive, emerging evidence suggests that when key features of the learning environment are coupled with instructional practices that build from them, preschool and elementary children can engage in science and engineering practices and learn sophisticated science ideas that are meaningful to their experiences and everyday life (Lehrer and Schauble, 2015; Metz, 2011; NRC, 2007). This chapter is organized around five features of the learning environment that support learning, which are summarized in Table 5-1. These are interacting parts of a system rather than features on a checklist. Furthermore, the elements synergistically support multiple dimensions of children's work; they are separated here for analytic purposes and organized to illustrate the activity that they can support.

Children Engage in Science and Engineering in a Caring Community

A productive science and engineering learning environment for preschool through elementary school is one where children feel safe, feel their contributions are valued, and see their work as important to others (Carlone, Haun-Frank, and Webb, 2011; Eshach and Fried, 2005; Jaber and Hammer, 2016; Krist and Suárez, 2018; Lee, 2017; Liston, 2008; McWayne et al., 2020; Scardamalia, 2002). This kind of learning environment centers equitable and respectful relationships among children, be-

TABLE 5-1 Features of the Learning Environment That Support Learning

Children...	Features of the Learning Environment
Engage in science and engineering in a caring community.	• Teachers and children set and revise norms. • The learning environment promotes a collective culture. • Teachers build relationships with children, families, and communities. • The learning environment invites the emotional dimension of science and engineering work.
Orient to investigation and design in contexts they find meaningful.	• Children's work is anchored in rich contexts, phenomena, and design challenges. • Teachers attend to and value children's initial ideas and experiences.
Refine their explanations and solutions through sensemaking with data.	• Children work with tools, resources, and data to test and refine ideas and solutions. • Children discuss and make decisions, including questioning and problematizing. • Children's activity is grounded in iterative refinement of artifacts and children are positioned as sensemakers.
Learn with and from each other.	• Teachers and curricula invite a wide range of semiotic resources and ways of showing thinking. • Teachers and curricula use flexible structures to support collaboration and collective thinking. • Teachers elicit and work with children's ideas.
Are assessed in ways that show their learning and inform instruction.	• Formative assessment is used for multiple purposes. • Formative assessment systems draw on multiple forms of evidence. • Formative assessment includes probes and support for children. • Teachers develop understanding of the interpretation and potential biases involved in formative assessment.

tween children and teachers, and with the community more broadly. These learning environments promote a collective culture and invite and respond to the emotional dimensions of science and engineering work (Jaber and Hammer, 2016; Larimore, 2020; Scardamalia, 2002). Teachers play a pivotal role shaping the classroom culture by working with children to set, reflect on, and revise norms and establishing relationships with children, families, and communities (Chinn, 2006, 2012; Esteban-Guitart and Moll, 2014; Herrenkohl et al., 1999).

Carefully attending to and supporting *norms and roles for participation* in the science and engineering community (Nasir et al., 2014) is important for supporting a collaborative, caring culture. Norms and practices that are effective in community building in preschool and elementary science and engineering—building in part on relevant literature in secondary levels—include

- Leveraging children's social identities in service of their scientific understanding and engagement (Carlone, Scott, and Lowder, 2014) so that "being me," "being scientific," and "being a good member of the classroom community" are synergistic.
- Emphasizing science and engineering as collectively constructed as opposed to individually owned (Stroupe, 2014; Zhang et al., 2009).
- Minimizing sorting mechanisms and hierarchies between children by celebrating a wide range of proficiencies beyond success in final-form science (e.g., innovative problem solving, unique scientific observations, persistence through a task, insightful inference, intense curiosity, risk taking, tolerance for ambiguity, ability to focus) (Bang et al., 2017; Rosebery et al., 2010).
- Explicitly discussing and supporting science and engineering practices while allowing children to shape those practices and recognizing a wide range of scientific and engineering performances (Agarwal and Sengupta-Irving, 2019; Herrenkohl et al., 1999; McNeill, 2011; Ryu and Sandoval, 2012).

A *caring, collective culture* can also influence the way that children relate to each other, how the class engages together in sensemaking, children's uptake of science and engineering practices, their sense of what constitutes a "smart science student," and their science and engineering identities (Carlone, Mercier, and Metzger, 2021; Kane, 2015, 2016; Varelas et al., 2008). Teachers who develop a collaborative science and engineering culture set up opportunities for children to work together in small groups and as a whole class, expecting them to share and listen to each other and jointly construct conceptual understanding (Carlone, Haun-Frank, and Webb, 2011; Engle and Conant, 2002; Herrenkohl and Mertl, 2010; Peterson and French, 2008; Sandoval et al., 2019). Such teachers also seek to disrupt normative views of knowledge as final form and individually owned, with the teacher as the implied audience and arbiter of children's contributions, ideas typically well established by the elementary years (Carlone, Scott, and Lowder, 2014). When sharing correct answers and seeking positive evaluation from teachers are the focus of children's activity, divisions among children become more pronounced and taking risks is more difficult. When all children feel they have a stake in and responsibility for their peers' learning and well-being, more children recognize themselves and get recognized by others as competent and capable.

As teachers develop positive *relationships* with children in moments of interaction, they position learners in their classrooms as important for the community (Kane, 2015, 2016; Watkins et al., 2017) while also potentially challenging their own beliefs about how children may learn best (Loucks-Horsley et al., 2009). These relationships are most likely to be supported when teachers are intentional about interrogating their own positionalities and identities and those of the children with whom they work (Mensah and Jackson, 2018). They can build these relationships through routines like morning greetings, demonstrating interest in their ideas, and checking in with them about difficulties and successes during the investigation and design process. Finally, teachers are able to develop respectful and equitable relationships with the communities and children's families by learning about children's and their families' lives—from the kinds of natural phenomena and design challenges that relate to their goals and needs (which can be helpful for contextualizing investigations and design) to their cultural norms for communicating and collaborating (Chinn, 2006, 2012; Esteban-Guitart and Moll, 2014; Hudicourt-Barnes, 2003; McWayne et al., 2020; Wright, 2019).

Moreover, scholars have increasingly highlighted *the role of emotion* in doing and learning science and engineering and have begun to develop accounts of classroom environments that draw on emotional dimensions to support individual and collective learning (Jaber and Hammer, 2016; Wright, 2019). Scientists and engineers experience a sense of puzzlement, frustration, and sometimes failure as they recognize the gaps in their thinking or as troublesome issues re-emerge (Kimmerer, 2013; Knorr Cetina, 2001; Radoff, 2017). They also, however, report joy as they think with new and exciting ideas and see new things (Fox, 1983; Kimmerer, 2003). So too are accounts of children's learning of science and engineering replete with descriptions of children's emotions (Engle and Conant, 2002; Jaber and Hammer, 2016). Davis and Schaeffer (2019) note that although children's experiences of environmental problems have affective dimensions, these are rarely elicited or studied, particularly among minoritized youth whose communities are directly impacted. Furthermore, minoritized children may fear repercussions of behaviors (such as Nick experienced in Box 3-1) that may lead them to proscribe their full engagement with the science or engineering work of the classroom (Wright, Wendell, and Paugh, 2018; see Box 5-1).

Preschool programs have historically been conceptualized to address the whole child (Bishop-Josef and Zigler, 2011; Larimore, 2020), intentionally focusing not only on academic learning but also on physical and social-emotional development, with health and family engagement as key components (U.S. Department of Health and Human Services, 2020). The

---

BOX 5-1
The Emotional Dimensions of Engineering Design for Black Children

Engineering designs often fail (Papert, 1980), meaning there is an emotional risk to engaging in this work. For Black children, though, the risk can be more about perceptions about being well behaved in school than based in the work of the discipline of engineering itself (Wright, Wendell, and Paugh, 2018). As an example, three fourth grade girls (two of whom were Black, and one who was white) were working together to design a water filter as part of an Engineering is Elementary unit. Each girl designed an initial solution, then all came together to develop a single team design. The group, like other groups in the study, simply combined their individual ideas, layering them on top of one another, rather than discussing each and deciding on the merits of each. One of the girls, who was Black, described the situation as such:

> Because, sometimes, I can get in arguments. Because you don't want Ms. Humphrey thinking you're in an argument with nobody. You get in an argument then it turns out to be a fight then you get suspended, and you get a whoopin' at home, you know? (p. 294)

Another child, a Black boy, similarly noted, "sometimes, people get real mad when you don't use their ideas [for the engineering design], and they just go off and just get real mad" (p. 295). These children worked to avoid the risk of the teacher perceiving them as troublemakers. For example, in the case of the three girls, previous experiences in the classroom led them to conclude that if they were to engage in argumentation in a particular way that it could be misinterpreted and result in additional consequences, suggesting that in this instance the learning environment may constrain opportunities for engaging in the practice of argumentation. This risk avoidance led to them engaging less fully in the engineering work at hand (Wright, Wendell, and Paugh, 2018).

SOURCE: Based on Wright, Wendell, and Paugh (2018).

preschool day offers multiple opportunities for collaborative learning; it includes whole-group discussions, guided small-group activities, free choice learning centers, and outdoor exploration and routines with opportunities for socially interactive learning. For these reasons, emotional and instructional support have both been identified as key dimensions of preschool classroom quality (LaParo, Pianta, and Hamre, 2008; Mashburn et al., 2008). Preschool educators have been found to use the most effective holistic instructional practices when facilitating science activities, in comparison to their practices in other subject areas (Cabell et al., 2013). Preschool thus has unique affordances for caring and collaborative science learning. The approaches described in this chapter appear to be just as important for elementary learners, though they are often less of a focus for research and professional learning.

Children's Activity Is Oriented to Investigation and Design in Meaningful Contexts

As described in Chapters 3 and 4, it is important to make connections across content areas and across sites of activity. Meaningful contexts serve as much more than a "hook"; they honor the student perspective by helping them to see that the work they are doing is helping to address the problems and questions they have raised. Thus, productive environments *anchor children's activity in meaningful contexts, phenomena, and design challenges*—linked to the experiences, knowledge, interests, and identities of children and their environments. Productive contexts for science and engineering can emerge from children's interests and observations in their classrooms, homes, and communities (Eshach and Fried, 2005; French, 2004; Katz, 2010; NRC, 2012; Tu, 2006). For example, McWayne and colleagues (2018) worked with preschool educators and parents to co-design a relationally and culturally situated science, technology, and engineering program. During Lunar New Year, families brought lucky bamboo into the classroom, spurring engineering activities to reinforce the concept of stability. Family activities, such as neighborhood walks, inspired the creation of scrapbooks that later guided engineering design activities in which children refined their understanding of force and motion. Research in kindergarten has similarly documented how neighborhood nature walks can springboard science investigations of organisms and their adaptations (Samarapungavan, Patrick, and Mantzicopoulos, 2011); furthermore, family walks can inspire intergenerational sensemaking about biological and physical phenomena (Marin and Bang, 2018). There are fewer examples of emergent uptake of children's interests and activities for upper elementary science and engineering learning (see Kelly, Brown, and Crawford, 2000, as an exception).

Problematizing phenomena in children's lives and introducing phenomena and design challenges that resonate with children's experiences (Penuel and Reiser, 2018) also support productive contexts for science and engineering. For example, by exploring the growth of a cob of corn left out in the rain, second grade children can apply their understanding of plant growth to a new phenomenon, addressing standards related to structure–function relationships and how plants and animals meet their needs (NASEM, 2017; Novak et al., 2019). By seeking to design toys for other children, they can explore ideas of force, motion, and magnetism (Krajcik et al., 2021). Children can explore water's different forms by pursuing the question, "what happens to rain after it hits the ground?" (Baumfalk et al., 2019). Contexts can also connect investigation and design to issues of justice and equity by incorporating phenomena and design challenges that are relevant in children's communities (Cody and Biggers, 2020; Dalvi, Wendell, and Johnson, 2016; Davis and Schaeffer, 2019; Haas et al., 2021; Mensah et al., 2018; Upadhyay, 2009).

Teachers in these environments *attend to and value children's initial ideas and experiences*, playing a crucial role in welcoming and valuing multiple ideas and experiences and working with children's ideas to develop disagreements and questions that will situate further design and investigation. As noted in Chapter 4, children (and adults) struggle to pose investigable questions in new contexts and do not always recognize disagreements or gaps in their understanding. Teachers can provide support by offering sustained exploration of the shared phenomenon or design challenge; eliciting children's ideas and experiences to make it clear that everyone has something to contribute; valuing uncertainty as indicating that there is "something to figure out"; asking probing questions; pointing out differences in ideas; and co-constructing problems and questions with children (Bismack and Haefner, 2020; McGill, Housman, and Reiser, 2021; Metz, 2011; Phillips et al., 2018; Reiser et al., 2017; Watkins et al., 2018; Zembal-Saul and Hershberger, 2020).

Overall, productive environments anchor children's activity in meaningful contexts, phenomena, and design challenges. Investigation and design can emerge from children's exploration of familiar contexts, such as the classroom's block area or their schoolyard (Fleer, Gomes, and March, 2014; Larimore, 2020). Instruction can also introduce phenomena and design challenges that connect to children's experiences and support subsequent investigation of disciplinary core ideas (Cunningham, 2017; Penuel and Reiser, 2018; Wright and Gotwals, 2017). Teachers may need to provide support by attending to and valuing children's interests and experiences and by helping children articulate questions and disagreements that establish a need for iterative investigation and design work.

Children Iteratively Refine Their Explanations and Designs

Productive science and engineering learning environments sustain investigation and design over time so that children can revise their thinking in response to new evidence and ideas. Although children's initial ideas about natural phenomena or design challenges are often productive, scientific accounts of the world often involve more causal complexity than everyday settings (Perkins and Grotzer, 2005) and involve invisible causal agents (i.e., forces and molecules). Consequently, children need opportunities to refine their ideas and iterate on proposed design solutions based on evidence and further information. Sustained opportunities for investigation and design provide repeated opportunities for children to grapple with science and engineering practices, engage with data, and develop deep conceptual understanding (Lehrer and Schauble, 2015; NRC, 2007, 2012). These opportunities frame science and engineering as a coherent endeavor unfolding over days, weeks, or months (Reiser et al., 2021; Schwarz, Passmore, and Reiser, 2017).

Access to *tools, resources, and data* can help children make progress on gathering information and *testing and revising their ideas.* Toys and manipulatives in preschool classrooms can promote exploration and building. Science and mathematical tools such journals, rulers, and magnifying glasses can support observation and data collection (Brenneman and Louro, 2008; Tu, 2006). Access to a range of texts, including informational text, can support children to identify with the goals, practices, and pursuits of science and engineering and provide support for developing explanations (see Chapter 6).

Technologies such as cameras and digital journals can provide unique affordances for documentation and support data visualization (Presser et al., 2017). Media, including simulations and games, can extend children's science and engineering learning by allowing children to manipulate variables and test hypotheses (Grindal et al., 2019; Presser et al., 2019; Smetana and Bell, 2012). Some of these technologies are particularly helpful for providing access to phenomena that are too large, small, slow, or fast to perceive without the tools (Presser et al., 2019). Tools accompanying public television programming also show promise (Xu and Warschauer, 2020). Designs based on embodied cognition use bodies themselves, and their movement, as resources for learning (Foglia and Wilson, 2013; Lindgren and Johnson-Glenberg, 2013; Ma, 2017; Samarapungavan, Bryan, and Wills, 2017; Shapiro, 2019); engaging children in dance, drama, or physical simulations support understanding of complex concepts (Danish et al., 2020; Georgen, 2019; Keifert et al., 2020; Varelas et al., 2010).

Science and engineering rely on a range of empirical methods (NRC, 2007) and these forms of investigation have different affordances in preschool through elementary school (Table 5-2). The forms of investigation each provide opportunities for engaging in the science and engineering practices and link back to children's own questions and problems, making them authentic and meaningful.

For example, observational methods may inform the development and refinement of questions and more controlled forms of investigation, and vice versa (Lehrer, Schauble, and Petrosino, 2001; Metz, 2011; Presser et al., 2017; Samarapungavan, Patrick, and Mantzicopoulos, 2011). To illustrate, Monteira and Jiménez-Aleixandre (2016) described a kindergarten class's inquiry into snails, where questions about feeding preferences emerging from long-term observation supported experiments to determine preferences. This snail experiment in turn opened up new questions, which children pursued by observing marks left on food to conjecture about snails' mouthparts, engaging with text, and finally, closely observing a limpet's mouth with a hand lens. Similarly, Manz (2015, 2016) described how third graders compared Wisconsin Fast Plants to understand whether the amount of light a seed received mattered for growth and reproduction. The children argued that their investigation did not adequately allow them to understand the growth of plants in a wild area behind their school—recognizing, first, that the plants in the backyard were different kinds than those studied in the investigation and, second, that the amount of light provided by the lightbox and sun might differ. The teacher supported children to propose a field-based investigation of different areas in the backyard to describe light and develop counts of the plants in plots. In each case, teachers supported children to make sense of how their investigations helped them make progress on their questions, what new gaps and questions investigations had surfaced, and what new data were needed.

Giving children opportunities to *discuss or make important decisions* about how to define the questions or problems they are exploring, how to go about that exploration, and how to evaluate their efforts is crucial to the development of a science and engineering classroom community for meaningful sensemaking (Duschl, 2008; Ford and Forman, 2006; Lehrer, Schauble, and Petrosino, 2001; Manz, 2016; Metz, 2008). Scientists and engineers face uncertainty not only about the best explanation for a phenomenon or the best design, but in how to define problems, how to design investigations, what measures or evidence to focus on, and how to make sense of variability in data. Children need to engage with this uncertainty to understand science and engineering practice (Driver et al., 1996; Ford, 2005; Manz, Lehrer, and Schauble, 2020). Further, a robust body of research in education and psychology shows the value of learners grappling with uncertainty and failure (e.g., Hiebert et al., 1996; Kapur and Bielaczyc, 2012; Reiser, 2004).

TABLE 5-2 Forms of Investigation and Material Resources

Investigation Type	Description: Children...
Field Study; Place-Based Work	Observe and interact with ecological and life cycle phenomena in their environment (e.g., nature walks, school gardens).
First-Hand Observational Studies Over Time	Observe a phenomenon over a period of time (e.g., examining plant growth or tracking weather).
Building, Tinkering, and Optimizing	Explore a phenomenon through interacting and trying out ideas (e.g., exploring ramps, force and motion).
First-Hand Comparisons and Experiments	Compare conditions, varying one factor and trying to understand causes or differences (e.g., plant growth in different conditions).
Simulations	Engage with a representation of a phenomenon, testing parameters.
Second-Hand Data	Use data collected by others to develop claims and explanations.

Affordances: Children...	Considerations
Observe phenomena and designs as they occur in the world, including in the school's immediate area; develop relationships with and within ecosystems; ask should-we questions.	Using outdoors for learning (as opposed to recess) may be unfamiliar to children and may require norm setting. Repeated visits to distant location may not be practical; lessons may benefit from visits to the schoolyard instead. Available outdoor spaces may not align with learning goals and planning may be needed to identify relevant phenomena.
Observe, pose questions, draw, and measure.	May be less useful for causal questions and may entail descriptive questions.
Explore materials and ideas, posing "what if" and "how can I" questions and gaining familiarity with ideas in contexts they co-create.	Hard to record ideas; may require planning for creative options. Work may not generate useful comparisons so may require complementary learning experiences.
Explore and see causal effects to support explanations; may measure, compare, and represent data.	May require extensive experience before causal questions are sensible. May yield inconsistent results when conducted by children, so may require contingency plans or improvement of investigative procedures.
Easily and efficiently manipulate variables and/or test design solutions.	Simulation meaning may be opaque to children, which may necessitate explication or complementary learning experiences. Simulations may demonstrate ideas rather than fostering sensemaking, which may necessitate different choices.
Analyze datasets that may be hard to collect within the constraints of classrooms.	Data collection and representation may be opaque to children and may require explication and scaffolding.

Children can understand and engage with several forms of uncertainty and decision making when

- Defining engineering problems (Atman et al., 2007; Hynes and Swenson, 2013; Watkins, Spencer, and Hammer, 2014)
- Deciding how to represent a phenomenon in an investigation to make progress on questions (Lehrer, Schauble, and Petrosino, 2001; Manz, 2015; Siry, Wilmes, and Haus, 2016; Sodian, Zaitchik, and Carey, 1991; Warren et al., 2001)
- Deciding what to use as evidence; deciding what and how to measure (Hapgood, Magnusson, and Palincsar, 2004; Lehrer and Schauble, 2012; Monteira and Jiménez-Aleixandre, 2016; Varelas et al., 2008)
- Deciding how to represent observations and data (Hapgood, Magnusson, and Palincsar, 2004; Lehrer and Schauble, 2004; Lehrer, Schauble, and Petrosino, 2001; Siry, 2013)
- Determining how to use findings from an investigation to develop an explanation and identify the limits of investigation or what other information is needed (Manz, 2015; Metz, 2004, 2011; Palincsar and Magnusson, 2001; Richards, Johnson, and Nyeggen, 2015)
- Exploring the ethical and social consequences of a decision, explanation, or design (Gunckel and Tolbert, 2018; McGowan and Bell, 2020)

Engineering learning experiences often emphasize problem solving without making space for children to engage in processes of identifying problems to be solved, identifying criteria and constraints, gathering more information to learn about the problem, and/or redefining the problem. Rather than allow children to engage in this work of "problem scoping" (Atman et al., 2007; Watkins, Spencer, and Hammer, 2014), often curricula present problems that are already well defined, or teachers do the work of problem scoping for children. Children need opportunities to do this work themselves, because practicing problem scoping can make space for them to engage in question-asking, identify creative solutions, and involve skills that need to be developed and practiced.

Boxes 5-2 and 5-3 illustrate some of these forms of uncertainty and show that engaging children in making decisions about investigations and designs are not equated with open exploration. Children need support from adults to consider decisions.

Organizing instruction around *developing and revising artifacts across lessons* can help orient instruction around sensemaking by connecting children's work to a broader conceptual context, and can help position children as sensemakers. Preschool and elementary science lessons often emphasize data collection and representation removed from efforts to construct explanations or models (Zangori, Forbes, and Biggers, 2013). Often, models, explanations, and even designs are developed at the end of a series of activities as a way to express or showcase what children have learned or to make the "correct explanation" public (Gouvea and Passmore, 2017; Schwarz et al., 2009). When children are asked to develop tentative models, explanations, or prototypes at the beginning of a unit, they make their ideas visible and have a chance to engage with each other's ideas, setting up a need to investigate and supporting a sense of coherence as they return to artifacts over time (Reiser et al., 2017) (see Box 5-4). Organizing investigation and design around constructing, using, evaluating, and refining explanations, models, and prototypes can also help focus children's efforts around disciplinary criteria, such as the explanation that best accounts for available data or the design prototype that best meets solution criteria (Schwarz, Passmore, and Reiser, 2017; Vo et al., 2015).

As children iteratively refine their ideas and artifacts, teachers use tools and resources and facilitate discussions and decision making to help maintain a focus on the purpose of investigative and design work by reminding children of where they are in their inquiry, articulating and/or posting the central challenge or question, and connecting children's ideas back to the purpose at hand (Manz, 2016; Winokur and Worth, 2006). Children benefit from support to interpret observations, reminding themselves of the

---

BOX 5-2
Decision Making in a First Grade Investigation

Attempting to discover more about the role of the sun in ripening fruit, a group of children decided to place one tomato on a windowsill and another in the "dark." Although all the children accepted placement on the windowsill as an acceptable operationalization of "light," many children were uncertain about what would count as "dark." They argued about its meaning but eventually settled upon placing a tomato under an opaque cover. . . Having settled on dark and light, another child objected, "But the sun is hot, not just light. Does heat matter?" Several children found this objection compelling, and someone pointed out that although the windowsill was light, it was also cold. The ensuing discussion eventually resulted in an expanded space of comparison: light and cool (the windowsill), light and warm (a well-lit location away from the sill), dark and warm (the covered tomato), and dark and cold (inside the refrigerator).

SOURCE: Adapted from Lehrer, Schauble, and Petrosino (2001, p. 263).

> **BOX 5-3**
> **Problem Defining and Problem Scoping in a Fourth Grade Engineering Design Activity**
>
> Two fourth graders were discussing how to make a periscope that would allow two characters in a book to see a statue (Watkins, Spencer, and Hammer, 2014).
>
> Mike: And do you wanna make this out of wood?
> Thomas: Mmm, wood would be more artificial but it would take longer.
> Mike: It would take longer, but it would be stronger, and um,
> Thomas: But how would um they, how would they get the wood?
> Mike: Do they have to?
> Thomas: Yeah, but if they get if- when like- but- you know how Jamie is really cheap?
> Mike: Yeah, he is.
> Thomas: So, if, they wouldn't probably get the wood. They would probably get the cardboard, cause. . .
> Mike: (softly) Yeah, I see what you're saying, I see what you're saying.
> Thomas: Cause Jamie's cheap and he, and that would probably cost a lot more than cardboard.
> Mike: (louder) But then cardboard wouldn't be as sturdy and um, you, you know how flimsy card board is. Yeah, I mean. . .
> Thomas: But then they, once they get the wood they'd have to get the cardbo- Like they'd have to get glue. They'd have to get all this other stuff.
>
> Watkins, Spencer, and Hammer (2014) interpret this exchange, stating:
>
> This exchange began with Mike asking about the primary material with which they would build their periscope. This question opened up a negotiation between the boys, in which they discussed not only different materials, but by arguing about the importance of different problem considerations, they also negotiated the content and boundaries of the problem space for which they were choosing these materials. (p. 7)
>
> The boys named elements of the problem space, negotiated different perspectives, and reflected on the problem space as they began to consider what would constitute a potential solution.
>
> SOURCE: Based on Watkins, Spencer, and Hammer (2014).

meaning of numbers and representations; they also need support to move beyond conclusions about trends in data to explanations of why and how findings occurred (Brenneman and Louro, 2008; Hapgood, Magnusson, and Palincsar, 2004; Herrenkohl, Tasker, and White, 2011; Presser et al., 2019; Zangori, Forbes, and Biggers 2013). Moreover, teachers acknowledge chil-

BOX 5-4
Children's Models as Artifacts

Artifacts can include two-dimensional models (e.g., drawings of the inside of a snail's mouth; Monteira and Jiménez-Aleixandre, 2016) or illustrations (e.g., sketches describing what happens to water as it hits the ground; Zangori, Forbes, and Schwarz, 2015), three-dimensional models (e.g., sculptures of bee pollination; Danish and Enyedy, 2007), plans and designs (Portsmore, Watkins, and McCormick, 2012), or written explanations co-constructed as a community or written individually (e.g., teacher documentation of preschoolers' verbal explanations about growth during observation and documentation of how pumpkins change over time; Brenneman and Louro, 2008). The figures here illustrate what children's artifacts can look like, at preschool (Figure B5-4a), second grade (Figure B5-4b), and fifth grade (Figure B5-4c).

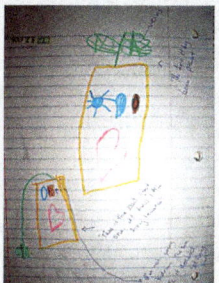

FIGURE B5-4a Preschool model of plant growth.
SOURCE: Brenneman and Louro (2008).

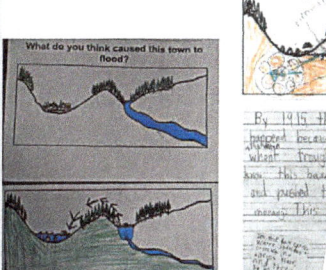
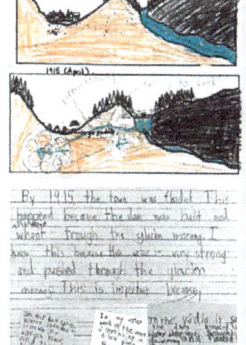

FIGURE B5-4b Second grade beginning and revised models of geologic water cycle.
SOURCE: Shim et al. (2018) Ambitious Science Teaching Unit.

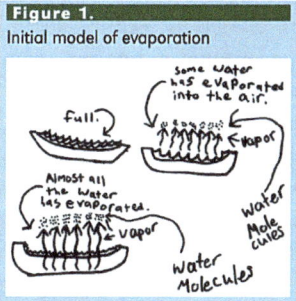
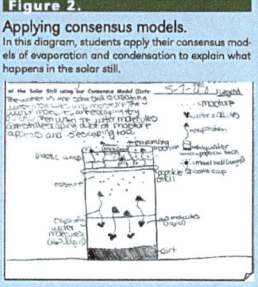

FIGURE B5-4c Fifth grade beginning and revised models of water cycle.
SOURCE: Kenyon, Schwarz, and Hug (2008).

dren's contributions, attributing observations, data, and ideas to individuals or the community (Monteira, Jiménez-Aleixandre, and Siry, 2020). Before introducing read-alouds that provide canonical information, teachers can review with children the progress they have made in their investigations and what questions remain; during read-alouds, they can connect information to children's discoveries and questions (Palincsar and Magnusson, 2001; Varelas et al., 2014; Zembal-Saul, McNeill, and Hershberger, 2013). Lastly, teachers need to make adjustments based on the class's progress and emerging questions. In this kind of responsive teaching, teachers attend to the substance of children's ideas and respond through opening up discussion and adjusting resources, support, and next steps (Colley and Windschitl, 2016; Peterson and French, 2008; Robertson, Hammer, and Scherr, 2016; Schwarz et al., 2020).

In summary, children's sensemaking can be supported by providing opportunities for them to produce and refine artifacts as they articulate explanations, develop models, and test designs. Children can engage with a range of information sources—including empirical investigation, second-hand data, and informational text—to revise their initial ideas. Within this work, children can be positioned as active sensemakers and can discuss decisions about investigations and criteria for their work; they can also question and problematize situations with data, allowing them to explore authentic local contexts and problems. Because children's iterative sensemaking is often unpredictable and nonlinear, instructional and assessment practices involve adjusting resources and support based on children's progress and emerging questions. Further, the creation and refinement of artifacts and the discussions that emerge from this process make children's sensemaking visible and can serve as formative assessment evidence for teachers, as described later in this chapter.

Children Learn with and from Each Other

The practices of science and engineering are inherently dialogic (Feinstein and Waddington, 2020; Kelly, 2014); scientists and engineers are able to ask questions about phenomena, define a problem space, propose methods of investigation or design, and co-construct explanations and solutions through collaborative negotiation and meaning making. Similarly, when children work together to investigate or design solutions, they engage in discourse and rely on a host of resources and productive strategies for communicating their observations, decisions, and reasoning (Ballenger and Carpenter, 2004; Colley and Windschitl, 2016; Mercer, Dawes, and Staarman, 2009; Paugh, Wendell, and Wright, 2018; Peterson and French, 2008; Rosebery et al., 2010; Suárez, 2020; Varelas et al., 2008; Warren et al., 2001).

Discourse needs to be intentionally supported in science and engineering learning environments. An important feature of this support is the acknowledgment and disruption of power hierarchies that operate in the classroom related to (1) the discourse that is allowed and valued in classrooms; (2) the roles that children and adults play in meaning making; and (3) the differential social status assigned to children and adults in collaborative discourse (Engle, 2012; Wendell, Wright, and Paugh, 2017). In such learning environments, the curriculum and teacher invite a wide range of semiotic resources (i.e., talk, representations, materials, and actions used for communicative purposes, including multiple languages and embodied actions) and ways of showing thinking, including drawing on different cultural repertoires. Teachers can use flexible structures that support collaboration, and within those, use talk moves to elicit and work with children's ideas toward sharing tentative explanations, planning investigations, and agreeing on or evaluating explanations, solutions, and actions.

Equitable science and engineering learning environments recognize the vast *range of communicative or semiotic resources* that children leverage in the service of figuring out natural phenomena and addressing design challenges, especially for multilingual learners (Bang et al., 2017; NASEM, 2018a; Nasir et al., 2014). Children bring and develop a range of semiotic resources. These do not always match the canonical forms of communication typical of learning environments (see Table 5-3). Centering academic English and technical vocabulary at the expense of other forms of communication can ignore or dismiss the meaning-making strategies that emergent multilingual children bring, and thus perpetuate inequities (Flores and Rosa, 2015; García and Kleifgen, 2019; Lee and Stephens, 2020; NASEM, 2018a).

For instance, Warren and colleagues (2001) observed that an upper elementary student, Jean-Charles, used lexical and grammatical structures from Haitian-Creole when distinguishing between growth and development in insects. Using Haitian-Creole, Jean-Charles made a conceptual distinction between the process of growing (*vin gran*) and a stage of development (*vin tounen*); without access to this familiar language, Jean-Charles's participation and learning could have been truncated.

Teachers and the curriculum materials they use to organize their instruction may use *flexible structures to support children's collaboration and collective thinking.* Through collective efforts to understand each other, children can meaningfully engage in science and engineering practices that develop their conceptual understanding of the world and of the disciplines (Engle and Conant, 2002; Kelly, 2014; Suárez, 2020). For this reason, equitable science and engineering in preschool through elementary learning environments use a range of participation structures (i.e., how children and teachers are expected to participate in tasks, as well as the roles and respon-

TABLE 5-3 Semiotic Resources Children May Develop and Use

Type of Semiotic Resource	Use in Context
Words in Other Named Languages	Bilingual fifth graders write a science report about elements in the periodic table using words associated with English and Spanish (Poza, 2016).
Gestures	Multilingual children (second and fourth graders) in an informal setting rely on a combination of pointing and metaphoric gestures, in conjunction with speech, to illustrate their model for how electrical energy is transmitted through a DC circuit (Suárez, 2020).
Artifacts and Materials	A multilingual kindergartner relies on objects (e.g., xylophones) and representations (e.g., drawings) to explain how and why bottles filled with water produce different sounds when blowing on them (Siry and Gorges, 2020).
Everyday Words	Multilingual third and fourth graders propose that "the coat traps the heat" when reflecting on the thermodynamic processes that underlie the insulating properties of coats (Rosebery et al., 2010).
Technical Term/Scientific Vocabulary	A monolingual third grader proposes placing a "velcrum" under a plank of wood to create a lever. The teacher uses this as an opportunity to introduce the technical term *fulcrum*, reinforcing the use of this term by labeling the fulcrum on a model of a lever, and encouraging children to use it during discussions (Hooper and Zembal-Saul, 2020).
Individual and Collective Whole-Body Movements	A small group of multilingual fifth graders plan and act out an interpretation of the water cycle, using their position, interaction, and motion to show water particles collecting, evaporating, forming clouds, and precipitating. A classmate suggests a change to better show the relationship between rain and clouds (Kotler, 2020).

SOURCE: Based on Hooper and Zembal-Saul (2020); Kotler (2020); Poza (2016); Rosebery et al. (2010); Siry and Gorges (2020); Suárez (2020).

sibilities participants take on) to promote talk (see Table 5-4). For instance, at the beginning of an investigation, children could individually develop their initial models of the water cycle, which they would later share with small groups and then the whole class. This combination of individual and group work can help unearth similarities and differences in children's conjectures and reasoning, and frame the kinds of investigations they need to conduct to better understand the relationships among evaporation, precipitation, and groundwater (Zangori et al., 2017). After completing their investigations, small groups of children can share their updated models with the rest of the class to represent their current understanding based on the evidence and to get feedback from their peers and the teacher (Zangori et al., 2017).

TABLE 5-4 Participation Structures for Investigation and Design

Participant Structure	Configuration	Teacher's Role	Affordances and Equity Considerations
Turn and Talks	Pairs or small groups	Draw on ideas for whole-group work	Enhanced discourse and engagement for children; share initial ideas and thoughts. Provides low-stakes ways of starting conversation and helps build a caring community.
Group Tasks (Herrenkohl and Guerra, 1998; Varelas et al., 2008)	Pairs or small groups	Decide structures and tasks; determine roles; circulate and support children	Enhanced discourse and engagement for children; collaborative engagement in science and engineering practices. Provides scaffolded ways of starting and sustaining conversation. Assigning or having children choose sensemaking roles (not just logistical roles) enhances learning opportunities. Can minimize hierarchies and competition between children with varying academic histories.
Collective Exploration (French, 2004; Siry, 2013)	Whole group, small group, or centers	Help children narrate investigation and design; highlight connections	Children work collectively with materials; children build on others' ideas. Can help to make visible contributions of children who may be marginalized in other subjects. Can minimize hierarchies and competition between children with varying academic histories.
Collectively Sharing Artifacts (Cartier et al., 2013)	Small group, jigsaw, or whole group (e.g., gallery walk)	Select and structure artifacts shared; highlight connections	Children learn about others' ideas and designs. Can help to make visible contributions of children who may be marginalized in other subjects. Can minimize hierarchies and competition between children with varying academic histories.
Open-Ended Discussion (Gallas, 1995; Warren and Rosebery, 2011)	Whole group	Attentive listener and participant	Teachers and children learn about children's ideas; children can pose questions and explore connections. Can provide a space for collectively developing and making visible the norms for science and engineering discourse, as well as welcoming a range of ways of knowing. Can minimize hierarchies and competition between children with varying academic histories.
Guided Discussions (Colley and Windschitl, 2016; Winokur and Worth, 2006)	Whole group	Invite and probe children's ideas; help children relate ideas to each other's; support sensemaking	Children move toward decisions and explanations. Can provide a space for collectively developing and making visible the norms for science and engineering discourse, as well as welcoming a range of ways of knowing. Can minimize hierarchies and competition between children with varying academic histories.

Learning environments are enhanced when teachers use targeted pedagogical strategies that invite children to make their thinking visible and encourage others to engage with those ideas; that is, teachers in these environments *elicit and work with children's ideas*. Cartier and colleagues (2013) describe the kinds of "focused talk" that teachers can rely on to engage children in a dialogue intended to develop their thinking toward the lesson's learning goals. Teachers' focused talk can serve to make children's thinking visible, such as when a kindergarten teacher supported children to graphically represent the forces they thought acted on a person as they sailed down a slide (Windschitl, Thompson, and Braaten, 2018). Additionally, focused talk can guide children's thinking in productive directions, such as when the teacher encouraged her fourth graders to explain how the flow of electrical energy through a bulb could be responsible for heat and light, and then highlighted a child's idea that electricity running through a wire would produce heat (Colley and Windschitl, 2016). Finally, teachers' focused talk can be useful for directing children's attention to salient features of the problem space, such as when the teacher asked her fourth graders to rub their hands together to experience how kinetic energy can be transformed into thermal energy, as a way of embodying what was happening in the bulb's filament (Colley and Windschitl, 2016).

Peterson and French (2008) examined how preschool educators supported young children's explanatory language during science activities. They found teachers used modeling and eliciting language, encouraged explanations through observation and prediction, and promoted collaborative discussion among children and peers. At the beginning of units, teachers modeled and elicited language by naming and describing objects and phenomena as children observed and/or experienced them. They also posed open-ended questions and later encouraged children to share their observations and predictions with questions such as "What happened?" and "What do you think will happen?" To ensure that results that contradicted children's predictions would not be discouraging, teachers emphasized the satisfaction of learning through science and praised children for making predictions (regardless of whether these were correct or not). Teachers modeled taking an open stance, using words such as "maybe" to highlight that uncertainty is an important part of exploration and investigation. Finally, teachers invited children to comment and respond to peers' ideas, highlighting how disagreements are a normal part of collaborative science learning.

Studies of elementary school classrooms have described how teachers can use pedagogical strategies that allow them to orchestrate discussion among children, with the intent of eliciting children's ideas and creating opportunities for their peers to engage with them. For instance, teachers can use "Talk Moves" (Michaels and O'Connor, 2012; Michaels, O'Connor, and Resnick, 2008) that are meant to make children accountable to (1) the learning community, as they listen intently to their peers' explanations and engage with them; (2) the standards of reasoning, as children evaluate the logic and plausibility of conclusions; and (3) knowledge. Being accountable to both the learning community and the standards of reasoning creates a situation in which children listen to their peers' ideas and assess the explanatory power of the models discussed (Engle and Conant, 2002). These talk moves, however, can be used in ways that are rote (without attention to the disciplinary substance of children's ideas) or to elicit and highlight the "correct" idea. In these cases, they do not support collaborative work, and can instead re-instantiate the teacher or text as authority and some children's ideas as more valuable than others (Colley and Windschitl, 2016; Manz and Renga, 2017; Schwarz et al., 2020; Zangori and Pinnow, 2019).

Equitable science and engineering preschool through elementary learning environments center and build on children's observations and experiences. This is especially important for children from nondominant and minoritized communities, where equitable learning opportunities require teachers "seeing and hearing students' ideas and reasoning as connected to science (as opposed to being off topic or, worse, disruptive)" (Bang et al., 2017, p. 36). Being able to notice children's ideas and hear the science in their thinking is a crucial aspect of this (e.g., NASEM, 2018a; Robertson, Hammer, Scherr, 2016).

Formative Assessment to Understand Children's Learning and Inform Instruction

Assessment is a systematic, multistep, and multifaceted process that involves collecting and interpreting data to make inferences about children's learning (NRC, 2014a). *A Framework for K-12 Science Education* (hereafter referred to as the *Framework*; NRC, 2012) discusses three common purposes for science assessment: *formative assessment* to guide science instructional processes, *summative assessment* to determine science attainment levels, and *assessment for program evaluation* to examine comparisons across classrooms, schools, districts, or countries. *Developing Assessments for the Next Generation Science Standards* (NRC, 2014a) also distinguishes between *classroom* or *internal* assessments (selected or designed by teachers and conducted as part of instruction) and *external* assessments (selected by schools, districts, states, or countries to monitor learning). This section primarily describes assessment processes that are *formative* in nature and can be designed and used in preschool through elementary classrooms and taken up by educators to inform and guide their work with children.

Most science assessment design and research that is aligned to the *Framework* has been conducted with grades 6–12. Within this work, there is a consensus that assessment design address the following principles: (1)

assessment methods and tasks must elicit and attend to multiple dimensions of science and engineering learning (i.e., practices, disciplinary core ideas, crosscutting concepts) simultaneously, (2) assessment systems must gather evidence of proficiency with science practices and ideas as they develop over time as the product of coherent systems of curriculum and instruction, and (3) assessment work must be underpinned by an understanding of the conceptual terrain, tasks, and supports that allow children to show their understanding, as well as by an understanding of how children's ideas/practices develop (NRC, 2014a). There is not yet a robust research base in preschool to fifth grade that assesses science in ways consistent with the principles above (Greenfield, 2015). Therefore, the committee drew from the principles developed in the NRC report, research on assessment more broadly, and emerging research in preschool and elementary school to briefly describe the basis of a formative assessment system for preschool through elementary science and engineering.

Formative assessment can be woven into the ongoing work that children are engaged in, reflecting how formative assessment is used for *multiple purposes*. Classroom artifacts—including science notebooks, design drawings, and models—and children's participation in classroom discussion can provide evidence for teachers to make inferences about children's interests, proficiency, and need for further support (Brenneman and Louro, 2008; NRC, 2014a; Smith et al., 2016). Teachers and designers of curricula can gather such evidence for a variety of different purposes. For instance, prior to or early in curricular sequences, teachers may benefit from information on the resources and interests children bring to particular design problems, phenomena, and classroom activities. Such assessments might include pre-interviews with children, family sharing and documentation projects, and assessment tasks to elicit children's initial explanations, models and/or drawings (McWayne et al., 2020; Russ and Sherin, 2013; Schwarz et al., 2009; Tzou and Bell, 2010). Subsequently, teachers can collect formative assessment evidence to determine the supports that will allow particular children to engage, contribute, and make progress by reflecting on discussions, examining artifacts, or using designed assessments tasks (NASEM, 2017; Shavelson et al., 2008). They may also aggregate data to determine the next instructional steps likely to benefit the classroom community in their design and investigation work (Atkin and Coffey, 2003; Sevian and Dini, 2019). Finally, a purpose that is less often highlighted is to monitor and adjust classroom's community norms and structures (Penuel and Watkins, 2019; Reiser et al., 2021).

Verbal explanations and writing provide an important source of data for understanding children's explanation and conceptual understanding, illustrating how formative assessments draw on *multiple forms of evidence*. McNeill (2011), for example, investigated fifth grade students' views of explanation, argument, and evidence across three contexts (what scientists do, what happens in science classrooms, and what happens in everyday life) and examined how children's argumentation changed over the course of the year by gathering multiple sources of written and verbal formative data (pre- and post-interviews, classroom conversations, and children's written explanations).

However, children, especially those in preschool and early elementary, are not always able to convey all their knowledge in writing, or even verbally. Young children are learning language and concepts of print as they develop understanding in science and engineering, and learning across these different domains is connected and mutually reinforcing (see Chapter 6). Young children's science discourse is enhanced when they are allowed and encouraged to document their learning through drawings, photographs, and diagrams, and later use those as resources in their explanations (Siry and Gorges, 2020). Formative assessment approaches therefore attend to how young children's engagement with materials and manipulatives and their use of gesture conveys their thinking and knowledge.

Although formative data appear to be easy to gather as part of children's ongoing work, teachers need to give careful consideration to the design of formative assessment probes posed during science and engineering activities (Keeley, 2018). *Formative assessment probes can be embedded into activities* to elicit children's thinking before and after they engage in investigations; when purposefully designed, such assessment probes become useful not only for gathering assessment data, but also for guiding elements of the learning activities themselves. Keeley (2018), for instance, described how P-E-O prompts (prediction, explanation [the justification for the prediction], and observation [testing the prediction]) can serve as formative assessment, while simultaneously providing a structure to guide children through science investigations. During the sensemaking conversations that follow the investigations, teachers can also invite children to revisit their answer to probes (for instance, their initial prediction) and revise their explanations, allowing teachers to better understand children's developing understanding.

Attention to the forms of support provided during activities is critical (Fine and Furtak, 2020; Gotwals and Songer, 2013; NRC, 2014a). For example, Ashbacher and Alonzo (2006) found that the value of using journals as a formative assessment depends heavily on the amount of support children receive from teachers (e.g., guidance about what information to include). Support ranged from minimal to overly prescriptive. Neither extreme was found helpful; moderate amounts of support—for instance, providing guiding prompts but also allowing the children freedom to draw and write what they learned in their own words—allowed better formative assessment and child learning.

Finally, teachers' effective use of formative assessment requires them to develop understanding of the *interpretation and potential biases* involved in formative assessment. Robust assessment is undergirded by a sense of the conceptual terrain of a unit of study or even year of instruction, including the goals for practice and understanding; the resources, interests, and experiences children might bring to instruction; and stepping stones toward reaching goals (Campbell, Schwarz, and Windschitl, 2016; Coffey et al., 2011; NRC, 2014a). NRC (2014a) concludes that assessment tasks for three-dimensional learning need to include interpretive systems and elaborates:

> NGSS-aligned assessments will also need to identify likely misunderstandings, productive ideas of children that can be built upon, and interim goals for learning. . . To teach toward the NGSS performance expectations, teachers will need a sense of the likely progression at a more micro level, to answer such questions as:
>
> - For this unit, where are the children expected to start, and where should they arrive?
> - What typical intermediate understandings emerge along this learning path?
> - What common logical errors or alternative conceptions present barriers to the desired learning or resources for beginning instruction?
> - What new aspects of a practice need to be developed in the context of this unit? (p. 91)

Teachers engaging in assessment—whether listening to children during whole-group discussion or small-group collaboration, examining children's artifacts such as models or design plans, or using planned assessment probes—will need to interpret children's discourse and productions in relation to the disciplinary substance (Coffey et al., 2011) they care about. Work that started in mathematics education (e.g., Sherin, Jacob, and Phillip, 2011) on teacher noticing has recently been extended to science education to understand how teachers attend to and interpret children thinking in talk (Cowie et al., 2018; Luna, Selmer, and Rye, 2018; Rosebery, Warren, and Tucker-Raymond, 2016; Schwarz et al., 2020; Sevian and Dini, 2019) and artifacts (Luna, Selmer, and Rye, 2018). Other work in early mathematics education (Clements and Sarama, 2021a) supports the development of formative assessments aligned with learning trajectories or learning progressions, and provides a model for future work in science and engineering, noting that high-quality formative assessment building on learning trajectories must identify the goal, determine where the child's thinking is presently, and what instruction will support movement along the progression.

The growing body of literature in elementary science and engineering education emphasizes the importance of teachers attending to the detail and substance of children's work, the understanding needed to attend to and interpret children's thinking, and the ways that teachers' attention can be drawn to other aspects of children's engagement (e.g., canonical correctness, fluency of talk, seriousness vs. silliness) (Lee and Stephens, 2020; Rosebery, Warren, and Tucker-Raymond, 2016; Russ et al., 2008; Sevian and Dini, 2019; Warren and Rosebery, 2011). There is emerging evidence that teachers' attention to the disciplinary substance in children's talk can be supported by (1) engaging with the science and engineering content (Manz and Suárez, 2018; Rosebery, Warren, and Tucker-Raymond, 2016; Watkins et al., 2018), (2) examining and discussing children's work with colleagues (Rosebery, Warren, and Tucker-Raymond, 2016), and (3) rubrics and educative materials that provide support for attending to and interpreting children's work (Arias et al., 2016).

Culturally and linguistically sensitive assessments are important and needed. Inferences from formative assessment are "subject to systematic, irrelevant influences that may be associated with gender, race, ethnicity, disability, English language proficiency, or other student characteristics" (Bennett, 2011; NASEM, 2018a). In other words, teachers may judge the skills of some children differently than others, which in turn may influence how children's instruction is facilitated and modified (Bennett et al., 1993; NASEM, 2018a). Multilingual children's learning during science investigations and engineering design activities is likely influenced both by children's linguistic and conceptual understanding of the questions and challenges presented and discussed. An emergent body of research is examining how teachers can recognize and disrupt biases toward particular ways of talking or demonstrating knowledge (Fine and Furtak, 2020; Lee and Stephens, 2020; NASEM, 2018a; Ruiz-Primo, Solano-Flores, and Li, 2014; Solano-Flores, 2016; Warren and Rosebery, 2011).

In formative assessment, teachers can aim to reduce potential bias in terms of cultural background by considering data from multiple sources and from different contexts, soliciting input from families and other educators with expertise working with groups of children they are less knowledgeable about (Bennett, 2011; NASEM, 2018b), and can ensure that assessment opportunities are not biased against children with learning disabilities and/or learning differences by providing multiple means of engagement, representation, action, and expression (Basham and Marino, 2013), as reflected in earlier parts of this chapter. Science and engineering professional development programs that address formative assessment along with pedagogical content knowledge (McNeill and Knight, 2013) and justice-oriented approaches (Mensah, 2009) could help ensure formative assessment efforts are grounded on teachers' understanding of disciplinary learning and less likely to be biased.

EQUITY AND THE DESIGN OF LEARNING ENVIRONMENTS

A great deal of the text of this chapter is focused on the design of learning environments that provide all children with *increased opportunities and access to high-quality science and engineering learning and instruction* (Approach #1). Designing such environments provides children with access to science and engineering and also offer a way of supporting children's *increased achievement, representation, and identification with science and engineering* (Approach #2). The characteristics emphasized are supported by empirical evidence that suggests their utility for supporting children's learning and have implications related to identity, as well. For example, developing a classroom culture oriented toward caring and collective well-being and knowledge building can shape how children engage in sensemaking together, how they take up the science and engineering practices, and their identities as people who do science and engineering (Carlone, Mercier, and Metzger, 2021; Kane, 2015, 2016; Varelas et al., 2008). At the same time, children—particularly children of color—are sensitive to the kinds of behaviors that are likely to get them labeled as troublemakers or earn them sanction in the classroom (Wright et al., 2018). Thus, the design of the learning environment and the teacher's instructional practices and norms within that environment can play important roles in how children learn and engage in identity development. Finally, by fostering and valuing a range of linguistic resources, the learning environment can help a range of children—including emergent multilingual learners—see themselves represented in the classroom.

Extensive work in this chapter provides guidance about how learning environments can work toward *expanding what counts as science and engineering* (Approach #3). Examples include

- Resetting norms so that hierarchies are minimized and a number of proficiencies (e.g., curiosity, risk taking) are valued, not only final-form science (Bang et al., 2017; Rosebery et al., 2010).
- Building on a wide range of semiotic resources and allowing children multiple ways of expressing sensemaking (Rosebery et al., 2010; Suárez, 2020; Warren et al., 2001).
- Instructional practice that requires and allows teachers to notice children's thinking and see and hear children's ideas as reasonable and fruitful, and not off topic or problematic (Bang et al., 2017)—thus building on children's ways of talking and sensemaking.
- Ensuring that assessments are culturally and linguistically sensitive, and working to disrupt biases based on race, gender, linguistic resources, learning disability/differences, or any of the myriad other ways teachers may inadvertently express preference for some children's ways of knowing or expressing their ideas over others

(Bennett, 2011; NASEM, 2018a; Ruiz-Primo, Solano-Flores, and Li, 2014; Warren and Rosebery, 2011).

These approaches are important for all children, in all grade levels and content areas—but they are particularly important for minoritized children and others who are often marginalized in science and engineering.

The chapter highlights a few ways that learning environments can support children (and teachers) in *seeing science and engineering as part of justice movements* (Approach #4). Such connections provide ways of drawing on real-world contexts for authentic sensemaking. For example, Davis and Schaeffer (2019), drawing on regional issues of water justice that were prominent in the news, highlight numerous strengths of such a focus. Engineering design challenges present similarly relevant local problems or phenomena; these can be used to explore issues of justice and engage in decision making (Cody and Biggers, 2020; Dalvi, Wendell, and Johnson, 2016; Haas et al., 2021; Upadhyay, 2009). Davis and Schaeffer note, however, that children's emotional responses to environmental issues are rarely elicited or studied, and that this is particularly true among minoritized youth who are often directly affected by the justice issues.

SUMMARY

This chapter has described the learning environment features that allow children to learn science and engineering in a caring community, orient to investigation and design in meaningful contexts, refine their explanations and solutions through sensemaking, learn with and from each other, and be assessed in ways that show their learning and inform instruction. Accomplishing these goals necessitates a learning environment that supports children's meaningful learning. The teacher, with support from and in partnership with children, curriculum materials, school context, and other elements of the learning environment, works with children to set and revise norms to support a collective culture. As part of this work, the teacher invites the emotional dimensions of science and engineering while also building relationships with children, families, and communities. Teachers also ground children's work in rich contexts and position them as sensemakers through eliciting, attending to, and valuing their initial ideas and experiences. Moreover, teachers help children to work with tools, resources, and data to refine their ideas and solutions and the artifacts that reflect their sensemaking while inviting a wide range of ways for children to show their thinking, using flexible structures to support collaboration as they engage children in discussing and making decisions. Lastly, teachers use formative assessments for multiple purposes, drawing on multiple forms of evidence and providing different forms of support for children, all while working against potential biases.

Recognizing the complexity of this work, the chapter describes a number of ways to accomplish these goals. Instruction can be based in rich phenomena and design challenges that orient children's investigation and design work. Whether these are emergent, planned, or adapted for local relevance, they can be meaningful contexts for children's work. Learning experiences can support children as sensemakers by allowing them to make their ideas visible through developing and refining artifacts. Children can engage, with appropriate support, in making and discussing decisions about aspects of their investigation and design process. Furthermore, children's collaboration and collective thinking can be strengthened by using different participation structures and explicitly inviting a wide set of resources into classroom work. Through these and other approaches, learning environments can support the kinds of meaningful opportunities to learn emphasized throughout this report.

6

The Potentials and Pitfalls of Integrating Across Domains

Main Messages

- Principles for making productive connections include engaging children in investigation and design experiences that draw on multiple domains, making integration explicit in designs and teaching, supporting children's knowledge in individual disciplines, and recognizing that more integration is not necessarily better.
- Integrating science and engineering with each other and with other content areas in preschool through elementary classrooms has the potential to enhance connections between subjects and effectively increase the amount of instructional time for science and engineering instruction.
- Integration can benefit all domains if the design (a) respects the unique content and disciplinary practices of all domains, (b) leverages meaningful and mutually supportive connections among the subject areas, and (c) is developmentally, culturally, and linguistically appropriate.
- There are key opportunities for integrating science and engineering with English language arts, mathematics, and computational thinking.

Scientists and engineers engage in investigation and work to solve problems in ways that are often interdisciplinary in nature. The same interdisciplinarity applies to children's science and engineering learning and activity. Children use both language and literacy and mathematics (and other content areas) as they engage in science and engineering. They talk, sketch, draw, and write as they observe, design, and communicate their thinking. Additionally, they draw on texts (including diagrams, television shows, and simulations) constructed by others as they ask questions and develop explanations (e.g., Duke, 2016) and use measures and quantitative comparisons as they develop understanding of phenomena (e.g., Lehrer and Schauble, 2015). Making connections across content areas can be challenging, but takes advantage of affordances of the structure of preschool through elementary teaching and learning systems. Children work with teachers who support their progress across multiple content areas. Time can be used more fluidly without the need for bells and movement to new classrooms that characterize the middle and upper grades.

Interdisciplinary connections can be capitalized on in ways that are supportive of children's learning within science and engineering, as well as in content areas like English language arts (ELA), mathematics, and social studies, and in other areas like social-emotional learning, approaches to learning, and executive function (Bustamante, Greenfield, and Nayfeld, 2018; Bustamante, White, and Greenfield, 2018; Pearson, Moje, and Greenleaf, 2010). In the chapter, the word *domains* is used to refer to these academic content areas and other areas related to children's learning, such as social-emotional learning. Interdisciplinary connections across domains support learning in science and engineering *and* learning in other areas.

That said, drawing connections across these domains, both disciplinary content and other areas related to learning, can be challenging and must be done with care. Each content area discipline has core ideas and practices that need to be developed deeply and systematically (Clements and Sarama, 2021b; English, 2016; Lederman and Niess, 1997; Picha, 2020; Rich et al., 2020). And connecting learning across domains is seldom addressed systematically in curricular materials and professional learning initiatives (see Chapters 7 and 8). This chapter offers some starting points for considering such instructional connections.

This chapter begins with a brief description of approaches that have been taken when science and engineering are promoted in connection with other domains (notably content area domains and the area of social-emotional learning). This discussion is followed by summaries of the evidence base regarding connections to specific content domains, including language and literacy, mathematics, and computational thinking and computer science. The chapter argues for the benefits of making meaningful connections to be made and presents guidance for doing so.

APPROACHES TO CONTENT INTEGRATION

There are a number of different approaches to the integration of content (Moore, Johnston, and Glancy, 2020). Terms like *interdisciplinary* and *integrated* are often used interchangeably to describe approaches that connect learning across content domains (Czerniak et al., 1999; National Research Council [NRC], 2014b). Based on a review of the literature (e.g., Couso, 2020; Czerniak et al., 1999; English, 2016; Moore et al., 2020; NRC, 2014b; Rennie, Wallace, and Venville, 2012; Sarama et al., 2017), the committee proposes four main approaches that have typically characterized efforts to connect content domains:

1. Superficial Connections (Add-On or Sequential)—activities that showcase another discipline is added into a unit with little connection other than the topic.
2. Partial Integration—Two or more domains are addressed simultaneously, sometimes with one playing a supportive role.
3. Full Integration—All major domains are combined in every major lesson, instructional activity, or project. An overarching, usually real-world problem situates the use of multiple domains, but domains may not be fully supported.
4. Interdisciplinary Integration—Domains are connected sometimes via partial and other times full integration, with the criterion that each retains their core conceptual and epistemological structures so that connections serve the goals of each discipline.

Henceforth, the term "connection" is used to indicate linkages between domains of any depth and type. "Integration" refers to designs where the connections are more than superficial (i.e., the second, third, and fourth categories, above).

Both within and across these four categories, there is variation in types, degree, and depth of integration and pedagogical structures. Approaches to integration may differ in terms of the authenticity of context used, the intentionality of the connections, and the capacity for maintaining the integrity of the disciplines involved. Table 6-1 provides an overview of the features and learning goals of the four approaches to integration and identifies the number of domains connected and how domains are selected for integration.

Although at first glance these categorizations may appear to constitute a scale of increasing pedagogical efficacy, existing evidence does not support such a hierarchy (Rennie, Wallace, and Venville, 2012). Instead, research suggests designing to make connections where activity across domains is mutually supportive of learning in each domain, with different approaches

TABLE 6-1 Dimensions of Connections in Domain Integration

Features and Learning Goals	Number of Domains Connected	Selection of Domains to Connect
Superficial Connections (Add-On or Sequential)		
May involve only *context integration* in which one discipline uses a problem from another discipline as the context, but only attempts to achieve learning goals in the primary discipline. Children do not experience the other discipline's core ideas or practices as useful.	2 or more	Less intentional selection
Alternatively, the two domains may be applied to the problem, but only sequentially.		
Partial Integration		
Content integration achieves learning goals in two or more disciplines simultaneously.	2 or more	Intentional selection
Often, one domain as the primary driver of the practices, concepts, and development, with the other used in support. Children's experiences within the secondary domain(s) may involve only review or skill application		
Alternatively, the two domains may be more connected, explicating some related concepts and shared practices.		
Full Integration		
A complex problem that requires multiple domains drives instruction.	All domains	Potentially less intentional
Ideas and practices are brought in as they are useful for addressing the problem.		
Often these are not based on learning trajectories in any domain and children's engagement and learning can vary widely across domains.		
Interdisciplinary Integration		
This approach blends the integration approaches and adds specific pedagogical principles.	2 or more	Intentional selection with criteria for selection
Classes are organized into multiple blocks of time, for each content domain, as well as integrated experiences, so that each domain retains its core conceptual, procedural, and epistemological structure but also fully connects to other domains in cross-cutting concepts and practices. Thus, educational experiences integrate two or more domains whenever, but only, when it serves the goals of each.		

being appropriate in different situations. The committee sees value in partial integration, full integration, or interdisciplinary approaches, but suggests eschewing superficial connections or add-on approaches without any meaningful integration.

Although research is limited and varies in quality, the *STEM Integration in K-12 Education* report (NRC, 2014b) and other relevant literature suggest four promising principles for connecting science and engineering with other domains:

1. *Engage children in investigation and design experiences that draw on multiple domains.* When instruction situates children's science and engineering learning in meaningful and rich contexts, children engage in activity that recruits—and potentially deepens—practices, skills, and knowledge developed in other parts of the school day and may build positive identities in science and engineering (e.g., English, 2016; McClure et al., 2017; Moore, Johnston, and Glancy, 2020; NRC, 2014b).
2. *Make integration explicit in designs and teaching.* Even in meaningful contexts that call for activity that transcends disciplines, integration may not automatically support productive learning experiences (NRC, 2014b). Therefore, designs need to consider the potential learning and identity development within the multiple domains, and make relationships across domains explicit for children.
3. *Support children's knowledge in individual disciplines.* Domains often need to be learned in and of themselves, with dedicated time for each subject and a basis in a learning trajectory for children's development of central understanding and practices (Clements and Sarama, 2021b; English, 2016). For example, teaching science within the context of literacy can be reduced to "content-rich literacy," where the target literacy knowledge and practices drive the work, and children do not learn meaningful science content or develop an understanding of science and engineering practice.
4. *More integration is not necessarily better.* Research comparing various types of integrated curricula does not always support full integration (NRC, 2014b). Focusing on opportunities to use the disciplines in mutually supportive ways can help to ensure that children are learning and developing practices in each.

These principles offer entrance points for beginning the work of content connections and integration in the preschool through elementary ages.

APPROACHES TO INTEGRATING WITH SPECIFIC DOMAINS

Choices about connections and integration should be based on the contexts, disciplines, and learning goals. Consistent with the committee's charge to examine instructional approaches that support and enhance learning in science and engineering, the next sections discuss empirical evidence for productive connections between science and engineering and other domains.

Table 6-2 summarizes the committee's findings from the literature around a set of key questions:

TABLE 6-2 Connections and Evidence of Efficacy

	Justification for Integration
English Language Arts	• Language and literacy help children develop tools and practices for making sense of and communicating about the world. • Children can use reading, writing, drawing, and speaking to acquire ideas and communicate their thinking about science and engineering. (Drawing on Cervetti et al., 2006; Duke, 2000; Lee and Stephens, 2020; Lemke, 1998; Palincsar and Magnusson, 2001; and others.)
Mathematics	• In preK–5, mathematics is one main tool for modeling in science and engineering. • Science practices involve counting, measuring, spatial thinking, working with data, multiplicative thinking and scaling, identifying patterns, and mathematical and logical reasoning. (Drawing on Gelman et al., 2010; Lehrer and Schauble, 2006; and others.)
Computational Thinking	• Computational thinking (CT) can support learning across domains and disciplinary learning provides a meaningful context for engaging in CT. (Drawing on Cooper and Cunningham, 2010; Grover and Pea, 2018; Weintrop et al., 2016; and others.)
Social Studies	• Potential connections to social issues as well as disciplinary practices in history. (Drawing on Davis and Schaeffer, 2019; Herrenkohl and Cornelius, 2013; Marino, 2019; Tzou et al., 2019; and others.)
Social-Emotional Learning	• Effective approaches to learning are positively associated with improvements in science. (Drawing on Bustamante et al., 2018.)

1. What are overlaps and connections in disciplinary activity in science/engineering and the other domain? What justifies integration between these domains?
2. How have science/engineering and the other domains been connected or integrated in preschool through elementary settings? What is the evidence that learning in science/engineering and learning in the other domain are mutually beneficial?
3. What are key productive opportunities for integration in preschool through elementary school?

Evidence of Effectiveness	Opportunities for Integration
• Substantial evidence that integrating literacy and science can support more time for science/engineering learning without detracting from children's literacy learning, including for emergent multilingual learners. • Building both process and content knowledge in science facilitates literacy development.	• Use texts to support explanation and understanding. • Use texts to support understanding of science and engineering practice and help children develop identities and interests. • Help children generate texts and inscriptions to represent their reasoning.
• Support for integration of science or engineering with mathematics is more logical than empirical. • Empirical evidence suggests that quantification is central to an understanding of matter and that understanding distribution and chance is central to understanding life sciences concepts.	• Help children engage in quantification (distinguishing and developing measures for attributes). • Help children engage in data analysis and representation.
• Emergent	• Use science or engineering contexts to highlight CT practices. • Use CT as the method for exploring a science or engineering concept.
• Emergent	• Use socioscientific issues and complex socioecological and political systems, across multiple social sciences (e.g., civics, economics). • Connect disciplinary practices like argumentation in history and science.
• Emergent	• Emergent

By far, the most literature is available for language and literacy and mathematics. However, because of the nature of teaching and learning in preschool through elementary classrooms, the committee thought it would be important to review the literature in other areas, as well. Emerging connections deserve further investigation and hold promise in areas such as computational thinking. The committee determined that the connections to social studies and social-emotional learning are too scant to warrant full inclusion and only a brief treatment is done, but notes the importance of further research in these areas. Regarding social-emotional learning, Bustamante and colleagues' (2018) work suggests the potential of early science learning in relation to positive approaches to learning in young children.

With regard to social studies (which includes the study of civics, economics, geography, and history), work situating science and engineering in socioscientific issues and complex socioecological and political systems, including work in secondary school classrooms and informal settings, suggests the potential for connecting science and engineering with social studies in elementary classrooms (Bang et al., 2012; Davis and Schaeffer, 2019; Morales-Doyle, 2017; Tzou et al., 2019; Zangori et al., 2020). This body of work, though emergent, suggests that connections between science and social studies in terms of *socioscientific issues* might be particularly relevant to justice-oriented science and engineering instructional approaches aiming to situate learning in contexts relevant to children's lives, supporting learning both of natural science and engineering *and* of ideas and practices related to the social sciences. Additionally, other work in social studies and science focuses on disciplinary practices such as argumentation across disciplines (Herrenkohl and Cornelius, 2013; Marino, 2019; Rebello, Asunda, and Wang, 2020). This work suggests that similarities across *disciplinary practices* related to argumentation in science and history, in particular, could have affordances for children's learning and disciplinary work.

The sections that follow review the literature that helps to elaborate the answers to the questions: *What are key productive areas of overlap and opportunities for integration in preschool through elementary school? What are potential pitfalls of that integration?* These two questions are addressed for language and literacy, mathematics, and computational thinking.

Connections to Language and Literacy[1]

As described throughout this report, science and engineering are social and multimodal enterprises. The collective development of understanding

---

[1] Portions of this section include content from a paper commissioned by the committee, titled "The Integration of Literacy, Science, and Engineering in Prekindergarten through Fifth Grade" (Palincsar et al., 2020).

and solutions relies on communicating through, for example, talk, writing, and visual representation. Further, scientists and engineers—and "regular people" doing science and engineering—draw on others' ideas by engaging with a variety of genres of text, such as field guides, research articles, and graphs. Rather than starting from scratch, they draw on and evaluate established ideas and make connections between their developing questions and findings and others' texts. Finally, people tend to draw on conventions and purposes for various text genres as they use and communicate scientific understanding in persuasive text, informational text, fiction, memoirs, and even poetry.

Literacy and language are practices. However, ELA, as a content area, is often taught separately from other areas. Increasingly, literacy educators question the wisdom of this instructional design. Cervetti and colleagues (2006) write, "In a perfect (or at least better) world, language and literacy—like learning—would be regarded as a means to learning in the disciplines rather than an end unto itself" (p. 3). For example, research shows that emergent multilingual learners are more likely to understand and learn English when it is embedded in meaningful, authentic science and engineering learning activities (NASEM, 2018a).

ELA is represented in the Common Core State Standards (CCSS) and is heavily included in accountability structures in states, districts, and schools in preschool through fifth grade. The CCSS for ELA and the Next Generation Science Standards (NGSS) have important areas of connection and overlap. The CCSS emphasizes that the teaching of literacy skills (e.g., identifying main ideas, drawing inferences, using text structure to summarize text) needs to occur in the context of reading disciplinary-specific texts for disciplinary-specific purposes. Children need to learn to engage in "close, attentive reading" of challenging text, including informational text in science. Furthermore, argumentation, including supporting claims with evidence, is identified as a central strand of the CCSS and is one of eight science and engineering practices in the NGSS, though the nature of evidence in the two subjects is different (see Lee [2017] for a discussion of distinctions). Indeed, although the eighth science and engineering practice of the NGSS—*Obtaining, Evaluating and Communicating Information*—has the closest connection to much of the work in literacy, most of the other science and engineering practices also intersect with language and literacy practices (e.g., engaging in evidence-based argumentation; developing and using models).

Approaches to Connecting Domains and Evidence of Effectiveness

Numerous programs have been developed to productively connect or integrate science/engineering and ELA, and these can serve as supports for educators interested in connecting across content areas. Tables 6-3 and 6-4 summarize those programs that have a substantial literature base, including quasi-experimental and experimental studies, pre-post studies of learning in literacy and/or science, and close, qualitative descriptions of children's engagement and reasoning. This work is more extensive in the connections between ELA and science. The work in science has provided evidence of outcomes in science, literacy, and noncognitive domains, while work to date in engineering has focused on learning in science and engineering but has not examined literacy outcomes.

Integrating science and literacy may be particularly beneficial for emergent multilingual learners. For example, third grade science domain knowledge was significantly associated with third grade reading comprehension, particularly for students classified as English language learners (Hwang and Duke, 2020) and particularly for higher-level comprehension skills such as building a situation model and building inferences (see also Best, Floyd, and McNamara, 2008; Droop and Verhoeven, 1998). As Hwang and Duke (2020) argue:

> Reading instruction can be more effective when it is situated in knowledge-building goals than in a generic context (e.g., Guthrie et al., 2004; Halvorsen et al., 2012). In this study [Hwang and Duke, 2020], science domain knowledge played a more important role in reading comprehension development in students who are ELs than in students who are monolingual. The results support recommendations of Lesaux and Harris (2015) to situate much of the instruction provided to students who are ELs within a content area context. *Results of this study also call into question the practice of pulling students who are ELs out of content area instruction in order to teach them basic reading and language skills at the expense of content knowledge development.* [emphasis added] (pp. 12–13)

Although this body of evidence is nascent, the committee draws attention to the implications: emergent multilingual learners would benefit from *remaining present for* science instruction, rather than being removed for remedial English instruction (also see NASEM, 2018a).

Taken together, research on programs that make strong connections between science or engineering and literacy show evidence that integrating can support more time for science and engineering learning without detracting from, and indeed making critical contributions to, children's literacy learning. Knowledge affects how one processes vocabulary, handles new vocabulary, makes inferences, handles incoherence, and creates a situation model of texts. Therefore, building both process and content knowledge in science facilitates literacy development (Anderson and Pearson, 1984; Hwang and Duke, 2020; Kintsch, 2013).

Opportunities for Integration

Opportunity 1: Incorporate text to help children develop and deepen explanations and to situate reading in conceptually coherent, meaningful pursuits of understanding and solutions.

Text—broadly defined to include a range of materials and genres—can be an important resource for helping children extend and deepen understanding developed as they explore empirical systems and engage with data. In addition, the data needed to support some scientific explanations is not possible or accessible within elementary classroom work. For example, consider the difficulty studying the solar system or directly observing organisms' different strategies and behaviors in tropical rainforests, temperate forests, and the Arctic.

There is evidence that this approach can support literacy learning and reading comprehension as well (Cervetti, Wright, and Hwang, 2016). For example, fourth grade children reading a set of conceptually coherent text sets demonstrate greater understanding, vocabulary knowledge, and learn more from a new text on a related topic than learners engaged in similar instruction with a variety of unconnected texts (Cervetti, Wright, and Hwang, 2016). Further, children benefit from support to understand the features of informational and multimodal text and to learn to navigate these forms of text effectively (Jian, 2016; Prain and Waldrip, 2006). Duke (personal communication, August 27, 2020) points out that science and engineering texts have particular informational text features that other areas of study do not. Therefore, using text to deepen understanding and explanations explored through first-hand investigation with data is a productive context for building children's comprehension and their motivation for reading to find out, and children's use of text features in the service of developing understanding (see Box 6-1). Literacy learning benefits from motivation, opportunity to build background knowledge, and conceptual coherence. Science learning benefits from incorporating understanding of text features and ways to help children learn to navigate expository text. Providing text to help children deepen their explanations *after* engaging in investigation, design, and sensemaking supports ongoing sensemaking without usurping it (as providing expository text prior to investigation or design might do). Opportunity 2, below, describes additional designs and uses of text.

Multimodal text (including representations, videos, photographs, interactive diagrams, and simulations) can play an important role in supporting children's learning. These forms of text can be approached as something children connect to phenomena and problems and learn to engage with critically (Dalton and Palincsar, 2013; DeFrance, 2008; Easley, 2020; Henderson, Klemes, and Eshet, 2000; Varelas and Pappas, 2006, 2013; Wilson and Bradbury, 2016). Texts can also facilitate connections

TABLE 6-3 Features of Integrations of Science and Literacy Interventions in Preschool Through Fifth Grade

Features of Integrated Curricula: Opportunities to…	In Science, for PreK–2
actively engage with scientific phenomena or engage with engineering design	ScienceStart![a] SOLID Start[b] Science Literacy Project[c] Integrated Science Literacy Enactments (ISLE)[d] Grades 1–2 Science IDEAS[e]
read and discuss a variety of texts: informational texts, including read-alouds, for preK–2, and informational, narrative, and hybrid texts, for 3–5 learn and apply comprehension strategies*	ScienceStart! SOLID Start Science Literacy Project ISLE Grades 1–2 Science IDEAS
draw and/or write about science or engineering (including the practice of dictating to an adult)	ScienceStart! SOLID Start Science Literacy Project ISLE Grades 1–2 Science IDEAS
discuss scientific phenomena or engineering design problems	ScienceStart! SOLID Start Science Literacy Project ISLE Grades 1–2 Science IDEAS
have an extended block of time for science instruction that replaces ELA instruction take home learning opportunities with family members	Science Literacy Project ISLE

NOTE: *Comprehension strategies include making predictions, using text structure, learning new vocabulary, identifying main ideas, asking questions, making inferences.
[a]French (2004), Peterson and French (2008)
[b]Wright and Gotwals (2017)
[c]Samarapungavan, Patrick, and Mantzicopoulos (2011)
[d]Varelas and Pappas (2013)
[e]Romance and Vitale (2001)
[f]Guthrie et al. (2004)
[g]Cervetti, Kulikowich, and Bravo (2015)

In Science, for 3–5	In Engineering, for PreK–5
Science IDEAS[e] CORI[f] Seeds of Science/Roots of Reading[g] ML-PBL[h]	Engineering is Elementary[i] Project Lead the Way Launch[j] PictureSTEM[k] EngrTEAMS[l] LEGO Engineering[m]
Science IDEAS CORI Seeds of Science/Roots of Reading ML-PBL	Engineering is Elementary Project Lead the Way Launch PictureSTEM
Science IDEAS CORI Seeds of Science/Roots of Reading ML-PBL	
Science IDEAS CORI Seeds of Science/Roots of Reading ML-PBL	Engineering is Elementary Project Lead the Way Launch City Technology[n] PictureSTEM EngrTEAMS
Science IDEAS CORI Seeds of Science/Roots of Reading ML-PBL	Engineering is Elementary Project Lead the Way Launch City Technology PictureSTEM EngrTEAMS
Science IDEAS	

[h]Fitzgerald (2018, 2020)
[i]Aguirre-Muñoz and Pantoya (2016); Cunningham et al. (2020); Hertel, Cunningham, and Kelly (2017)
[j]https://www.pltw.org
[k]Guzey et al. (2014)
[l]Douglas et al. (2018)
[m]http://www.legoengineering.com
[n]Beneson, Stewart-Dawkins, and White (2012)
SOURCE: Adapted from Tables 2, 3, and 13 in Palincsar et al. (2020) commissioned paper.

TABLE 6-4 Learning Gains from Integrations of Science and Literacy in Preschool Through Fifth Grade

Gains Following Use of Integrated Curricula	In Science, for PreK–2
Science or Engineering Content	ScienceStart! SOLID Start Scientific Literacy Project
Science or Engineering Practices	SOLID Start
Science Vocabulary	ScienceStart! SOLID Start
Reading Achievement	
Connections Across the Unit and to Children's Lived Experiences	ISLE
Noncognitive Gains[a]	ScienceStart! Scientific Literacy Project
Long-Term Benefits[b]	

[a]Noncognitive gains include reading motivation, reading engagement, attitude toward science, attitude toward reading, self-confidence, motivation, and engagement.
[b]Long-term benefits include benefits specific to science knowledge and reading comprehension measured years later.
SOURCE: Adapted from Tables 4, 5, and 14 in Palincsar et al. (2020) commissioned paper.

across home and school (Shymansky, Yore, and Hand, 2000; Strickler-Eppard, Czerniak, and Kaderavek, 2019).

Opportunity 2: Incorporate text describing doing and using science and engineering to provide expansive views of science and engineering and help children develop identities and interests.

Text can also be an important resource for helping children develop an understanding of the connections of science and engineering to their lives, including constructing images of the practices that scientists and engineers engage in, developing understanding of who is and can be a scientist and engineer, and understanding the problems that science and engineering have relevance for. In classroom studies that have supported teachers to use text, children developed broader and more nuanced understanding of who does science, where science is done, and what activities scientists engage in, and

In Science, for 3–5	In Engineering, for PreK–5
CORI Science IDEAS Seeds of Science/Roots of Reading ML-PBL	Benenson, Stewart-Dawkins, and White (2012) Cunningham et al. (2020)
ML-PBL	Benenson, Stewart-Dawkins, and White (2012) Cunningham et al. (2020) Douglas et al. (2018) Hertel, Cunningham, and Kelly (2017)
Seeds of Science/Roots of Reading	
Science IDEAS CORI Seeds of Science/Roots of Reading ML-PBL	
	Benenson, Stewart-Dawkins, and White (2012)
CORI Science IDEAS	Aguirre-Muñoz and Pantoya (2016)
Science IDEAS	

the nature of scientific understanding—for example as tentative and social (Farland, 2006; Tucker-Raymond et al., 2007).

Studies that analyzed the content of science texts designed for young readers have demonstrated that teachers and curriculum designers must choose text carefully and then support engagement with text to develop expansive views of what science and engineering are and who does science and engineering (Ford, 2006; Kelly, 2018; Rivera and Oliveira, 2021). Texts are more likely to represent science knowledge than the doing of science and to present knowledge as facts (Ford, 2006; May et al., 2020), emphasize experiment or observation over other methods of science knowledge development (Ford, 2006), and represent scientists as white and/or male (Kelly, 2018; May et al., 2020). They vary widely in their reference to science practice and science knowledge development, with biographies and other books that emphasize the "lived lives of sci-

> **BOX 6-1**
> **Multiple Literacies in Project-Based Learning:**
> **Braiding Literacy and First-Hand Investigation**
>
> The Multiple Literacies in Project-based Learning (ML-PBL) curriculum integrates science, English language arts, and mathematics and is designed to address the three-dimensional learning goals of the NGSS and select CCSS. The ML-PBL approach to integrating science and literacy braids reading, writing, and oral language with first-hand investigations to create opportunities for students to engage in science practices and build knowledge about core ideas.
>
> The third grade ML-PBL curriculum includes four 6-to-9-week units that are designed to address the three dimensions of the NGSS. Each unit is framed by a driving question that is meaningful to students and anchored in real-world problems (e.g., *How can we help the birds around here grow up and thrive? How can we design gardens to grow food for our community?*). Within and across ML-PBL units of instruction, students have multiple and varied opportunities to read and interpret a variety of traditional print, multimodal, and digital texts as they engage in project-based learning.
>
> Fitzgerald (2018, 2020) examined the design, placement, and teacher enactment of texts and tasks. For example, findings indicated that the design, placement, and pairing of texts and tasks—in hand with the teacher's enactment—created meaningful purposes for third graders to read and interpret informational texts across ML-PBL units. To illustrate: in the first third grade unit, children viewed videos and participated in an interactive read-aloud of a researcher-designed, informational text to build upon their first-hand observations of squirrels around their school. The teacher supported children to identify and use information from the text to revise models they constructed to answer the question: *How do squirrels survive in their environment?* The design and inte-

entists" through fictional accounts of science work, descriptions of the history of science ideas, and descriptions of contemporary science problem solving more likely to provide descriptions of science practice (Kelly, 2018; May et al., 2020).

Integration may also generate new genres of text. Palincsar and Magnusson (2001) conducted a program of research that culminated in the development and study of an innovative genre of text—one written as a scientist's notebook—that was specifically designed to support children and teachers to approach science text as an inquiry. A hybrid of exposition, narration, description, and argumentation, the notebooks included multiple ways of representing data, including tables, figures, and diagrams. The authors' quasi-experimental study found that both the traditional texts and these "notebook texts" supported learning, but that the children found the notebook texts more enjoyable. Subsequent observational research revealed gration of texts in the units also provided opportunities for children to read strategically to support skills in reading and interpreting text. In the second ML-PBL unit, as the teacher facilitated an interactive read-aloud of a researcher-designed, biographical text about the Black engineer who designed the Super Soaker, she supported children to make predictions based on ideas in the text and to make connections to their prior knowledge and experience while reading. The design and integration of texts in ML-PBL also engaged children in using text in the service of disciplinary knowledge building and engaging in science practices. Children then participated in an interactive read-aloud of a researcher-designed text about two children who troubleshoot the design of a toy and observe how friction affects objects' motion. The text illustrated scientific practices, such as planning and conducting fair tests and closely observing phenomena, and also provided a context for and motivated children to plan and conduct their own investigations of moving toys they built in the classroom.

A randomized controlled trial conducted in 23 treatment and 23 control schools showed significant and substantial effects of the curriculum materials, professional learning experiences, and assessments (Krajcik et al., 2021). The authors used a three-level hierarchical model to determine the difference between conditions, while accounting for the clustering of students in schools. Third graders in the treatment condition outperformed those in the control condition by more than 0.25 standard deviation on a summative science assessment designed to align with the NGSS and not associated with the research project. This corresponds to an eight-percentage-point increase in student achievement scores, and the treatment effect holds when accounting for numerous factors, including initial student reading ability, gender, race [school level], ethnicity, and socioecomonic status. Positive effects were also seen for social and emotional learning.

SOURCE: Adapted from Palincsar et al. (2020) commissioned paper.

the ways teachers used notebook texts to help children more effectively represent data from their own first-hand investigations, assume a more critical stance toward texts, and acquire vocabulary.

Opportunity 3: Support children in producing texts and inscriptions to represent their reasoning for themselves, the classroom community, and the wider community.

Children's ongoing work to document and share their thinking, observations, designs, and findings in science and engineering is a natural fit for developing multimodal composition strategies (which support literacy). Similarly, recent research has found multiple benefits to young children engaging in multimodal composition (e.g., drawing, creating models) to document science observations, including deepening thinking and learning with data (supporting science and engineering).

Thus, first, supporting learners in engaging in multimodal composition supports their learning. Traditional definitions of literacy often consider the four primary modalities of literacy to be reading, writing, speaking, and listening (National Governors Association, 2010). However, many literacy scholars have encouraged expanding the modality of "writing" to include multimodal composition, including using drawing or other image-based media (e.g., images, symbols, audio, graphical displays, and/or animation) to represent ideas (Dalton, 2012; Dalton and Palincsar, 2013; Siegel, 2006), which is similar to what professional scientists do (Krajcik et al., 2021; Lemke, 2004; Suárez, 2020).

In preschool through elementary school, science journals or notebooks provide young children opportunities to observe closely and to represent their observations of objects and phenomena (Brenneman and Louro, 2008; Romance and Vitale, 2001). Engineering programs similarly involve children maintaining some variety of engineering journal or notebook, either hand drawn (Cunningham et al., 2020; Douglas et al., 2018; English and King, 2017; Hertel, Cunningham, and Kelly, 2017; King and English, 2016) or digital (Wendell, Andrews, and Paugh, 2019). Children are often guided with prompts, graphic organizers, suggested headings, or other supports, and reflective prompts support children's learning of key understanding and development of vocabulary (Rouse and Rouse, 2019).

Second, supporting learners in writing explanations and supporting claims with evidence engages and develops science and engineering concepts and also literacy skills relevant to writing persuasive text and supporting claims. Research on written explanations of learners in grades 3–5 suggest that writing explanations and descriptions of engineering designs supports improved understanding of engineering and science models and ideas (Chambliss, Christenson, and Parker, 2003; Rouse and Rouse, 2019; Songer and Gotwals, 2012) and improvement in learners' explanations and understanding of evidence (McNeill, 2011; Yang and Wang, 2014). This research indicates the need for a coherent and dual focus on the science/engineering and literacy practices. For example, a teacher might engage children in developing explanations in contexts where there is more than one plausible explanation and so they must generate their own explanation/rationale (Zangori and Forbes, 2014), supporting children to both connect and distinguish everyday and scientific argumentation (McNeill, 2011) and providing supports, including models and peer feedback, for particular linguistic features of scientific explanations (Chambliss, Christenson, and Parker, 2003; McNeill, 2011; Seah, 2016).

Other uses and genres of text can also be beneficial. Numerous studies have documented the role of drawing—both observational records and engaging in developing and revising models—in supporting children's learning in science (e.g., diSessa et al., 1991; Fox and Lee, 2013; Samarapungavan et al., 2017). Science and engineering can be a context where children write persuasive texts to convince community members of the importance of problems and propose solutions (Calabrese Barton and Tan, 2010; Davis and Schaeffer, 2019). Finally, some work explores imaginative narrative-based writing, theater, poetry, and art as a context for children to deepen and explore science and engineering (Danish and Enyedy, 2006; Gallas, 1995; Varelas et al., 2010).

Potential Pitfalls

One key pitfall is that even with curricular materials that have been designed for integration, teachers may still experience difficulties with supporting both literacy and science and engineering practices. Another area of concern is that at times, "best practices" in literacy and science/engineering seem to be contradictory. Although full treatment of these pitfalls is beyond the scope of this report, the committee names two issues, based mainly on committee members' work in classrooms and with teachers and children.

1. The "I Do, We Do, You Do" model of literacy instruction—emphasizing teacher modeling, then scaffolded support to engage in a practice together, then children using that practice independently—comes in tension with models of science and engineering instruction that emphasize children engaging with ill-structured problems, putting forward their own tentative design ideas and explanations, and revising those through activity. Teachers may be able to navigate this apparent tension through using interactive modeling to support children in learning new aspects of science practice (Arias and Davis, 2016; Hapgood et al., 2004; Palincsar and Magnusson, 2001) but allowing more child-driven investigation of phenomena.
2. Vocabulary practices can seem at first contradictory but have been negotiated with success (e.g., Warren et al., 2001) when there is a focus on sensemaking (NASEM, 2018a). For example, in literacy, particularly with emergent multilingual learners, teachers often preteach key vocabulary, often perceived as a recommended strategy in English language development. In science, teachers promote experience with a phenomenon and develop conceptual underpinnings about it, then introduce the "science term." Supporting language-rich sensemaking could take the form of recognizing that it can be useful to know certain kinds of words (e.g., the names of tools being used, such as "thermometer" or "hand lens") and holding off on preteaching other kinds of conceptual vocabulary (e.g., "conductor" or "adaptation") until children have made meaning of the concepts embedded in these terms.

In contrast, the early literacy practice of "invented spelling," which emphasizes that children learn word patterns as meaningful chunks and rules and reveal their understanding through trying out writing, is more consistent with resource-based accounts of children's development of understanding (Russ and Berland, 2019). Teachers may need support to make sense of apparent differences and contradictions, as well as areas where literacy and science/engineering are well aligned.

Connections to Mathematics

Mathematics is an essential foundation for engaging in any domain of science and engineering. Many models in science and engineering are mathematical in expression (ideal gas law, models in climate science) or rely on mathematical relationships (simulations of predator/prey relationships; exponential growth). Engineers develop models of bridges and apply mathematical models of stress to them. Scientists and engineers collect numerical and categorical data and make use of mathematical ideas and tools to tabulate, organize, and interpret data.

A goal of mathematics education is for children to view mathematics as sensible, useful, and worthwhile—to see themselves as capable of thinking mathematically and to appreciate the beauty and creativity that is at the heart of mathematics. One way to accomplish this is to have mathematics be learned and applied to help address questions from the other STEM domains. Ideally, children gain exposure to prerequisite math competencies in an appropriate sequence and then science serves as a context for children to experience mathematical concepts and skills as meaningful and useful. Similarly, engineering relies on mathematics, but also has contributed to mathematics with its inventions (from physical to digital) and, perhaps most significantly, can be a meaningful context for learning mathematics, although empirical results are mixed (National Academy of Engineering and National Research Council, 2009).

The NGSS and CCSS for Mathematics have areas of overlap that are relevant to children's work. Two of the science and engineering practices highlighted in the NGSS are mathematical in nature (analyzing and interpreting data and using mathematics and computational data). Furthermore, a crosscutting concept focuses on scale, quantity, and proportion. The CCSS have a strand focused on measurement and data. From kindergarten to second grade, children engage with different representations (e.g., bar graphs, picture graphs) and ask and answer questions using graphs. In third grade, children begin to scale measurements and graphs and ask and answer comparative questions (how many more, how many less) and explore measurements for attributes such as volume and weight. Over grades 3–5, children solve problems using and comparing measurements, and compare and convert between units.

Approaches to Connecting or Integrating and Evidence of Effectiveness

Mathematics is often included in most contexts in which children learn science or engineering. Science and engineering curricula regularly engage children, for example, in comparing attributes or measures, working with measures of length, height, area, volume, or weight, examining graphs, and making calculations. The types and depths of these connections (as described in Table 6-1) often vary substantially. For example, some uses of mathematics (e.g., measuring the distance traveled from the bottom of a ramp) demonstrate the usefulness of mathematics but are unlikely to serve *learning goals* in mathematics. In other contexts, connections are designed so that mathematical understanding and practices are deepened by providing contexts for considering what children are doing and why (Clements and Sarama, 2021a; Lehrer and Schauble, 2006). Making the role of mathematics explicit by repeatedly foregrounding the desired mathematical content and temporarily backgrounding other STEM content is one way that all disciplines might be advanced—a principle of the interdisciplinary approach of Table 6-1.

Unlike ELA, there are few programs that have systematically sought to support the integration of mathematics and science or have collected evidence on children's learning in both mathematics and science/engineering, though a few programs of research have sought to examine how mathematical reasoning and skills contribute to the learning of a particular science understanding at the preschool and elementary level. Wiser and colleagues (2006, 2009) developed a learning progression for understanding of matter, positing that quantification is central to an understanding of matter. They describe the progression of understanding of attributes and measures of matter, from the idea that objects have properties (weight, length, area, and volume) that can be described, compared, and measured to weight as an additive property that can be measured and is a function of both volume and material. These ideas, in turn, support the development of ideas such as transformations of matter that conserve weight or that matter exists even when broken into pieces too small to see. Lehrer and Schauble (2004, 2012) have argued that (a) identifying and relating attributes and (b) developing understanding of mathematical models of distribution and chance are central to understanding core concepts in the life sciences; this research shows that elementary-age children benefit from engaging with identifying and mathematizing attributes.

Opportunities for Integration

Opportunity 1: Help children engage in quantification (distinguishing and developing measures for attributes).

Measurement is an important topic in mathematics, science, and engineering, and helps develop other competencies, including reasoning and logic. By its very nature, geometric measurement (length, area, and volume) connects the two critical domains of mathematics, geometry and number, and also connects mathematics to science and engineering. In particular, science and engineering are contexts where children can come to see and distinguish attributes as they wrestle with which attributes are important for helping them answer questions or orient design (Jin et al., 2019; Lehrer, Giles, and Schauble, 2002). These attributes include basic units such as length (height, perimeter, girth, etc.) and weight, as well as derived (computed) units such as density, speed, and acceleration. This work to distinguish attributes and determine a unit of that attribute are critical components of the development of measure. Unfortunately, typical measurement instruction in the United States does not address these components, and many children are taught to measure in a rote and decontextualized fashion, engaging in tasks such as children seeing a picture of a pencil above a ruler (aligned at the zero point) and asked to tell the measure (reading the numeral at the other end of the pencil).

Children investigating science phenomena or designing solutions to engineering problems, however, are measuring for a purpose in situations in which the principles of measurement must be constructed, followed, and articulated. Science and engineering can provide a context where discussions—about what to measure, how to measure, and whether measurements are comparable—are meaningful, as children recognize that their measurement tools and methods have import for what they can see and conclude (Lehrer and Schauble, 2012; Lehrer, Giles, and Schauble, 2002; Masnick and Klahr, 2003; NRC, 2008). Measuring in meaningful contexts requires accuracy, resulting in feedback that is intrinsic to the situation itself, and building concept images (Vinner and Hershkowitz, 1980) that provide firm conceptual foundations for future development.

The teaching of measurement within science or engineering projects can benefit from consideration of the mathematical principles of measurement *and* the learning trajectories that have been developed within mathematics education (Barrett, Clements, and Sarama, 2017; Clements and Sarama, 2021a). These learning trajectories explicate levels of thinking along a birth to sixth grade development progression that, if ignored, can lead to rote use of measurement tools within science and engineering. These trajectories describe how children can be supported to discuss attributes and amounts in their play and learn to measure, connecting number to quantity in both geometric measurement—length, area, volume, and angle/rotation (Barrett, Clements, and Sarama, 2017; Clements and Sarama, 2021a; Gao, 2001)—and other scientific measurements, such as mass (weight) and time. They uncover the work of learning to measure, identifying an attribute, developing a concept of the attribute, identifying and iterating units of measure, understanding how a particular tool would allow one to measure that attribute, and using measures to make meaningful comparisons between objects and processes. As children begin to explore new science contexts, they can be supported to engage in this work. For example, Lehrer, Giles, and Schauble (2002) reported how the "size" of a pumpkin was initially taken to mean height for some first graders and width for others. This difference provided a context for the teachers to help children discuss similarities and differences in attributes and consider how each might be measured. Such work is precluded in curricula that choose measures for children to use.

Opportunity 2: Support children in transforming and analyzing data, as well as in understanding the foundational concepts of data representation and statistics.

Each year of mathematics in elementary school often includes a unit on graphing, with children typically collecting preferences or conducting counts in their classrooms (e.g., what classmate's favorite meal is, how many pockets children have) or examining, calculating with, and interpreting pre-made graphs. In contrast, organizing and interpreting data to solve a problem is central to work in science and engineering contexts, where a key strategy for managing uncertainty and error is to look for patterns and aggregate across cases. For example, Lehrer and Schauble's program of research demonstrated that mathematical and scientific reasoning can be mutually supportive in the context of children's inventing and revising representations related to plant growth, as shown in Box 6-2.

Potential Pitfalls

This work must be carefully constructed to understand the contexts where children find it sensible to draw on mathematical ideas and to make sure that they have developed the prerequisite skills and understanding, which are sometimes best accomplished outside of the context of a complex phenomenon that children are seeking to understand and explain. From a mathematics perspective, mode, median, proportion, and measure are concepts (rather than simply procedures or calculations). Many science curricula introduce and ask children to use mathematical representations and processes (e.g., bar charts, line plots, calculating the mean of multiple trials) to help children efficiently see what they are supposed to from an investigation, without much attention to whether children understand the reasons for these processes or have been introduced to them systematically. For example, statistical concepts such as mode and median (and related calculations) are not introduced until sixth grade in CCSS, based on a principled development of ideas over time—but children in grades 3–5 are often asked to use line plots and calculate means or modes in their science work.

Three key pitfalls warrant particular attention. As with ELA, full treatment of these pitfalls is beyond the scope of this report.

1. Sequencing of ideas: Mathematics, in particular, often suffers from attempts at STEM integration (Clements et al., 2021; English, 2016). This can happen if simple application of already-learned

---

BOX 6-2
Mutually Supporting Mathematical and Scientific Reasoning

Lehrer and Schauble's program of research has demonstrated how mathematical and scientific reasoning can be mutually supportive as children work on inventing and revising their representations related to plant growth. The study was conducted across multiple grades, first through fifth.

First graders used strips of paper to represent the heights of different species of plants over time. At first, they needed the strips to be green to represent the stem and insisted on drawing leaves and the flower on the strips. With the teachers' support, they came to see the strips as representing one dimension of plant growth (height) and began to use comparisons across species and over time to make claims about plant growth (Lehrer and Schauble, 2000). In contrast, third and fourth graders used line graphs, where the slopes of the lines directed student attention to different heights at different points in the plant's life cycle, prompting an exploration of rate of change and ratio (Lehrer and Schauble, 2000). Further, comparing across different children's graphs led to a discussion of scale as children recognized that the same slope of line represented different rates of growth because children had constructed their graphs using different scales in the x- and y-axes.

Additionally, third through fifth graders were supported to develop line plots that allowed them to compare cases to answer questions about conditions for growth. This work supported children in considering what "most of the plants were doing," as well as think about the role of a consistent scale in identifying outliers and to consider various explanations for variability and difference in outcomes (Lehrer and Schauble, 2000, 2004); in fifth grade, this work also supported children to propose and refine nascent statistical procedures (e.g., sampling; measures of spread and center).

SOURCE: Based on Lehrer and Schauble (2000, 2004).

math procedures within a STEM project are accepted as the mathematics children are "learning" for an extended period; such a design can serve to trivialize aspects of math learning. Another concern is the way that mathematical understanding and skills might be integrated into science and engineering activity before children understand their conceptual underpinnings and in a way that undermines the development of those ideas.
2. Developing conceptual (rather than utilitarian) understanding of attributes: Sometimes easy-to-measure numerical attributes are used as a stand-in for more powerful conceptual values; this can inhibit children's sensemaking (Manz and Renga, 2017).
3. Treatment of early mathematical ideas and practices in the NGSS: Several authors have critiqued the development of mathematical concepts and practices within the NGSS appendices and performance expectations, in particular at the early grades—arguing that mathematical ideas and practices, including ideas related to quantification, proportion, and scale, are often implicit or unevenly treated at the early grades (Jin et al., 2019; Osborne et al., 2018).

Connections to Computational Thinking[2]

Compared with ELA and mathematics, research on the remaining domains for potential integration with science and engineering is relatively nascent. This is true for computational thinking (CT). Wing (2006) defines CT as "a universally applicable attitude and skill set" that helps solve problems and design solutions in ways that make them amenable to being solved with computational systems (p. 33). CT involves a range of skills including problem solving, logical and algorithmic thinking, abstraction, pattern generalization, and others (Dong et al., 2019; Grover and Pea, 2013; NASEM, 2021). Most of the research on CT has focused on middle and high school students; there is, however, an emerging body of literature focused on preschool and elementary aged children (e.g., Metcalf et al., 2021). For example, ScratchJr and KIBO (a tangible robotics kit) have been developed to support children in engaging in engineering in early childhood spaces. These programs allow children to learn and apply programming concepts, design, and problem solving even before they can read (Bers, 2018; NASEM, 2021).

---

[2] Portions of this section include content from two papers commissioned by the committee, titled "The Integration of Computational Thinking in Early Childhood and Elementary Science and Engineering Education" (Ketelhut and Cabrera, 2020) and "The Integration of Computational Thinking in Early Childhood and Elementary Education" (Moore and Ottenbreit-Leftwich, 2020).

Some scholars argue that CT can support learning across content domains (Grover and Pea, 2013; Henderson, Cortina, and Wing, 2007; Lee et al., 2020; Weintrop et al., 2016) and that disciplinary learning provides a meaningful context for engaging in CT (Cooper and Cunningham, 2010). For example, using computational tools has been shown to support learning science (e.g., diSessa, 2001; Hambrusch et al., 2009; NASEM, 2021).

Overall, there are few empirical articles that investigate the integration of CT with science and/or engineering at the preschool through elementary levels (see NASEM, 2021). Several projects investigate these connections, but most are not yet mature enough to have empirical publications. What research there is tends to focus on less rich forms of connection (as briefly described in Table 6-1). Some of this work maps children's activity back onto CT practices, *using science or engineering contexts as a way of highlighting CT practices*. For example, Ehsan and colleagues (2020) created an engineering design exhibit ("build a puppy play yard") at a family science center. They then analyzed the actions of ten 5- to 7-year-old children as they interacted with this exhibit to see if they demonstrated computational thinking. As one example, the authors identified the CT skill of abstraction when a child said they would build something for the puppy to play with and add a fence in response to the repeated parent question of what they will build. Other studies did something similar: look at curriculum or children's behavior and then map it onto CT practices.

In other work, *CT is an integral part of lessons and activities—the method for exploring a scientific or engineering concept.* In many cases, this integration is enacted through programming—learners use a developmentally appropriate programming environment to create models, test scenarios, and design solutions within disciplinary topics. For example, Dickes et al. (2019) created a 15-lesson unit where third grade children explored an ecosystem within an immersive virtual environment. Children were also engaged with a 2D agent-based modeling environment where they used programming to control the behaviors of animals as they saw the outcomes in the ecosystem. The authors demonstrated different moments where children transform the disciplinary content from one type of representation to another. Overall, this implementation resulted in children advancing their understanding of both the scientific concepts of the curriculum and the purpose and mechanisms of computational models.

WORKING TOWARD EQUITY AND INTEGRATING ACROSS DOMAINS

At a basic level, *increasing opportunities for and access to high-quality science and engineering* is a matter of instructional time (Approach #1). As argued in this chapter, integration is one important way to address the issue of instructional time, a problem that is exacerbated in lower-resourced schools, which tend to serve more Black, Brown, Indigenous, and other children of color.

Integration has the potential to improve *achievement, representation, and identification with science and engineering*, as well (Approach #2). Texts can help to increase representation (Kelly, 2018; May et al., 2020); for example, children's books can show the work of Black scientists or illustrate girls following their interest in engineering. Such representation allows a broader range of children to "see themselves" in these disciplines. Integrating science with ELA can also help to improve achievement outcomes for emergent multilingual learners (Hwang and Duke, 2020).

Integrating science and engineering with language arts and mathematics can *expand the concept of what constitutes science and engineering*, and how these subjects are done (Approach #3). Multimodal text can be used to support children's learning, and children can also generate multimodal ways of expressing their ideas. These approaches provide multiple ways of engaging children's sensemaking (e.g., Cunningham et al., 2019). Similarly, allowing multiple ways for children to make measurements gives them a range of ways of representing their observations and their ideas (e.g., Lehrer and Schauble, 2012).

Finally, integration has potential for helping to make *science and engineering an integral part of justice movements* (Approach #4). Children can use literacy practices to generate texts that reach a broader audience than the classroom (Calabrese Barton and Tan, 2010; Davis and Schaeffer, 2019)—a way of working collectively toward justice in a public way (e.g., for the neighborhood or community). The committee also notes the potential for the integration of science or engineering with social studies in working to help children see science and engineering as part of justice movements while benefiting children's science and social studies (e.g., history, civics, economics) learning; however, the committee did not find much research here, and so calls out this area as one for future research.

SUMMARY

Children often have a disjointed experience of the school subjects throughout the day, perhaps because they have limited opportunities to synthesize their learning across content areas or make connections among them (Stevens et al., 2005). Integrating science and engineering with other content areas and domains of importance in the preschool and elementary day has the potential for addressing this issue and enhancing the amount of instructional time spent in science and engineering, as argued throughout this chapter. Table 6-5 summarizes some of the ways integration may be undertaken. These approaches may support educators in embarking on making these connections with children.

TABLE 6-5 Integrating Science and Engineering with Other Domains

	Key Ideas
Overarching Principles	• Engage children in investigation and design experiences that draw on multiple domains. • Make integration explicit in design and teaching. • Support children's knowledge in individual disciplines. • More integration is not necessarily better.
Integrating with English Language Arts	• Use texts to support explanation and understanding. • Use texts to support understanding of science and engineering practice and help children develop identities and interests. • Help children generate texts and inscriptions to represent their reasoning.
Integrating with Mathematics	• Help children engage in quantification (distinguishing and developing measures for attributes). • Help children transform and analyze data and understand data representation and statistics.
Integrating with Computational Thinking (CT)	• Use science or engineering contexts to highlight CT practices. • Use CT as the method for exploring a science or engineering concept.

7

The Role of Curriculum Materials and Instructional Resources

Main Messages

- High-quality instruction in preschool through elementary science and engineering requires curriculum materials that build toward the vision of the *Framework*; are grounded in investigation and design; are coherent, flexible, adaptable, equitable, responsive; and have evidence supporting their effectiveness.
- It is unreasonable to expect preschool through elementary teachers to develop such materials independently.
- States and districts play a role in the selection of curriculum materials at the elementary level, weighing multiple factors and using a range of tools and processes.
- Teachers' use and adaptation of science and engineering curriculum materials is influenced by their knowledge, beliefs, and attitudes about the disciplines, teaching science and engineering, and learners; by the characteristics of the materials themselves; and by the school and classroom contexts in which the materials are being used.
- Physical instructional resources and facilities are crucial for preschool through elementary science and engineering instruction, but are often in short supply, particularly in under-resourced schools.

"Curriculum materials" refers to the resources designed to be used by teachers in classrooms to guide their instruction (Stein, Remillard, and Smith, 2007; also see Tyler, 1949, and Pinar et al., 1995, for foundational perspectives). Why is it important for teachers to have access to curriculum materials to use for preschool through elementary science and engineering? These educators—in contrast to their secondary counterparts—are typically responsible for the teaching of all academic subject areas. It is unreasonable to expect them to develop—from scratch—coherent, equitable science and engineering units that build toward the vision of *A Framework for K–12 Science Education* (hereafter referred to as the *Framework*; National Research Council [NRC], 2012). Instead, teachers need high-quality starting places that they can use and adapt.

Curriculum materials are ubiquitous in classrooms and have long been recognized for their capacity to help to make change in the educational system (Ball and Cohen, 1996). Curriculum materials are limited, however, in *how much* change they can effect in the larger educational system. Curriculum materials in preschool through elementary grades are still "catching up" to be able to build toward the vision of the *Framework* (NRC, 2012) and to demonstrate genuine alignment with it and the Next Generation Science Standards (NGSS; NGSS Lead States, 2013).[1] For example, some curriculum materials continue to emphasize hands-on activity without supporting explanation and the development of explanations over time (e.g., Zangori, Forbes, and Biggers, 2013). Furthermore, because these materials may look different from how teachers were taught and how they have taught in the past, teachers need to have opportunities for teacher education and professional learning so they can learn how to use these materials effectively, as discussed in Chapter 8. System-level concerns that may limit the effects of curriculum materials include the complex political and technical aspects of implementation, discontinuous streams of reform, mismatches between the goals of the initiatives and assessments, and insufficient and inequitable material resources devoted to education and reform (Berliner, 2006; Kozol, 2005; Spillane, 2001).

Despite these concerns, curriculum materials also have great promise for supporting science and engineering learning in preschool through elementary, particularly as development and refinement continues. Indeed, curricular interventions are a potentially stronger lever for change than other approaches commonly adopted in the educational system (Whitehurst, 2009). At the most basic level, they can provide an entry point for subjects that many teachers of younger grades find challenging (Banilower et al., 2018; Davis, Petish, and Smithey, 2006). Building on that, teachers can use lesson and unit plans as something to start from and adapt for their own contexts (e.g., Arias et al., 2016; Bismack et al., 2014; Sullivan-Watts et al.,

---

[1] The *Framework* and the NGSS do not include preschool/prekindergarten.

2013). Ideally, these materials provide recommendations for opportunities to learn (see Chapters 4, 5, and 6) that can work toward the vision of the *Framework*. Sometimes, these materials come with the physical resources that are needed to conduct first-hand, hands-on investigations or design challenges—physical resources that might be commonplace in a high school laboratory but can be hard to come by in a typical preschool or elementary classroom (e.g., Jones et al., 2012). Finally, these curricular materials sometimes support teacher learning as well as children's learning, working as one approach to making change in instruction over time (Davis and Krajcik, 2005; Davis et al., 2017). These educative curriculum materials may also be used in conjunction with professional learning experiences, as research across grade bands suggests (Edelson et al., 2021; Short and Hirsh, 2020).

This chapter pulls together ideas from Chapters 4, 5, and 6 to yield design insight for curriculum materials that are based on what the literature says about learning environments, instructional practices, and integration of domains (see Box 7-1). Furthermore, research on curriculum and curriculum materials across grade levels shows that curriculum materials need to support teachers' adaptation, including adaptation based on children's thinking and interests (Broderick and Hong, 2020; Clements, 2007; Davis et al., 2017); identify, introduce, and integrate fundamental concepts and practices coherently and in a sensible order (Kesidou and Roseman, 2002; Schmidt, Wang, and McKnight, 2005); and be designed for equity (Confrey and Lachance, 2000). Building across these ideas, *high-quality science and engineering curriculum materials* (a) have evidence supporting their effectiveness, (b) build toward the vision of the *Framework*, and are (c) grounded in investigation and design, (d) coherent (build toward big ideas sensibly and connect across ideas and activity), (e) flexible and adaptable, and (f) equitable, including that they support teachers in being responsive to children's ideas.

According to the 2018 National Survey of Science and Mathematics Education (NSSME+), 77 percent of elementary classrooms report using commercially published materials (Banilower et al., 2018). Nearly half of elementary science classes are using textbooks or modules that were published over a decade ago, meaning they predate or have not been reviewed for alignment with NGSS or the vision of the *Framework* (Plumley, 2019). Furthermore, although the use of these materials serves as the basis for the overall structure and content emphasis of their instructional units, teachers also often incorporate other materials to modify their lessons, including resources from subscription-based websites or individually created materials (Banilower et al., 2018; Doan and Lucero, 2021; National Academies of Sciences, Engineering, and Medicine [NASEM], 2020). Materials from sources such as Teachers Pay Teachers account for about 39 percent of the designated materials in elementary classrooms and are used weekly in about 49 percent of elementary classrooms (Plumley, 2019). Such idiosyncratic, one-off materials do not systematically meet the characteristics of high-quality curriculum materials. These findings suggest that a majority of teachers are not currently using curriculum materials that reflect the guidance identified in Box 7-1; therefore, the focus in this chapter is on studies of more coherent curricular materials or programs. Box 7-2 provides an example of an effort that reflects some of the guidance presented in Box 7-1.

The sections that follow review the literature on preschool and then elementary curricular efforts.[2] The chapter then turns to a review of the

---

BOX 7-1
Implications for the Design of Curriculum Materials

To support children in developing and demonstrating proficiency in investigation and design, effective curriculum materials help children...

- Orient to phenomena and design challenges
- Collect and analyze data and information
- Develop explanations and design solutions
- Communicate reasoning
- Connect learning across content areas and sites of activity

To support productive learning environments, effective curriculum materials help teachers...

- Engage children in science and engineering in a caring community
- Orient children to investigation and design in contexts they find meaningful
- Support children in refining their explanations and solutions through sensemaking with data
- Support children in learning with and from each other
- Assess children in ways that show their learning and inform instruction

To support effective integration, effective curriculum materials...

- Engage children in investigation and design experiences that draw on multiple domains
- Make integration explicit in design and teaching
- Support children's knowledge in individual disciplines
- Recognize that more integration is not necessarily better

SOURCE: Drawn directly from Chapters 4, 5, and 6.

---

[2] Because selection of materials is largely an issue in the K–12 realm, the elementary section includes a treatment of districts' selection of materials, and because of the nature of the evidentiary base, the elementary section also includes a discussion of the insufficiency of instructional materials for investigations and design challenges.

> **BOX 7-2**
> **Engineering is Elementary (EiE)**
>
> Engineering is Elementary (EiE) is designed for first through fifth grade classrooms. The series has recently been expanded to include EiE for kindergarten, a preschool curriculum called Wee Engineer, and several products intended for use in informal settings. EiE's 20 elementary units each focus on a different type of engineering, such as structural engineering or biomechanical engineering. Each unit is mapped to the NGSS, ITEEA Standards for Technological Literacy, Common Core Math Standards, and Common Core English Language Arts Standards. A four-lesson framework provides common structure across the set of units, reflecting intentional connections to other domains and disciplines (Cunningham, Lachapelle, and Davis, 2018), for example:
>
> - Lesson 1 integrates engineering with literacy and begins with an illustrated storybook that presents a rich narrative, often situated in another part of the world, to provide context for the unit and its design challenge.
> - Lesson 2 introduces a particular subfield of engineering and provides an activity connected to science or engineering concepts relevant to the design challenge.
> - Lesson 3 often integrates engineering with science content and practice, typically featuring an exploration of phenomena, materials, or systems that will inform the designs children create. The lesson typically involves data collection and analysis and sometimes connects to mathematical standards.
> - Lesson 4 presents children with an engineering design challenge that builds on the previous lessons. Children engage in the five-step EiE engineering design process—Ask, Imagine, Plan, Create, and Improve—often drawing on content and practices from science and mathematics.
>
> EiE is well established, having started in 2003, with extensive field trials and other studies. Recently, an efficacy study showed that children who engaged in EiE had greater learning gains in both engineering and science than children who engaged in a control curriculum, with girls yielding larger engineering learning gains than boys (Cunningham et al., 2020).
>
> SOURCE: Based on commissioned paper by Cardella, Svarovsky, and Pattison (2020).

literature on preschool through elementary teachers' use of and learning with curriculum materials. The chapter closes with a brief discussion of how curriculum materials can be used to work toward equity and justice in science and engineering education.

PRESCHOOL CURRICULUM AND INSTRUCTIONAL RESOURCES

Early childhood researchers and practitioners have created multiple professional development programs and curricular resources that promote science teaching and learning in preschool classrooms and, more recently, programs and resources that promote engineering teaching and learning. Science curriculum efforts initially focused on specific content themes or on scientific method and inquiry; they highlighted science "inquiry skills" or "process skills" (rather than science practices and crosscutting ideas) as "skills that one could develop independently from content knowledge" (Larimore, 2020, p. 708). Recent curricular efforts have more closely aligned to current science frameworks. For example, Greenfield and colleagues (2017) have adapted the *Framework* for use in preschool classrooms. However, research that explores how science and engineering can be cohesively supported across preschool through elementary grades is needed.

Some of the curricular and professional development programs initially developed include The Young Scientists Series (Chalufour and Worth, 2003, 2004, 2005), Science Start! (French, 2004), and Preschool Pathways (PrePS) to Science (Gelman and Brenneman, 2004; Gelman et al., 2009). These programs (which focus on science, not engineering) were developed based on strong theoretical foundations, emphasize the importance of integrating science throughout the day, and provide supports for teachers to integrate science with other domains. These programs, however, pre-date and do not always clearly align with current science frameworks, and research examining their impact on science teaching and learning has been limited. A study examining the promise of Science Start! reported significant gains in vocabulary (PPVT) in a (single group) study in Head Start classrooms and a small (experimental) study with three prekindergarten classrooms (French, 2004). Although it is known generally that there is often a relationship between science learning and language learning (as discussed in Chapter 6), less is known about how that relationship played out in this curriculum and whether this led to improvements in science learning.

When these programs were developed and evaluated, there were few instruments available for measuring science learning in preschool, although recent work has begun to fill that gap. Greenfield (see Clements et al., 2015; Greenfield, 2015, for a review) developed and field-tested equated English and Spanish adaptive science assessments. These two assessments (Lens on Science; Enfoque en Ciencia) were specifically designed to measure science learning throughout preschool, including core content, practices, and crosscutting concepts.

In recent years, additional science curricular programs have been designed and evaluated; these include My Teaching Partner-Math/Science (MTP-M/S; Whittaker et al., 2020), the interdisciplinary Connect4Learning (C4L) curriculum (Sarama et al., 2016), and the Next Generation Preschool Science/Science with Nico and Nor curricular program (Domínguez and Goldstein, 2020). These programs focus on science practices for the purpose of developing both conceptual understanding and an appreciation for how to do science. This focus helps align these programs with the kinds of characteristics highlighted in Box 7-1. Furthermore, this science-as-practice approach is a good match for preschool, where children's curiosity about the natural world acts as a powerful catalyst for exploration of natural phenomena.

Most of these recent curriculum development efforts have included implementation studies and examinations of teacher and child outcomes. For instance, a randomized controlled trial conducted to examine the effects of the MTP-M/S intervention in 140 prekindergarten classrooms found that teachers who participated in the intervention exhibited higher quality and quantity of science instruction and that children in intervention classrooms outperformed children in comparison classrooms on a science assessment after 2 years of implementation (Whittaker et al., 2020). Similar findings are reported for Science with Nico and Nor: results from a randomized controlled study in 20 public preschool classrooms indicate the curriculum program, which included science curricular activities and digital media, was used appropriately, and that children in classrooms that implemented the program made significant improvements in science learning relative to children in comparison classrooms (Domínguez and Goldstein, 2020). A pilot study and a subsequent quasi-experimental study of the C4L curriculum, which promotes mathematics, science, literacy, and social-emotional learning, indicate that children exposed to the curriculum outperformed children in comparison classrooms in science, literacy, mathematics, and social-emotional vocabulary (Sarama et al., 2017).

Although findings on science learning are encouraging, reported effect sizes are small (e.g., the effect size for MTP-M/S was .20, and the Science with Nico and Nor intervention accounted for 5% of the overall variance in science learning). These findings highlight the need to identify child-level variables that contribute to children's science learning, such as the experiences that young children engage in at home and other informal learning contexts (Domínguez and Goldstein, 2020). Overall, the evidence from these studies reflects a shift from research-based materials toward research-validated materials.

Complementing these examples in preschool science is an example of a preschool curriculum program focused on engineering: Wee Engineer, developed as part of the Engineering is Elementary curriculum series (Cunningham, Lachapelle, and Davis, 2018; see Box 7-2). Using a simplified three-step engineering design process, Explore-Create-Improve, Wee Engineer units provide prekindergarten educators and children with a meaningful design context, a clear design challenge, simple materials to explore and use for design solutions, and connections to play. This new program does not yet have extensive evidence supporting its efficacy.

Although these efforts have attended to current science and engineering frameworks, they have not used the science and engineering practices, disciplinary core ideas, and crosscutting concepts in the NGSS specifically. All of them have attempted to align to the NGSS while also attending to preschool and prekindergarten standards, resulting in slightly different learning goals. Two recent programs that focus on both science and engineering have used a version of the *Framework* adapted for use in infant, toddler, and preschool classrooms (Greenfield, Alexander, and Frechette, 2017). One is a preschool program with dual language learners enrolled in a Head Start Program: RISE (Readiness through Integrated Science and Engineering) STE curriculum (McWayne et al., 2020). The other, the Early Science Initiative, is a new multisite project within the Educare Learning Network.

ELEMENTARY GRADES CURRICULUM AND STANDARDS EFFORTS

In recent decades, there has been an emphasis on hands-on learning and engagement with materials as supporting engagement and children's "doing science" at the elementary level (NRC, 2007).[3] The field has called this "hands on rather than minds on." Until the release of the *Framework* in 2012, there had not, in general, been a focus on research-based learning progressions over long periods of time. In addition, the materials were built around assumptions that younger children could only engage in particular kinds of activities (e.g., observing, categorizing, describing) before others (e.g., explaining, designing investigations). The *Framework*'s emphasis on science and engineering practices, even with young children, pushes against this constraint-based and deficit-oriented approach. The *Framework* emphasizes sensemaking and puts forward coherent learning progressions starting in kindergarten. Thus, building on arguments originally put forward in *Taking Science to School*, the *Framework* pushes for changes in elementary science (and engineering) instruction and thus, curriculum materials.

The introduction of the *Framework* and subsequent adoption or adaptation of the NGSS by 44 states (see Chapter 2) have spurred the development of new curricular programs at the elementary level (e.g., Haas et al., 2021; Krajcik et al., 2021; Wright and Gotwals, 2017). Some of these elementary development efforts are working toward alignment with the *Framework* and the standards, and their vision; they are in some ways working toward the vision of learning environments put forward in Chapter 5. These programs

---

[3] *Taking Science to School* (NRC, 2007) summarized the history of curriculum development.

tend to be *phenomenon* and/or *problem based*; children in K–5 use phenomena and models in ways similar to how scientists do and solve design challenges in ways similar to how engineers do. These programs emphasize *sensemaking*. Using the science and engineering practices, disciplinary core ideas, and crosscutting concepts, children attempt to make sense of phenomena and develop solutions to problems; in this approach, teachers, instead of emphasizing facts and terminology, support children in that three-dimensional sensemaking process. Furthermore, these programs *build on and allow responsiveness to children's ideas*. These programs emphasize *relevance and authenticity* (such as described in Chapter 5) and the importance of *equitable and just learning experiences and outcomes* for every child. The materials may provide support aimed directly at supporting *teacher learning*, as well (Davis et al., 2017). A final key characteristic, based on research across grade levels, is *coherence*, in which ideas connect to and build on one another (e.g., Kesidou and Roseman, 2002; Weiss et al., 2003). New elementary materials are being developed now to reflect these characteristics and the vision of the *Framework*. Some efforts take up guidance provided in the NGSS, as well, including support for equity, assessment, the nature of science, and addressing learning progressions, though issues of whose knowledge is included in curriculum materials are still in play. Developing such materials is challenging and these efforts will need to demonstrate useful impact on teachers and children. Box 7-3 illustrates an example of how the SOLID Start curriculum has attended to some of these issues.

District Selection of Materials

According to the 2018 NSSME+ Horizon report, 72 percent of elementary classes use instructional materials for science instruction that have been designated by the district, and of these classes, 67 percent of teachers report having textbooks designated for their elementary science instruction, 51 percent of teachers report having kits or modules designated, and 43 percent of teachers report having state, country, district, or diocese-developed units and lessons designated (Banilower et al., 2018). Additionally, roughly 30–40 percent of teachers reported that they used either textbooks, kits/modules or state, county, district, or diocese-developed units and lessons for science instruction at least once a week (Plumley, 2019).

Considering Characteristics of Materials

Materials take different approaches to content delineation. Most assume that there is a designated science (or engineering) time (which is aligned with the typical structure of the school day in most districts). Some are integrated, connecting science to other academic subject areas includ-

BOX 7-3
SOLID Start

The SOLID Start (Science, Oral Language, and Literacy Development from the Start of School) curriculum is aimed at early elementary children. The curriculum, which integrates science and literacy, is based on practices likely to support young children in expressing their ideas through science talk: driving questions, active engagement with science phenomena, interactive read-alouds, and the incorporation of drawing and writing, echoing several of the characteristics of newer curriculum efforts (e.g., phenomenon or problem based, emphasizing sensemaking, building on and responsive to children's ideas, equitable and just, and coherent; the materials are also designed to support teacher learning). The curriculum is mapped onto both the Next Generation Science Standards and some strands of the Common Core State Standards ELA standards—namely standards for oral language, informational text, and writing. The curriculum is designed around five common components:

1. Ask: The teacher poses a daily driving question, such as "what is wind?"
2. Explore: Children explore a scientific phenomenon through dramatic play and other activities and gather evidence to help them respond to the driving question. For example, children might catch air using a plastic bag and make air move using paper and straws.
3. Read: The teacher reads aloud from an informational trade book (e.g., *I Face the Wind* by Vicki Cobb), using questions to support children in discussing ideas and providing support for learning vocabulary for science practices (e.g., evidence) and science content (e.g., blow).
4. Discuss: The teacher supports children in discussion throughout the lesson. For example, the teacher may ask questions like, "What evidence did you find in the book that we read? What did you observe during your exploration?"
5. Write: Some lessons include a portion where the teacher models science writing (such as on a class chart that says "Our Question, Our Claims, Our Evidence") or children draw and write in a science journal.

A quasi-experimental study involving 147 children found that kindergartners developed important science and literacy knowledge and practices and could engage in sophisticated science talk. Children who experienced the SOLID Start curriculum outperformed the comparison condition on all four dimensions of the interview-based posttest: claim, evidence-based support, receptive vocabulary, and vocabulary application in a science context, with large and educationally meaningfully effect sizes.

SOURCE: Wright and Gotwals (2017), particularly Table 2.

ing language arts, mathematics, or engineering. Curriculum materials also vary along other dimensions. Curricular programs can be comprehensive or supplemental. They can be kit based or not. Finally, they can be free and open source, or they can be commercially available. This section briefly explores the reasons schools or districts might choose materials with different combinations of these various characteristics.

Comprehensive materials cover the entire school year and typically are billed as addressing all of the relevant standards for a given grade level. Thus, teachers using comprehensive materials have access to lesson plans and unit plans for their instruction for the year—a boon for elementary teachers who are, as emphasized throughout this report, typically responsible for all academic subjects as well as other aspects of their children's development. These materials also enhance the consistency of children's experience over the elementary years.

Any materials, but particularly comprehensive materials, may be kit-based—a loose term that does not fully capture the complexity of obtaining materials for science and engineering instruction. Kit-based science (or engineering) curricular programs provide all or almost all of the physical resources that teachers need for engaging children in the lessons in the units, including both consumable and nonconsumable materials. This provision of materials is key in working toward the vision of the *Framework*, given the centrality of phenomena and design challenges and thus the importance of children engaging in first-hand investigations. Examples of comprehensive, kit-based materials include FOSS, Amplify, and Science and Technology Concepts (STC) (Banilower et al., 2018).

More than one-half of elementary teachers report having access to kits (Banilower et al., 2018), and research suggests that kits make the teaching of science feasible in the elementary grades. For example, a study conducted by Jones and colleagues (2012) explored teachers' reported use of kits. In this large-scale study of 503 practicing elementary teachers in the United States, teachers who reported more use of kits also reported more use of innovative or reform-oriented practices such as having learners support claims with evidence, analyze data, and work in groups. This study is consistent with others that demonstrate the utility of kits for elementary science *teaching* (e.g., Nowicki et al., 2013). On the other hand, Slavin and colleagues (2014) conducted a meta-analysis and found minimal positive effects of kit use on children's *learning*. Many teachers use kits and seem to appreciate how they make the teaching of science more feasible for them, and children are unlikely to learn science if teachers do not teach science.

In contrast to comprehensive materials, many materials, including some developed by research projects, are incomplete—that is, they do not include units that address all of the standards across a school year—and thus they serve as de facto supplemental materials. The incomplete nature of these materials can be a challenge for districts, schools, and teachers. That said, the materials developed by research projects tend to be of high quality, and in particular, tend to work toward not just technical alignment with the standards but also alignment with the vision of the *Framework* for elementary grades. Examples of such materials include NextGen Storylines (aimed at developing tools to support teachers in developing sequences of lessons that unfold coherently around science practices for children; Reiser et al., 2021), Multiple Literacies in Project-Based Learning (aimed at upper elementary and integrating science, engineering, language arts, and mathematics; e.g., Easley, 2020; Fitzgerald, 2018; Krajcik et al., 2021; Miller, Severance, and Krajcik, 2021; see Box 6-1), SOLID Start (aimed at kindergarten and integrating science, engineering, and language arts; Wright and Gotwals, 2017; see Box 7-3), Lee's NGSS-aligned curricular materials (aimed at upper elementary grades, integrating science and ELA, and emphasizing support for emergent multilingual learners; Haas et al., 2021), and Engineering is Elementary (Cunningham et al., 2020; see Box 7-2). Each of these materials is research based, and these materials have varying degrees of empirical evidence of efficacy, though in all cases, studies are ongoing.

Materials also may be free and open source, or commercially available. Clearly, free materials have an advantage for schools and districts, in that the budgetary impact of the materials is alleviated, leaving—perhaps—money to be allocated for physical investigation materials and/or professional development experiences for teachers. (It must be acknowledged, as well, that "free" materials still present substantial expenses for districts, in the form of professional learning sessions, kits, and resources; science funds still need to be budgeted for the curriculum to be taught as intended.) Another potential benefit of some open-source materials is that they are designed to allow teacher adaptation. Examples of research-based materials that are freely available include NextGen Storylines, Multiple Literacies for Project-Based Learning, and SOLID Start. OpenSciEd, which will begin development of elementary materials around the time of the publication of this report, is also built on the open-source model.

Materials vary in terms of how much evidence supports their efficacy and who generated that evidence (i.e., the developers or an outside party). Looking for evidence beyond what a commercial developer provides from in-house studies is key. Research-based materials typically provide evidence that goes beyond what most commercial publishers provide, such as evidence about teachers' use and children's learning.

Materials also vary in terms of their attention to issues of equity and justice. For example, the developers of the NextGen Storylines argue that providing their materials as open—educational resources that can be freely downloaded allows them to be adapted for local contexts (Reiser et al., 2021)—an important characteristic for working toward equity. SOLID Start reflects several of the equity-oriented characteristics depicted in Box 7-1, including being anchored in contexts, providing multimodal opportunities for expression of children's ideas, and using texts (through interactive read-alouds) for both explanation and identity work (Wright and Gotwals, 2017).

Additional Considerations for Review and Selection

Other criteria for considering and eventually selecting instructional materials include (1) support for children to develop coherent science explanations, (2) strategies for assessing learners' progress and understanding (i.e., embedded formative assessment), (3) intentionally attending to the importance of language in science learning, and (4) support for teacher learning (NASEM, 2018b). Materials that support coherent explanations and solutions help children understand what they are working on and why, and more importantly, help teachers recognize the key moments that need to occur for the lesson to build toward the vision of the *Framework* (Reiser et al., 2021). Formative assessment-embedded materials allow children to share their understanding in multiple modalities, while providing guidance to teachers on ways to elicit and respond to children's thinking (Fine and Furtak, 2020). Curriculum materials that attend to science and engineering and language integration recognize that language is actually a means to investigate phenomena, solve problems, and accomplish tasks in the classroom through various modalities—talk, text, and diagrams (Haas et al., 2021). This approach particularly supports the participation of emergent multilingual learners in robust science learning (Lee and Stephens, 2020; NASEM, 2018a). Lastly, educative materials (Davis et al., 2017) are designed to facilitate both student and teacher learning, afford multiple ways to adapt lessons to meet the range of learners' and teachers' needs, and may include features that help teachers see what an enacted lesson looks like, including the anticipated thinking and decision-making roles for teachers during a particular lesson.

District Review Processes

Districts have many criteria to consider and choices to make when deciding about curricular programs to adopt; at the same time, though, districts may have to make decisions about instructional materials under time pressure after only cursory reviews of textbooks or presentations of materials, with budgetary considerations determining the final choice (NASEM, 2018b). Relying on a robust review process is critical in decision making. EdReports,[4] for example, conducts curricular reviews. At this time, it seems that even elementary materials designed with the NGSS in mind are not yet fully aligned with the vision of the *Framework*. The Educators Evaluating the Quality of Instructional Products (EQuIP) rubric and its associated tools can be used to determine how well lessons and units are aligned to the NGSS and other state standards informed by the *Framework*, and to inform teachers' own adaptations to the materials as well as informing designers' ongoing development work. Other tools that help teachers and districts select materials to use as they implement the NGSS in their classrooms and schools include (1) the NGSS Lesson Screener, (2) Primary Evaluation of Essential Criteria (PEEC) for NGSS Instructional Materials Design, and (3) NextGen Toolkit for Instructional Materials Evaluation (NextGen TIME; adapted from an earlier tool, Next Generation Analyzing Instructional Materials, or NGSS AIM). Tools vary in their complexity and can be challenging for curriculum adoption committees to use; new resources are regularly being developed in part to support the tools' ease of use.[5]

The NGSS Lesson Screener is used to analyze a single science lesson for alignment to the NGSS, where a lesson is defined as a learning sequence that might extend from one or two classes to one or two weeks. PEEC is a three-step evaluation tool for full programs, measuring how well materials are designed to support teaching to meet the goals of the *Framework* and the NGSS. PEEC incorporates the EQuIP rubric, and establishes whether materials for a given program involve (1) making sense of phenomena and designing solutions to problems; (2) 3D learning; (3) K–12 learning progressions; (4) connection to ELA and mathematics; and (5) reaching all students with all standards (NASEM, 2018b). NextGen TIME[6] is a five-step tool that involves assessing the district's readiness for the review process, identifying curricular programs to examine in depth, refining those choices by understanding the strengths and limitations of each program, piloting one or two options, and then planning the professional learning opportunities that would be needed for teachers as well as what adaptations may need to be made to better fit the context of the district.

States and districts may have their own curricular review processes, as well. For example, Louisiana's instructional materials review process uses committees composed of Louisiana educators who evaluate materials

---

[4] For more information, see http://www.edreports.org.

[5] For example, see https://www.nextgenscience.org/resources/critical-features-instructional-materials-design-today's-science-standards and https://www.wested.org/resources/toward-ngss-design-equip-guidance/.

[6] NextGen TIME was developed collaboratively by Biological Sciences Curriculum Study (BSCS), Achieve, Inc., and WestED. Next Gen AIM, a foundation for NextGen TIME, was developed collaboratively by BSCS, Achieve, Inc., and the K–12 Alliance.

based on a set of state-developed rubrics. The rubrics provide a structure for the educators to evaluate the quality of the curricular program and its alignment to the state's standards. The reviews fall in three tiers, with the top tier indicating a program that has met all of the criteria on the rubric. After the evaluation process, publishers have the opportunity to respond to the evaluation before the evaluation is published. The state department of education publishes a compilation of the results of these evaluations, updated weekly. Districts can purchase top-tier materials under a state contract; lower-tier materials are not eligible for the state contract, but can be purchased and used. Other states use different (often less stringent) instructional materials review processes, or expect districts to take the lead entirely on instructional review.

Once materials have been adopted, the capacity for teacher adaptation is key. Teachers' use of and adaptation of curriculum materials are addressed in more depth later. District and school leaders need to have a sense of how the curriculum materials should be used, including recognizing adaptation that is in keeping with the vision of the materials and understanding of the physical materials needed to engage children in first-hand investigation and design.

Insufficiency of Instructional Materials for Investigations and Design Challenges

Although having high-quality curriculum materials is key in supporting science and engineering for children, another factor also matters: the availability of the physical instructional resources one needs for conducting investigations and the facilities that make those investigations possible. For example, children may need hand lenses to support careful observation or balances that are accurate enough to capture small changes in mass; they also need consumable supplies (e.g., seeds, cups, batteries) that are used and must be replenished. Their classrooms need access to water, electricity, physical workspace, and other utilities and infrastructure to support their investigation and design work. Furthermore, some phenomena occur on scales that are too large, small, slow, or fast to be directly viewed, and so computer technology for access to videos or simulations may be needed. These critical resources and facilities are not always available for teachers. The committee did not find parallel systematic evidence on this issue for preschool settings; however, the NSSME+ report (Banilower et al., 2018) provides a window into elementary classrooms across the United States.

In terms of physical instructional resources, 80 percent of elementary classrooms have access to some kind of balance (e.g., a pan scale or digital scale). Most elementary classrooms do have access to electric outlets (93%)

and faucets and sinks (83%). These rooms are much less likely, however, to have laboratory tables (29%), and elementary seating arrangements can make conducting collaborative investigations a challenge in some settings. Most elementary schools have schoolwide wifi (98%) and laptop or tablet carts available (89%).

The funding available for equipment, consumable supplies, and software can signal how science is prioritized in elementary schools. The NSSME+ found that at the elementary level, the median amount that schools spent per pupil on science resources (specifically equipment, consumable supplies, and software) was $1.98—considerably lower than the $6.88/pupil spent at the high school level, and also much lower than the $6.45/pupil spent on math resources at the elementary level. These expenditures are inequitably distributed based on a number of factors: number of students on free and reduced-price lunch, school size, locality (urban/rural), and geographic region.[7]

Elementary teachers perceive the resources they have available for science as inadequate. When asked to comment on whether their access to resources is adequate, only 39 percent agreed with regard to equipment (e.g., thermometers, magnifying glasses); 38 percent with regard to facilities; 49 percent with regard to instructional technology (e.g., calculators, computers); and 30 percent with regard to consumable supplies (e.g., living organisms, batteries). Middle and high school science teachers are much more likely to rate their access to resources as adequate. Perhaps more saliently, elementary teachers are much more likely to rate their access to resources for *mathematics* as adequate, in comparison to *science*; the parallel figures for teachers' perceived adequacy of their access to instructional technology, measurement tools, consumable supplies, and manipulatives, in elementary mathematics, range from 65 to 87 percent.

Overall, these findings show that science instruction is under-resourced and not highly prioritized in elementary classrooms, and that these concerns are exacerbated in under-resourced schools (Banilower et al., 2018).

TEACHERS' USE OF AND LEARNING WITH CURRICULUM MATERIALS

Besides being an important resource for children's learning, curriculum materials are a key lever for supporting teachers and their learning. Specifically, curriculum materials are an important form of support for preschool and elementary teachers of science (and, by extension, for teachers of engineering, although there is less research related to engineering), supporting multiple domains of teachers' knowledge and practice. They can comple-

---

[7] Currently available data from the NSSME+ Horizon report do not disaggregate these factors to elementary grades.

ment initial teacher education and ongoing professional learning, taken up in Chapter 8. In this section, some of the relevant scholarship is reviewed, drawing largely on a recent review of the literature on elementary and secondary science teachers' use of curriculum materials (Davis, Janssen, and van Driel, 2016) and focusing on the findings from that review related to elementary teaching and learning, as well as on other scholarship exploring preschool teachers' use of curriculum materials (e.g., Whittaker et al., 2020).

Ways Curriculum Materials Support Teachers

Although curriculum materials are typically thought of as a way to provide learning activities or, at most, to support teachers' learning of subject-matter knowledge, in fact using curriculum materials also helps to build preschool through elementary teachers' pedagogical content knowledge and their pedagogical design capacity (Beyer and Davis, 2012a, 2012b; Whittaker et al., 2016; 2020), as well as other aspects of their knowledge and practice (Davis and Krajcik, 2005; Davis et al., 2017). Preschool teachers have been found to effectively use science curricular materials that embed within-activity curricular supports, such as recommendations for language, teaching tips and adaptation ideas, and online supports such as brief video demonstrations of high-quality teacher–child interactions around science and mathematics (Whittaker et al., 2016). Elementary teachers can use curriculum materials effectively (e.g., Forbes, 2011; Forbes and Davis, 2010), including educative curriculum materials (e.g., Arias, Davis, and Palincsar, 2014; Bismack et al., 2014, 2015) or curriculum materials that are designed to support teacher learning as well as student learning. For example, teachers using educative curriculum materials can use them to support children in engaging in certain science practices (e.g., Arias, Davis, and Palincsar, 2014; Enfield, Smith, and Grueber, 2008) and to provide emergent multilingual learners with ambitious opportunities to learn (Cervetti, Kulikowich, and Bravo, 2015).

That said, preschool through elementary teachers may struggle with using curriculum materials to support sensemaking and engagement in science practices (e.g., Beyer and Davis, 2008; Biggers, Forbes, and Zangori, 2013; Bismack et al., 2014; 2015; Domínguez and Goldstein, 2020; Zangori, Forbes, and Biggers, 2013), including the kinds of proficiencies around investigation and design specified in Chapter 4. Studies in elementary school consistently show that beginning (preservice and early career) elementary teachers were able to use some aspects of their curriculum materials effectively but struggled to use or enhance existing supports for explanation, argumentation, and other science practices or to build new supports for sensemaking. Studies examining outcomes of preschool science curricula report similar findings, with teachers successfully promoting engagement in observation and investigation, but less frequently facilitating discourse to promote explanation (e.g., Domínguez and Goldstein, 2020).

Furthermore, teachers may use curriculum materials in a way that aligns with their current practice, rather than pushing toward the reforms intended by and embedded within the materials (e.g., Davis, 2006; Schwarz et al., 2008). In addition, elementary teachers may recognize the positives of "opening up" the curriculum for scientific uncertainty, but also experience some tensions around doing so (Manz and Suárez, 2018).

Some research has explored how educative curriculum materials can support effective integration of science and literacy (Chapter 6). A study of educative features within science curriculum materials aimed at upper elementary grades looked at a range of educative features, including learning goals that outlined the conceptual focus of the reading, interactive reading guides, graphic aids to support teachers' and children's understanding of texts, and narratives that described how fictional teachers chose to support children during reading and discussions of readings (Arias, Palincsar, and Davis, 2015). Another pair of studies looked at the effects of modified trade books that connected the texts to the nature of science and provided discussion prompts (Brunner, 2019; Brunner and Abd-El-Khalick, 2020). Finally, another study explored educative features aimed at supporting teachers in integrating science and literacy with emergent multilingual learners; the features included science background information, instructional suggestions and rationales, and specific instructional strategies for supporting emergent multilingual learners (Cervetti, Kulikowich, and Bravo, 2015). Across these studies, the researchers found that teachers drew on the educative features and were able to incorporate some of the ideas and strategies suggested therein. Box 7-4 summarizes some of the strengths and limitations of how curriculum materials can support teachers.

The above discussion has focused on how educative curriculum materials could be designed to support teacher learning directly. In addition to this, teachers also learn through the combination of curriculum materials and professional learning experiences provided to schools adopting those curriculum materials (see Short and Hirsh, 2020). When a district adopts a curricular program, they typically are able to obtain professional development to support teachers in learning to use the program in their teaching. In these cases, the curriculum materials become, in essence, the phenomenon under investigation, and teachers explore them in multiple ways: as students, but also as teachers, sometimes examining children's work and/or videos of enactment and sometimes engaging in practice-based rehearsals themselves (e.g., Lee et al., 2008; Roth et al., 2011; see NRC, 2015b, for a review).

> **BOX 7-4**
> **Strengths and Limitations of Curriculum Materials' Support for Teachers**
>
> Strengths: What does evidence suggest curriculum materials may support?
>
> - Teachers' subject-matter knowledge, pedagogical content knowledge, pedagogical design capacity, and other aspects of their knowledge and practice
> - Supporting children in engaging in some science practices
> - Providing emergent multilingual learners with meaningful opportunities to learn
> - Supporting the integration of science and literacy
>
> Limitations in how curriculum materials may support teachers
>
> - Idiosyncratic or isolated materials are unlikely to support teachers' professional learning
> - Curriculum materials may not uniformly help teachers to support students' sensemaking practices
> - Teachers may use curriculum materials in ways that align with their current practice and feel tensions in opening up opportunities for scientific uncertainty

Teachers' Use and Adaptation of Curriculum Materials

Teachers use the same science curriculum materials in quite variable ways (e.g., Arias, Palincsar, and Davis, 2015; Arias et al., 2016; Bismack et al., 2015), suggesting that expecting "fidelity of implementation" (O'Donnell, 2008) is likely unrealistic. Furthermore, some scholarship suggests that enacting curriculum materials with "fidelity" may be unrelated to students' science achievement gains (Lee, Penfield, and Maerten-Rivera, 2009), though the use of curriculum materials in general seems supportive of student learning (Lee et al., 2008). Generally, teachers adapt curriculum materials for their own use (Davis, Janssen, and van Driel, 2016; Stein, Remillard, and Smith, 2007), and fidelity to the *vision* of the curriculum may be a more appropriate goal (e.g., McNeill et al., 2018).

Preschool through elementary teachers need to engage in active and principled adaptation of any materials (e.g., Davis, 2006; Schwarz et al., 2008). Often, for example, materials need changing to better infuse opportunities for children's sensemaking (rather than being told "the answer"), to meaningfully engage children in the science and engineering practices, to connect to local contexts, and to fit within one's own classroom and with one's own learners. Teachers say they make changes to curriculum materials based on time constraints and the needs of their learners (Davis et al., 2017). Such curricular adaptation can be engaged solely by the classroom teacher, or it can involve co-design work in which researchers and teachers partner, often to make local connections and/or to shift the epistemic work of the materials (e.g., Manz and Suárez, 2018; McWayne et al., 2021; Stromholt and Bell, 2017).

What influences elementary teachers' use of science curriculum materials? The teachers' own knowledge and beliefs shape how they use the materials, as do characteristics of the materials themselves and the contexts in which they are being used. Table 7-1 summarizes some of these factors. The first of these factors, teachers' understanding of the science practices, is related to their uptake of ideas from educative curriculum materials; teachers were (not surprisingly) more likely to incorporate practices that they understood better (e.g., Arias et al., 2016; Bismack et al., 2015; Zangori, Forbes, and Biggers, 2013). For example, given curriculum materials that offered opportunities for first-hand investigation and the development of mechanistic explanations, preservice teachers were more likely to emphasize hands-on data collection and the description of cause and effect relationships (i.e., what happened), but not the mechanisms underlying a phenomenon (the how or why)—which aligned with their understanding of evidence and explanation (Zangori, Forbes, and Biggers, 2013). Furthermore, beliefs—about what children can do (Zangori, Forbes, and Biggers, 2013), assessment or lesson design (Beyer and Davis, 2012b), or classroom management (Kelly and Staver, 2005)—have been found to be related to teachers' decision making about how to enact curriculum materials. Teachers who do not believe that science practices should be assessed, for example, were unlikely to use or add opportunities for assessment of science practices (Beyer and Davis, 2012b). On the other hand, teachers who understood the value of personal relevance in lesson design could make appropriate changes to enhance this aspect (e.g., changing the lesson purpose from "keep a cotton ball dry" to "keep me dry when it's raining"; Beyer and Davis, 2012b).

A second factor in teachers' use of curriculum materials is the design of the materials themselves. Although there is variation in how teachers take up specific characteristics of the curriculum materials, some research suggests that teachers using kit-based curriculum materials were more likely to teach accurate content (Nowicki et al., 2013). How inquiry-oriented curriculum materials are tends also to predict how much a teacher is likely to engage children in scientific inquiry (or what might now be called science practice) (e.g., Beyer and Davis, 2012b; Forbes, 2013; Forbes and Davis, 2010; Zangori, Forbes, and Biggers, 2013). These studies consistently demonstrate the value of access to high-quality, coherent, practice-oriented curriculum

TABLE 7-1 Factors Shaping Teachers' Adaptations of Curriculum Materials

Factors	Examples of Results
Teachers' Knowledge and Beliefs	
Teachers' understanding of the science practices	Stronger understanding of certain practices may lead teachers to include those practices.
Teachers' beliefs (e.g., about learners' capabilities, assessment, classroom management)	A belief that children cannot engage in sophisticated sensemaking may lead teachers to omit opportunities for sensemaking.
Perceptions of time constraints	Limited time may lead teachers to omit lesson segments.
Characteristics of the Curriculum Materials	
Comprehensive or kit-based materials	May support teachers in teaching accurate science content; no clear effect on children's learning.
Inquiry or practice orientation	Greater orientation toward science practice may lead to engaging children with the practices.
Specific educative features yield different effects	More situated educative features and features that support principled adaptation and engagement in sensemaking seem helpful.
Contexts of Curriculum Material Use	
Classroom contexts (e.g., mentors) as supportive or not supportive of adaptation	Having mentor teachers who model the importance of principled adaptation of curriculum materials seems helpful.

materials in elementary classrooms. That said, as Slavin and colleagues (2014) note, there are relatively few strong, large-scale studies of effects of elementary science curricular programs.

Furthermore, a close look at one dimension of this second factor reveals that specific types of educative features appear to have different effects on how teachers use the curriculum materials. For example, teachers with access to curriculum materials that incorporated narratives of how other educators used the materials themselves were likely to draw on the narratives frequently; other, less situated, but more explicit, educative features were used less often but were more likely to support teachers in learning specific educational principles of practice (Beyer and Davis, 2009). Educative features may support the *how* of engaging in science instruction—providing a clear, step-by-step roadmap—or the *what*—showing what this kind of instruction can look like (Drayton et al., 2020). With preschool teachers, online supports were used far less than other forms of support (Whittaker et al., 2016).

In general, preschool through elementary teachers seem to use educative features that are centrally situated within lessons—such as narratives, rubrics, and examples—more often than they use other, less situated elements (Arias et al., 2016; Bismack et al., 2015; Whittaker et al., 2016), though some teachers also found utility in content supports such as concept maps and content storylines (Arias et al., 2016). Which educative elements teachers take up seems related to the teachers' purposes and instructional goals (which are idiosyncratic) as well as to the nature of the educative features themselves (Arias et al., 2016). That said, generally scholarship suggests benefits of incorporating educative features into curriculum materials for elementary science (Cervetti, Kulikowich, and Bravo, 2015; Enfield, Smith, and Grueber, 2008; Lin et al., 2012).

Recent work (Davis et al., 2017) has developed an empirically grounded set of design principles for educative curriculum materials. These design principles recommend using multiple forms of support, providing suggestions for productive adaptations of the materials, providing supports that are situated in teachers' practice, incorporating educative features that can be applied directly as teaching tools, and—directly related to elementary science and engineering—focusing on supporting sensemaking and using instrumental science and engineering practices to incrementally work toward change in teachers' practice.

A third factor in how elementary teachers use science curriculum materials is the classroom context. Much of this work has taken place with preservice elementary teachers. Preservice teachers may not adapt curriculum materials; some research suggests that it is relatively rare for preservice elementary teachers to see their mentor teachers making such adaptations (Beyer and Davis, 2012a), which can make preservice teachers unlikely to engage in curricular modification themselves. That said, when preservice teachers do perceive their field placements to be supportive of that modification, they may be in a better position to enact more reform-oriented instruction, by virtue of adapting curriculum materials toward that goal (Forbes, 2013).

In summary, this research shows an important role that curriculum materials—particularly those that are designed to support teacher learning as well as children's learning—can play for teachers who are responsible for science and engineering with the younger grades.

WORKING TOWARD EQUITY WITH CURRICULUM MATERIALS

Having curriculum materials available for preschool through elementary teachers provides an important support for them in *increasing access to high-quality opportunities for science and engineering learning* available for children (Approach #1). Furthermore, kits and the physical and/or digital resources needed for science investigations and engineering design challenges serve a similar role—without the "stuff" needed for investigation and design, it is far more difficult for teachers to do that kind of work. Yet the NSSME+ report shows that some schools are less likely to have access to the range of physical resources, and these under-resourced schools are also likely to spend less, per pupil, on such materials (Banilower et al., 2018). Thus, learners in under-resourced schools are less likely to have the kinds of opportunities to learn science and engineering as compared to their counterparts in higher-resourced schools. Likewise, curriculum materials serve to support children with learning disabilities and/or learning differences; however, the committee did not find literature specific to adapting or differentiating science or engineering curriculum materials for preschool through elementary children with learning disabilities and/or learning differences, so this is an area for future research.

Curriculum materials and instructional resources can shape the *emphasis on increased student achievement, representation, and identification with science and engineering* (Approach #2). For decades, textbooks reinforced the idea that science and engineering were realms of white men. A related concern is whose knowledge is represented in the materials. Although these are ongoing issues, curriculum materials now can be a way of highlighting the contributions of a wide range of scientists and engineers (e.g., Fitzgerald, 2018, 2020). In addition, educative curriculum materials may be able to support teachers in recognizing the capabilities of their learners, which could, in turn, allow the children to see themselves as people who do science and engineering (e.g., Arias et al., 2016).

Furthermore, curriculum materials can support *expanding what counts as science and engineering* (Approach #3). Educative features can support teachers in learning about how they can support emergent multilingual learners in science (Cervetti, Kulikowich, and Bravo, 2015; Lee et al., 2008). This support helps set up a learning environment in which multiple forms of expressing sensemaking are valued and supported. The Learning in Places Collaborative (2020) curriculum for the lower elementary grades provides an emergent example of how curriculum materials—involving culturally based learning experiences oriented toward sustainable decision making and using the outdoors to learn about socioecological systems—can expand what counts as science; such experiences may also support learning outside of the natural sciences (e.g., economics, ethics, civics).

Although the committee did not find many examples of preschool or elementary science or engineering curriculum materials that were explicitly aimed at *seeing science and engineering as part of justice movements* (Approach #4), several projects are working toward (a) orientation around local phenomena or designs with (b) educative support for teacher adaptation for using those local phenomena or designs (Haas et al., 2021; Reiser et al.,

2021; Stromholt and Bell, 2017). Teachers' adaptations of such materials could focus on local justice issues. One example of curriculum designed explicitly toward seeing science as a part of justice movements is the collaborative work done around the disproportionate effects of the COVID-19 pandemic for Black, Brown, and Indigenous communities (Housman et al, 2021).

SUMMARY

Curriculum materials are not a panacea to the challenges of preschool through elementary science and engineering instruction, but cannot be discounted as a substantial influence on that instruction. High-quality curriculum materials have evidence supporting their effectiveness; support teachers in being responsive to children's ideas; are coherent, flexible, adaptable, equitable, and grounded in investigation and design; and build toward the vision of the *Framework*. These materials can support teachers in developing learning environments that in turn support children's sensemaking. Yet not all teachers have access to high-quality curriculum materials or to the physical materials needed for science and engineering teaching.

Newer curriculum development efforts emphasize using science and engineering practices as a way of developing conceptual understanding and making sense of the natural and designed worlds. These materials are often organized around phenomena and problems that are meaningful to children. States and districts engage in review processes to select curriculum materials to be used in local schools. Districts might more highly prioritize open-source materials (because they are free); materials that are comprehensive (covering the entirety of the grade bands) as opposed to incomplete programs for consistency of children's experience; kits over standalone materials for teachers' ease of use; and materials that are research based in their design and research supported in their efficacy for likelihood of success. Although new materials are being developed, the creation of materials that meet the design recommendations presented takes time and requires infrastructure.

Teachers learn from and with curriculum materials, and they adapt them to meet their needs. Curriculum materials can support teachers' learning with regard to many dimensions of teachers' work (e.g., supporting emergent multilingual learners); educative curriculum materials, in particular, are designed to support teachers' learning and show positive effects. How teachers use and adapt curriculum materials depends on the teachers' knowledge and beliefs, the characteristics of the materials themselves, and the contexts in which they are being used. The work of building toward the vision of the *Framework* in curriculum materials while deepening attention to equity and justice is a significant challenge. The design of curriculum materials that specifically support the goal of teaching toward equity and justice in science and engineering in preschool and elementary settings is an area for further research and development and will require substantial investment of time and effort.

8

Supporting Educators to Center Children, Investigation, and Design

---

Main Messages

- Preschool through elementary school teachers benefit from having strong teacher preparation and coherent professional learning opportunities. These supports provide opportunities to expand on teachers' strengths.
- The demographics of the preschool and elementary teacher workforce are starkly different from the demographics of the children being taught. This discrepancy means that there are often cultural mismatches between teachers and the children in their classrooms.
- To support teachers in enacting science and engineering instruction that is responsive to and supportive of the cultural and linguistic backgrounds of the children in their classrooms, a growing body of research highlights the importance of diversifying the teacher educator workforce, placing preservice teachers in supportive field placements involving children from a range of linguistic and cultural backgrounds, and using sustained professional learning experiences synergistically with educative curriculum materials.

Preschool and elementary teachers have an extraordinarily challenging job, as they are responsible for children's learning across *all* academic content areas—English language arts, literacy, mathematics, social studies, and all disciplines of science. Furthermore, they face other demands that are often seen as less pressing in the secondary grades, but are of paramount importance with younger children, such as supporting social-emotional learning, physical well-being, and well-roundedness (such as through art and music) (Institute of Medicine [IOM] and National Research Council [NRC], 2012). Most preschool and elementary teachers do not go into the teaching profession because they love science and engineering, and they may have little preparation for teaching science and engineering. Furthermore, as noted elsewhere in the report, they may lack the time and resources for engaging in the work; this is particularly true of teachers working in under-resourced schools, which, as has been shown, typically serve larger numbers of Black, Brown, Indigenous, and other children of color.

Throughout this chapter, the committee is oriented toward the assets preschool and elementary teachers bring to the work of teaching science and engineering to young children (Zembal-Saul, Carlone, and Brown, 2020; see also Gray, McDonald, and Stroupe, 2021). This asset orientation pushes against a standard narrative that sees preschool and elementary teachers as generally weak with regard to the teaching of science and engineering. Zembal-Saul, Carlone, and Brown (2020) describe how characterizing elementary teachers as having limited science backgrounds and troubled science identities can perpetuate damaging narratives about these educators as teachers of science and engineering. These deficit narratives can interfere with the design of powerful professional learning.

Instead, repositioning elementary teachers using a lens focused on *possibility* allows seeing them as uniquely equipped to support children's rigorous, responsive, and just sensemaking in science. As teachers create a trusting classroom environment where children feel safe to speak out and contributions are valued (see Brackett et al., 2019; Castagno, 2019), opportunities can open up for teachers to explore and connect with children's cultural and linguistic resources and lived experience in families and communities (Moll et al., 1992; Warren et al., 2001) (see Chapter 5). In addition, expertise across language domains of speaking, listening, writing, and reading can be reframed as an asset that can facilitate sensemaking in science as discussed in Chapter 6.

Teachers build expertise individually and collectively, across time and across multiple settings and contexts (National Academies of Sciences, Engineering, and Medicine [NASEM], 2015). Moreover, the committee acknowledges, and tries to account for, the historical systems in which preschool and elementary educators work—systems that have historically held teachers of young children in low esteem and have not, for several decades, privileged the teaching of science (much less engineering) to young children (see Box 8-1) (Carlone, Haun-Frank, and Kimmel, 2010).

TEACHER LEARNING

Teachers are learners. The committee draws on the discussion of what teachers need to know and be able to do in Chapter 5 of *Science Teachers' Learning* (NASEM, 2015) to provide a primer on teacher learning. Issues that seem especially salient in understanding preschool and elementary teachers of science and engineering are the focus.

As *Science Teachers' Learning* specified, teachers need to develop professional knowledge and practices that extend beyond understanding of content, to reach the vision of science and engineering learning put forward by the *Framework*. Three elements are particularly key; these relate to teaching "a diverse range of students," having expertise around the three dimensions of the *Framework*, and having pedagogical content knowledge and practice to "support students in rigorous and consequential learning of science" (NASEM, 2015, p. 95). Though *Science Teachers' Learning* focused on science, those dimensions are extended here to include engineering as well.

Similar to *Science Teachers' Learning*, in this report, the committee explores "knowledge, skills, competencies, habits of mind, and beliefs" (p. 95) and related constructs that are central in the teaching of science and engineering with young learners, recognizing that these foci are not static. Identities, dispositions, and beliefs are seen as potentially central with this population, because the standard narrative would paint preschool and elementary teachers as, if not antiscience, at least antiscience teaching. The key constructs used in this chapter are defined as follows:

- Identity: "the ways in which a teacher represents herself/himself through her/his views, orientations, attitudes, knowledge, and beliefs about science teaching, the kind of science teacher she/he envisions to be, and the ways in which she/he is recognized by others" (Avraamidou, 2016, p. 863)
- Dispositions: "professional attitudes, values, and beliefs that support student learning and development" (Eick and Stewart, 2010, p. 785); similar to habits of mind
- Beliefs: teachers' perspectives (about science and engineering or science and engineering teaching, for example) that can be distinguished from their knowledge (Pajares, 1992), which change over time, across moments, and across contexts (Louca, Hammer, and Elby, 2004)
- Knowledge: content knowledge for teaching (Ball, Thames, and Phelps, 2008), or the subject-matter knowledge and pedagogical

BOX 8-1
Historicizing Preschool and Elementary Teachers

Normative definitions of "teacher" are simultaneously and historically rooted and produced in moment-to-moment interactions. Most preschool and elementary teachers are white women and, because of the central role elementary schools play in cultural reproduction, heteronormative, white, gender roles are the most valued and available for teachers in elementary settings. Elementary teachers are often celebrated for their compliance, nurturing, and people pleasing, and also thrive from positive recognition from administrators who, too, are often hesitant to work against established norms (Carlone, Haun-Frank, and Kimmel, 2010). There are also privileged ways to perform "teacher" that malign minoritized teachers. Ladson-Billings (2009) provides a compelling case for why and how Black women are rarely held up as exemplary teachers. For example, a "warm demander" style, often attributed to Black teachers who work with mostly minoritized, socioeconomically disadvantaged children, is a culturally responsive communication style that may look to be no-nonsense, severe, or overly structured to outsiders, but is a way to demand high expectations and communicate unwavering care for and belief in all children's abilities to succeed. Warm demanders act as strong but compassionate teachers, incorporating humor and straightforward communication that is firm but does not demean students (Bondy et al., 2007). Warm demanders' style of nurturing diverges from images borne of white, upper-middle class values (e.g., clear and firm directives as opposed to gentle suggestions for children's behaviors) and therefore may be unrecognizable to some teachers, administrators, or families as nurturing. Critically examining the hidden values of a "good" elementary teacher can surface inequities and lead to more just pedagogies for professional learning.

Those whose teaching looks different than historical and local norms are increasingly at risk of being marginalized, ostracized, and even punished (Giroux and Giroux, 2006). The literature about elementary teaching alludes to the hesitance of teachers to take up practices that go against the grain and roles that violate gendered and raced models of "good teacher." For instance, Carlone, Haun-Frank, and Kimmel (2010) spent 2 years in a teacher's fourth grade classroom, located in a school serving mostly minoritized youth. A Southern, white teacher from a self-proclaimed "poor, rural" background, Ms. Carpenter (a pseudonym) had a style that observers sometimes found jarring. For example, she encouraged the children to treat a class pet's death pragmatically because "that's what we would do on our farm growing up." She also resisted the normative teacher role by engaging her learners with problems that administrators and other teachers deemed too advanced and not aligned with the curriculum; her curriculum was strongly student driven. Her unconventional practices like regularly taking science outside and allotting time for all-day science explorations brought critique and derision from peers. Ms. Carpenter was professionally isolated, which was difficult for her. Research suggests that even those who deliberately teach against the grain express self-doubt about engaging in unsanctioned practices (Carlone, Haun-Frank, and Kimmel, 2010). Historical meanings of *good elementary teacher* make science and engineering teaching that is equitable and meaningful difficult, but an awareness of these historical meanings can lay the foundation for change.

SOURCE: Adapted from Carlone, Huan-Frank, and Kimmel (2010).

content knowledge related to both science and engineering content and science and engineering practices (Bismack, 2019; Johnson and Cotterman, 2015)
- Practice: the work done by a teacher (e.g., eliciting children's ideas) or the act of getting better at that work (e.g., through rehearsals; Lampert, 2010; see also, for a focus in science teaching, Arias and Davis, 2017; Kloser, 2014; Windschitl et al., 2012).

Each of these elements has the potential for shaping how a teacher engages in the work of teaching. For example, an elementary teacher's self-efficacy for science teaching and her identity as a teacher of science might influence how often she teaches science. Her beliefs about children might influence what expectations she sets for which children in her classroom. Her content knowledge for science teaching might help her push children toward sensemaking, or might constrain her from doing so, and in particular her knowledge of science practices might lead her to engage children in the forms of activity put forward in Chapter 4. Further, her capacities with regard to certain science teaching practices might support her in engaging children in sensemaking discussions. This chapter discusses what the literature shows about these potential influences. Box 8-2 illustrates how an elementary teacher might plan and enact a lesson built around a fairly typical elementary investigation—observing condensation forming on a cold can.

Teachers at all positions on the teacher professional continuum (Feiman-Nemser, 2001) may be novices when it comes to reaching the vision of the *Framework* and may need well-designed supports for learning to do this work. They benefit from learning opportunities that zero in on helping them develop the kinds of knowledge, skills, and proficiencies outlined above. These opportunities to learn support outcomes such as enhanced teacher capacity for engaging in effective instruction that meets the needs of every learner. That capacity for instruction, in turn, helps to support children's learning and development. In *Science Teachers' Learning*, this is referred to as the "connect the dots" model (connecting teachers' opportunities to learn to their knowledge, beliefs, attitudes, and practice, to their students' outcomes), and the model is used in this chapter in exploring the literature on how teacher education and professional learning experiences can support preschool and elementary educators' learning.

Connecting teacher learning to teacher outcomes and children's outcomes is not linear; rather, learning is both iterative and dynamic and "embedded in contexts what teachers learn and how they exercise their knowledge and skill" (NASEM, 2015, p. 116). This suggests that many teacher learning opportunities do not take place in formal professional development experiences but, rather, occur in school with children and colleagues, whether in the classroom or as teachers work as a team to look closely at their learners' work. Thus, teachers must be conceptualized as

> **BOX 8-2**
> **Building on Teachers' Assets: Toward the Vision of the *Framework* and Toward Justice**
>
> Ms. Green, a fifth grade teacher, is planning a lesson exploring the phenomenon of condensation (the change of state from water vapor to liquid water). The children will observe condensation forming on the outside of a cold can and will engage in the science practice of developing and using scientific models. Ms. Green is a white, monolingual teacher teaching in a school with sizeable numbers of emergent multilingual speakers; Ms. Green's class, roughly evenly split across Black, Latinx, and white children, includes several Spanish-speaking children as well as a handful of children with learning disabilities/differences, including one who has an auditory-processing disorder. Ms. Green believes in her learners' capacities, and she identifies as a teacher who wants to support the success of all of her students. She seeks out ways of connecting with children and their families. Although she took few science courses in college, she believes in the value of science learning for children.
>
> Ms. Green works to understand each child in her classroom. She knows she wants to anchor her instruction to connect with her learners' interests, experiences, and knowledge. At the same time, she knows that a range of decisions—including seemingly simple ones, such as what kind of container to use for illustrating the phenomenon of condensation forming—have cultural ramifications she needs to think through in light of her students.
>
> In terms of her scientific knowledge, Ms. Green needs to understand the mechanism of the process of condensation (that when water vapor in the surrounding air cools, its molecules lose energy, and thus it forms liquid water on a cold surface). In fact, she is excited to explore it alongside the children, to further her own understanding. She also needs to be able to anticipate typical ideas that children may have about condensation (such as thinking that water leaks through a can of ice water). She needs to "hear the science" in what the children have to say, and to have ideas about how she can respond.
>
> Ms. Green needs to plan a set of experiences with the phenomenon that could help children develop their thinking (such as putting food coloring in the water, or showing condensation forming on a cold hand-mirror). She should be able to draw on existing curriculum materials to help her devise these experiences—her district's curriculum materials, although not perfect, are an important starting place for her. Based on experience, she knows that she will need to make two key kinds of adaptations. First, she will make changes to the end of the lesson, to make sure that the children are doing the sensemaking. Second, she will make adaptations to address the specific needs of her learners, such as adding multiple kinds of language supports and making local connections.
>
> To make sure she is providing the linguistic resources her learners need, she thinks about the language demands of the lesson. She knows she can con-

nect to the word *condensación* for her Spanish-speaking children, plans ways of incorporating visual and multimodal supports (such as showing photographs and drawings of the observations, as well as building on the drawn models children will generate), and intends to encourage children to use multiple languages in their discussion—but she recognizes that she will need to develop additional ideas for language supports, to better support her emergent multilingual learners and her learners with auditory-processing challenges or language-based learning differences.

Ms. Green also needs to have strong content knowledge around the scientific practice of developing and using models, and she needs to know typical problems her students are likely to encounter as they engage in scientific modeling, as well as techniques she can use to support them in doing so. She wants to engage them in iterative model building, so she plans to have children develop an initial diagrammatic model, then return to develop a consensus model after the condensation lesson—and again after further lessons in the unit. One practice already in place in Ms. Green's classroom is having the children discuss conventions they will use in their models; this serves to advance their engagement in the disciplinary practice (helping them see the congruence between their ways of thinking and scientific ways of thinking), and also provides a way for the children to make choices about their own work. This helps them see themselves as knowledge generators and doers of science, which is important to Ms. Green in terms of helping the children develop identities as people who do science. Their models will be a key way that the children engage in sensemaking *and* demonstrate their understanding.

Ms. Green likes to engage her students in thinking about the purpose of an investigation, and the class has a series of thinking questions that they routinely use to make some key decisions about, for example, making and recording observations. To foster children's sensemaking through discourse, she will leverage a range of participation structures, including turn-and-talks for eliciting children's initial ideas about the source(s) of the condensate, small-group investigations, and whole-class guided discussions. She will reinforce the class' discourse norms of science, such as asking for evidence to support claims. Toward the end of the lesson, she will engage the children in a whole-class guided sensemaking discussion, during which she will elicit children's ideas, compile the small-groups' data (recording the data on the board systematically to allow children to see patterns across groups), and move children toward constructing their consensus model. She will make sure to highlight the work of some of her emergent multilingual learners, to make their contributions public. Later, Ms. Green will draw on individuals' and groups' written explanations and drawn models as a form of assessment to inform her next moves and also as a way to help the children develop science affinities.

SOURCE: Adapted from NASEM (2015, Box 5-1).

learners throughout their career and their experiences (e.g., Berland, Russ, and West, 2020; Rosebery, Warren, and Tucker-Raymond, 2016). This may be particularly true for preschool and elementary teachers, given how many subject areas and topics they teach.

PRESCHOOL AND ELEMENTARY SCIENCE AND ENGINEERING EDUCATORS

The last two decades have seen some shifts in the composition of the teacher workforce, but it has not kept up with the changing student demographics (NASEM, 2020). There are approximately 1.8 million public elementary school teachers in the United States (U.S. Department of Education, 2019), and another 2 million or so early childhood educators and caregivers (Early Childhood Workforce Index, 2018). Most elementary teachers are women (89%) and most identify as white (79%) (U.S. Department of Education, 2019). Among their many other responsibilities, these preschool and elementary educators largely are responsible for teaching all academic subjects, including science and engineering. That said, some schools and districts have dedicated specialists who teach these subjects, especially for grades 3–5 (Brobst et al., 2017).

These general findings also apply to early childhood teachers (AACTE, 2019; IOM and NRC, 2012). Additionally, most early childhood educators do not speak a language other than English (Early Childhood Workforce Index, 2018). More early childhood educators are people of color—around 40 percent—when the full range of these educators are accounted for, including those working in infant care and in home-based settings (Early Childhood Workforce Index, 2018).

Preschool and elementary teachers tend not to have degrees, extensive coursework, or certifications in science or engineering, due to the nature of elementary certification in most states; furthermore, elementary teachers tend to receive fewer opportunities for professional learning in science as compared to in other areas (Banilower et al., 2018; Doan and Lucero, 2021; Plumley, 2019). (Although these data stem from studies of elementary teachers, there is little reason to believe that preschool teachers are any more likely to have strong science backgrounds.) In addition, teachers with strong science backgrounds are not evenly distributed across schools in the U.S. (Banilower et al., 2018; NASEM, 2020). Given that an average of about 20 minutes per day is devoted to science teaching in elementary classrooms (Plumley, 2019), children today are less likely to experience science teaching at all, and when they do, most are unlikely to be taught by a teacher with a strong background in science. Furthermore, the uneven distribution of teachers has implications for the professional learning needs of teachers in higher-poverty elementary schools and for the availability of expertise with which to build collective capacity in those schools (NASEM, 2020; Sleeter and Owour, 2011), perpetuating long-term lack of access to science and engineering (Mensah and Jackson, 2018).

Identities and Dispositions[1]

Preservice early childhood teachers[2] may have unique motivations for becoming teachers. These can include wanting to emulate an influential teacher (Chang-Kredl and Kingsley, 2014) or wanting to take part in creating an equitable future for children (Goller et al., 2019), or perceiving oneself as good at teaching (Goller et al., 2019). Extrinsic motivations, such as job security or a job that allows time for family are sometimes in play as well (Goller et al., 2019; Liu and Boyd, 2018; Yüce et al., 2013).

As a standard narrative, preschool and elementary teachers are viewed as generalists who do not know or care much about science or engineering (Davis, Petish, and Smithey, 2006). In sizeable numbers, science representatives surveyed for the 2018 NSSME+ perceive lack of teacher interest in science as a problematic factor for science instruction in their school or district (Banilower et al., 2018; Plumley, 2019). Although the standard narrative about elementary teachers of science shows them as antiscience, lacking of knowledge of science, and/or fearful of science, research suggests that some elementary teachers have important characteristics or dispositions and knowledge that can enable them to further develop as teachers of science (Davis, Petish, and Smithey, 2006). For example, when in-service elementary teachers self-identified as scientists, their learners were more likely to document observations pre- and post-inquiry compared to respective learners of other teachers within the same grade level (Madden et al., 2010). Eick and Stewart (2010) showed that preservice elementary teachers were able to make up for not having a strong science subject-matter background by having positive dispositions. Specifically, four preservice elementary teachers in a teacher education program were studied, and each had dispositions that supported them in being able to use reform-based curriculum materials, such as inquisitiveness, investigation, and the inclination to learn alongside the learners in the classroom.

---

[1] This section draws in part on syntheses of the literature by Davis and Haverly (in press) and Zembal-Saul et al. (in press).

[2] In this chapter, and elsewhere where indicating preservice teachers who could teach preschool, the committee uses "preservice early childhood teacher" in recognition of the fact that teacher education programs for this population are typically termed "early childhood teacher education." Furthermore, for simplicity, the report used "preschool teacher" or "early childhood teacher" as a more inclusive term, rather than distinguishing between preschool teachers and aides. This necessarily glosses some differences in preparation and certification.

Beliefs Related to Science and Engineering Teaching

Generally, preschool and elementary teachers are assumed to have unsophisticated beliefs about both science and science teaching and to be scared of science (or engineering) teaching (Davis, Petish, and Smithey, 2006). For example, 31 percent of elementary teachers felt very well prepared to teach science as compared to their preparedness to teach mathematics (73%) and reading (77%), and they felt more prepared to teach life or earth science than physical science or engineering (Plumley, 2019). Yet beliefs are emergent in practice and change over time and across contexts (Hammer and Elby, 2002; Louca et al., 2004). As educators gain practice in teaching science and engineering, learning theory suggests that they will become more confident (e.g., Lave and Wenger, 1991). Work by Appleton and Kindt (2002) has shown that the adoption of reform-based science teaching practices by in-service elementary teachers is linked to self-efficacy, confidence, and support from colleagues.

Scholarship has looked at preservice and in-service elementary teachers' self-efficacy beliefs for teaching science (e.g., Bautista, 2011; Cartwright and Atwood, 2014; Gunning and Mensah, 2011; Menon and Sadler, 2016; Palmer, 2011; Sackes et al., 2012) and engineering and/or computer science (Hammack and Ivey, 2017; Ottenbreit-Leftwich and Biggers, 2017; Ozturk, Dooley, and Welch, 2018; Rich et al., 2017; Webb and LoFaro, 2020), including work that connected these self-efficacy beliefs to pedagogical content knowledge for teaching engineering (Perkins Coppola, 2019) or computer science (Israel et al., 2020; Ray et al., 2018). Generally, these studies suggest that elementary teachers' self-efficacy for science and engineering teaching is initially relatively low but can develop with time and experience. Additional research has examined other aspects of teachers' beliefs (Danielsson et al., 2016; Metz, 2009; Steele et al., 2013; Wilson and Kittleson, 2012), including beliefs of early childhood preservice teachers (Akerson, Buzelli, and Eastwood, 2010; Gullberg et al., 2018; Küçükaydın, and Gökbulut, 2020) and views of engineering and design (Hsu, Purzer, and Cardella, 2011).

Science and engineering teaching may also be shaped by teacher beliefs about children, and particularly children of color. In general, scholarship that does not specifically focus on elementary science or engineering suggests that white teachers tend to hold lower expectations for their students of color, that it is challenging for teachers to change their expectations of students, and that these low expectations can negatively impact students' learning (e.g., López, 2017). Rivera Maulucci (2010) found that the three participating fifth grade teachers' expectations of minoritized children as well as other characteristics of the school context and culture shaped the quality of the science learning experiences they provided; science was marginalized (in favor of mathematics and English language arts), and instructional quality, teacher morale, and teacher beliefs also suffered. Focusing on issues related to justice in teacher preparation, including for preschool and elementary educators of science and engineering, may support developing learning environments that are in turn supportive of children of color and children from other groups historically marginalized in science and engineering.

Knowledge Related to Science and Engineering

Generally, preschool and elementary teachers of science and engineering are assumed to have insufficient understanding of science and engineering subject-matter knowledge. Indeed, there is some literature that suggests that elementary teachers have some of the same non-normative ideas as their students do (see Davis, Petish, and Smithey, 2006, for a review). The subject-matter knowledge expected for elementary teachers is extraordinarily broad, making some of the expectations on these teachers unreasonable. Being able to position teachers as learners, furthermore, can open space for shared epistemic agency in classrooms (Berland, Russ, and West, 2020).

Cobern and colleagues (2014) tested the validity of an assessment instrument for measuring pedagogical content knowledge with 28 preservice elementary teachers. The authors found that the preservice teachers were able to make reasonable choices about different instructional approaches regardless of their science subject-matter knowledge, suggesting that elementary teachers may successfully compensate for shaky subject-matter knowledge. Exploring preservice elementary teachers' subject-matter knowledge, Nixon, Smith, and Sudweeks (2019) compared the knowledge of 169 preservice elementary teachers to the knowledge of 439 fifth and sixth grade practicing teachers. The authors found that preservice teachers scored worse on an assessment of their knowledge of science topics that in-service teachers were implementing. The authors conclude that elementary teachers are able to (and do) learn the science topics they are responsible for teaching, even without intervention. Together these studies and others suggest some important strengths of elementary teachers in terms of their knowledge for science teaching.

Other scholars looked at early childhood and elementary teachers' knowledge of specific topics or science areas, including greenhouse effect, wind, anatomy, biotechnology, species identification, evolution, the environment, energy in physical systems, and lunar phases (e.g., Palmberg et al., 2018; Rice and Kaya, 2012; Saçkes and Trundle, 2014)—demonstrating the broad (and sometimes esoteric) set of topics these teachers are apparently expected to understand, and some of these studies showed ways the teachers' knowledge was lacking. Some of these studies also show, however, how preservice preschool and elementary teachers can develop their knowledge with carefully designed experiences and that they do have important knowledge of many fundamental ideas in science (e.g., Rice and Kaya, 2012).

Overall, although many of these studies of subject-matter knowledge show areas where preservice teachers may struggle or lack knowledge, they also show that preservice teachers bring important resources to their understanding of the science and that they can learn science content through teaching and compensate for missing subject-matter knowledge when necessary.

SUPPORTING EDUCATOR LEARNING

As discussed in the previous sections, evidence suggests that preschool and elementary teachers bring strengths to the work of teaching science and engineering and that they also face some challenges. It is essential that teacher educators build on the strengths of those they educate and consider how to best support teachers in developing their knowledge, practice, and confidence. Furthermore, because these teachers teach multiple subjects (typically all academic subjects) and children receiving different levels of support (e.g., accommodations/services described in Individualized Education Programs), these educators are in the position of needing to balance a myriad of demands. This section addresses approaches of supporting educators in being prepared to engage in this complex work. The section turns first to preservice teacher education and then to ongoing professional learning for in-service teachers.

Preservice Teacher Education[3]

This section explores the roles of specific structures in initial teacher education, including content coursework, methods course, field experiences, and programmatic efforts. These efforts take place across contexts, including schools of education in universities, other university-based units (including, importantly, science departments, where content courses are typically taught), field placement schools or informal settings, and alternative certification programs. This section does not explore in-depth how to recruit teachers (particularly teachers of color) to preservice teacher education programs. It is important to note that there is less research examining the preparation of preschool teachers. In general, the reviewed research shows that most work in teacher education focuses on supporting preservice teachers' knowledge and beliefs, and less on their actual practice. This research also uncovers a relative dearth of work focused on equity- or

---

[3] The subsections draw heavily on recent reviews by Davis and Haverly (in press) and Zembal-Saul and colleagues (in press).

justice-oriented pedagogies in preschool and elementary science and engineering, though a few important examples of such work exist. The section turns first to research on the science content courses taken by preservice elementary teachers and how they learn science content.

Science Content Courses and Related Experiences

A key finding related to the role of science content courses is that they can support a range of outcomes, not just the development of subject-matter knowledge. This research explores a number of foci for teachers' needs, including how science content courses seem to

- build preservice teachers' subject-matter knowledge (e.g., Parker and Heywood, 2013);
- develop preservice teachers' self-efficacy, attitudes, and beliefs (e.g., d'Alessio, 2018; Menon et al., 2020);
- engage preservice teachers in science practices (e.g., Kim, Anthony, and Blades, 2014; Saribas and Akdemir, 2019); and
- help preservice teachers develop their instructional practices (e.g., Sabel, Forbes, and Zangori, 2015).

Overall, findings from these studies suggest that some designs can promote preservice teachers' subject-matter knowledge and self-efficacy beliefs and help them improve in their attitudes about science; some of this work shows positive relationships between subject-matter knowledge and self-efficacy beliefs (e.g., d'Alessio, 2018). Findings also suggest some approaches preservice teachers can take that are *less* supportive of their learning. For example, d'Alessio found that individuals who opted not to discuss science content when given the opportunity also decreased in self-efficacy after an intervention involving microteaching.

This body of research also explores other aspects of the courses themselves, including

- how science content courses can provide innovative models of instruction (e.g., Crowl et al., 2013; Powiertrzynska and Gangii, 2016; Riegle-Crumb et al., 2015); and
- the role of science content classes or other nature of science (NOS) experiences on views of the NOS (e.g., Akerson, Erumit, and Kaynak, 2019; Akerson et al., 2012; Bell, Matkins, and Gansneder, 2011; Hanuscin, 2013).

Findings from this work focused on innovative course design suggest that certain approaches—such as increasing engagement, providing hands-on experiences, or even incorporating a mindfulness component—may have positive effects not only on the preservice teachers' knowledge, but also on their beliefs and attitudes. To elaborate on one example, Riegle-Crumb and colleagues (2015) conducted a quasi-experiment comparing 238 preservice elementary teachers in the experimental group (hands-on science sequence) and 263 nonscience and non-education major students in the comparison group (regular lecture-based science course). The regular courses were similar to what the preservice teachers would have taken if the hands-on science class was not in place. Controlling for differences in the characteristics of the individuals in the groups, the study found that the students in the hands-on science coursework reported more confidence as science learners and an increased sense of science as relevant to their own lives, as well as more enjoyment of and less anxiety toward science. This was in contrast to the students in the comparison group, whose attitudes toward science declined after experiencing the traditional course. The researchers concluded that the use of a hands-on science sequence was associated with positive attitudes toward science learning.

Related to the learning of science content is the understanding of the NOS. For example, preservice teachers designed children's books to teach different aspects of the NOS to children during field placements (Akerson, Erumit and Kaynak, 2019). This strategy supported early childhood preservice teachers' understanding of the NOS and related pedagogical content knowledge. The studies related to the NOS suggest that explicit instruction in the NOS is important in shaping preservice teachers' views of the NOS—but they also show the importance of other kinds of experiences, including experiences that bring preservice teachers into the world of science (e.g., through science research or through interviewing scientists) and into the world of science teaching (e.g., through analyzing children's work or designing instructional materials).

Science Methods Courses

Elementary science methods courses positively shape aspects of preservice elementary science teachers' knowledge, beliefs, identities, and performances related to science teaching. Some of these studies focus on how science methods courses can affect (typically improve) aspects that matter in preservice teachers learning, including their

- beliefs and attitudes about science and science teaching (e.g., Avraamidou, 2013, 2015; Frisch, 2018; Wagler, 2010);
- beliefs and attitudes about science and science teaching, with regard to equity and justice (e.g., Bravo et al., 2014; Mensah and Jackson, 2018);

- identity development (e.g., Avraamidou, 2014; Naidoo, 2017; Settlage, 2011);
- knowledge (e.g., Buck, Trauth-Nare, and Kaftan, 2010; Mensah et al., 2018); and
- engagement in, beliefs about, or understanding of inquiry and/or science practices (e.g., Biggers and Forbes, 2012; Kaya, 2013; Kazempour; 2018; Wang and Sneed, 2019).

Some of these studies focus directly on equity and justice and suggest the importance of diversifying science teacher educators (Mensah and Jackson, 2018) and equity- and justice-oriented curricular design (Bravo et al., 2014; Mensah et al., 2018; Settlage, 2011).

Other studies take on important aspects of how science methods courses support preservice teachers in learning to do important aspects of teaching, including

- how they connect science and literacy (e.g., Carrier, 2013; Carrier and Grifenhagen, 2020; Wallace and Coffey, 2019), and
- how they plan lessons and use curriculum materials (e.g., Gunckel, 2011; McLaughlin and Calabrese Barton, 2013; Plummer and Ozcelik, 2015; Zangori et al., 2017).

For example, in a mixed-methods study of 55 preservice teachers, Carrier (2013) found that although preservice teachers entered the science methods course with limited subject-matter knowledge of science vocabulary, they improved in their knowledge during the course. They demonstrated, however, problematic vocabulary instructional strategies during their peer teaching experiences in the course (e.g., decontextualized use of vocabulary, introducing vocabulary at the start of a lesson and not returning to it). Results of the study highlight the importance of supporting novice teachers in learning effective instructional strategies for working on science academic language with children.

A third group of studies explore effects of more specific features of the science methods courses themselves, including:

- innovative uses of technology (e.g., Bautista, 2011; Bautista and Boone, 2015; Dalvi and Wendell, 2017; Olson, Bruxvoort, and Haar, 2016),
- approximations of practice and other features of practice-based teacher education and preservice teachers' characteristics (e.g., Bautista and Boone, 2015; Bottoms, Ciechanowski, and Hartman, 2015; d'Alessio, 2018; Wenner and Kittleson, 2018), and
- approximations of practice and other features of practice-based teacher education and preservice teachers' performance or practice (e.g., Arias

and Davis, 2017; Benedict-Chambers, 2016; Benedict-Chambers and Aram, 2017; Kademian and Davis, 2018; Lewis, 2019).

For example, Bautista and Boone (2015; see also Bautista, 2011) used mixed methods to study 62 preservice teachers in an early childhood program science methods class that was using a mixed reality avatar system for supporting the preservice teachers in learning to teach. The preservice teachers' self-efficacy increased over the course of the semester; factors that seemed to shape that self-efficacy included preservice teachers' sense of their subject-matter knowledge and whether they were being observed by their peers. The mixed reality avatar experiences seemed to complement and extend the preservice teachers' other opportunities for teaching, such as micro-teaching experiences with their peers. Together, this research on innovative uses of technologies suggests some promise of technologies in supporting preservice teachers' learning and enhancing their self-efficacy for teaching science and engineering.

Further work explored how approximations of practice and other features of practice-based teacher education—usually within science methods courses—could shape preservice teachers' characteristics or their performance or practice. (Practice-based teacher education emphasizes preservice teachers learning to do the responsive work of teaching and not only developing knowledge or beliefs related to teaching.)

For example, in a qualitative study looking at 22 preservice elementary teachers, Kademian and Davis (2018) found that preservice teachers planned to use a range of teaching practices likely to be supportive of leveraging children's contributions and that using carefully designed tools during planning a discussion seemed to support the development of their content knowledge for teaching as well as their teaching practice. Bottoms and colleagues (2015) explored how small-scale teaching experiences in an after-school STEM club in a dual immersion Spanish/English setting supported preservice teachers in developing their thinking about the teaching of science for equity. Together, the papers on practice-based teacher education listed above suggest that providing structured teaching experiences as approximations of practice can support preservice teachers in their development of their knowledge, beliefs, self-efficacy, and practice, although preservice teachers still struggled in some areas. These experiences were variously strengthened through the use of tools, virtual or technology-mediated experiences, or settings that included children with a variety of cultural and linguistic backgrounds.

Areas for further research include studies that explore how elementary science methods courses can shift preservice teachers' knowledge of or beliefs related to justice-oriented or antiracist pedagogies. Thompson and colleagues (2020) put forward a framework of four principles for practice-

and equity-based science methods experiences, including developing critical consciousness, learning about children's cultures and communities, designing for each child's full participation in the culture of science, and challenging the culture of science through restorative justice; frameworks of this sort warrant further empirical research. Another area for further work is the need for more studies to unpack the impact of using curriculum materials on preservice teachers' readiness for and ability to plan inquiry-based instruction and to differentiate instruction (e.g., by group size or by the intensity of instruction).

Field Experiences

Two key findings with regard to field experiences are that (1) they are crucial in supporting learning to teach preschool or elementary science and engineering and that (2) coherence between the field experience and the teacher education program can enhance opportunities to learn. Some of this research has focused on the roles of the practicum or student teaching in

- shaping preservice teachers' self-efficacy, beliefs, knowledge, and identities as science teachers (e.g., Chen and Mensah, 2018; Hanuscin and Zangori, 2016; Siry and Lara, 2012);
- shaping preservice teachers' practice or performance (e.g., Canipe and Gunckel, 2020; Forbes, 2013; Gunckel and Wood, 2016; Plonczak, 2010; Subramaniam, 2013); and
- shaping preservice teachers' characteristics *and* performance (e.g., Akerson et al., 2012; Biggers and Forbes, 2012; Cartwright and Haller, 2018; Forbes, 2013; Gunckel, 2013; Hawkins and Park Rogers, 2016; Olson, Bruxvoort, and Vande Haar, 2016; Smith and Jang, 2011; Sullivan-Watts et al., 2013).

Some of this work highlights the role of the mentor teacher (e.g., Canipe and Gunckel, 2020; Chen and Mensah, 2018; Gunckel, 2013). Other studies highlight the role of curriculum materials (e.g., Biggers and Forbes, 2012; Forbes, 2013; Sullivan-Watts et al., 2013). For example, Sullivan-Watts and colleagues (2013) followed 27 preservice teachers from their science methods class into student teaching. In this mixed-methods study exploring many of the dimensions that shape elementary science teaching, the authors found that most of the preservice teachers' lessons involved inquiry in some way. However, initially, many of these lessons focused only on observation or classifying and not more sophisticated sensemaking practices. The authors found that science subject-matter knowledge and preference for science teaching were both strong predictors of the quality of science lessons. The authors also found that using kit-based curriculum materials seemed to support structuring questions and investigations; the kits did not, however, seem to support sensemaking around data.

Further work explored particular characteristics of the practicum experience, including the roles of

- informal science teaching experiences (e.g., Bottoms, Ciechanowski, and Hartman, 2015; Harlow, 2012; Wallace and Brooks, 2015);
- cogenerative dialogue (e.g., Siry and Lang, 2010; Siry and Lara, 2011); and
- other kinds of characteristics, including linguistic diversity (e.g., Cone, 2012; Rivera Maulucci, 2011; Weller, 2019).

These studies add to the evidentiary base about the importance of the field and show how specific characteristics of that field experience can be important to name and nurture. For example, cogenerative dialogue during co-teaching in the field, or other purposeful experiences in the field, may offer a way for preservice preschool teachers to shift their perspectives to center children and their learning. Siry and Lang (2010) and then Siry and Lara (2011) showed how dialogue expanded children's action in the course of science investigations, and preservice teachers' awareness of children's learning. These experiences of co-planning and co-teaching with their mentors also seemed to foster identity development. These studies, together, point to the importance of experiences that allow preservice teachers to deeply engage with children and colleagues. These studies contribute to a key theme across this set of papers, namely, the importance of coherence between the program's stance and the field experiences.

Box 8-3 examines work that explores the supports needed for novice elementary teachers to work toward justice in science teaching—one focusing on the role of the cooperating teacher (Chen and Mensah, 2018) and the other focusing on the linguistic diversity of the field placement (Rivera Maulucci, 2011).

Programmatic Approaches

Thus far, the chapter has focused on discrete parts of a teacher education program that can support preservice teachers' learning; now, the attention shifts to the role of the program as a whole and the importance of coherence within the design and organization of programs. Programs can promote their particular vision through coordinated design and enactment efforts, and this may be particularly important in elementary and early childhood teacher education, given the nature of preschool and elementary teaching (e.g., Davis and Boerst, 2014; Sandoval et al., 2020; Zembal-Saul, 2009). Some studies of early childhood and elementary science and engineering teacher educa-

> **BOX 8-3**
> **Field Experiences in Support of Working Toward Justice in Elementary Science Teaching**
>
> Two examples illustrate some of the work that supports novice elementary teachers in working toward equity and justice in their science teaching. First, looking at the role of mentor or cooperating teachers, Chen and Mensah (2018) examined the role of the cooperating teacher in supporting the identity development of three preservice teachers in a social justice focused elementary teacher education program. The authors found that in this case study the preservice teachers' cooperating teachers had a particularly important role in shaping their identities as science teachers and as social justice teachers. For example, one cooperating teacher helped her preservice teacher become more comfortable in adapting lessons to children's interests. The cooperating teacher provided supportive feedback and positioned the preservice teacher as a role model. This helped to build the preservice teacher's confidence as a science teacher. Observing how their cooperating teachers did and did not enact social justice teaching informed how the participating preservice teachers saw themselves as positioned for engaging in social justice science teaching.
>
> A second example is from Rivera Maulucci (2011). Rivera Maulucci studied one preservice teacher and her identity as an urban science teacher. The practicum experiences were based in two dual language elementary classrooms. The preservice teacher herself was bilingual and was an immigrant. The author found that the preservice teacher's early experiences as a Spanish speaker and as a learner of English shaped how she viewed the intersections of language learning and science learning, her knowledge of which became more sophisticated as she participated in the dual language program field placements.
>
> These two small studies point toward approaches in the field that may support more justice-oriented science (and engineering) teaching in the elementary grades: placements with cooperating teachers who reflect the justice-oriented stance of the program in their science or engineering teaching, and placements in dual language contexts that can highlight synergies between science and language. Such placements may be particularly important in light of a finding from Gunckel and Wood (2016): the learning experiences the authors fostered between preservice teachers and cooperating teachers yielded rich conversations about inquiry—but very rarely included discussions of equity, despite the authors' encouragement of such discussions.
>
> SOURCE: Based on Chen and Mensah (2018), Gunckel and Wood (2016), Rivera Maulucci (2011).

tion experiences focus at the level of the teacher education program. These studies take up how a teacher education program can support

- development of self-efficacy, confidence, and beliefs (e.g., Ford et al., 2013);

- development of knowledge, beliefs, and practice (e.g., Arias and Davis, 2017; Bartels, Rupe, and Lederman, 2019; Todorova et al., 2017);
- cross-content efforts (e.g., Davis, Palincsar, and Kademian, 2019, integrating science and literacy; McGinnis et al., 2020, integrating computational thinking and science);
- school–university partnerships (e.g., Zembal-Saul et al., 2020); and
- efforts around equity and justice (e.g., Hernandez and Shroyer, 2017).

For example, Ford and colleagues (2013) studied the effects of an approach of a "science semester" in an elementary teacher education program. In this mixed-methods study, the authors studied 312 preservice elementary teachers. The authors were interested in the preservice teachers' self-efficacy and beliefs about science and science teaching. In the "science semester," preservice teachers were immersed in science for a semester of the teacher education program, taking courses in earth, life, and physical science as well as elementary science methods. The courses share an inquiry-based and problem-based learning approach, and the instructors make purposeful cross-disciplinary connections, involving extensive co-planning and co-design across instructors. By the end of the semester, the preservice teachers showed improved personal science teaching efficacy (confidence in their ability to be an effective teacher of science), some knowledge of inquiry-based instruction, and appreciation of problem-based learning. As with many studies of self-efficacy, they did not show improved science teaching outcome expectancy (confidence in the connection between their teaching practices and children's learning). The preservice teachers also expressed some concerns about their own experiences with learning through inquiry. Although some of the typical concerns lingered—most notably here, about engaging children in investigations—the integrated and immersive experience shows numerous benefits and much promise.

Examining the development of knowledge and skill of a high-leverage practice across a practice-based teacher education program, Arias and Davis (2017) used a case study approach to longitudinally study four preservice teachers across a 2-year practice-based teacher education program. The authors found that the preservice teachers became more sophisticated in how they were able to enact the high-leverage science teaching practice of supporting children in making evidence-based claims. The preservice teachers' prior experiences and backgrounds and the pedagogies of practice incorporated throughout the program were found to shape that development. The authors also identified some areas for further growth. Most notably, the preservice teachers tended to do some of the intellectual work for the children they were teaching. The preservice teachers' successes, though, suggest that practice-based pedagogies can support this challenging work, even for novices.

Hernandez and Shroyer (2017) conducted a qualitative study involving 12 Latinx preservice teachers who were generally bilingual, nontraditional, first-generation students. The participants were enrolled in a teacher education program with a purposeful pipeline design intended to diversify the teaching force. The authors looked at the participants' use of culturally responsive teaching strategies in their science and math instruction when teaching children with a range of cultural and linguistic backgrounds. The preservice teachers were mostly successful with some dimensions of culturally responsive teaching (e.g., connecting content to children's lives and building relationships with children), though they also experienced some struggles (e.g., facilitating knowledge construction). As with the science semester (Ford et al., 2013), the whole-program practice-based approach (Arias and Davis, 2017), and other papers in this section, as well as other literature focused on justice in elementary teacher education (e.g., Sandoval et al., 2020), the programmatic approach afforded some important strengths, while not, of course, addressing every area of need in elementary science teacher education.

Initial Teacher Education Summary

In summary, the literature makes clear how different facets of teacher education can support preservice teachers' own learning and development in areas related to the teaching of science and engineering. *Science content courses* can support the development of subject-matter knowledge, knowledge and beliefs about how scientists construct knowledge through engaging in practices, beliefs about science and science teaching, attitudes toward science and science teaching, and science teaching practice. *Science methods courses,* including practice-based teacher education experiences, can support the development of more positive beliefs, self-efficacy, attitudes, and science identities; knowledge; understanding of and engagement in science and engineering practices; instructional planning and the use of curriculum materials; and engagement in science and engineering instructional practices (including some regarding supporting children of color and emergent bilingual children). *Field experiences* can support preservice teachers' self-efficacy, beliefs, identities, knowledge, instructional practice, and use of curriculum materials. *Programmatic approaches* can support the development of self-efficacy, beliefs, knowledge, practice, cross-content work, and efforts around equity and justice.

Based on this analysis of the literature, it is important that the design of teacher education experiences for preservice early childhood and elementary teachers of science and engineering consider the following:

1. Incorporate opportunities for preservice teachers to develop knowledge, beliefs, identities, and practice, around...

    - *The value of science and engineering* for young children—to promote motivation for teaching these subjects in the first place
    - *Science and engineering content and disciplinary practice*—to work toward the vision for science and engineering teaching put forward in the *Framework*
    - *Equity and justice in science and engineering*—to ensure meaningful learning experiences for every child and to work to redress systemic forms of oppression
    - *The integration of science and engineering with other subjects or domains*—to improve the time available for meaningful science and engineering teaching and support children to make connections among content areas
    - *The effective use of science and engineering curriculum materials,* including for supporting sensemaking—to improve teachers' abilities to use curriculum materials
    - *Engagement in instructional practices,* such as eliciting and working with children's ideas and supporting children to use tools, make decisions, and refine their explanations and design solutions—to support preservice teachers' ability to promote children's sensemaking and identity development

2. Work toward coherence across the structures involved in initial teacher education, which could include science and engineering content classes, science (or engineering) methods classes, other content area methods classes, field experiences, and others, as well as coherence with future school workplaces
3. Build on preservice preschool and elementary teachers' strengths

Professional Learning Opportunities for In-service Classroom Teachers[4]

In *Science Teachers Learning* (NASEM, 2015), professional learning was described as being situated in formally organized programs offered by a wide range of individuals and organizations both within and often

---

[4] Portions of this section include content from multiple papers commissioned by the committee: "Engineering Education in Pre-Kindergarten through Fifth Grade: An Overview" (Cardella, Svarovsky, and Pattison, 2020); "The Integration of Literacy, Science, and Engineering in Prekindergarten through Fifth Grade" (Palincsar et al., 2020); "The Integration of Computational Thinking in Early Childhood and Elementary Engineering Education" (Ketelhut and Cabrera, 2020); and "The Integration of Computational Thinking in Early Childhood and Elementary Education" (Moore and Ottenbreit-Leftwich, 2020).

outside of school systems. That said, even when there were diverse and numerous professional learning opportunities available for K–12 teachers, they were shown as overwhelmingly disconnected from district curricula, removed from school contexts, and rarely provided coherent opportunities for teachers to develop increasingly sophisticated knowledge and practices over time. Much teacher learning, then, takes place outside of those formal programs. Rather than foregrounding descriptive accounts of professional development programs, that report focused on "connecting the dots" across teachers' opportunities to learn, teacher learning, and student outcomes. This serves as a jumping off point for exploring the literature more specific to this report's charge.

Overall, the evidence base on teachers' professional learning in science was not robust when the *Science Teachers' Learning* (NASEM, 2015) report was written. However, with the available evidence, a consensus model of effective professional learning experiences (*Science Teachers' Learning* Conclusion 5) was proposed. The consensus model put forward includes the following features (p. 118):

- content focus: learning opportunities for teachers that focus on subject-matter content and how students learn that content;
- active learning: can take a number of forms, including observing expert teachers, followed by interactive feedback and discussion, reviewing student work, or leading discussions;
- coherence: consistency with other learning experiences and with school, district, and state policy;
- sufficient duration: both the total number of hours and the span of time over which the hours take place; and
- collective participation: participation of teachers from the same school, grade, or department.

Studies that were intentionally designed to "connect the dots" (which included two studies focused on elementary science; see Heller et al., 2012; Roth et al., 2011) informed an extension of the consensus model. The extended consensus model included the following program characteristics (pp. 134–135):

- Teachers' science content learning is intertwined with pedagogical activities such as analysis of practice.
- Teachers are engaged in analysis of student learning and science teaching using artifacts of practice such as student work and lesson videos.
- There is a focus on specific, targeted teaching strategies.

- Teachers are given opportunities to reflect on and grapple with their current practice.
- Learning is scaffolded by knowledgeable professional development leaders.
- Analytical tools support collaborative, focused, and deep analysis of science teaching, student learning, and science content.

The Next Generation Science Exemplar System (NGSX) offers an example of a professional learning experience that aligns with many of these ideas and that is aimed directly at supporting the kind of instruction recommended throughout this report (Reiser et al., 2017). NGSX is designed based on the consensus model outlined above, and incorporates five design principles (Reiser et al., 2017, pp. 282–283):

1. Situate teacher learning in tasks requiring sensemaking of classroom cases.
2. Focus professional development on the science practices of argumentation, explanation, and modeling.
3. Help teachers connect what is new about the science, student thinking about the science, and pedagogical supports for the science.
4. Organize teacher study groups to apply the reforms to their own classroom practice.
5. Develop peer facilitators' expertise in knowledge-building facilitation.

In the design, face-to-face teacher groups work with an array of online resources, including rich video cases, to explore three-dimensional (3D) learning and teaching. Participants experience 3D learning themselves, examine student thinking and practices, and analyze how other teachers support students in those practices. The authors describe the theory of action as assuming that teachers "need to understand the core shifts in the reform by investigating examples of practice, and then work on how to apply them to their own practice" (Reiser et al., 2017, p. 294). As an example of a partial connect-the-dots study, examining how teachers' confidence, beliefs, and knowledge related to 3D learning shifted as a result of the professional learning experiences, the initial results are promising. Participating teachers (who included some elementary teachers, as well as middle and high school teachers) became more able to use disciplinary core ideas themselves to explain phenomena and became more confident about their ability to engage in this kind of teaching. They shifted in their beliefs about some teaching strategies (e.g., diminishing how they valued the pre-teaching of vocabulary). Finally, they became more sophisticated in their ability to reason about pedagogical scenarios involving science practices. The approach reflects the promise of focused professional learning experiences aimed at supporting instruction that centers children, investigation, and design.

Several focal areas are reviewed next: professional learning experiences to support preschool and elementary teachers in learning to teach engineering (and computational thinking); learning to integrate science and engineering with language art; opportunities for preschool teachers; and teaching toward equity and justice in preschool and elementary science and engineering.

Engineering Education Professional Learning Experiences

Universities and STEM education centers often serve as providers of engineering education professional learning experiences, and a few studies out of those organizations have explored the effects of professional learning experiences aimed at supporting elementary teachers in learning to teach engineering (e.g., Capobianco, DeLisi, and Radloff, 2018; Duncan, Diefes-Dux, and Genry, 2011; Guzey et al., 2014; Sun and Strobel, 2013; Watkins et al., 2018). These studies yield insights about the development of teachers' expertise around engineering education (e.g., Sun and Strobel, 2013) and the possible effects of professional learning experiences on their knowledge, beliefs, and/or practice with regard to engineering teaching (e.g., Capobianco, DeLisi, and Radloff, 2018; Duncan, Diefes-Dux, and Genry, 2011; Guzey et al., 2014; Watkins et al., 2018). Furthermore, in an example of professional learning experiences to support computational thinking, an after-school year-long professional learning opportunity was connected to work with both preservice and in-service teachers. The preservice teachers participating in the experience often integrated computational thinking into typical science lessons, but also saw an increase in their self-efficacy for teaching computational thinking (Cabrera et al., 2019, 2020; Ketelhut et al., 2019).

Research shows that these experiences vary widely; most common are in-person workshops (from 1-hour to multiweek programs), sometimes designed based on the consensus model for professional learning experiences (i.e., engaging teachers as learners in engineering activities, modeling effective practice, and making connections to teachers' work) (e.g., Sargianis, Yang, and Cunningham, 2012). Some of these experiences capitalize on the research happening at universities to bring preschool and elementary educators into engineering education (e.g., Duncan, Diefes-Dux, and Gentry, 2011; Guzey et al., 2014). Teaching engineering in the preschool and elementary grades is so new that this continues to be an important area for future research. However, Engineering is Elementary (EiE) provides one of the most extensive forms of support for teachers in learning to incorporate engineering into their elementary classrooms (Cunningham, Lachapelle, and Lindgren-Streicher, 2006). (A new curriculum, Wee Engineer, takes this work to preschool, as discussed in Chapter 7.) The EiE workshops incorporate many of the characteristics of effective professional learning experiences as described above. Over time, EiE developed first a train-the-trainer program and later a national network of certified professional learning opportunities providers to extend their reach (Sargianis, Yang, and Cunningham, 2012). These efforts help to build the expertise of the facilitators, one of the keys of the extended consensus model.

Museums and other sites of informal learning often serve as providers of engineering education professional learning experiences for preschool and/or elementary teachers. Several museums work as a part of the EiE network, including the Museum of Science in Boston (where the curriculum was developed), the Science Museum of Minnesota, and the Arizona Science Center. The Lawrence Hall of Science, the Exploratorium, and the Children's Museum of Pittsburgh also offer their own programs and partnerships for professional learning; for example, the Exploratorium partners with a California district to work with all of the elementary schools in the district. The New York Hall of Science engages both formal and informal educators in professional learning experiences using its Design-Make-Play framework that informs integrated STEM activity (Honey and Kanter, 2013) and in the STEM Educators Academy run by ExpandED Schools. Head Start on Engineering aims at engineering-focused professional learning experiences for preschool teachers.

Professional Learning Experiences Supporting Content Integration

Numerous scholars have studied professional learning opportunities for elementary teachers to learn to integrate science and literacy. Some of these include opportunities for teachers to ask questions, give feedback, and reflect on their personal beliefs and practices or to practice implementing instructional activities and pedagogical strategies (e.g., Hart and Lee, 2003). Some provide a range of forms of support across the year (e.g., Paprzycki et al., 2017). Some provide ongoing access to consultants such as science content experts or practicing scientists (e.g., Shymansky et al., 2013). Still others provide opportunities for co-design involving teachers and researchers (e.g., Fazio and Gallagher, 2019). Such experiences variously lead to more coherent and elaborate conceptions of both literacy and science instruction, improved knowledge and practices for teaching science with English learners, improved scores on standardized mathematics, reading, and/or science tests, and/or teacher-reported professional growth (e.g., Hart and Lee, 2003; Lee and Maerten-Rivera, 2012; Paprzycki et al., 2017; Shymansky et al., 2013).

In-service elementary teachers often express concern about their lack of science or engineering subject-matter knowledge. For example, in Stoddart and colleagues (2002) study of a professional development project to encourage in-service elementary teachers in rural California to focus on inquiry and language acquisition, researchers found that, initially, the majority of their 24 participants felt well prepared to teach either science or language, but not both. After the professional learning experiences, however, the majority of teachers believed they had improved in the domain initially perceived to be their weak domain. (See also Cahnmann and Remillard, 2002; Lee et al., 2016.)

Professional Learning Experiences for Preschool Teachers

Given the argument made throughout this report about the importance of engaging even very young children in science and engineering, what is known about professional learning opportunities for preschool teachers in terms of teaching science and/or engineering? Two recent articles provide some insight into this realm. Hollingsworth and Vandermaas-Peeler (2017) found that, after training in what the authors call "inquiry methods," the participating teachers reported using some inquiry practices, including observing and questioning; they did not, however, support children in more sophisticated practices, such as making predictions or evaluating evidence. The teachers noted that scheduling and time constraints as well as lack of materials all pose challenges to them in engaging children in inquiry-based science teaching. Brenneman, Lange, and Nayfield (2019) designed and iteratively refined a professional learning experiences model aimed at empowering preschool teachers in providing high-quality STEM learning experiences, particularly within schools serving children with a variety of cultural and linguistic backgrounds. Grounded in much the same literature as the consensus model presented above, the model included workshops, reflective coaching cycles (to provide individualized coaching), and professional learning communities. Taken together, these two papers suggest the importance of social supports (e.g., coaches, colleagues) and structural or systemic supports (e.g., materials, instructional time), as well as support for teaching strategies likely to be of importance in the preschool setting.

Other studies have examined the impact of professional learning experiences that aim to support preschool teachers' instructional practices for science. For example, studies of MyTeachingPartner—Math/Science (Kinzie et al., 2014; Whittaker et al., 2020) show positive effects of the combination of curriculum materials and professional learning experiences (designed drawing on the consensus model for professional learning). Findings from a 2-year quasi-experiment comparing the intervention to a business-as-usual comparison condition, involving 140 teachers in a range of early childhood settings, showed positive effects on children's science skills after the second year of the intervention, though the findings cannot clearly distinguish between possible effects of the *amount* of science taught from the effects of the *quality* of the science taught (Whittaker et al., 2020). An earlier study, comparing a business-as-usual condition, a curriculum-only condition, and a curriculum-plus-teacher-supports condition, found positive effects of the inclusion of teacher support—but only for mathematics outcomes, not for science outcomes (Kinzie et al., 2014).

Foundations for Science Literacy (FSL; Gropen et al., 2017) supports teachers as they plan and facilitate science learning experiences and assess children's conceptual understanding during science investigations. The program includes coursework, curriculum guidance, classroom-based assignments, and coaching. Findings from a randomized controlled trial with 142 preschool teachers indicated that teachers in the FSL professional learning program demonstrated higher quality of science teaching and improved pedagogical content knowledge in physical science relative to teachers in comparison classrooms. Furthermore, findings from an instrumental variable analysis suggest that the quality of science instruction mediated the relationship between FSL participation and children's science learning.

These large-scale studies reflect how the consensus model (or extended consensus model) for professional learning experiences, particularly in conjunction with supportive curriculum materials and coaching, can support preschool teachers in their science teaching.

McWayne and colleagues (2018) have also recently worked to co-design Readiness through Integrative Science and Engineering (RISE) (McWayne et al., 2020)—a relationally and culturally situated science, technology, and engineering professional development program—with Head Start preschool teachers and families with a variety of cultural and linguistic backgrounds. The RISE Home-School Connection component aims to "flip the scripts" on traditional notions of family engagement, bringing children's experiences outside of school into the classroom. The program suggests three strategies for teachers to learn what families know and do in science and engineering: (1) observe, talk with, and listen to children, (2) learn indirectly from families via neighborhood walks, and (3) learn directly from families by planning joint activities, family discussion groups and home visits.

Professional Learning Experiences and Equity

Relatively little work since the publication of *Science Teachers' Learning* (NASEM, 2015) has pushed forward with a focus specifically on teaching toward equity and justice in preschool or elementary science and engineering.

As one example, Lee and colleagues (2016) conducted a cluster randomized controlled trial study involving 103 fifth grade teachers. The study explored the effects of the P-SELL (Promoting Science among English Language Learners) intervention. The intervention combined educative curriculum materials—designed to promote teacher learning as well as children's learning—with teacher professional learning workshops taking place during the summer and throughout the school year. The workshops reflected many of the characteristics described above as the extended consensus model. The findings demonstrated positive effects on teachers' subject-matter knowledge and their (self-reported) instructional practices (including teaching for understanding, teaching for inquiry, language development strategies, and use of home language). Thus, the study connected some of the dots between teacher knowledge, teachers' opportunities to learn via professional learning experiences and educative curriculum materials, and teacher practice.

Marin and Bang's (2015) work with Indigenous educators in an out-of-school setting shows that connecting to "storywork" while designing science curriculum became part of a "decolonizing pathway" that reclaimed and situated Indigenous stories as part of science teaching and learning. Rosebery, Warren, and Tucker-Raymond (2015) worked with early career prekindergarten to seventh grade teachers serving learners from historically nondominant communities. As part of a 30-hour professional development program, they were able to cultivate *interpretive power*, or teachers' attunement to the diversity of children's sensemaking and ability to see their ideas as generative in science.

The ACESSE: Advancing Coherent and Equitable Systems of Science Education project (Penuel, Bell, and Neill, 2020) is a networked improvement community that involves science education leaders from several states with researchers from two universities, with the goal of enhancing vertical and horizontal coherence within and across state systems. A focus of the network is to enhance teachers' professional learning opportunities around formative assessment and equitable science teaching. Team members co-design and share resources and modules across state systems, to be used broadly to support teachers' professional learning. The team's framework for equitable science learning provides a guidepost for dimensions to which professional learning experiences around equity and justice should attend (Bell, 2019).

Professional Learning Opportunities for Classroom Teachers Summary

In summary, the extended consensus model put forward in *Science Teachers' Learning* (NASEM, 2015) is supportive of in-service teachers' learning. Models of professional development experiences or other professional learning opportunities for teachers typically build on the consensus model or the extended consensus model, wholly or in part, and results of studies of these experiences add to the evidence showing the efficacy of such models.

SUPPORTING EDUCATORS IN WORKING TOWARD EQUITY

Children's *increasing opportunities and access to high-quality science and engineering learning and instruction* (Approach #1) hinge on teachers teaching these subjects. If teachers do not see themselves as people who can do science and engineering or who can teach science and engineering, then they are unlikely to do so. Thus, bolstering preschool and elementary teachers' self-efficacy for science and engineering teaching and their identities as people who teach science and engineering, as explored in several studies reported in the chapter, is key. In addition, teachers need opportunities to learn to make these experiences accessible for children, yet the committee found little research on learning to support children with learning disabilities and/or learning differences (e.g., through differentiation) in science and engineering.

Toward the goal of *emphasizing increased achievement, representation, and identification with science and engineering* (Approach #2), work by both Mensah (e.g., Mensah and Jackson, 2018) and Avraamidou (2013, 2014) shows the importance of diversifying the teacher education workforce. These studies highlight the importance of seeing "people like you" in science teacher education, particularly for preservice elementary teachers. Representation also matters in terms of who the preservice teachers themselves are. This chapter highlighted one example of a teacher education program that is working purposefully to diversify the teaching workforce for elementary education (Hernandez and Shroyer, 2017); more scholarship in this area could be helpful. (An initiative of the American Indian College Fund aimed at increasing the pipeline of Indigenous early childhood teachers and improving Native early childhood education, for example, warrants further study in relation to science and engineering education.)[5]

Expanding what constitutes science and engineering (Approach #3) can include expanding teachers' perspectives on how a wide range of children engage in this work meaningfully. Several papers reviewed in this chapter show, in different ways, the power of placing preservice preschool and elementary teachers in field settings that include children with a variety of linguistic and cultural backgrounds (Bottoms et al., 2015; Brenneman et al., 2019; Rivera Maulucci, 2011). Furthermore, studies with practicing teachers emphasize the importance of providing focused supports for

---

[5] For more information, see https://collegefund.org/wp-content/uploads/2019/12/Early-Childhood-Education-Initiatives_B.pdf.

emergent multilingual learners. Lee and colleagues (2016), for example, used professional learning experiences in concert with educative curriculum materials to support teachers in learning teaching strategies for emergent multilingual learners, and Rosebery and colleagues supported teachers in coming to value a range of approaches to sensemaking.

The committee found few studies of preservice or in-service teachers with regard to *seeing science and engineering as part of justice movements* (Approach #4), though Marin and Bang's (2015) work with Indigenous educators would help position them to do so. The committee did identify a few studies that looked at teachers' identity as a social justice teacher (Chen and Mensah, 2018; Rivera Maulucci, 2011), which could be a step toward such work, as well as a framework that warrants further empirical exploration (Thompson et al., 2020).

SUMMARY

Preschool and elementary teachers bring numerous assets to their work in teaching science and engineering. Recognizing these teachers' assets—including aspects of their identities, dispositions, beliefs, and knowledge—and not focusing exclusively on what they may lack can help to flip the narrative about how to enhance science and engineering instruction in the early years.

Professional learning opportunities for preservice and in-service teachers need to build on their strengths. These learning opportunities can take a number of forms, but must provide a degree of coherence with teachers' professional contexts. In preservice teacher education, structures including science content courses, science methods courses, field experiences, and programmatic approaches can, collectively, support preservice preschool and elementary teachers in developing their knowledge, beliefs, identities, and practice. In-service professional learning experiences that focus on content and pedagogy, promote teachers' active engagement (e.g., reviewing children's work), focus on specific teaching strategies and ensure opportunities to grapple with practice, and build on analytic tools can support similar kinds of outcomes. Figure 8-1 summarizes how preservice teacher education and in-service professional learning experiences "connect the dots" from opportunities to learn to teaching outcomes.

As shown throughout this chapter, designing and providing experiences like these requires teacher educators and professional learning facilitators to have strong knowledge and expertise. For example, to teach preservice or in-service teachers about justice-oriented science or engineering education, one must have strong expertise about justice-oriented science or engineering education oneself. Similarly, to support teachers in learning about the teaching of engineering, one needs rich expertise around engineering teaching.

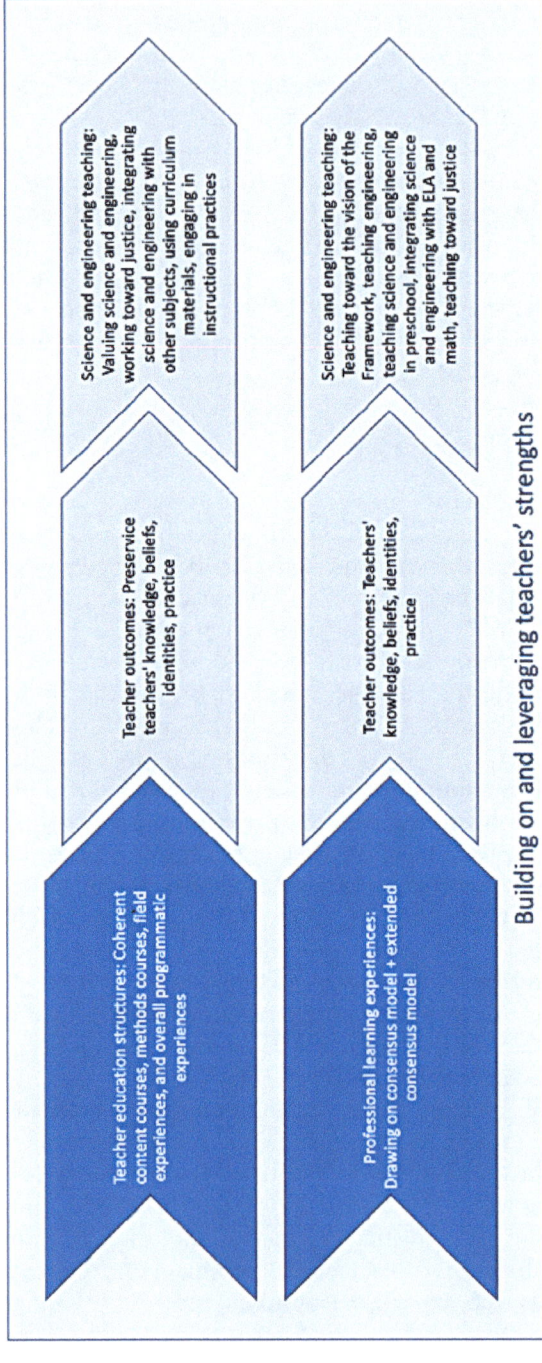

FIGURE 8-1 Connecting the dots: Designing learning experiences for preservice and in-service preschool and elementary teachers of science and engineering.
SOURCE: Adapted from NASEM (2015, Fig. 6-1).

9

Transformative Leadership

Main Messages

- Organizational culture, policy and management, and educator capability interact to shape instructional reform efforts in school districts.
- When preschool and elementary school and district leaders emphasize the importance of science and engineering education and foster shared responsibility for science and engineering instruction among teachers, science and engineering instruction is included as a strong part of the curriculum. These leaders also allocate time and resources and provide professional learning opportunities for teachers to develop expertise around science and engineering instruction.
- Although specialists can provide preschool and elementary science and engineering instruction when it may not otherwise be available, specialist positions appear to have the greatest impact when school and district administrators and other leaders are involved in science education and the overall district and school culture places value on science and provides resources to support it.

Providing robust science and engineering learning opportunities to all preschool through fifth grade children across gender and racial identities and socioeconomic and linguistic backgrounds requires considerable shifts in classroom instruction and leadership practices. Previous chapters outlined evidence-based instructional practices that center children, investigation, and design in preschool through elementary, but teachers' enactment of these practices can only happen if leaders create supportive conditions outside the classroom. These conditions are influenced by policies and practices at local, state, and national levels of the education system. Chapter 2 highlighted how some national and state policies have constrained time and resources for preschool through elementary science and engineering, while others have offered renewed consideration of the teaching and learning of science and engineering (i.e., as outlined in *A Framework for K–12 Science Education*; National Research Council [NRC], 2012).

This chapter focuses on how leaders at the local level, specifically in public districts and schools, have navigated this broader policy environment in efforts to transform preschool through elementary science and engineering education. There is not a significant research base on local leadership practices that support meaningful and equitable science and engineering instruction; thus, there is not sufficient causal evidence related to the effectiveness of particular practices. The committee thus considered descriptive evidence from diverse sources, including peer-reviewed journal articles, evaluation reports and other grey literature, and presentations made to the committee by experts and practitioners. Moreover, there is limited literature on the role of leadership in preschool and a dearth of literature on science and engineering. The literature that does exist examines professional development for leaders and the impact more generally on teachers, school climate, and outcomes; given that this research examines the early childhood education space there is some overlap with early elementary grades. Anecdotal accounts yield similar findings as described throughout this chapter—there is greater teacher participation when leaders are involved.

The chapter is organized around a framework for district and school leadership that considers three interrelated areas around which transformative change efforts align: (1) organizational culture, (2) policy and management, and (3) educator capability (Blumenfeld et al., 2000). Throughout, this chapter emphasizes transformation—specifically, the potential for leadership to create new organizational approaches to preschool through elementary science and engineering rather than adapting what already exists. However, few research and evaluation efforts focus specifically on transformative leadership practices that support science and engineering teaching that works toward justice, or on how leaders design systems around the assets and strengths of children with various racial, cultural, and linguistic backgrounds. Thus, this is an area for future research.

A FRAMEWORK FOR TRANSFORMATIVE LEADERSHIP

Scholars studying systemic instructional reform efforts in science education have identified three dimensions that interact to influence how these efforts unfold in U.S. school districts: (1) organizational culture, (2) policy and management, and (3) educator capability (Blumenfeld et al., 2000). This framework was originally applied to work bringing a middle school inquiry and technology science innovation to scale in a large urban school district; here, the committee uses it to organize the available evidence on local leadership practices that enable meaningful and equitable preschool through elementary science and engineering instruction. Figure 9-1 illustrates the framework, showing that the three dimensions are distinct yet related, with each affecting the other. The committee describes each dimension briefly in this section, then expands on each dimension in subsequent sections, including relevant examples based on the literature or committee member experience and expertise.

As described in prior National Academies of Sciences, Engineering, and Medicine publications focused on STEM education (see *Science and Engineering for Grades 6–12* [NASEM, 2019b] and *English Learners in STEM Subjects* [NASEM, 2018a]), the available research suggests that attention to all three dimensions is necessary to support transformative change in districts and schools. Although the vast majority of literature examining systemic change focuses on the K–12 education system, the framework also aligns with calls for a unified foundation in early childhood education that (1) is based on a sound vision and theory of child development and early learning; (2) attends to leadership, systems, policies, and resource allocation; and (3) provides support for high-quality professional practice (Institute of Medicine [IOM] and National Research Council [NRC], 2015). Given the emphasis on the K–12 system in the literature, the focus here is on transformative leadership across grades K–5; however, the committee

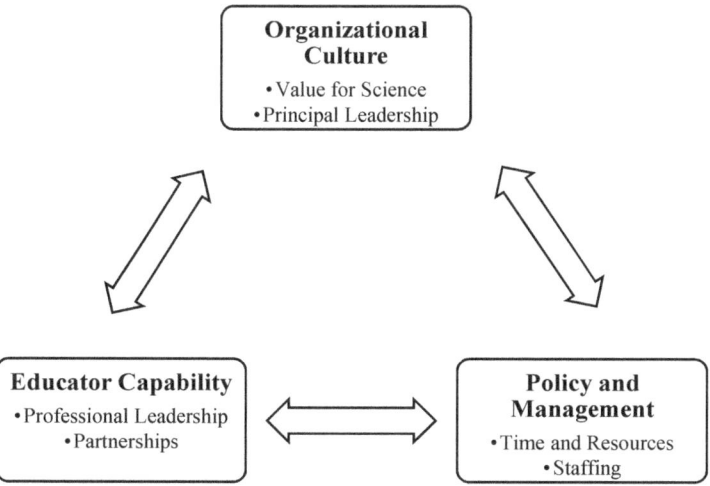

FIGURE 9-1 Dimensions of leadership.

recognizes the need for alignment and coherence from preschool through elementary school, and addresses this as an area for future research in Chapter 10.

Organizational culture encompasses norms, values, and expectations that shape educators' collective work. These norms, values, and expectations can operate to background or foreground the teaching of science and engineering in preschool through elementary schools. For instance, in elementary schools serving children of color from low socioeconomic backgrounds, science may be undervalued by educators because of a shared, implicit assumption that children need to develop basic skills in language arts and mathematics (Spillane et al., 2001). In other schools in high-poverty neighborhoods where science instruction is evident, principals have been found to foster school cultures that support teacher collaboration and distributed leadership, and that set clear goals and expectations making science a priority (Alarcón, 2012). Box 9-1 discusses how a new elementary school principal supported her school's organizational culture by focusing teachers' attention on science instruction during collaborative routines.

Enacting clear goals and expectations requires attention to *policy and management*, which includes funding, resources, and staffing. Instructional time policies and school scheduling are also important considerations. In districts and schools where there is an expectation that science and engineering will be taught in preschool through elementary grades, leaders can support this goal by allocating fiscal and human resources to purchase instructional materials, secure classroom space, and hire science coordinators or science support teachers (Alarcón, 2012; Casey et al., 2016; Miller, 2010; Spillane et al., 2001) or teachers' aides to raise staff-to-child ratios and allow instructional focus on STEM (IOM and NRC, 2015). This is also discussed in Box 9-1, which shows how the featured principal allocated specific time for science instruction across grade levels and encouraged teachers to take on instructional leadership roles focused on science. She also accessed resources for science instruction for her school through connections to external organizations (such as local universities) and grants (such as her district's Systemic Initiative).

Ensuring that these fiscal and human resources are used to teach science and engineering equitably and justly necessitates a focus on *educator capability*, or the beliefs, skills, and expertise that influence leadership and teaching practices. Although much literature indicates that many preschool and elementary teachers have limited preparation in teaching science and engineering (see Chapter 8), school principals also often lack the necessary knowledge and skills to make sense of and support instructional change in science (Halverson, Feinstein, and Meshoulam, 2011; Spillane, 2005). Overall, building on teachers' and leaders' strengths to develop educator capability specific to preschool through elementary science and engineer-

> **BOX 9-1**
> **How a School Leader Fostered Science Instructional Reform**
>
> Accountability measures in the public-school system contributed to Adams School, a K–8 school where 90 percent of the children received free or reduced-priced lunch, placing great emphasis on language arts and mathematics instruction. Other subject areas, such as science, were only intermittently emphasized as part of general efforts to improve instruction across subjects. Yet over a 12-year period, efforts to improve student achievement at Adams were successful, according to improvement in test scores, and the district recognized these gains by selecting Adams as a mathematics and science academy. In a district where the priorities and incentives emphasized mathematics and language arts instruction, and there was a strong conviction among staff that these children needed to master the basics in mathematics and language arts, how did science education become central to the work of Adams educators?
>
> Spillane and colleagues (2001) describe how attention to organizational culture, policy and management, and educator capability generated transformative change at the school. With respect to *organizational culture,* the Adams School principal, Ms. Williams, supported ongoing instructional initiatives to focus teachers' attention on curriculum and instruction and created opportunities for teachers to interact with and learn from one another. Efforts to build relationships and collaboration among the staff included the establishment of monthly grade-level meetings and school-wide mathematics and science committees. In terms of *policy and management,* time was allocated to science instruction at each grade level, and Ms. Williams encouraged willing teachers, including two teachers with an interest in science, to take instructional leadership roles. These science leaders, in turn, drew on existing science initiatives in the school, notably the science fair, to create time and space for science and to identify and activate the resources for science leadership.
>
> Although most of the initial instructional resources for leading change in science teaching were connected to the school's instructional agendas for mathematics and language arts, school leaders accessed and mobilized resources for improving science instruction through connections with local universities, colleges, and science institutions, as well as the district's Systemic Initiative, which focused on improving science instruction in district schools. Augmenting *educator capability,* relationships with these external partners created opportunities for professional development among teachers that were encouraged and supported by school leaders. For example, teachers participated in collaborative design projects involving the development and testing of project-based science curriculum units with local universities, who also sponsored an after-school program to help children prepare science fair projects.
>
> Overall, subject-specific instructional leadership, teacher leadership and collaboration, and external resources worked in tandem to develop the Adams School science program. These features of transformative leadership are explicated further in this chapter, drawing on the available literature.
>
> SOURCE: Adapted from Spillane et al. (2001).

ing instruction can support positive organizational cultures that express value for science and engineering for all children, as well as the creation of appropriate policies and the allocation of sufficient resources that ensure instruction is grounded in children's ideas and competencies. Box 9-1 also shows this aspect of the featured principal's work, highlighting how she leveraged the connections to universities to provide professional learning opportunities and experiences for the teachers at her school. The sections below expand on each dimension of the framework.

Organizational Culture

Schein (1985) describes organizational culture as "the deeper level of basic assumptions and beliefs that are shared by members of an organization, that operate unconsciously" (p. 6); Deal and Peterson (1999) define school culture as "an underground river of feelings, folkways, norms, and values that influence how people go about their daily work" (p. 9). Although the evidence base is small, findings from the extant literature focused on elementary science instruction point to the importance of a positive school culture that places a value on science teaching and learning for ensuring that science is taught in grades K–5. Some research examines implementation of the Next Generation Science Standards (NGSS) and therefore presumably encompasses science and engineering, but no studies of which the committee is aware focus exclusively on how school culture supports elementary engineering. In general, a positive school culture emphasizes a value for elementary science (Sikma and Osborne, 2015) and is characterized by strong principal leadership (Peters-Burton et al., 2019).

Value for Science

Qualitative studies of science teaching in elementary schools have found that when science is viewed as secondary to teaching language arts and mathematics, science is either not taught or is taught poorly, for example by providing decontextualized hands-on experiences (Meier, 2012; Spillane et al., 2001). Science may be undervalued due to a school's emphasis on high-stakes testing in other subject areas, or because of concerns that the school's student population needs more support in basic core subjects (i.e., language arts and mathematics). Overall, school values may influence teachers' expectations, with the beliefs system held by leaders concerning the importance of a curriculum area shaping the ethos for that area (Lewthwaite, 2006).

In an interview study examining leadership for science education in 25 K–8 schools in Massachusetts, researchers found that science was minimized due to the influences of state-level testing and teacher evaluation policies, conflicting district-level priorities, and limited time for teaching science in early, untested grade levels (Lowenhaupt and McNeill, 2019). As one principal in the study noted, "If they don't test it, it gets neglected," because "if we bomb science and do well in ELA and math, we are a high-performing school. That is the reality of where we are in education" (p. 473). These realities shaped the value placed on science education and thus the extent to which it was taught.

The extent to which the school culture supports a vision and value for science also shapes the resources and learning opportunities available for science teaching and learning (Spillane et al., 2001). As illustrated in Box 9-1, Spillane and colleagues (2001) describe how a new principal in a Chicago elementary school worked to concentrate attention on science by articulating a vision that included science inquiry for the primary grades, and identifying and procuring resources to build a science laboratory and hire a specialist teacher. Indeed, having both a vision and resources appears to be important for motivating the teaching of science (Alarcón, 2012). In a Canadian school district where there was a shared vision for science education *and* strategies and resources were in place to accomplish this vision (e.g., instructional materials, professional learning opportunities, coaches), teachers reported high rates of adequacy, knowledge, and motivation to teach science (Lewthwaite, 2006). Context and resources have been shown to make a large difference in the quality of preschool science education as well (James, Stears, and Moolman, 2012).

Principal Leadership

In the broader educational reform literature, principal leadership has been positively associated with student achievement (Hallinger and Heck, 2011; Wahlstrom and Louis, 2008), and has been found to have an indirect effect on elementary student outcomes through actions that shape school culture (Hallinger, Bickman, and Davis, 1996). Some of these actions are often referred to as *instructional leadership* (Leithwood and Mascall, 2008; Leithwood et al., 2009; Spillane and Hunt, 2010), which includes transforming school structures around new organizational routines that foster teacher learning and collaboration (Spillane, Parise, and Sherer, 2011) and implementing systems of instructional supervision (Camburn, Rowan, and Taylor, 2003; Donaldson, 2009; Hallinger, 2005). Principals can also play an important role as agents of science education policy implementation, buffering their schools and teachers from competing external demands and adjusting school structures to accommodate science instruction (Wenner and Settlage, 2015).

In a small survey study, Casey and colleagues (2016) describe how elementary principals in high-performing North Texas schools worked as effective instructional leaders by giving teachers time to write science curriculum, emphasizing the importance of alignment, and ensuring that science was taught at each grade level. They took a flexible approach to staffing when it came to science instruction and opted to departmentalize or use self-contained approaches based on teachers' and children's needs. Further, the principals reported focusing communication to teachers on science instruction, collaborating with them, observing instruction, and providing coaching.

The school principal appears to play an important role in creating an organizational culture that supports elementary science and engineering. However, research suggests that some elementary principals, and their administrative staff more broadly, lack expertise in science and thus the confidence to supervise teachers' science instruction (Lowenhaupt and McNeill, 2019). When asked about providing formative teaching observations and feedback as part of their instructional leadership, few principals described conducting observations focused on science, and noted that few teachers set instructional goals focused on science. When science teaching was observed, principals indicated taking a content-neutral approach that emphasized general aspects of teaching and learning. Thus, teachers had few opportunities for feedback specific to science teaching practices.

Given that principals tend to be prominent sources of advice and information for teachers in the area of science education, especially compared to other subject areas where specialists often serve as formal instructional leaders (Spillane and Hopkins, 2013), more research is needed to understand principals' roles in facilitating or hindering science (and particularly engineering) instruction in their schools and to identify effective leadership capacity building efforts (see Educator Capability section below). The next section discusses how district and school administrators have attended to policy and management in efforts to transform elementary science and engineering education.

Policy and Management

Policies and management structures that address instructional time, resources, and staffing are foundational to fostering an organizational culture that prioritizes preschool through elementary science and engineering instruction for all children.

Time and Resources

Aligned with the evidence reviewed in Chapter 2, a recent study of grade 3–5 teachers' uses of the practices articulated in the NGSS noted that teachers felt there was insufficient time to teach science and that they were not given adequate instructional resources to engage children with the practices (Smith and Nadelson, 2017). The NGSS Early Implementers Initiative attempted to address these barriers to elementary science instruction through a 6-year project in which the K–12 Alliance at WestEd provided eight California school districts and two charter management organizations support with NGSS implementation in grades K–8.

Findings from the project evaluation indicated that one of the most effective ways that district administrators communicated to all teachers that science was an instructional priority was by mandating a minimum number of weekly minutes of science instruction for each grade (Tyler et al., 2020). The majority of districts established new policies mandating 60 to 90 minutes of science per week in grades K–5, although one district mandated a full 2 hours of science in grades K–2 and 2.5 hours in grades 3–5. Some districts also officially sanctioned the integration of science during the allotted instructional time for English language arts and/or English language development. Results from evaluation surveys showed increases over time in the extent to which teachers were encouraged to teach science and felt that science was a priority at their schools (Iveland et al., 2017). These increases in time allocation for science were accompanied with substantial amounts of professional learning for administrators and teacher leaders to support NGSS-aligned instruction. Almost all participating teachers and administrators reported a positive change in the general quality of children's science learning and engagement as a result of their participation in the initiative, and children reported positive views about science beginning in grades K–2 (Tyler and DiRanna, 2018).

Systematically increasing instructional time has also been identified as an effective strategy for advancing science learning for children identified as English learners (Feldman and Malagon, 2017). This Education Trust-West study identified six California districts where more than the state average of English learners and children qualified for free and/or reduced-price meals and whose English learners scored higher than the state average for English learners on the 2015 standardized assessment in science. Findings from interviews and observations described how leaders in some districts made explicit commitments to increasing instructional time for science and to supporting English language development (ELD) through science learning. In one elementary school, teachers reported an increase from 1.5 days per week teaching science to 3 days per week, noting the affordances of integrating science and ELD instruction for children's learning (Feldman and Malagon, 2017).

Beyond designated instructional time, another important factor in supporting science and engineering instruction is administrators' provision of funding and the allocation of resources. In the NGSS Early Implementers Initiative, district and school administrators described advocating for the earmarking of district funds to support NGSS implementation and ensuring that school funds were channeled to provide resources specific to the standards being taught (Iveland et al., 2017). Principals also described allocating resources to create dedicated science spaces at their schools (often unused classroom spaces), buying new supplies and equipment for the space, and providing release time for teachers to arrange the room and add supplies.

These findings align with the leadership practices described in Spillane andcolleagues' (2001) study examining schoolwide efforts to transform science instruction in 13 K–8 public schools in Chicago. They described how principals identified and procured resources to build elementary science rooms or laboratories. Securing a science classroom was also found to be an important part of the critical resourcing school principals engaged in to support science education across three high-poverty bilingual elementary schools, in addition to purchasing bilingual materials for science (Alarcón, 2012). These descriptive studies also noted that some school leaders allocated resources to supporting science coordinator specialists or science support teachers. Such formal positions are an important aspect of staffing, the focus of the next section.

Staffing

A small body of literature examines the role of science specialists in the management of elementary science instruction. There are three general models around which specialists are incorporated into a school's science instructional approach. The first has been variously labeled departmentalization (Schwartz and Gess-Newsom, 2008), team teaching (Brobst et al., 2017), and a collaborative specialist model (Nelson and Landel, 2007). It does not require hiring additional staff, as teachers at a grade level (or sometimes multiple grades) divide up responsibility for specific subject areas, with one or more assigned as the science teacher(s). Then, children rotate through teachers' classrooms during the day. Although this model helps to ensure there is time allocated for science (and engineering) instruction, it does not necessarily support integration across content areas or foster shared responsibility for the teaching of science and/or engineering.

In the second model, often referred to as a pull-out or special area model, one teacher provides science instruction to children across grade levels. These teachers can be based in a single school (Brobst et al., 2017; Marco-Bujosa and Levy, 2016; Schwartz and Gess-Newsom, 2008) or assigned to multiple schools in a district (Schwartz, Lederman, and Abd-El-Khalick, 2000). This model requires additional staffing and resources, as specialists often have a dedicated laboratory or classroom space. This model also ensures that instructional time is dedicated to science and engineering, at least for some grade levels, and that it is taught by a teacher with subject-matter expertise. As in the departmentalized approach described above, this model does not necessarily support integration across content areas or foster teachers' capacity in the areas of science and engineering. This separation can be mitigated, however, if teachers are required to teach an integrated science unit in their classrooms, as supported by the specialist (Marco-Bujosa and Levy, 2016).

The third model utilizes school-based coaching (Berg and Mensah, 2014) or a district science coordinator (Whitworth et al., 2017a, b). There are fewer studies examining science coaching than the above described models, especially when considering the burgeoning literature on literacy and math coaching (e.g., Coburn and Woulfin, 2012; Hopkins, Ozimek, and Sweet, 2017; Mangin and Dunsmore, 2015; Mayer, Woulfin, and Warhol, 2015; Sun et al., 2014). Coaches provide mentoring and professional development to teachers, which may include co-planning and co-teaching in addition to resource provision (Schwartz and Gess-Newsom, 2008). The specialist can be a full-time instructional coach, or a part-time teacher leader who has content expertise and provides coaching to teachers in their school (Klein et al., 2018; Wenner, 2017) or district (Whitworth et al., 2017a, b).

The committee found a small body of literature examining the effectiveness of these science specialist models, and no literature on elementary engineering specialists. One study conducted in seven districts in the Pacific Northwest compared the knowledge, preparedness, and instructional quality of elementary science specialists (n = 19) and self-contained classroom teachers (n = 16) in grades K–5 (Brobst et al., 2017). The specialists in the study, who taught either in a team-teaching or pull-out model, were more likely to have subject-matter expertise in science than self-contained teachers and to indicate higher ratings on content knowledge, feelings of preparedness to teach science, and familiarity with science standards. Based on observations of their teaching, specialists also scored higher on some measures of instructional quality than self-contained teachers. These measures were associated with the time participants were given to plan for and teach science, suggesting that the time afforded to specialists to engage with science curricula enabled higher-quality teaching.

In another study of 30 schools in one large northeastern urban district, researchers examined whether the quality, quantity, and/or cost of science instruction differed when that instruction was provided by a science specialist or by a self-contained classroom teacher, using children's scores on statewide science achievement tests and children's engagement in science lessons as outcome measures (Levy et al., 2016). Focused on fourth and fifth grade student outcomes, the results showed greater differences at the school level than across classrooms. Although funding mattered (i.e., schools where science was poorly funded typically produced poor student outcomes but the reverse was not always true), the best outcomes were associated with the value placed on science and principal support (e.g., instructional leadership, materials, support for ancillary activities), regardless of whether the science instruction was being provided by a science specialist.

Based on a follow-up study of five schools from the larger sample where specialist models were in place, Marco-Bujosa and Levy (2016) noted that, although the science specialist model ensures that science will be taught, a lack of support from self-contained classroom teachers and especially the principal could marginalize science as a subject area. Thus, although the specialist model provided time and space for science instruction, strong principal leadership was necessary to provide appropriate resources, foster shared responsibility for science instruction, and prioritize external pressures in ways that made sure that science was taught.

In another study examining pull-out specialist models, Schwartz and colleagues (2000) compared instructional planning between science specialists and self-contained classroom teachers, as well as student achievement between a specialist-led district and a nonspecialist district. In the specialist-led district, children in fourth through sixth grades had two 45–55-minute science lessons each week, taught by a specialist in a fully equipped science room. Collaboration between the specialist (who had completed a greater number of science credits than teachers) and classroom teachers was expected, with co-facilitation of lessons and follow-up provided to children who missed science lessons. In this district, the instructional planning of science specialists was better aligned with reform-based practices when compared to classroom teachers, and children taught by the specialists were more engaged in inquiry-oriented activities and demonstrated critical thinking abilities. However, when comparing children's outcomes between the specialist-led and nonspecialist district, findings revealed no significant differences in outcomes on state science tests for children.

Finally, Miller (2010) described how a high-achieving school district utilized a combined coordinator and coaching model. The district had a K–12 science department that included a coordinator at each of the district's five school buildings as well as teachers from each grade K–5 from both elementary schools who were the "go-to" science people for teachers on their grade level teams. Building coordinators received extra compensation and oversaw efforts to teach science in their schools, which included ordering textbooks and kits. This K–12 departmental structure "resulted in a network of teacher leaders throughout the district that ensured that science had an advocate in every grade and linked every grade with the expertise of the high school science teachers" (Miller, 2010, p. 25). This cascading specialist structure contrasted with a similarly sized yet lower achieving district, where leadership for elementary science was left up to principals and a district curriculum director. Although the director reorganized the science curriculum around kits and provided professional learning opportunities for teachers, the lack of school-based specialists limited teachers' implementation of the new curriculum.

Taken together, the evidence base focused on policy and management for elementary science and engineering education signal the importance of district- and school-level supports in the form of funding, resources, and staffing. Although studies on elementary science specialists indicate that these positions have the potential to ensure the allocation of instructional time for science and engineering and to positively shape science instruction, they are not a panacea. The literature suggests that, to transform teaching and learning, when specialist positions are employed, they must be accompanied by strong leadership that expresses value for science and engineering, affords sufficient resources, and fosters shared responsibility. The literature also suggests that these values are important when classroom teachers are responsible for science instruction (i.e., in the absence of specialist). The next section examines how attending to educator capability may engender these positive changes in the teaching and learning of science and engineering.

Educator Capability

Like other educational change efforts, transforming science and engineering instruction necessitates deep teacher learning and shifts in teachers' knowledge and beliefs (Cohen, 1990; Spillane, 2004). Support for these shifts often comes from embedded, ongoing professional learning opportunities supported by strong instructional leadership (Hallinger, 2005; Lowenhaupt, 2014). Yet, as noted above, school principals and other leaders may lack the necessary knowledge, resources, and skills to make sense of such reforms, particularly in science (Halverson, Feinstein, and Meshoulam, 2011; Spillane, 2005). Chapter 8 focused on the development of educator capacity through the support of teachers' professional learning. This section reviews the available literature on professional learning for leaders in elementary science and engineering, as well as the role of partnerships in supporting educator capability.

Professional Learning for Leaders

When leaders lack sufficient knowledge, they are not able to support teachers in transforming their instruction. Supporting a cascading leadership model may be important for developing educator capability, where both administrators and teacher leaders are supported in advancing instructional change in science and engineering. Shymansky et al. (2013) described a professional development model focused on developing local leadership and gradually transferring responsibilities from experts external to districts to teacher and administrator leadership teams within each district. The first year of professional development focused exclusively on working with these leadership teams. After the first year, the teacher members worked in cross-district professional learning communities to build portfolios of adapted lesson plans on selected science topics, which they then supported fellow teachers in their home schools to implement with principal support. Science achievement scores of grade 3 and grade 6 student cohorts on the two forms of the Trends in International Mathematics and Science Study administered at the beginning, middle, and end of the professional development effort revealed a V-shaped pattern of scores, suggesting that teachers struggled with the newly adapted science inquiries at first but then became more effective in their use.

Teacher leadership was also an important component of the NGSS Early Implementers Initiative (Tyler et al., 2019). In each district involved in the Initiative, a Core Leadership Team of nine teachers and three administrators was established to work with the district's Project Director in planning and leading NGSS implementation. The teachers on these teams were called the "Core Teacher Leaders." At the end of the first year, each district recruited between 30 and 60 Teacher Leaders, depending on the size of the district, with the understanding that they would be responsible for sharing their expertise with other teachers of science in their districts. Teacher Leaders were provided extensive professional development in the NGSS practices, with the Core Teacher Leaders also receiving leadership training. Core Teacher Leaders facilitated learning communities for Teacher Leaders; in addition, all Teacher Leaders led professional learning activities at their school sites and collaborated with colleagues at their schools to co-plan and co-teach lessons. These findings suggest that, in general, building capacity for teacher leadership among teachers and providing formal structures for them to engage with colleagues can be helpful in fostering teacher collaboration and learning more broadly.

Beyond teacher leadership, the literature suggests that attending to the capability of administrators is also important. Based on findings from a study of instructional supervision in science involving 25 K–8 principals, McNeill, Lowenhaupt, and Katsch-Singer (2018) found that principals were more likely to attend to science practices focused on investigation as opposed to science practices that supported sensemaking or critique. To principals, investigating meant engaging in any hands-on science activity or general exploration. When asked to discuss their observations of classroom videos, principals focused on general pedagogy and children's engagement rather than specific science practices, and their evaluations of the videos did not align with science practices (e.g., some rated a video using direct instruction as aligned with the science practices).

The NGSS Early Implementers Initiative supported principal professional learning in several ways (Iveland et al., 2017). Initially, all administrators attended an annual Summer Institute for Teacher Leaders as well as biannual leader trainings, yet project directors found that some site leaders still lacked an understanding about NGSS. As such, project staff planned a 2-day Academy that provided principals opportunities to learn and talk with their peers about the pedagogical shifts required by the NGSS and how to support NGSS implementation in their schools. To assist principals in communicating with teachers about science and engineering instruction, the Initiative also developed an "Evidence of Learning" protocol for use when observing Teacher Leaders' lessons.

Similarly examining leadership engagement in professional development for elementary science instruction, Whitworth and Chiu (2015) share preliminary results from VISTA, a project aimed to build an infrastructure to support sustained, intensive science teacher professional development to increase learners' performance. VISTA included an Elementary Science Institute that specifically included school principals and district science coordinators in professional development activities, during which they engaged with teams of teachers who were focused on understanding problem-based learning, inquiry, and nature of science. Following the professional development, principals reported an increased understanding of how to support science teachers, and teachers rated their principals higher at being effective in supporting science instruction following the professional development.

Overall, these studies suggest that attention to district and school leadership structures is important for fostering educators' capability to transform elementary science and engineering instruction. They describe how professional learning aligns across district, school, and teacher leaders, and thus shapes principal supervision and supports teacher learning. The next section discusses nascent research on how partnerships can also support this work.

Partnerships

Partnerships with science and engineering institutions and organizations, as well as institutes of higher education, may help to support district- and state-level efforts to advance educator capability. For instance, informal learning organizations such as science centers, nature centers, and botanical gardens have been an important source for coaching and capacity building for elementary science teachers (Bevan et al., 2010; Chiu, Price, and Ovrahim, 2015). Collaborations between these kinds of institutions and both pre- and in-service teachers can include sustained interactions that have the potential to have significant impact on teachers' capacities and practices, although most evidence of effectiveness to date is found in evaluations of specific programs. Feldman and Malagon (2017) describe how science centers, such as the Lawrence Hall of Science at the University of California at Berkeley and the Exploratorium in San Francisco, worked with school districts and university partners in the BaySci program to provide in-person and virtual professional learning opportunities for teachers, teacher leaders, and district leaders. An evaluation of the program (Remold et al., 2014) drew on interviews and surveys with participants to report that the program had been largely successful in producing meaningful shifts in teachers' instructional practices in the nine participating districts, shifting district leadership and culture regarding science teaching, and building district capacity to engage in reform of current district policies regarding science teaching and learning.

Another example of how districts can partner with organizations to build educators' capacities is found in the collaborative model that has been used by ExpandEDSchools to leverage the expertise of teacher educators from the informal sector. Their Design2Learn and STEM Educators Academy programs (Murchison and Banay, 2019) both bring classroom teachers and community educators to learn from museum educators and to work together to develop aligned approaches to engineering education across childrens' formal and informal science learning experiences. Evaluations of ExpandEd's STEM Educators Academy Program have demonstrated growth in classroom teachers' sense of self-efficacy, and participating teachers perceived greater enthusiasm and understanding of the target science concepts among their children (Banay, 2021).

The evidence base regarding effective methods for partnering universities with K–12 school districts to support elementary science teaching is broad but diffuse. Much of the work in this domain was done in the context of Math–Science Partnerships (MSPs), a federally targeted program funded by the National Science Foundation through formula grants that supported the development and study of a wide range of university–school partnerships, all seeking to improve science teaching in some or all of the K–12 grades. Much of the literature on MSPs is evaluative—many program models have been piloted and some have been shown to have positive effects on student achievement in mathematics and science (e.g., Dimitrov, 2009)—but there is little evidence that identifies specific, scalable approaches to organizing, implementing, and sustaining these kinds of partnerships (Yin, 2008). With the passage of the Every Student Succeeds Act, the MSP program was eliminated and combined with several other formula grant programs. The loss of MSP funds significantly impacted state-level implementation efforts; thus, these programs are now under the purview of local districts to continue implementing with their own resources.

In discussing university-based partnership initiatives involving several school districts, Avendano and colleagues (2019) points to the example of the work of the Center for Innovation in STEM Education (CISE) at California State University of Dominguez Hills. CISE provides programs for elementary and secondary children that foster a pipeline for undergraduate STEM majors. These undergraduates are supported to become teachers and offered continued support through Teacher Leader Programs that are also available to other teachers at their schools. CISE also offers STEM Lab Schools within high-poverty schools that serve as a training ground for teachers and invite parents and community members to workshops and training. This example illustrates the potential of a university partnership for creating multiple opportunities that attend to educator capability.

Several initiatives have sought to create broad, multistakeholder approaches to building what Fuller (2020) calls "innovation clusters," in which schools or districts partner with multiple actors in their local communities to build coherent networks of STEM learning opportunities for young people. Pittsburgh's Remake Learning initiative, for example, has worked at a regional level to bring children, teachers, administrators, and families into contact with a broad range of STEM learning experience outside of the school building and school day, but systematic investigations of the impact of these efforts, or the mechanisms of their influence, are not available. The Noyce Foundation-funded STEM Ecosystem Network, a different model that also seeks to support diverse partnerships with schools, has primarily focused on youth outcomes, rather than on building school or educator capacity and has generally focused on middle- and high-school age youth (Allen et al., 2020). Models such as these, which include "the influence of families and peers; out-of-school-time offerings such as afterschool programs; and community resources such as science centers, libraries and media" (Krishnamurthi et al., 2014), could be explored as potential strategies to support and expand more focused collaborations with elementary science teachers.

Leaders of the NGSS Early Implementers Initiative also recognized the importance of engaging the community in their capacity-building efforts (Iveland et al., 2017). One-third of district and school administrators in the project reported doing some kind of community outreach as a way to support NGSS implementation. One elementary school principal from the project was quoted in Rammer and colleagues (2017), noting "Administrators can help establish the bridges that connect teachers to resources throughout the community. They can devote time to making the phone calls and weaving through the possibilities for community connections that will partner with the teachers to make their work relevant to students and the community."[1] Additionally, Project Directors reported reaching out to

---

[1] See https://classroomscience.org/articles/ngss/ngss-early-implementers/supporting-and-enhancing-ngss-implementation-tale-two-principals-efforts.

science-oriented companies, museums, and other organizations, with one Director bringing together several local organizations to discuss how the organizations might support teachers with NGSS implementation. Further, some Early Implementer districts indicated that they were working on family science nights to help introduce the community to the NGSS and coordinating with local businesses to support the NGSS by providing resources or information about local science topics.

Although these examples suggest the importance of creating an ecosystem for preschool through elementary science and engineering education for fostering educator capability across districts and schools, more research is needed that examines how, and under what conditions, community partnerships can contribute most powerfully to leadership and instructional transformation. Moreover, given that the committee found no studies explicitly examining how family partnerships play a role in supporting educator capability, this is also a much-needed area of research.

TRANSFORMATIVE LEADERSHIP AND EQUITY

Leaders can support children's *increased opportunities and access to high-quality science and engineering* (Approach #1). As emphasized throughout this report, children have the right to engage with science and engineering. Principals and other leaders play an important role in setting up the conditions that allow that to happen. Principals who foster school cultures that support teacher collaboration and distributed leadership and who make it clear that science is a priority—for example by setting expectations around instructional time—can support the teaching of science even in settings where science would typically be rare (Alarcón, 2012; Iveland et al., 2017; Spillane et al., 2001; Tyler et al., 2020).

Although the committee did not find any research that explicitly focused on the connections between leadership and *increase achievement, representation, and identification with science and engineering* in preschool and elementary settings (Approach #2), it is clear that focusing on educator capability (such as through providing professional learning experiences or through using science specialists) has the potential to support teachers as they endeavor to engage children in higher-quality learning opportunities, which would in turn support children's achievement.

Because organizational culture encompasses the norms, values, and expectations that shape educators' work, taking an *expansive perspective on what constitutes science and engineering* should in turn shape the organizational culture (Approach #3). Thus, principals have a role to play in expanding what counts as science and engineering (even though the committee found no work directly related to this issue in terms of the marginalization of certain children). The committee *did* find literature related to expanding a perspective on what constitutes science and engineering in a more general sense (McNeill et al., 2018)—suggesting that principals need support in expanding their own perspectives on what constitutes science and engineering.

The committee did not find evidence related to how leaders could support schools in recognizing *science and engineering as part of justice movements* (Approach #4). Logically, though, principals' leadership could extend to this issue, and they could promote this as a school value; this is an area for further research.

SUMMARY

The evidence presented in this chapter illustrates the importance of district and school leadership in developing contexts that support science and engineering education in preschool through elementary. Ensuring that district and school leaders have instructional expertise in science and engineering is helpful but insufficient. The literature suggests that successful reform efforts include formal structures (e.g., time), resources, and routines (e.g., learning communities) that prioritize and demonstrate value for science and engineering instruction across grade levels. These efforts can be supplemented by science (and engineering) specialists and via external partnerships, but simply adding specialist positions or partnering with outside institutions is not likely to result in the transformative change that is necessary for all children to have access to robust learning opportunities. Each dimension of transformative leadership explored in this chapter—organizational culture, policy and management, and educator capacity—must be considered, as well as how these dimensions connect to and interact with one another.

10

Progressing Toward a Vision for Science and Engineering in Preschool Through Elementary Grades

The committee was charged with examining the available evidence on science and engineering in preschool through elementary grades, including the approaches and strategies that can be used by teachers, providers of professional learning opportunities, administrative leaders, education researchers, and policy makers to provide all children with high-quality learning experiences. Science and engineering have contributed to systemic injustices against historically marginalized communities, shaping the relationships these individuals and communities have with science and engineering and how they engage with learning. Engaging all children in science and engineering requires significant changes to what both children and teachers do in the typical classroom, what curricular materials promote, and what school systems value. Because many aspects of science and engineering are part of children's daily lives, contextualizing science learning by integrating what children bring to the classroom into science and engineering instruction can support learning.

The committee considered the four approaches to equity outlined in Chapter 1 and threaded throughout the report: (1) increasing opportunity and access to high-quality science and engineering learning and instruction; (2) emphasizing increased achievement, representation, and identification with science and engineering; (3) expanding what constitutes science and engineering; and (4) seeing science and engineering as part of justice movements. Together, these four approaches comprise a spectrum of ways that the field can work toward equity and justice in preschool and elementary science and engineering, with the third and fourth centering more squarely on justice.

Individual educators, districts, and states differ in how they orient to and address issues of equity and justice, both in general and in the specific context of preschool through elementary science and engineering. Furthermore, any efforts—whether they are focused on increasing the amount of science or engineering taught to children, improving the quality of that instruction, providing wider representation of who does science and engineering, recognizing a wider variety of ways of knowing in science and engineering, or full-on taking up issues of, for example, environmental justice or health disparities—can serve to help schools and other settings for learning work toward equity and justice in important ways. Therefore, the report has attempted to make visible approaches to engaging in the full range of facets of this work, and has aimed to be supportive of educators interested in working toward change or in expanding on their existing work. The committee recognizes that the kind of curricular, instructional, and relational work described in this report can be hard and uncomfortable. It can require difficult introspection on one's own (perhaps unconscious) biases, reflection on current and past practices and their effects on children, tough conversations with colleagues or administrators, and perhaps challenging relationships with families. At the same time, this work may lead to positive impacts for children and educators as well as the fields of science and engineering. Toward these ends, individuals or groups of individuals (e.g., teachers, leaders, grade-level teams, state science coordinators, policy makers) may work for change via these four approaches to equity; ultimately, systemic change will be needed to help move those smaller efforts along.

Using a similar structure to the report's Summary, this chapter synthesizes the committee's conclusions and recommendations for policy, practice, and research drawn across the full report and presents steps toward a new vision for science and engineering in preschool through elementary grades that emphasizes equity and justice in the work. The chapter concludes with areas for future research.

CONCLUSIONS

What follows first are the committee's conclusions based on the review of the available evidence on science and engineering in preschool through elementary grades, organized by key themes. The committee first articulates issues with respect to the prioritization of science and engineering in these early grades. Then, the committee more explicitly emphasizes how children learn and become more proficient in science and engineering and how the design of learning environments can support children's engagement in investigation and design; this is followed by a discussion of the roles of curriculum and content integration. The committee then describes conclusions related to how to support educators in their work and the role of district and school leadership. These collectively describe the approaches that actors at different levels of the system need to consider for enhancing science and engineering teaching and learning throughout preschool and elementary school.

The committee notes that efforts to build toward the vision of the *Framework* while deepening attention to justice are nascent. These conclusions identify promising starting points for this integrative work. In subsequent sections, the committee makes recommendations and points to areas for further research to move these connected visions closer to reality.

Prioritizing Science and Engineering in Preschool Through Elementary Grades

The research described throughout this report has highlighted how children explore phenomena, designs, materials, and relationships in their worlds. Despite the research showing that children can engage in science and engineering from a young age and that they find such activity interesting and meaningful, for a number of different reasons, science and engineering are often not attended to in robust and comprehensive ways in state policies, particularly for preschool through elementary grades (see Chapter 2). The lack of attention in policies constrains the time and resources (e.g., curriculum materials, assessments, physical and digital resources, professional learning experiences) for teaching science and engineering in preschool through elementary grades. Chapter 2 also describes the impact of high-stakes accountability policies and how emphasis on performance on these measures has decreased the time overall for science in elementary classrooms. High-stakes accountability policies have also led to children who receive support services being tracked or pulled out from instruction in other content areas (e.g., science and social studies); the burgeoning growth of policies such as third grade reading laws exacerbates some of these issues. The neglect of science and engineering education in the preschool through elementary years deprives children of opportunities to develop understanding and skills that are building blocks for success in subsequent grade levels and for active participation in a democratic society; it further deprives them of their right to engage with the wonders of the natural and designed worlds.

CONCLUSION 1: Children engage in meaningful science and engineering from a very young age, across multiple contexts and settings.

CONCLUSION 2: Science and engineering instruction is under-resourced and not highly prioritized in preschool through elementary schools, with engineering receiving even less attention. These concerns are exacerbated in under-resourced schools, which disproportionately impacts children and communities of color.

CONCLUSION 3: On average, there is substantially less instructional time devoted to science and engineering compared to English language arts and mathematics. The evidence is not clear about the most effective ways to structure the frequency and duration of science (or engineering) instructional time in preschool through elementary grades.

CONCLUSION 4: Science and engineering instructional policies, standards, and teaching practices from preschool to elementary grades lack alignment and coherence. Research and curricular design efforts that focus on the transition from preschool to elementary school, in science and engineering, are needed.

CONCLUSION 5: There is limited research on how children with learning disabilities and/or learning differences engage in and experience science and engineering learning in preschool through elementary grades and forms of support that might be helpful. Further, children receiving academic supports often have been excluded or pulled out from key science and engineering learning experiences, limiting not just the research base but children's opportunities to learn.

Supporting Children's Learning, Engagement, and Proficiency in Science and Engineering

From infancy, children can engage in everyday practices that form the foundations of scientific and engineering practice—they explore, discover, and investigate the world and develop explanations; construct representations; scope problems and develop and refine solutions; communicate their reasoning and learn from others; and consider actions based on fairness, impact, or justice. These can be developed into disciplinary practices with support, instruction, and guidance.

As children enter schools, they bring with them important prior experiences, reasoning strategies, funds of knowledge drawn from their families and communities, multiple ways of knowing about the world, and a broad range of communicative repertoires to the learning experiences. These are particularly important to value in historically marginalized learners in science and engineering, which the committee recognizes as including Black, Brown, and Indigenous children and other children of color; children with learning disabilities and/or learning differences; emergent multilingual learners; and children marginalized on the basis of gender.

Chapter 3 emphasizes four big ideas for conceptualizing preschool through elementary science and engineering learning: that learning is a social and cultural process, that learning in science and engineering is a process of identity formation, that science and engineering learning occurs across contexts, and that learning science and engineering is non-neutral—that is, what is learned, how it is learned, and what counts as competence in learning is shaped by the values, practices, norms, and opportunities in a given setting. One key context, for children, is family, broadly defined; here, learners begin to develop their knowledge and cultural frames that they will use to organize their understanding of the world and of themselves as learners. Furthermore, children's play, from infancy through elementary school and beyond, affords important opportunities for authentic engagement in science and engineering—authentic both to children's lives and to the disciplines.

Chapter 4 builds upon these ideas to describe how children have, demonstrate, and build proficiencies with investigation and design, and that their opportunities to learn can resonate meaningfully with their everyday lives. To become robust scientific thinkers, as envisioned in the *Framework*, children need frequent opportunities to engage in high-quality science and engineering activities, supported by adults and other children. Because children have proficiencies with investigation and design, educators can develop learning environments that support the demonstration and further development of those proficiencies.

Chapter 5 highlights how learning environments can emphasize caring and respect, meaningful and rich contexts for investigation and design, iterative refinement of ideas and sensemaking, and meaningful assessment. Teachers' use of instructional practices aimed at facilitating children's engagement in investigation and design helps to nurture these environments. Moreover, engaging in science and engineering is a social endeavor—one where children can practice important collaboration skills that can support social-emotional development and foster adaptive approaches to learning.

CONCLUSION 6: Science and engineering learning experiences provide unique opportunities for children to identify as people who do and value science and engineering along with their other identities (e.g., racial, ethnic, linguistic, learning [dis]ability, and gender). When children are provided opportunities to explore questions that matter to them and are recognized as knowledge producers and problem solvers, increases in motivation and disciplinary affiliation are observed.

CONCLUSION 7: The broadly defined family context is a child's primary learning community; therefore, families are essential partners in the learning of science and engineering in preschool through elementary grades.

CONCLUSION 8: The development and expression of children's proficiencies in science and engineering is related to their knowledge, experiences, their cultural and linguistic backgrounds, and the characteristics of the instructional environment and pedagogical approaches. Their engagement in science and engineering looks different across preschool through fifth grade.

CONCLUSION 9: Across the many contexts in which children engage in science and engineering activity, children's development of ideas and practices is supported by their own intuitive and imaginative ways of investigating and designing as well as by long-term, sustained experiences, rich settings and materials (including use of age-appropriate technologies), and engagement with peers and knowledgeable others.

CONCLUSION 10: Children can share, use, connect, and develop their understanding of big conceptual ideas in science and engineering when instruction (1) is anchored in design problems and phenomena that are conceptually rich, accessible, and meaningful to children and (2) provides supports for children to iteratively refine their explanations and solutions, making progress on questions and problems they have identified.

CONCLUSION 11: Science and engineering learning are social endeavors. Instructional and curricular supports are needed to promote relationships, collective meaning-making, and discourse across children's development and learning contexts.

CONCLUSION 12: When teachers of science and engineering are able to elicit, notice, value, and build on the many ideas, experiences, and communicative resources that children bring to the classroom, they can organize connections between children's existing knowledge and curiosity and the environment around them, supporting children to continue to make sense of the natural and designed world.

CONCLUSION 13: A robust formative assessment approach for preschool through elementary school provides appropriate supports for children to show their understanding and skill, includes ways for children to show their understanding in multiple modalities, and specifies a way of making inferences about children's understanding.

Curriculum and Content Integration

Science and engineering can be integrated with other subject areas, such as language arts, mathematics, and computational thinking. As discussed in Chapter 6, integration, if done well, can effectively add time to the day for science and engineering. It can build meaningful bridges across content areas, eliminating the silos that are less reflective of how scientists and engineers work. Orienting instruction toward rich phenomena and design problems provides opportunities to motivate, use, and develop practices and ideas in other content domains. In addition, research suggests that curricula that intentionally integrate science and literacy can increase children's time on science without decreasing children's development of reading and writing skills and that some literacy and mathematical skills and understanding are enhanced by connections to science and engineering. However, superficial integration can limit children's engagement in authentic disciplinary practices (in any discipline).

As described in Chapter 7, preschool and elementary teachers benefit from access to high-quality curriculum materials. The committee frames *high-quality curriculum materials* as grounded in investigation and design, coherent (i.e., they build toward big ideas sensibly and connect across ideas and activity), flexible and adaptable, equitable and responsive, and building toward the vision of the *Framework*; further, high-quality curriculum materials have evidence supporting their effectiveness. These materials, rather than providing a script for teachers to follow step by step, support teachers in being responsive to children's thinking and ideas. Using high-quality curriculum materials selected by districts and states provides an important starting point for instruction, and teachers make adaptations to even high-quality materials. Often, teachers make changes due to concerns about time, resources, and their perceptions of children's needs. These adaptations should be in keeping with the developers' vision of the materials and grounded in the teacher's priorities, principles, and context. Teachers also benefit from having adequate physical and digital resources, including access to technology that would allow for examination of phenomena that occur on scales too large, small, slow, or fast to be directly viewed; however, these critical physical and digital resources are not always available for teachers.

CONCLUSION 14: High-quality instruction in preschool through elementary science and engineering requires curriculum materials that build toward the vision of the *Framework*; are grounded in investigation and design; are coherent, flexible, adaptable, equitable, responsive; and have evidence supporting their effectiveness. It is unreasonable to expect preschool through elementary teachers to develop such materials independently.

CONCLUSION 15: Educators' use and adaptation of science and engineering curriculum materials is influenced by their knowledge, beliefs, and attitudes about the disciplines, teaching science and engineering, and learners; by the characteristics of the materials themselves; and by the school and classroom contexts in which the materials are being used.

CONCLUSION 16: Integrating science and engineering with each other and with other content areas in preschool through elementary classrooms has the potential to enhance connections between subjects and effectively increase the amount of instructional time for science and engineering instruction. Such integration can benefit all domains if the design (a) respects the unique content and disciplinary practices of all domains, (b) leverages meaningful and mutually supportive connections among the subject areas, and (c) is developmentally, culturally, and linguistically appropriate.

Supporting Educators

Chapter 8 describes the enormous role preschool through elementary educators play in fostering children's learning of science and engineering, alongside their many other responsibilities in supporting children's growth. Preschool through elementary school teachers typically teach all subject areas, including all areas of science and engineering. The chapter recognizes that the elementary teacher workforce of the United States overwhelmingly comprises white women and that they typically have limited preparation in science and engineering. These teachers bring many assets to the work, including care for children, capacity in building relationships with children and families, and inquisitiveness about the world. To build on those assets to get to the vision of science and engineering teaching described in this report, teachers need a constellation of supports across their preservice and professional career. These supports for working toward this vision of science and engineering teaching, particularly with regard to working toward equity and justice, must be framed as part and parcel of the everyday work of classrooms, rather than extraordinary or tacked on as extras for those who are interested.

Preservice teacher education for early childhood and elementary teachers includes science content coursework (whether taught in schools or education or in science departments), science methods courses, and field experiences. Each of these can contribute to the development of preservice teachers' beliefs, identities, knowledge, and practice with regard to teaching science and engineering and can enable teachers to build on the assets, experiences, and curiosity of children. Coherence across the initial teacher education system—for example, across science content courses, science methods courses, and field experiences—is key, and attention to quality within each element is important as well (e.g., ensuring that science content courses for preservice elementary teachers teach science in ways that are consistent with the vision of the *Framework*). Professional learning experiences for teachers include a myriad of experiences, including professional learning communities, professional learning sessions connected to curriculum materials, and partnership with science specialists and coaches, among others. The extended consensus model for professional learning names multiple key characteristics of these experiences, such as bringing together content and pedagogy and working on targeted teaching strategies—all of which prepare teachers to explore the connections among canonical science and engineering knowledge, science and engineering practices, crosscutting concepts, and the lived worlds and experiences of their learners.

CONCLUSION 17: Preschool through elementary school teachers need multiple kinds of supports to provide effective, engaging science and engineering learning opportunities to children. Teachers benefit from having strong teacher preparation, curriculum materials, physical and digital resources, coherent professional learning opportunities, and supportive school leadership. These supports provide opportunities to expand on teachers' strengths.

CONCLUSION 18: The demographics of the preschool and elementary teacher workforce are starkly different from the demographics of the children being taught. This discrepancy means that there are often cultural mismatches between teachers and the children in their classrooms. These can make salient any differences in teachers' and children's relationships to science and engineering and can be reflected in instruction.

CONCLUSION 19: Teachers need support in enacting science and engineering instruction that is responsive to and supportive of the cultural and linguistic backgrounds of the children in their classrooms. To address this need, a growing body of research highlights the importance of diversifying the teacher educator workforce, placing preservice teachers in mentored and supportive field placements that involve children from a range of linguistic and cultural backgrounds, and using sustained professional learning experiences synergistically with educative curriculum materials.

CONCLUSION 20: Preservice early childhood and elementary teachers demonstrate positive shifts in their beliefs, knowledge, and practice related to science and engineering teaching when they have opportunities to engage in science and engineering practices themselves and have opportunities to support children in engaging in these practices.

CONCLUSION 21: Professional learning experiences that engage preschool through elementary teachers in (a) collaboratively analyzing practice and children's thinking, (b) making connections among professional learning opportunities such as educative curriculum materials and workshops to their classrooms, (c) engaging in instructional co-design, and (d) working with supportive coaches or facilitators all support the development of these teachers' knowledge, attitudes, beliefs, and practice.

District and School Leadership

Chapter 9 shows that organizational culture, policy and management, and educator capability interact to shape instructional reform efforts in school districts. These three dimensions are distinct but related, and, together, they allow analysis of local leadership practices that enable equitable preschool through elementary science and engineering instruction that builds toward the vision of the *Framework*. School and district leaders play an important role in providing advice and information for teachers, particularly in the area of science education. Moreover, these leaders set policy and management structures that impact preschool through elementary science and engineering instruction, including structures around instructional time, resources, and staffing. One key dimension of staffing structures is the use of science specialists, or, more generally, organizational approaches such as departmentalization or team teaching. Lastly, professional learning experiences that align across the levels of district, school, and teacher leaders can shape principals' supervision of teachers and thus teachers' opportunities to learn. Partnerships with science and engineering organizations and universities can play an important role in supporting such professional learning opportunities.

CONCLUSION 22: When preschool and elementary school and district leaders emphasize the importance of science and engineering education and foster shared responsibility for science and engineering instruction among teachers, science and engineering instruction is included as a strong part of the curriculum. These leaders also allocate time and resources and provide professional learning opportunities for teachers to develop expertise around science and engineering instruction.

CONCLUSION 23: Although specialists can provide preschool and elementary science and engineering instruction when it may not otherwise be available, specialist positions appear to have the greatest impact when school and district administrators and other leaders are involved in science education and the overall district and school culture places value on science and provides resources to support it.

RECOMMENDATIONS

A prevailing issue emphasized by this committee is the lack of attention to science and engineering in preschool through elementary grades. It is imperative that all children receive opportunities to engage with science and engineering that builds toward the vision of the *Framework*. Toward that goal, the committee recognizes that a shift toward equity and justice in science and engineering education is needed and requires systemic change. Such systemic change involves a wide range of actors at all levels (schools of education and other higher education units supporting teacher education, professional learning opportunity providers, curriculum developers, funding agencies, states and districts, schools) to make a commitment to support the development of all educators' and leaders' knowledge, capabilities, and capacities for science and engineering teaching that works toward equity and justice.

Analyses at the end of the chapters of the report explore each chapter's focus in light of the four approaches to equity named in Chapter 1. These analyses suggest that, overall, there has been substantial effort made in the first two approaches, some significant pockets of progress in the third, and relatively little regarding the fourth. Across the educational endeavor as a whole, all four approaches are necessary to fully and genuinely work toward disrupting systemic oppression, and yet, as noted above, incremental and individual steps can work in concert with bolder actions and with broader systemic change.

Based upon the committee's conclusions and this vision to enhance children's opportunities and move toward equity and justice, the following recommendations (organized around the same themes used for the Conclusions) are intended to be steps to meeting this objective. Because of the emerging scholarship in the work on equity and justice, the recommendations working specifically toward this are based on inferences from the existing evidence. A section of the research agenda that follows focuses on how this literature base can and should be further bolstered.

Prioritizing Science and Engineering in Preschool Through Elementary Grades

RECOMMENDATION 1: State policy makers should establish policies that ensure science and engineering are comprehensively, frequently, and consistently taught in all preschool through elementary settings. The policies should also ensure that children are not being pulled out of science and engineering instruction for remediation in other subjects.

RECOMMENDATION 2: District and school leaders in elementary and preschool settings should examine the amount of time and resources allocated to science and engineering instruction and then (a) develop schedules that allow a comprehensive, frequent, and consistent focus on science and engineering, (b) create coherence from preschool through elementary, and (c) allocate the necessary resources (fiscal, material, and human) to support equitable science and engineering learning opportunities.

RECOMMENDATION 3: Preschool and elementary school leaders should evaluate the characteristics of classroom instruction, the qualifications of teachers hired and whether the hiring practices serve to promote educator diversity, and the professional learning opportunities offered to teachers so that adjustments can be made as needed to support and enhance teachers' capacities for teaching science and engineering well.

RECOMMENDATION 4: State leaders, district leaders, and researchers should work together to build connections across preschool and elementary school and to conduct research to investigate how alignment and coherence across preschool through elementary supports children's learning of science and engineering.

Supporting Children's Learning, Engagement, and Proficiency in Science and Engineering

RECOMMENDATION 5: To draw on and further develop children's science and engineering proficiencies and identities, teachers should arrange their instruction around interesting and relevant phenomena and design problems that leverage children's natural curiosity and give children opportunities for decision making, sensemaking, and problem solving.

RECOMMENDATION 6: Teachers should enact science and engineering learning experiences that establish norms for a caring, collective culture and position children as active thinkers and doers while also providing opportunities to support collaboration and collective thinking.

RECOMMENDATION 7: Teachers should include formative assessment processes that gather multiple forms of evidence at multiple timepoints, with the goal of informing instruction.

RECOMMENDATION 8: Teachers should seek out opportunities to continue to build their expertise in working toward equity and justice in their science and engineering teaching.

RECOMMENDATION 9: Preschool and elementary school leaders and teachers should engage and collaborate with families and local community leaders to mutually support children's opportunities for engaging in science and engineering. Such collaboration allows for leaders and teachers to design learning experiences that are meaningful and relevant to children and helps families to better support their children's learning outside of the school.

Curriculum and Content Integration

RECOMMENDATION 10: Curriculum developers should work in partnership with researchers, teachers, school or district leaders, and families and community leaders to develop preschool through elementary science and engineering curriculum materials that are coherent and equitable, that build toward the vision of the *Framework*, and that

- provide opportunities for children's sensemaking around investigation and design;
- build on children's interests and repertoires of practice;
- provide educative supports for teachers;
- provide opportunities for teachers to make productive adaptations to meet contextual needs;
- provide supports for teachers to make meaningful connections to communities and families;
- explore integrating science and engineering with other domains in ways that benefit children's learning and use instructional time effectively;
- are manageable for use in preschool and elementary settings;
- align preschool and elementary instruction; and
- show evidence of effectiveness.

RECOMMENDATION 11: State and district leaders should rely on a robust evidence-based review, selection, and implementation process when making decisions about preschool through elementary curricular programs to adopt to ensure that the science and engineering units build toward the vision of the *Framework* and are grounded in investigation and design, coherent, flexible, adaptable, and equitable.

RECOMMENDATION 12: State and district leaders should provide teachers with sustained professional learning opportunities for using and adapting curriculum materials, and should ensure that they have adequate access to materials, equipment, and other physical and digital resources needed for children to engage in investigation and design.

RECOMMENDATION 13: As materials become available, state and district leaders should ensure that every school has the curriculum materials and instructional resources needed for engaging in science and engineering teaching that works toward equity and justice.

Supporting Educators

RECOMMENDATION 14: Teacher educators (in and outside of schools of education), facilitators of professional learning experiences, and school and district leaders should

- help preschool through elementary teachers to recognize the importance and value of teaching science and engineering;
- understand and address the needs and goals of classroom teachers;
- support teachers in connecting their professional learning with their classroom practice;
- foreground authentic and equitable science and engineering content and disciplinary practice;
- allow for meaningful integration of science and/or engineering with other subjects; and
- support teachers' effective use and adaptation of science and engineering curriculum materials.

RECOMMENDATION 15: Designers and facilitators of professional learning opportunities should ensure that sustained opportunities to work on science and engineering teaching that works toward equity and justice, in conjunction with supportive curriculum materials, are offered. These experiences should support teachers in developing the ability to recognize and value their learners' conceptual, linguistic, and cultural resources, such as funds of knowledge stemming from their families and communities and their sensemaking repertoires.

RECOMMENDATION 16: Schools of education should provide professional learning opportunities for science teacher education faculty on how to work toward equity and justice in teacher education.

RECOMMENDATION 17: Federal agencies should reassess how funds are allocated for research and development efforts to enhance teaching and learning of science and engineering within preschool through elementary classrooms and prioritize efforts that

- diversify the preschool through elementary teacher workforce;

- recognize the unique character of preschool through elementary teachers and teaching;
- develop teachers as leaders;
- support research and development that works across content areas to support teacher educators, teachers, and children in making meaningful connections; and
- elevate the study of equitable curricular resources and initial and ongoing teacher professional learning experiences that support teachers in working toward equity and justice in preschool and elementary science and engineering.

District and School Leadership

RECOMMENDATION 18: District leaders should provide professional learning opportunities for principals, center directors, and other school leaders to enhance leaders' capacity for providing instructional leadership for science and engineering. These professional learning opportunities should focus on science and engineering practices and support leaders in seeing multiple ways science and engineering are valuable for children.

AREAS FOR FUTURE RESEARCH

Considerable research exists that shows the potential of children in learning science and engineering. At the same time, much remains to be learned. The unique character of science and engineering teaching and learning in preschool through elementary grades shapes what research is able to be conducted. Those factors cause challenges for conducting research in this arena. Some of these include

- **Issues stemming from the rarity of teaching of science and engineering:** As has been established throughout this report, science and engineering are taught infrequently in many elementary schools and preschool settings. Furthermore, when these subjects are taught, they are scheduled idiosyncratically. This means it can be difficult for any research focused on science and engineering in these age bands to occur, and in particular, it makes getting commitments for conducting large-scale in-classroom research difficult and the logistics of doing so quite challenging.
- **Issues of systemic exclusion:** The research base undergirding much of the scholarship on science and engineering education has systematically excluded groups of learners (e.g., children of color,

children with learning disabilities and/or learning differences). Thus, research on instruction is grounded in incomplete and inadequate representations of children's repertoires of practice, and ideas about how and why children learn science and engineering must be expanded.

- **Issues of assessment and measurement:** Because of the age of the children of focus in the charge, it can be challenging for scholars to design effective assessments. Interpreting data generated with young children—for example, young children's talk, written artifacts, and/or embodiments—can be difficult as well. The nature of children's talk is often discursive and rambling, and their written literacy is, of course, developing. In part due to these challenges, it can be difficult to develop reliable measures to make valid inferences about young children's thinking. Thus, it is worth considering how teachers use formative assessment to support children in their learning and summative assessment to determine what children have learned.
- **Issues of informal learning:** Informal learning offers challenges in terms of looking at children within family groups or classes, rather than as individuals.
- **Issues of funding:** Funding has been unevenly distributed in terms of the kinds of questions that have been supported for exploration as well as the scholars who receive funding (i.e., scholars of color receiving funding less often)—leading to limited evidence in some areas.

Next, the section turns to the key areas of focus for future research. The committee orients these recommendations around key foci or themes across this report, including issues of equity and justice; engaging families and communities; curriculum, instruction, learning environments, and assessment; teacher education and professional learning; systems and policies; and approaches to research. These areas are overlapping and interconnected.

Working Toward Equity and Justice

The committee urges that research be conducted to understand and support how learning science and engineering can contribute to equity and justice.

Areas of focus here include first and foremost, **science and engineering pedagogies, curriculum, and teacher education and professional learning for preschool through elementary school that emphasize equity and justice,** including seeing science and engineering as a part of justice movements. This includes connections to short- and long-term learning of educators and children, the development of identities in science and engineering, and developing ideas about the value of science and engineering in children's lives and communities. For instance, what constitutes relevance, or consequential learning, in preschool through elementary school? What can preschool through elementary children do toward community transformation through science and engineering?

Scholarship on antiracist pedagogy is crucial to examine as researchers continue to work toward justice in preschool through elementary science and engineering. Given that prioritizing antiracism necessitates a broader perspective on the intent of learning experiences, what does an expansive set of learning goals or outcomes look like for science and engineering at this age? Focusing on teachers, this includes the development and testing of learning trajectories in becoming oriented to antiracist science and engineering approaches, and the development of tools and frameworks to support teaching at the intersection of preschool through elementary science, engineering, and antiracism. It also includes the exploration of design principles for antiracist work and identifying focal areas that represent likely "hotspots" for curriculum and instruction that works toward justice (e.g., the environment and natural world, health and the human body).

A second key focus here would be exploring in more depth **science and engineering learning with particular groups of children:** Black and Brown children, Indigenous children, children with learning disabilities and/or learning differences, emergent multilingual learners, girls, and others who are often marginalized from science and engineering as professions and as school subject areas. This research must recognize that children's experiences are influenced by their intersecting identities and must not essentialize or assume homogeneity within groups. As one example of this area of need, the committee found little literature documenting the removal of children from science class for children to receive special education or English as a Second Language services—yet most committee members had anecdotal experiences of that happening time and again. Black and Brown children, in particular, are often excluded from science and engineering class due to supposed behavioral infractions. To help inform design efforts that would work toward equity and justice, further scholarship should explore (a) **how to effectively support children who belong to these groups in foundational science and engineering opportunities to learn, (b) their experiences when provided those opportunities, and (c) how preschool through elementary science and engineering can provide opportunities to work to dismantle white supremacy, even in majority white spaces.**

A third key focus involves **exploring science and engineering learning with diverse groups of children.** Accounting for the heterogeneity within any given classroom or group is important for effecting change in instruction. This may entail studies in settings with children who come from a range of cultural and/or linguistic backgrounds and/or are different ages. For example, how can classroom teachers best support making cultural connections in their science or engineering instruction when children in the classroom represent multiple, perhaps quite different, cultural backgrounds?

Engaging Families and Communities

The committee urges that research focus additional attention on understanding families' and communities' contributions to the teaching and learning of science and engineering with children.

Specifically, the committee recommends that research focus on **how families negotiate and navigate among their local ways of knowing, informal engagements with science and engineering, and more formal school-based ways of knowing** science and engineering. Research must also focus on the complementary side—that is, **how schools and districts elicit, acknowledge, and leverage families' ways of knowing** and connect these to more formal school-based ways of knowing.

A second area of focus is to explore **how partnerships across schools or districts, community-serving learning organizations like museums, and families and community members can promote equity- and justice-oriented science and engineering instruction** with preschool through elementary aged children. What do models for such partnerships look like? What policy contexts are necessary to build and sustain these partnerships? How do the unique material and historical conditions in different communities shape their opportunities to build and sustain partnerships in locally distinct and sustainable ways? What kinds of effects can such partnerships have on learners and on communities, and what is the evidence of those effects?

Curriculum, Instruction, Learning Environments, and Assessment

The committee urges that research be conducted to understand and support curriculum, instruction, and assessment that supports children in engaging meaningfully in investigation and design.

One area of focus here should be further work on **the forms of activity named in Chapter 4, and on what they look like when they are taken up by a range of children**: across ages, backgrounds, and contexts. Beyond looking at this cross-sectionally, the field needs research that looks longitudinally at how these forms of activity are taken up and evolve over time as children move from grade to grade. This work would help to inform instructional design: What helps children to engage in these forms of activity, across grade levels? This would also contribute to bolstering the literature base supporting the learning progressions that are presented in the *Framework* and would support the possible extension of the *Framework* to preschool in a developmentally appropriate way that maintains a child-centered focus on play.

Another area of focus should **zoom in on the youngest learners, specifically.** What do these forms of activity look like for preschool children? What is the intersection among science and engineering and play? Furthermore, the field needs research that articulates science and engineering learning goals for preschool. What would learning progressions around the science and engineering practices, such as those in the *Framework*, look like if they started in preschool? How can efforts in preschool support later efforts to engage children in science and engineering?

An additional area of focus should be on **children with learning disabilities and/or learning differences and how they learn science and engineering.** The committee found relatively little work here. What are the experiences of children with learning disabilities and/or learning differences in preschool and elementary science and engineering, and how can instruction in and learning environments for these subject areas support them well? What does effective "differentiation" look like for the kind of three-dimensional, phenomenon- or design challenge-based learning emphasized in the *Framework*? Related also to the next topic of teacher education and professional learning, what kinds of opportunities to learn are important for preschool through elementary teachers of science and engineering, in learning to teach children with learning disabilities and/or learning differences?

Another area of focus should be on **integration**. This report has highlighted the potential for integration across domains (including science and engineering, along with English language arts [ELA], mathematics, computational thinking, social studies, social-emotional learning, and others). Yet relatively little research exists to guide this kind of curricular and instructional work, particularly outside of mathematics and ELA. How can teachers be supported in learning to do this kind of integration? What should curriculum development look like for authentic and meaningful integration? What might it look like with social studies, in particular—another often-marginalized subject? What types of combinations and what degree of combination maximizes the advantages and minimizes the challenges? How do different models of integration work—who do they benefit, and under what conditions are they beneficial, equitable, and sustainable? How do these models relate to how time is spent in preschool and elementary classrooms? Furthermore, more research is needed on several of the potential pitfalls named for integration with mathematics and ELA. Research on the integration of mathematics, science, and engineering yields variable effect sizes. Research and development efforts often describe connections across content areas but do not address precisely how and why those connections function educationally.

A fourth area of focus should be on **the design of curriculum materials that support preschool through elementary science and engineering.** Although the research base seems to show how curriculum materials are supportive of teachers, it is less clear about the effects on learning and identity development for children. Given the committee's definition of high-quality curriculum materials, what specific features are centrally important for this age group? What learning goals, scaffolding, and instructional designs are most appropriate for the different grade bands? How can curriculum materials support the development of crosscutting concepts across units and across years? How, and under what conditions, can the use of technology facilitate science and engineering learning? What do educative curriculum materials look like that support teachers in equity- and justice-oriented pedagogy in science and engineering?

An additional area of focus should be on the **incorporation of engineering in preschool through elementary settings.** Too little research has focused here, and the inclusion of engineering in younger grades is quite new. More work is needed to guide design of curriculum materials and instructional practice for engineering education at these ages. How do young children take up the disciplinary practices of engineering? How do they develop identities as people who do engineering? What unique opportunities does engineering offer, and how can curriculum designers take advantage of those opportunities?

A final area of focus should be **assessment.** What does three-dimensional assessment in science and engineering look like with young children? How can different forms of assessment be constructed and used for effective teaching and learning in preschool through elementary school? What does assessment for preschool through elementary science and engineering look like when it privileges not just three-dimensional learning and the vision of the *Framework*, but also a justice-oriented stance? What does accountability look like in preschool through elementary science and engineering, and what are the implications for instruction?

The kind of design work alluded to here takes time. Teachers must take risks to engage in this work with children. Researchers and teachers, working together, must learn from children and engage in iterative redesign.

Teacher Education and Professional Learning

The committee urges that research be conducted to better understand how teachers learn to engage in high-quality, equitable science and engineering instruction with young learners.

A key assumption of the committee is that the field needs to move beyond research that emphasizes preschool through elementary teachers' supposed deficits vis-à-vis science and engineering teaching, and toward **research that explores how to leverage teachers' strengths and how to support them in developing their instructional practice.** For example, assumptions are typically made about elementary teachers' need for very wide and very deep subject-matter knowledge in science; to what extent are those assumptions well founded? How does teachers' inquisitiveness about children's thinking play into their practice? Research should explore connections among teachers' characteristics (e.g., knowledge, beliefs, identity), their relational work and instructional practice, and their efficacy in supporting children's learning and identity development; what teacher characteristics and practices are most central in supporting children's growth in science and engineering?

A second area of focus should include better understanding the **synergies among the relational work and the disciplinary work in science and engineering that preschool through elementary teachers do on a daily basis.** How do teachers make connections between children and investigation and design, and how should teacher educators support them in learning to make those connections?

There is little research that connects equity- and justice-oriented teaching with preschool through elementary science and engineering teaching. In addition, there is little research in teacher education that tracks teachers' justice-oriented practice; most of this scholarship focuses on teachers' beliefs. Thus, another area of focus should be on these **teachers' enacted practice, particularly with regard to using pedagogies that work toward equity and justice for preschool through elementary science and engineering**. More generally, research should focus on how teacher education experiences (including field experiences as well as science methods courses and other program structures) can shift preservice teachers' understanding of systemic oppression and educational injustices, and help develop their knowledge and practice around pedagogies for science and engineering that work toward equity and justice. What are the roles of tools or frameworks in supporting this work? How do novice teachers internalize and use such tools and frameworks over time?

Scholarship needs to further explore **a range of dimensions of preservice teacher education and ongoing professional learning for in-service teachers**. This work needs to take seriously the nature of early childhood and elementary teaching. For example, how do teachers conceptualize the science and engineering practices, and how do these conceptions connect to how they conceptualize their teaching of the disciplinary practices of other subjects? How can teachers be supported in integrating science and engineering with other subjects, through initial teacher education, ongoing professional learning, and/or educative curriculum materials? How does using innovative, high-quality curriculum materials shape teachers' readiness for and ability to plan for science and engineering instruction that foregrounds the proficiencies associated with investigation and design? What is the role of coherence in preservice teacher education and what dimensions of coherence matter the most? What should teacher education (including methods courses, content courses, and field experiences) look like for preservice teachers of color, and how can whiteness be decentered in contexts where many of the participants are white? Structurally, what does the preparation in science and engineering look like in initial teacher education compared to ELA and mathematics (e.g., how many methods classes, content classes, field experiences), and what is the effect of those structural differences in early childhood and elementary teachers' science and engineering teaching? How can early childhood teachers, in particular, be supported in learning to teach science and engineering, and what should preparation for teaching preschool through third grade or preschool through fourth grade look like? What are the effects of efforts (e.g., of tribal colleges and universities to prepare early childhood teachers, or of district partnerships to bring in Latinx elementary teachers) to diversify the teacher workforce and strengthen the teacher of color pipeline? The committee also found no recent work on induction support for early career preschool through elementary teachers of science and engineering, and so this, too, is an area for focus.

Finally, the committee found that most scholarship in science teacher education focuses on preschool through elementary teachers' knowledge or beliefs, whereas **little work focused on teachers' actual enacted practice.** Yet it is enactment that directly shapes children's opportunities to learn in science and engineering. More research, in both preservice teacher education and in-service professional learning, should focus on supporting and characterizing teachers' practice and how it develops over time. Furthermore, research that connects the dots from teachers' professional learning experiences (e.g., coaching) to their instructional practices to children's learning and identity development is needed.

Systems, Policies, and Leadership

The committee urges that research be conducted to better understand the roles of systems and policies in supporting the teaching and learning of science and engineering in preschool through elementary school.

The committee highlights four main areas of focus here. The first recognizes the **interconnections among different elements and levels of the system, and the need to understand those interconnections more fully.** There is a need to better understand the connections between the work occurring at the system (e.g., district or state) level and at the classroom level, and to articulate how system-level policies and practices shape science and engineering instruction in preschool through elementary classrooms. For instance, research should explore how large-scale assessments are used in comparison to their intended use. How do these assessments impact teacher evaluation? How do state and district policies impact—positively or negatively—children's access to science and engineering instruction? Furthermore, relatively little work has been done exploring the role of partnerships that reflect children's multiple cultural identities. Research should characterize the workings of multi-institutional community and school partnerships, exploring questions about how multiple actors in a system can engage in iterative design and learning.

A related area of focus is **improvement efforts.** Building capacity for early childhood and elementary teachers to be able to engage in the work of teaching science and engineering requires systemic efforts, as does putting factors in place that support that work (including funding, time, curricular resources, instructional resources, and facilities). Relatively little research has focused on teacher networks for preschool or elementary science or engineering—right now a largely untested, low priority in schools, yet one that has so much promise for children's growth and development in becoming agentic change makers in their communities—seems crucial. Similarly, there is relatively little research on partnerships contributing to transformational leadership, including research-practice partnerships. At the systems level, exploring what multitiered systems of support could look like for these subjects would help districts in designing for capacity building.

A third important area of focus in the systems and policy area focuses on **time** and the related issue of **the classroom schedule.** Instructional time limits how much science (and even more so, how much engineering) is taught in elementary schools and how that time is scheduled shapes what can be done. Yet the committee found relatively little classroom-level research illustrating how instructional time is being used for these subjects. Questions around time, then, become central in considering how the teaching and learning of science and engineering can be enhanced in the preschool through elementary grades. For example, what scheduling practices in elementary schools support investigation and design in the preschool or elementary classroom? What are the comparative effects—on teacher and child experiences and outcomes—of scheduling blocks of time daily or weekly for individual disciplines, versus scheduling times for integration of domains (and providing curricular supports for that integration)? What are the effects on multiple disciplines—for example, if the time spent on science increases in concert with a decrease in time for ELA, do learner outcomes in ELA change?

A final important area of focus is to learn more about **the effects of systems, policies, and leadership with regard to the teaching and learning of science and engineering in preschool, specifically.** Most of the systems-level work has taken place in K–12 contexts and thus excludes the preschool setting. Research that looks at connections between preschool systems and K–5 systems, coupled with longitudinal studies, is needed.

Approaches to Research

The committee urges that research be conducted to better understand the intricacies of how putting children, investigation, and design at the center of consideration can shape children's learning and development and how a range of factors facilitate that work. This leads to the need to develop improved research methodologies to be able to conduct this work.

First, investment must be made in **supporting scholars in learning to engage in and sustaining the research necessary**. This could take the form of postdoctoral fellow programs, multi-institutional centers, summer research methodology workshops, or virtual training programs. Further, institutions must provide support for learning and collaboration. Such support can take the form of (1) recognizing the time it takes for researchers to develop collaborative and trusting relationships with partners and (2) providing support for collaborations with community organizations, school districts, and interdisciplinary groups of researchers. A related point is to **broaden the field's viewpoints of relevant research methodologies or of applications of methodologies to focus on children and equity and justice**, leveraging a full range of approaches, including quasi-experimental comparison studies, qualitative case studies, randomized controlled trials, ethnographic and field studies, and large-scale surveys. These synergistic efforts could center on some of the issues raised at the start of this section. How can researchers interpret very young children's talk and written artifacts related to science and engineering? How can researchers interpret children's embodiment of ideas? What kinds of partnership strategies can foster wide-scale research with enough schools or districts for large-scale efficacy studies? How can scholars learn to "hear the science" in Indigenous, Black, or Brown children's utterances and recognize the cultural connections? How can scholars ethically and effectively study diverse populations in free choice environments, or work meaningfully in communities, around science and engineering? How can scholars look at efficacy in new ways, or look at fidelity and adaptation in new ways? For example, how best can scholars study an intervention in different locations and make sense of the local adaptations teachers or other educators make?

Second, the committee noted that many of the pressing needs for research require the **development of partnerships**, where groups of researchers, educators, families, and community members collaborate. Methodologies such as design-based implementation research, improvement science, networked-improvement communities, and social design experiments show potential, though have not been employed much within science and engineering at preschool through elementary. How can these methodologies or others be employed in studying preschool through elementary science and engineering? What kinds of partnership strategies can foster wide-scale research with enough schools or districts for large-scale efficacy studies?

How can research-practice partnerships develop and study the instructional materials and related infrastructure that support the kinds of opportunities to learn that this report details?

Third, the committee noted, across the scope of the work of the report, **the dearth of longitudinal studies and recommends this as a methodology to prioritize in the coming decade.** For example, given what the report has shown about the interaction between children's competence on the one hand and children's opportunities for learning on the other, studies could explore questions such as: How do teachers engage in this work over time, and what do they come to value about teaching science and engineering to children? What do preschool through elementary teachers' learning trajectories look like, for equity- and justice-oriented science and engineering teaching? What are the consequences of sustained opportunities for children's rich science and engineering engagement, year by year? How do children who experience rich engagement with science and engineering practice in preschool grow in terms of the science or engineering identities, by the time they reach fifth grade? Large scale and long term (preschool through high school), what is the impact of receiving effective, inspiring, and equitable science and engineering instruction over time, on children's learning, identity development, or engagement in justice-oriented community science and engineering work? Is there a difference between groups of children (e.g., children of color, children who receive special education services, children who do or do not receive free and reduced-price meals) who do or do not receive science and engineering instruction? An additional area to explore is how cross-sequential research, combining shorter-term longitudinal cohorts with overlapping cross-sectional cohorts, could help to address these longitudinal issues in a potentially more cost-effective way.

FINAL REFLECTION

In summary, this report builds on the assumption that every child has the right to experience the wonder of science and the satisfaction of engineering, shows that children are wholly capable of engaging meaningfully in science and engineering, and illustrates how they can be supported in doing so. Doing this well is urgent in light of the ongoing crises the nation faces—and has been facing throughout its history—around systemic racism, health inequities, and environmental peril. Educators who take children seriously in their endeavors are uniquely positioned to support them in making sense of the natural and designed world and in making the world a more just and equitable place. Recognizing and leveraging children's and educators' strengths will help move preschool through elementary science and engineering closer to the vision put forward in this report.

References

Achieve. (2017). *Leverage ESSA to Promote Science and STEM Education in States.* Available: https://www.achieve.org/files/Achieve_STEMreport7.12.17.pdf.

Agarwal, P., and Sengupta-Irving, T. (2019). Integrating power to advance the study of connective and productive disciplinary engagement in mathematics and science. *Cognition and Instruction, 37*(3), 349–366.

Aguirre-Muñoz, Z., and Pantoya, M.L. (2016). Engineering literacy and engagement in kindergarten classrooms. *Journal of Engineering Education, 105*(4), 630–654.

Aikenhead, G.S. (2006). *Science Education for Everyday Life: Evidence-Based Practice.* New York: Teachers College Press.

Akerson, V., Buzellii, C., and Eastwood, J. (2010). The relationship between preservice early childhood teachers' cultural values and their perceptions of scientists' cultural values. *Journal of Science Teacher Education, 21*(2), 205–214.

Akerson, V., Buzellii, C., and Eastwood, J. (2012). Bridging the gap between preservice early childhood teachers' cultural values, perceptions of values held by scientists, and the relationships of these values to conceptions of nature of science. *Journal of Science Teacher Education, 23*(2), 133–157.

Akerson, V., Erumit, B.A., and Kaynak, N.E. (2019). Teaching nature of science through children's literature: An early childhood preservice teacher study. *International Journal of Science Education, 41*(18), 1–23.

Akerson, V., Donnelly, L., Riggs, M., and Eastwood, J. (2012). Developing a community of practice to support preservice elementary teachers' nature of science instruction. *International Journal of Science Education, 34*(9), 1371–1392.

Alarcón, M.H. (2012). *Urban School Leadership for Elementary Science Education: Meeting the Needs of English Language Learners.* Unpublished doctoral dissertation, University of Texas at San Antonio.

Allen, S., Kastelein, K., Mokros, J., Atkinson, J., and Byrd, S. (2020). STEM guides: Professional brokers in rural STEM ecosystems. *International Journal of Science Education, Part B, 10*(1), 17–35.

American Association for the Advancement of Science. (1989). *Science for All Americans: A Project 2061 Report on Literacy Goals in Science, Mathematics, and Technology.* Washington, DC: Author.

———(1993). *Benchmarks for Science Literacy.* New York: Oxford University Press.

American Association of Colleges for Teacher Education. (2019). *Education Students and Diversity: A Review of New Evidence.* Available: https://aacte.org/resources/research-reports-and-briefs/education-students-and-diversity-a-review-of-new-evidence/.

Amrein, A.L., and Berliner, D.C. (2002). *An Analysis of Some Unintended and Negative Consequences of High Stakes Testing.* Tempe: Arizona State University Education Policy Research Unit. Available: http://nepc.colorado.edu/files/EPSL-0211-125-EPRU.pdf.

Anderson, K.J.B. (2012). Science education and test-based accountability: Reviewing their relationship and exploring implications for future policy. *Science Education, 96,* 104–129.

Anderson, R.C., and Pearson, P.D. (1988). A schema-theoretic view of basic processes in reading comprehension. In P.L. Carrell, J. Devine, and D.E. Eskey (Eds.), *Interactive Approaches to Second Language Reading* (pp. 37–55). Cambridge, UK: Cambridge University Press.

Appleton, K., and Kindt, I. (2002). Beginning elementary teachers' development as teachers of science. *Journal of Science Teacher Education, 13*(1), 43–61.

Archer, L., DeWitt, J., Osborne, J., Dillon, J., Willis, B., and Wong, B. (2010). "Doing" science versus "being" a scientist: Examining 10/11-year-old schoolchildren's constructions of science through the lens of identity. *Science Education, 94*(4), 617–639.

Archibald, J.A. (2008). *Indigenous Storywork: Educating the Heart, Mind, Body, and Spirit.* Vancouver, BC: UBC Press.

Arias, A.M., and Davis, E.A. (2016). Making and recording observations. *Science and Children, 53*(8), 54–60.

Arias, A., and Davis, E.A. (2017). Supporting children to construct evidence-based claims in science: Individual learning trajectories in a practice-based program. *Teaching and Teacher Education, 66,* 204–218.

Arias, A., Davis, E.A., and Palincsar, A.S. (2014). Using educative curriculum materials to support teachers in engaging students to justify predictions. In J. Polman, E. Kyza, K. O'Neill, I. Tabak, W. Penuel, S. Jurow, K. O'Connor, T. Lee, and L. D'Amico (Eds.), *The 11th International Conference of the Learning Sciences* (vol. 3, pp. 1429–1431). Boulder, CO: International Society of the Learning Sciences.

Arias, A., Palincsar, A.S., and Davis, E.A. (2015). The design and use of educative curricular supports for text-based discussions in science. *Journal of Education, 195*(1), 21–35.

Arias, A., Bismack, A., Davis, E.A., and Palincsar, A.S. (2016). Interacting with a suite of educative features: Elementary science teachers' use of educative curriculum materials. *Journal of Research in Science Teaching, 53*(3), 422–449.

Aschbacher, P., and Alonzo, A. (2006). Examining the utility of elementary science notebooks for formative assessment purposes. *Educational Assessment, 11*(3&4), 179–203.

ASCD. (2015). *Elementary and Secondary Education Act: Comparison of the No Child Left Behind Act to the Every Student Succeeds Act.* Available: https://www.ascd.org/ASCD/pdf/siteASCD/policy/ESEA_NCLB_ComparisonChart_2015.pdf.

Atkin, J.M., and Coffey, J. (Eds.). (2003). *Everyday Assessment in the Science Classroom.* Arlington, VA: NSTA Press.

Atman, C.J., Adams, R.S., Cardella, M.E., Turns, J., Mosborg, S., and Saleem, J. (2007). Engineering design processes: A comparison of students and expert practitioners. *Journal of Engineering, 96*(4), 359–379.

Au, W. (2007). High stakes testing and curricular control: A qualitative metasynthesis. *Education Researcher, 7*(5), 258–267.

Avendano, L., Renteria, J., Kwon, S., and Hamdan, K. (2019). Bringing equity to underserved communities through STEM education: Implications for leadership development. *Journal of Educational Administration and History, 51*(1), 66–82.

Avraamidou, L. (2013). Prospective elementary teachers' science teaching orientations and experiences that impacted their development. *International Journal of Science Education, 35*(10), 1698–1724.

Avraamidou, L. (2014). Tracing a beginning elementary teacher's development of identity for science teaching. *Journal of Teacher Education, 65*(3), 223–240.

Avraamidou, L. (2015). Reconceptualizing elementary teacher preparation: A case for informal science education. *International Journal of Science Education, 37*(1), 108–135.

Avraamidou, L. (2016). Intersections of life histories and science identities: The stories of three preservice elementary teachers. *International Journal of Science Education, 38*(5), 861–884.

Bacon, J. (2015). The impact of standards-based reform on special education and the creation of the 'dividual. *Critical Studies in Education, 56*(3), 366–383.

Bacon, J., and Ferri, B. (2013). The impact of standards-based reform: Applying Brantlinger's critique of "hierarchical ideologies." *International Journal of Inclusive Education, 17*(12), 1312–1325.

Bagiati, A., and Evangelou, D. (2011). Starting young: Learning outcomes of a developmentally appropriate PreK engineering curriculum. In W. Hernandez (Ed.), *Proceedings of the Research in Engineering Education Symposium*. Madrid, Spain: Universidad Politecnica de Madres.

Bairaktarova, D., Evangelou, D., Bagiati, A., and Brophy, S. (2011). Early engineering in young children's exploratory play with tangible materials. *Children, Youth and Environments, 21*(2), 212–235.

Baker, B.D., and Corcoran, S.P. (2012). *The Stealth Inequities of School Funding: How State and Local School Finance Systems Perpetuate Inequitable Student Spending*. Washington, DC: Center for American Progress.

Ball, D.L., and Cohen, D.K. (1996). Reform by the book: What is—or might be—the role of curriculum materials in teacher learning and instructional reform? *Educational Researcher, 25*(9), 6–8.

Ball, D., Thames, M., and Phelps, G. (2008). Content knowledge for teaching: What makes it special? *Journal of Teacher Education, 59*(5), 389–407.

Ballenger, C., and Carpenter, M. (2004). The puzzling child: Challenging assumptions about participation and meaning in talking science. *Language Arts, 81*(4), 303.

Banay, E. (2021). *The Research Is In: STEM Educators Academy Demonstrates Success*. Expanded Schools. Available: https://www.expandedschools.org/blog/research-stem-educators-academy-demonstrates-success#sthash.IHv7MpCb.BZ1axZdx.dpbs.

Bang, M., and Medin, D. (2010). Cultural processes in science education: Supporting the navigation of multiple epistemologies. *Science Education, 94*(6), 1008–1026.

Bang, M., Medin, D.L., and Atran, A. (2007). Cultural mosaics and mental models of nature. *Proceedings of the National Academy of Sciences of the United States of America, 104*(35), 13868–13874.

Bang, M., Montaño Nolan, C., and McDaid-Morgan, N. (2018). Indigenous family engagement: Strong families, strong nations. In E.A. McKinley and L.T. Smith (Eds.), *Handbook of Indigenous Education* (pp. 1–22). Singapore: Springer Nature.

Bang, M., Warren, B., Rosebery, A.S., and Medin, D. (2012). Desettling expectations in science education. *Human Development, 55*(5–6), 302–318.

Bang, M., Brown, B., Calabrese Barton, A., Rosebery, A., and Warren, A. (2017). Toward more equitable learning in science: Expanding relationships among students, teachers, and science practices. In C.V. Schwarz, C. Passmore, and B.J. Reiser (Eds.), *Helping Students Make Sense of the World Using Next Generation Science and Engineering Practices* (pp. 33–58). Arlington, VA: NSTA Press.

Banilower, E.R., Smith, P.S., Malzahn, K.A., Plumley, C.L., Gordon, E.M., and Hayes, M.L. (2018). *Report of the 2018 NSSME+*. Chapel Hill, NC: Horizon Research, Inc.

Barajas-López, F., and Bang, M. (2018). Indigenous making and sharing: Claywork in an Indigenous STEAM program. *Equity & Excellence in Education, 51*(1), 7–20.

Barrett, J.E., Clements, D.H., and Sarama, J. (2017). Children's measurement: A longitudinal study of children's knowledge and learning of length, area, and volume. *Journal for Research in Mathematics Education Monograph Series, 16.*

Bartels, S., Rupe, K., and Lederman, J. (2019). Shaping preservice teachers' understandings of STEM: A collaborative math and science methods approach. *Journal of Science Teacher Education, 30*(6), 666–680.

Basham, J.D., and Marino, M.T. (2013). Understanding STEM education and supporting students through universal design for learning. *Teaching Exceptional Children, 45*(4), 8–15.

Basile, V. (2021). Decriminalizing practices: Disrupting punitive-based racial oppression of boys of color in elementary school classrooms. *International Journal of Qualitative Studies in Education, 34*(3), 228–242.

Baumfalk, B., Bhattacharya, D., Vo, T., Forbes, C., Zangori, L., and Schwarz, C. (2019). Impact of model based science curriculum and instruction on elementary students' explanations for the hydrosphere. *Journal of Research in Science Teaching, 56*(5), 570–597.

Bautista, N. (2011). Investigating the use of vicarious and mastery experiences in influencing early childhood education majors' self-efficacy beliefs. *Journal of Science Teacher Education, 22*(4), 333–349.

Bautista, N., and Boone, W. (2015). Exploring the impact of TeachME™ Lab virtual classroom teaching simulation on early childhood education majors' self-efficacy beliefs. *Journal of Science Teacher Education, 26*(3), 237–262.

Bell, P. (2019). Infrastructuring teacher learning about equitable science instruction. *Journal of Science Teacher Education, 30*(7), 681–690.

Bell, P., Van Horne, K., and Cheng, B.H. (2017). Designing learning environments for equitable disciplinary identification. *Journal of the Learning Sciences, 26*(3), 367–375.

Bell, P., Bricker, L., Tzou, C., Lee, T., and Van Horne, K. (2012). Exploring the science framework: Engaging learners in scientific practices related to obtaining, evaluating, and communicating information. *Science and Children, 50*(3), 11.

Bell, R., Matkins, J., and Gansneder, B. (2011). Impacts of contextual and explicit instruction on preservice elementary teachers' understandings of the nature of science. *Journal of Research in Science Teaching, 48*(4), 414–436.

Bencze, L., Pouliot, C., Pedretti, E., Simonneaux, L., Simonneaux, J., and Zeidler, D. (2020). SAQ, SSI and STSE education: Defending and extending "science-in-context." *Cultural Studies of Science Education, 15*, 825–851.

Benedict-Chambers, A. (2016). Using tools to promote novice teacher noticing of science teaching practices in post-rehearsal discussions. *Teaching and Teacher Education, 59*, 28–44.

Benedict-Chambers, A., and Aram, R. (2017). Tools for teacher noticing: Helping preservice teachers notice and analyze student thinking and scientific practice use. *Journal of Science Teacher Education, 28*(3), 294–318.

Benenson, G., Stewart-Dawkins, S., and White, G. (2012). Engineering design of cars and gadgets in K–5 as a vehicle for integrating math, science and literacy. *Advances in Engineering Education, 3*(2), 1–25.

Bennett, D., and Monahan, M. (2013). NYSCI Design Lab: No bored kids. In M. Honey and D. Kanter (Eds.), *Design, Make, Play: Growing the Next Generation of STEM Innovators* (pp. 151–168). New York: Routledge.

Bennett, R.E. (2011). Formative assessment: A critical review. *Assessment in Education: Principles, Policy & Practice, 18*(1), 5–25.

Bennett, R.E., Gottesman, R.L., Rock, D.A., and Cerullo, F.M. (1993). The influence of behavior and gender on teachers' judgments of students' academic skill. *Journal of Educational Psychology, 85*(2), 347–356.

Berg, A., and Mensah, F.M. (2014). De-marginalizing science in the elementary classroom by coaching teachers to address perceived dilemmas. *Education Policy Analysis Archives, 22*(57), 1–35.

Berland, L.K., and Forte, A. (2010). When students speak, who listens? Constructing audience in classroom argumentation. In K. Gomez, L. Lyons, and J. Radinsky (Eds.), *Learning in the Disciplines: Proceedings of the 9th International Conference of the Learning Sciences (ICLS 2010)* (vol. 2, pp. 314–315). Chicago, IL: International Society of the Learning Sciences.

Berland, L.K., and Hammer, D. (2012). Framing for scientific argumentation. *Journal of Research in Science Teaching, 49*(1), 68–94.

Berland, L.K., and Reiser, B.J. (2009). Making sense of argumentation and explanation. *Science Education, 93*(1), 26–55.

Berland, L.K., Russ, R.S., and West, C. (2020). Supporting the scientific practices through responsive teaching. *Journal of Science Teacher Education, 31*(3), 264–290.

Berland, L.K., Schwarz, C.V., Krist, C., Kenyon, L., Lo, A.S., and Reiser, B.J. (2016). Epistemologies in practice: Making scientific practices meaningful for students. *Journal of Research in Science Teaching, 53*, 1082–1112.

Berliner, D.C. (2006). Our impoverished view of educational reform. *Teachers College Record, 8*(6), 949–995.

Bers, M.U., González-González, C., and Armas-Torres, M.B. (2019). Coding as a playground: Promoting positive learning experiences in childhood classrooms. *Computers & Education, 138*(1), 130–145.

Best, R.M., Floyd, R.G., and McNamara, D.S. (2008). Differential competencies contributing to children's comprehension of narrative and expository texts. *Reading Psychology, 29*(2), 137–164.

Bevan, B., Michalchik, V., Bhanot, R., Rauch, N., Remold, J., Semper, R., and Shields, P. (2010). *Out-of-School Time STEM: Building Experience, Building Bridges*. San Francisco: The Exploratorium.

Beyer, C., and Davis, E.A. (2008). Fostering second-graders' scientific explanations: A beginning elementary teacher's knowledge, beliefs, and practice. *Journal of the Learning Sciences, 17*(3), 381–414.

Beyer, C., and Davis, E.A. (2009). Using educative curriculum materials to support preservice elementary teachers' curricular planning: A comparison between two different forms of support. *Curriculum Inquiry, 39*(5), 679–703.

Beyer, C., and Davis, E.A. (2012a). Developing preservice elementary teachers' pedagogical design capacity for reform-based curriculum design. *Curriculum Inquiry, 42*(3), 386–413.

Beyer, C., and Davis, E.A. (2012b). Learning to critique and adapt science curriculum materials: Examining the development of preservice elementary teachers' pedagogical content knowledge. *Science Education, 96*(1), 130–157.

Biggers, M., and Forbes, C. (2012). Balancing teacher and student roles in elementary classrooms: Preservice elementary teachers' learning about the inquiry continuum. *International Journal of Science Education, 34*(14), 2205–2229.

Biggers, M., Forbes, C., and Zangori, L. (2013). Elementary teachers' curriculum design and pedagogical reasoning for supporting students' comparison and evaluation of evidence-based explanations. *Elementary School Journal, 114*, 48–72.

Bishop-Josef, S.J., and Zigler, E. (2011). The cognitive/academic emphasis versus the whole child approach: The 50-year debate. In E. Zigler, W. Gilliam, and W.S. Barnett (Eds.), *The Pre-K Debates: Current Controversies and Issues* (pp. 83–88). Baltimore, MD: Paul H. Brookes.

Bismack, A. (2019). *Content Knowledge for Teaching Science: A Longitudinal Study of Novice Elementary Teachers' Knowledge Development in a Practice-Based Teacher Education Program and School Contexts.* Unpublished doctoral dissertation, University of Michigan, Ann Arbor.

Bismack, A., and Haefner, L.A. (2020). Portrait of a first-grade teacher: Using science practices to leverage young children's sensemaking in science. In E.A. Davis, C. Zembal-Saul, and S.M. Kademian (Eds.), *Sensemaking in Elementary Science: Supporting Teacher Learning.* New York: Routledge.

Bismack, A.S., Arias, A.M., Davis, E.A., and Palincsar, A.S. (2014). Connecting curriculum materials and teachers: Elementary science teachers' enactment of a reform-based curricular unit. *Journal of Science Teacher Education, 25*(4), 489–512.

Bismack, A.S., Arias, A., Davis, E.A., and Palincsar, A.S. (2015). Examining student work for evidence of teacher uptake of educative curriculum materials. *Journal of Research in Science Teaching, 52*(6), 816–846.

Bjorklund, D.F., and Causey, K.B. (2018). *Children's Thinking: Cognitive Development and Individual Differences.* Los Angeles, CA: SAGE.

Blank, R.K. (2013). Science instructional time is declining in elementary schools: What are the implications for student achievement and closing the gap? *Science Education, 97*(6), 830–847.

Blumenfeld, P., Fishman, B.J., Krajcik, J., Marx, R.W., and Soloway, E. (2000). Creating usable innovations in systemic reform: Scaling up technology-embedded project-based science in urban schools. *Educational Psychologist, 35*(3), 149–164.

Bondy, E., Ross, D.D., Gallingame, C., and Hambacher, E. (2007). Creating environments of success and resilience: Culturally responsive classroom management and more. *Urban Education, 42*(4), 326–348.

Bottoms, S., Ciechanowski, K., and Hartman, B. (2015). Learning to teach elementary science through iterative cycles of enactment in culturally and linguistically diverse contexts. *Journal of Science Teacher Education, 26*(8), 715–742.

Braaten, M., and Windschitl, M. (2011). Working toward a stronger conceptualization of scientific explanation for science education. *Science Education, 95*(4), 639–669.

Brackett, M.A., Bailey, C.S., Hoffmann, J.D., and Simmons, D.N. (2019). RULER: A theory-driven, systemic approach to social, emotional, and academic learning. *Educational Psychologist, 54*(3), 144–161.

Bravo, M., Mosqueda, E., Solís, J., and Stoddart, T. (2014). Possibilities and limits of integrating science and diversity education in preservice elementary teacher preparation. *Journal of Science Teacher Education, 25*(5), 601–619.

Brenneman, K., and Louro, I.F. (2008). Science journals in the preschool classroom. *Early Childhood Education Journal, 36*(2), 113–119.

Brenneman, K., Lange, A. and Nayfeld, I. (2019). Integrating STEM into preschool education: Designing a professional development model in diverse settings. *Early Childhood Education Journal, 47,* 15–28.

Bricker, L.A., and Bell, P. (2008). Conceptualizations of argumentation from science studies and the learning sciences and their implications for the practices of science education. *Science Education, 92*(3), 473–498.

Bricker, L.A., and Bell, P. (2014). "What comes to mind when you think of science? The perfumery!": Documenting science related cultural learning pathways across contexts and timescales. *Journal of Research in Science Teaching, 51*(3), 260–285.

Brobst, J., Markworth, K., Tasker, T., and Ohana, C. (2017). Comparing the preparedness, content knowledge, and instructional quality of elementary science specialists and self contained teachers. *Journal of Research in Science Teaching, 54*(10), 1302–1321.

Broderick, J.T., and Hong, S.B. (2020). *From Children's Interests to Children's Thinking: Using a Cycle of Inquiry to Plan Curriculum.* Washington, DC: National Association for the Education of Young Children.

Brophy, S., and Evangelou, D. (2007). Precursors to engineering thinking (PET) project: Intentional designs with experimental artifacts (IDEA). In *Proceedings of the 2007 American Society for Engineering Education Annual Conference and Exposition* (pp. 12.1169.1–12.1169.11). Washington, DC: American Society for Engineering Education. https://peer.asee.org/precursors-to-engineering-thinking-pet.

Brown, B.A., and Spang, E. (2008). Double talk: Synthesizing everyday and science language in the classroom. *Science Education, 92*(4), 708–732.

Brown, C.S., Mistry, R.S., and Yip, T. (2019). Moving from the margins to the mainstream: Equity and justice as key considerations for developmental science. *Child Development Perspectives, 13*(4), 235–240.

Brunner, J.L. (2019). Teachers' use of educative features in guides for nature of science read-alouds. *Science & Education, 28*(3), 413–437.

Brunner, J.L., and Abd-El-Khalick, F. (2020). Improving nature of science instruction in elementary classes with modified science trade books and educative curriculum materials. *Journal of Research in Science Teaching, 57*(2), 154–183.

Bryk, A.S. (2010). Organizing schools for improvement. *Phi Delta Kappan, 91*(7), 23–30.

Buck, G., Trauth-Nare, A., and Kaftan, J. (2010). Making formative assessment discernable to pre-service teachers of science. *Journal of Research in Science Teaching, 47*(4), 402–421.

Bullock, M., Sodian, B., and Koerber, S. (2009). Doing experiments and understanding science: Development of scientific reasoning from childhood to adulthood. In W. Schneider and M. Bullock (Eds.), *Human Development from Early Childhood to Early Adulthood: Findings from a 20-Year Longitudinal Study* (pp. 173–197). New York: Psychology Press.

Bulunuz, M. (2013). Teaching science through play in kindergarten: Does integrated play and science instruction build understanding? *European Early Childhood Education Research Journal, 21*(2), 226–249.

Bustamante, A.S., Greenfield, D.B., and Nayfeld, I. (2018). Early childhood science and engineering: Engaging platforms for fostering domain-general learning skills. *Journal of Education Sciences, 8*(3), 144–157.

Bustamante, A.S., White, L.J., and Greenfield, D.B. (2017). Approaches to learning and school readiness in Head Start: Applications to preschool science. *Learning and Individual Differences, 56*, 112–118.

Bustamante, A.S., White, L.J., and Greenfield, D.B. (2018). Science and approaches to learning in Head Start: Examining bi-directionality. *Early Child Research Quarterly, 44*, 34–42.

Bustamante, A.S., Hindman, A.H., Champagne, C., and Wasik, B.A. (2018). Circle time revisited: How do preschool classrooms use this part of the day? *Elementary School Journal, 118*(4), 610–631.

Cabell, S.Q., DeCoster, J., LoCasale-Crouch, J., Hamre, B.K., and Pianta, R.C. (2013). Variation in the effectiveness of instructional interactions across preschool classroom settings and learning activities. *Early Childhood Research Quarterly, 28*(4), 820–830.

Cabrera, L., McGinnis, J.R., Ketelhut, D.J., Hestness, E.E., Mills, K.M., and Jeong, H. (2019). *Preservice Teachers' Changes in Self-Efficacy Regarding Computational Thinking.* Paper presented at the National Association for Research in Science Teaching (NARST) 92nd Annual International Conference, Baltimore, MD.

Cabrera, L., Coenraad, M., Mills, K.M., McGinnis, J.R., and Ketelhut, D.J. (2020). *Preservice Teachers' Self-Efficacy and Computational Thinking: A Mixed-Methods Approach.* Paper presented at the American Educational Research Association Conference, San Francisco, CA.

Cahnmann, M.S., and Remillard, J.T. (2002). What counts and how: Mathematics teaching in culturally, linguistically, and socioeconomically diverse urban settings. *The Urban Review, 34*(3), 179–204.

Cajete, G., and Bear, L.L. (2000). *Native Science: Natural Laws of Interdependence* (vol. 315). Santa Fe, NM: Clear Light.

Calabrese Barton, A., and Tan, E. (2010). We be burnin'! Agency, identity, and science learning. *Journal of the Learning Sciences, 19*(2), 187–229.

Calabrese Barton, A., and Tan, E. (2019). Designing for rightful presence in STEM: The role of making present practices. *Journal of the Learning Sciences, 28*(4–5), 616–658.

Calabrese Barton, A., and Tan, E. (2020). Beyond equity as inclusion: A framework of "rightful presence" for guiding justice-oriented studies in teaching and learning. *Educational Researcher, 49*(6), 433–440.

Callaghan, T., and Corbit, J. (2015). The development of symbolic representation. In L.S. Liben, U. Müller, and R.M. Lerner (Eds.), *Handbook of Child Psychology and Developmental Science* (4th ed., vol. 2, pp. 1–46). Hoboken, NJ: John Wiley & Sons.

Callanan, M.A. (2012). Conducting cognitive developmental research in museums: Theoretical issues and practical considerations. *Journal of Cognition and Development, 13*(2), 137–151.

Callanan, M., Martin, J., and Luce, M. (2015). Two decades of families learning in a children's museum. In D.M. Sobel and J.L. Jipson (Eds.), *Cognitive Development in Museum Settings: Relating Research and Practice* (pp. 15–35). New York and Abingdon, UK: Routledge.

Camburn, E., Rowan, B., and Taylor, E. (2003). Distributed leadership in schools: The case of elementary schools adopting comprehensive school reform models. *Educational Evaluation and Policy Analysis, 25*(4), 347–373.

Campbell, T., Schwarz, C., and Windschitl, M. (2016). What we call misconceptions may be necessary stepping-stones toward making sense of the world. *The Science Teacher, 83*(3), 69.

Canipe, M., and Gunckel, K. (2020). Imagination, brokers, and boundary objects: Interrupting the mentor–preservice teacher hierarchy when negotiating meanings. *Journal of Teacher Education, 71*(1), 80–93.

Capobianco, B.M., DeLisi, J., and Radloff, J. (2018). Characterizing elementary teachers' enactment of high-leverage practices through engineering design-based science instruction. *Science Education, 102*(2), 342–376.

Cardella, M.E., Svarovsky, G.N., and Pattison, S. (2020). *Engineering Education in Pre-Kindergarten through Fifth Grade: An Overview*. Washington, DC: The National Academies Press.

Carey, S., and Smith, C. (1993). On understanding the nature of scientific knowledge. *Educational Psychologist, 28*(3), 235–251.

Carlone, H.B., Haun-Frank, J., and Kimmel, S.C. (2010). Tempered radicals: Elementary teachers' narratives of teaching science within and against prevailing meanings of schooling. *Cultural Studies of Science Education, 5*(4), 941–965.

Carlone, H.B., Kimmel, S., and Tschida, C. (2010). A rural math, science, and technology elementary school tangled up in global networks of practice. *Cultural Studies of Science Education, 5*, 447–476.

Carlone, H.B., Haun-Frank, J. and Webb, A. (2011). Assessing equity beyond knowledge- and skills-based outcomes: A comparative ethnography of two fourth-grade reform-based science classrooms. *Journal of Research in Science Teaching, 48*, 459–485.

Carlone, H.B., Scott, C.M., and Lowder, C. (2014). Becoming (less) scientific: A longitudinal study of students' identity work from elementary to middle school science. *Journal of Research in Science Teaching, 51*(7), 836–869.

Carlone, H.B., Mercier, A.K., and Metzger, S.R. (2021). The production of epistemic culture and agency during a first-grade engineering design unit in an urban emergent school. *Journal of Pre-College Engineering Education Research*, 11(1), 1–20.

Carrier, S. (2013). Elementary preservice teachers' science vocabulary: Knowledge and application. *Journal of Science Teacher Education*, 24(2), 405–425.

Carrier, S., and Grifenhagen, J. (2020). Academic vocabulary support for elementary science pre-service teachers. *Journal of Science Teacher Education*, 31(2), 115–133.

Carrier, S.J., Tugurian, L.P., and Thomson, M.M. (2013). Elementary science indoors and out: Teachers, time, and testing. *Research in Science Education*, 43(5), 2059–2083.

Cartier, J.L., Smith, M.S., Stein, M.K., and Ross, D. (2013). *Five Practices for Orchestrating Task-Based Discussions in Science*. Reston, VA: National Council of Teachers of Mathematics.

Cartwright, T., and Atwood, J. (2014). Elementary pre-service teachers' response-shift bias: Self-efficacy and attitudes toward science. *International Journal of Science Education*, 36(14), 2421–2437.

Cartwright, T.J., and Hallar, B. (2018). Taking risks with a growth mindset: Long-term influence of an elementary pre-service after school science practicum. *International Journal of Science Education*, 40(3), 348–370.

Casey, P., Dunlap, K., Brown, K., and Davison, M. (2016). Elementary principal's role in science instruction. *Administrative Issues Journal: Education, Practice, and Research*, 2(2), 57–62.

Castagno, A. (Ed.) (2019). *The Price of Nice: How Good Intentions Maintain Educational Inequality*. Minneapolis, MN: University of Minnesota Press.

Cervetti, G., Kulikowich, J., and Bravo, M. (2015). The effects of educative curriculum materials on teachers' use of instructional strategies for English language learners in science and on student learning. *Contemporary Educational Psychology*, 40, 86–98.

Cervetti, G.N., Wright, T.S., and Hwang, H. (2016). Conceptual coherence, comprehension, and vocabulary acquisition: A knowledge effect? *Reading & Writing*, 29, 761–779.

Cervetti, G.N., Pearson, P.D., Bravo, M.A., and Barber, J. (2006). Reading and writing in the service of inquiry-based science. In R. Douglas, M.P. Klentschy, K. Worth, and W. Binder (Eds.), *Linking Science & Literacy in the K–8 Classroom* (pp. 221–244). Arlington, VA: NSTA Press.

Chalufour, I., and Worth, K. (2003). *Discovering Nature with Young Children* (The Young Scientist Series). St. Paul, MN: Red Leaf Press.

Chalufour, I., and Worth, K. (2004). *Building Structures with Young Children* (The Young Scientist Series). St. Paul, MN: Red Leaf Press.

Chalufour, I., and Worth, K. (2005). *Exploring Water with Young Children, Trainer's Guide*. St. Paul, MN: Red Leaf Press.

Chambliss, M.J., Christenson, L.A., and Parker, C. (2003). Fourth graders composing scientific explanations about the effects of pollutants: Writing to understand. *Written Communication*, 20(4), 426–454.

Chang-Kredl, S., and Kingsley, S. (2014). Identity expectations in early childhood teacher education: Pre-service teachers' memories of prior experiences and reasons for entry into the profession. *Teaching and Teacher Education*, 43, 27–36.

Charara, J., Miller, E., and Krajcik, J. (2021). Knowledge in use: Designing for play in kindergarten contexts. *Journal of Leadership, Equity, and Research*, 7(1), 1–28.

Chen, J., and Mensah, F.M. (2018). Teaching contexts that influence elementary preservice teachers' teacher and science teacher identity development. *Journal of Science Teacher Education*, 29(5), 420–439.

Cherbow, K., McKinley, M.T., McNeill, K.L., and Lowenhaupt, R. (2020). An analysis of science instruction for the science practices: Examining coherence across system levels and components in current systems of science education in K–8 schools. *Science Education, 104*, 446–478.

Chin, C., Brown, D.E., and Bruce, B.C. (2002). Student-generated questions: A meaningful aspect of learning in science. *International Journal of Science Education, 24*(5), 521–549.

Chinn, P.W. (2006). Preparing science teachers for culturally diverse students: Developing cultural literacy through cultural immersion, cultural translators and communities of practice. *Cultural Studies of Science Education, 1*(2), 367–402.

Chinn, P.W. (2012). Developing teachers' place-based and culture-based pedagogical content knowledge and agency. In B. Fraser, K. Tobin, and J.C. McRobbie (Eds.), *Second International Handbook of Science Education* (pp. 323–334). Dordrecht, The Netherlands: Springer.

Chiu, A., Price, A., and Ovrahim, E. (2015). *Supporting Elementary and Middle School STEM Education at the Whole-School Level: A Review of the Literature.* Paper presented at the National Association for Research in Science Teaching (NARST) 2015 Annual Conference, Chicago, IL.

Christenson, S., Decker, D., Triezenberg, H., Ysseldyke, J., and Reschly, A. (2007). Consequences of high-stakes assessment for students with and without disabilities. *Educational Policy, 21*, 662–690.

Clements, D.H. (2007). Curriculum research: Toward a framework for research-based curricula. *Journal for Research in Mathematics Education, 38*(1), 35–70.

Clements, D.H., and Sarama, J. (Eds.). (2004). *Engaging Young Children in Mathematics: Standards for Early Childhood Mathematics Education.* Mahwah, NJ: Lawrence Erlbaum Associates.

Clements, D.H., and Sarama, J. (2021a). *Learning and Teaching Early Math: The Learning Trajectories Approach* (3rd ed.). New York and Abingdon, UK: Routledge.

Clements, D.H., and Sarama, J. (2021b). STEM or STEAM or STREAM? Integrated or interdisciplinary? In C. Cohrssen and S. Garvis (Eds.), *Embedding STEAM in Early Childhood Education and Care.* Cham, Switzerland: Palgrave Macmillan.

Clements, D., Greenfield, D.B., Landry, S.H., and Sarama, J. (2015). Assessment and evaluation using technology: Formative assessment with young children. In O.N. Saracho (Ed.), *Educational Assessment and Evaluation* (pp. 339–371), in the series, *Contemporary Perspectives in Early Childhood Education.* Charlotte, NC: Information Age.

Clements, D.H., Vinh, M., Lim, C.-I., and Sarama, J. (2021). STEM for inclusive excellence and equity. *Early Education and Development, 2*(1), 148–171.

Cobern, W., Schuster, D., Adams, B., Skjold, B., Muğaloğlu, E., Bentz, A., and Sparks, K. (2014). Pedagogy of science teaching tests: Formative assessments of science teaching orientations. *International Journal of Science Education, 36*(13), 2265–2288.

Coburn, C.E., and Woulfin, S.L. (2012). Reading coaches and the relationship between policy and practice. *Reading Research Quarterly, 47*, 5–30.

Cody, J., and Biggers, M. (2020). Science, engineering, literacy, and place-based education: Powerful practices for integration. In E.A. Davis, C. Zembal-Saul, and S.M. Kademian (Eds.), *Sensemaking in Elementary Science: Supporting Teacher Learning* (pp. 46–63). New York: Routledge.

Coffey, J.E., Hammer, D., Levin, D.M., and Grant, T. (2011). The missing disciplinary substance of formative assessment. *Journal of Research in Science Teaching, 48*(10), 1109–1136.

Cohen, D.K. (1990). A revolution in one classroom: The case of Mrs. Oublier. *Educational Evaluation and Policy Analysis, 12*(3), 311–329.

Colley, C., and Windschitl, M. (2016). Rigor in elementary science students' discourse: The role of responsiveness and supportive conditions for talk. *Science Education, 100*(6), 1009–1038.

Cone, N. (2012). The effects of community-based service learning on preservice teachers' beliefs about the characteristics of effective science teachers of diverse students. *Journal of Science Teacher Education, 23*(8), 889–907.

Confrey, J., and Lachance, A. (2000). Transformative teaching experiments through conjecture-driven research design. In A.E. Kelly and R.A. Lesh (Eds.), *Handbook of Research Design in Mathematics and Science Education* (pp. 231–265). Mahwah, NJ: Lawrence Erlbaum Associates.

Cook, C., Goodman, N.D., and Schulz, L.E. (2011). Where science starts: Spontaneous experiments in preschoolers' exploratory play. *Cognition, 120*(3), 341–349.

Cooper, S., and Cunningham, S. (2010). Teaching computer science in context. *ACM Inroads, 1*(1), 5–8.

Counsell, S., Peat, F., Vaughan, R., and Johnson, T. (2015). Inventing mystery machines. *Science and Children, 52*(7), 64.

Couso, D., and Simarro, C. (2020). STEM education through the epistemological lens. In C.C. Johnson, M.J. Mohr-Schroeder, T.J. Moore, and L.D. English (Eds.), *Handbook of Research on STEM Education* (pp. 17–28). New York: Routledge.

Cowie, A.L., Orr, B.J., Sanchez, V.M.C., Chasek, P., Crossman, N.D., Erlewein, A., Louwagie, G., Maron, M., Metternicht, G.I., Minellie, S., Tengberg, A.E., Walter, S., and Welton, S. (2018). Land in balance: The scientific conceptual framework for Land Degradation Neutrality. *Environmental Science & Policy, 79*, 25–35.

Crowl, M., Devitt, A., Jansen, H., van Zee, E., and Winograd, K. (2013). Encouraging prospective teachers to engage friends and family in exploring physical phenomena. *Journal of Science Teacher Education, 24*(1), 93–110.

Cunningham, C.M. (2017). *Engineering in Elementary STEM Education: Curriculum Design, Instruction, Learning, and Assessment*. New York: Teachers College Press.

Cunningham, C.M., Lachapelle, C.P., and Davis, M.E. (2018). Engineering concepts, practices, and trajectories for early childhood education. In L.D. English and T. Moore (Eds.), *Early Engineering Learning* (pp. 135–174). Singapore: Springer.

Cunningham, C., Lachapelle, C., and Lindgren-Streicher, A. (2006). Elementary teachers' understandings of engineering and technology. *Proceedings of the 2006 American Society for Engineering Education Annual Conference and Exposition* (pp. 11.528.1–11.528.15). Washington, DC: American Society for Engineering Education.

Cunningham, C.M., Lachapelle, C.P., Brennan, R.T., Kelly, G.J., Tunis, C.S.A., and Gentry, C.A. (2020). The impact of engineering curriculum design principles on elementary students' engineering and science learning. *Journal of Research in Science Teaching, 57*(3), 423–453.

Czerniak, C.M., Weber, W.B., Jr., Sandmann, A., and Ahern, J. (1999). A literature review of science and mathematics integration. *School Science and Mathematics, 99*(8), 421–430.

d'Alessio, M. (2018). The effect of microteaching on science teaching self-efficacy beliefs in preservice elementary teachers. *Journal of Science Teacher Education, 29*(6), 441–467.

Dalton, B. (2012). Multimodal composition and the common core state standards. *The Reading Teacher, 66*(4), 333–339.

Dalton, B., and Palincsar, A.S. (2013). Investigating text–reader interactions in the context of supported eText. In R. Azevedo and V. Aleven (Eds.), *International Handbook of Metacognition and Learning Technologies* (pp. 533–544). New York: Springer.

Dalvi, T., and Wendell, K. (2017). Using student video cases to assess pre-service elementary teachers' engineering teaching responsiveness. *Research in Science Education, 47*, 1101–1125.

Dalvi, T., Wendell, K.B., and Johnson, J. (2016). Community-based engineering. *YC Young Children, 71*(5), 8.

Danielsson, A., Andersson, K., Gullberg, A., Hussénius, A., and Scantlebury, K. (2016). "In biology class we would just sit indoors...": Experiences of insideness and outsideness in the places student teachers' associate with science. *Cultural Studies of Science Education, 11*, 1115–1134.

Danish, J.A. (2014). Applying an activity theory lens to designing instruction for learning about the structure, behavior, and function of a honeybee system. *Journal of the Learning Sciences, 23*(2), 100–148.

Danish, J.A., and Enyedy, N. (2006). Unpacking the mediation of invented representations. In S. Barab, K. Hay, and D. Hickey (Eds.), *Proceedings of the 7th International Conference on Learning Sciences* (pp. 113–119). Bloomington, IN: International Society of the Learning Sciences.

Danish, J.A., and Enyedy, N. (2007). Negotiated representational mediators: How young children decide what to include in their science representations. *Science Education, 91*(1), 1–35.

Danish, J.A., Enyedy, N., Saleh, A., and Humburg, M. (2020). Learning in embodied activity framework: A sociocultural framework for embodied cognition. *International Journal of Computer-Supported Collaborative Learning, 5*(1), 49–87.

Darling-Hammond, L., Banks, J., Zumwalt, K., Gomez, L., Sherin, M.G., Griesdorn, J., and Finn, L.-E. (2005). Educational goals and purposes: Developing a curricular vision for teaching. In L. Darling-Hammond and J. Bransford (Eds.), *Preparing Teachers for a Changing World: What Teachers Should Learn and Be Able to Do* (pp. 169–200). San Francisco: John Wiley & Sons.

Darling-Hammond, S., Fronius, T.A., Sutherland, H., Guckenburg, S., Petrosino, A., and Hurley, N. (2020). Effectiveness of restorative justice in U.S. K–12 schools: A review of quantitative research. *Contemporary School Psychology, 24*, 295–308.

Davis, E.A. (2006). Preservice elementary teachers' critique of instructional materials for science. *Science Education, 90*(2), 348–375.

Davis, E.A., and Boerst, T. (2014). *Designing Elementary Teacher Education to Prepare Well-started Beginners*. Teaching Works, University of Michigan School of Education.

Davis, E.A., and Haverly, C. (in press). Well-started beginners: Preparing elementary teachers for rigorous, consequential, just, and equitable science teaching. In J. Luft and G. Jones (Eds.), *Handbook of Research on Science Teacher Education*. New York: Routledge.

Davis, E.A., and Krajcik, J. (2005). Designing educative curriculum materials to promote teacher learning. *Educational Researcher, 34*(3), 3–14.

Davis, E.A., Janssen, F., and Van Driel, J. (2016). Teachers and science curriculum materials: Where we are and where we need to go. *Studies in Science Education, 52*(2), 127–160.

Davis, E.A., Palincsar, A.S., and Kademian, S.M. (2020). Designing a practice-based elementary teacher education program and supporting professional learning in science teaching. In E.A. Davis, C. Zembal-Saul, and S.M. Kademian (Eds.), *Sensemaking in Elementary Science: Supporting Teacher Learning* (pp. 189–203). New York: Routledge.

Davis, E.A., Petish, D., and Smithey, J. (2006). Challenges new science teachers face. *Review of Educational Research, 76*(4), 607–651.

Davis, E.A., Palincsar, A.S., Smith, P.S., Arias, A., and Kademian, S. (2017). Educative curriculum materials: Uptake, impact, and implications for research and design. *Educational Researcher, 46*(6), 293–304.

Davis, N.R., and Schaeffer, J. (2019). Troubling troubled waters in elementary science education: Politics, ethics, & black children's conceptions of water [justice] in the era of Flint. *Cognition and Instruction, 37*(3), 367–389.

Dawson, E. (2014). "Not designed for us": How science museums and science centers socially exclude low-income, minority ethnic groups. *Science Education, 98*(6), 981–1008.

Deal, T.E., and Peterson, K.D. (1999). *Shaping School Culture: The Heart of Leadership.* San Francisco: John Wiley & Sons.

DeFrance, N.L. (2008). *Struggling Readers Learning with Graphic-Rich Digital Science Text: Effects of a Highlight and Animate Feature and Manipulable Graphics.* Unpublished doctoral dissertation, University of Michigan, Ann Arbor.

Delgado-Gaitan, C. (1990). *Literacy for Empowerment: The Role of Parents in Children's Education.* New York: Routledge.

DeLiema, D., Enyedy, N., and Danish, J.A. (2019). Roles, rules, and keys: How different play configurations shape collaborative science inquiry. *Journal of the Learning Sciences, 28*(4–5), 513–555.

DeLoache, J.S. (2004). Becoming symbol-minded. *Trends in Cognitive Sciences, 8*(2), 66–70.

Diamond, J.B., and Spillane, J.P. (2004). High-stakes accountability in urban elementary schools: Challenging or reproducing inequality? *Teachers College Record, 106*(6), 1145–1176.

Dickes, A.C., Sengupta, P., Farris, A.V., and Basu, S. (2016). Development of mechanistic reasoning and multilevel explanations of ecology in third grade using agent-based models. *Science Education, 100*, 734–776.

Dimitrov, M. (2009). Intermediate trends in math and science partnership–related changes in student achievement with management information system data. *Journal of Educational Research & Policy Studies, 9*(2), 97–138.

diSessa, A.A. (2001). *Changing Minds: Computers, Learning, and Literacy.* Cambridge, MA: MIT Press.

diSessa, A.A. (2014). The construction of causal schemes: Learning mechanisms at the knowledge level. *Cognitive Science, 38*(5), 795–850.

diSessa, A.A., and Wagner, J.F. (2005). What coordination has to say about transfer. In J.P. Mestre (Ed.), *Transfer of Learning from a Modern Multi-Disciplinary Perspective* (pp. 121–154). Greenwich, CT: Information Age.

diSessa, A., Hammer, D., Sherin, B., and Kolpakowski, T. (1991). Inventing graphing: Meta-representational expertise in children. *Journal of Mathematical Behavior, 10*, 117–160.

Doan, S., and Lucero, A. (2021). *Changing the Subject: K–12 Teachers' Use of and Access to Science-Specific Instructional Materials, Feedback, and Professional Learning.* Available: https://www.rand.org/pubs/research_reports/RRA134-7.html.

Domínguez, X., and Goldstein, M. (2020). *Next Generation Preschool Science: Findings from Design-based Research to Inform Iterative Development of an Innovative Curricular Program and a Field Study to Examine Implementation and Efficacy.* Society for Research on Educational Effectiveness.

Donaldson, M.L. (2009). *So Long, Lake Wobegon? Using Teacher Evaluation to Raise Teacher Quality.* Washington, DC: Center for American Progress.

Dong, Y., Catete, V., Jocius, R., Lytle, N., Barnes, T., Albert, J., Joshi, D., Robinson, R., and Andrews, A. (2019). PRADA: A practical model for integrating computational thinking in K–12 education. In *SIGCSE '19: Proceedings of the 50th ACM Technical Symposium on Computer Science Education* (pp. 906–912). New York: Association for Computing Machinery.

Douglas, K.A., Moore, T.J., Johnston, A.C., and Merzdorf, H.E. (2018). Informed designers? Students' reflections on their engineering design process. *International Journal of Education in Mathematics, Science and Technology, 6*, 443–459.

Drayton, B., Bernstein, D., Schunn, C., and McKenney, S. (2020). Consequences of curricular adaptation strategies for implementation at scale. *Science Education, 104*, 983–1007.

Driver, R., Leach, J., Millar, R., and Scott, P. (1996). *Young People's Images of Science*. Buckingham, UK: Open University Press.

Droop, M., and Verhoeven, L. (1998). Background knowledge, linguistic complexity, and second-language reading comprehension. *Journal of Literacy Research, 30*(2), 253–271.

Duckworth, E. (1972). The having of wonderful ideas. *Harvard Educational Review, 42*(2), 217–231.

Duke, N.K. (2000). 3.6 minutes per day: The scarcity of informational texts in first grade. *Reading Research Quarterly, 35*, 202–224.

Duke, N.K. (2016). Project-based learning: A great match for informational texts. *American Educator, 40*(3), 4–11, 42.

Duncan, D., Diefes-Dux, H., and Gentry, M. (2011). Professional development through engineering academies: An examination of elementary teachers' recognition and understanding of engineering. *Journal of Engineering Education, 100*(3), 520–539.

Duschl, R. (2008). Science education in three-part harmony: Balancing conceptual, epistemic, and social learning goals. *Review of Research in Education, 32*(1), 268–291.

Early, D.M., Iruka, I.U., Ritchie, S., Barbarin, O.A., Winn, D.M.C., Crawford, G.M., Frome, P.M., Clifford, R.M., Burchinal, M., Howes, C., Bryant, D.M., and Pianta, R.C. (2010). How do pre-kindergarteners spend their time? Gender, ethnicity, and income as predictors of experiences in pre-kindergarten classrooms. *Early Childhood Research Quarterly, 25*(2), 177–193.

Easley, K.M. (2020). *Simulations and Sensemaking in Elementary Project-Based Science*. Unpublished doctoral dissertation, University of Michigan, Ann Arbor.

Eberbach, C., and Crowley, K. (2009). From everyday to scientific observation: How children learn to observe the biologists world. *Review of Educational Research, 79*(1), 39–68.

Edelson, D., Reiser, B., McNeill, K., Mohan, A., Novak, M., Mohan, L., Affolter, R., McGill, T., Bracey, Z.B., Noll, J.D., Kowalski, S., Novak, D., Lo, A., Landel, C., Krumm, A., Penuel, W.R., Van Horne, K., Gonzalez-Howard, M., and Suárez, E. (2021). Developing research-based instructional materials to support large-scale transformation of science teaching and learning: The approach of the OpenSciEd middle school program. *Journal of Science Teacher Education, 32*(7), 780–804.

Edwards, K., Gotwals, A., and Wright, T. (2020). The Boxcar Challenge Unit: Integrating engineering design, science, and literacy for kindergarten. *Science and Children, 57*(5).

Ehsan, H., Fagundes, B., Moore, T.J., Tank, K.M., and Cardella, M.E. (2020). WIP: First-graders' computational thinking in informal learning settings. In *Proceedings of the 2020 American Society for Engineering Education Virtual Annual Conference*. Washington, DC: American Society for Engineering Education. https://www.asee.org/public/conferences/172/papers/30871/view.

Eick, C., and Stewart, B. (2010). Dispositions supporting elementary interns in the teaching of reform-based science materials. *Journal of Science Teacher Education, 21*(7), 783–800.

Eisenhart, M. (2001). Educational ethnography past, present, and future: Ideas to think with. *Educational Researcher, 30*(8), 16–27.

Enfield, M., Smith, E., and Grueber, D. (2008). "A sketch is like a sentence": Curriculum structures that support teaching epistemic practices of science. *Science Education, 92*, 608–630.

Engle, R.A. (2012). The productive disciplinary engagement framework: Origins, key concepts, and developments. In *Design Research on Learning and Thinking in Educational Settings: Enhancing Intellectual Growth and Functioning* (pp. 161–200). New York: Routledge.

Engle, R.A., and Conant, F.R. (2002). Guiding principles for fostering productive disciplinary engagement: Explaining an emergent argument in a Community of Learners classroom. *Cognition and Instruction, 20*(4), 399–483.

English, L.D. (2016). STEM education K–12: Perspectives on integration. *International Journal of STEM Education, 3*(1), 3.

English, L.D., and King, D.T. (2017). Engineering education with fourth-grade students: Introducing design-based problem solving. *International Journal of Engineering Education, 33*(1), 346–360.

Epstein, J.L., and Sheldon, S.B. (2016). Necessary but not sufficient: The role of policy for advancing programs of school, family, and community partnerships. *RSF: The Russell Sage Foundation Journal of the Social Sciences, 2*(5), 202–219.

Eshach, H., and Fried, M.N. (2005). Should science be taught in early childhood? *Journal of Science Education and Technology, 14*(3), 315–336.

Esteban-Guitart, M., and Moll, L.C. (2014). Lived experience, funds of identity and education. *Culture & Psychology, 20*(1), 70–81.

Falk, J.H. (2009). *Identity and the Museum Visitor Experience*. Walnut Creek, CA: Left Coast Press.

Falk, J.H., and Dierking, L.D. (2002). *Lessons Without Limit: How Free-Choice Learning is Transforming Education*. Lanham, MD: Altamira.

Falk, J., and Storksdieck, M. (2005). Using the contextual model of learning to understand visitor learning from a science center exhibition. *Science Education, 89*(5), 744–778.

Falloon, G. (2019). Using simulations to teach young students science concepts: An experiential learning theoretical analysis. *Computers & Education, 135*, 138–159.

Farland, D. (2006). The effect of historical, nonfiction trade books on elementary students' perceptions of scientists. *Journal of Elementary Science Education, 18*(2), 31–48.

Fazio, X., and Gallagher, T.L. (2019). Science and language integration in elementary classrooms: Instructional enactments and student learning outcomes. *Research in Science Education, 49*(4), 959–976.

Feiman-Nemser, S. (2001). From preparation to practice: Designing a continuum to strengthen and sustain teaching. *Teachers College Record, 103*(6), 1013–1055.

Feinstein, N.W., and Waddington, D.I. (2020). Individual truth judgments or purposeful, collective sensemaking? Rethinking science education's response to the post-truth era. *Educational Psychologist, 55*(3), 155–166.

Feldman, S., and Malagon, V.F. (2017). *Unlocking Learning: Science as a Lever for English Learner Equity*. Oakland, CA: Education Trust-West.

Fine, C., and Furtak, E. (2020). A framework for science classroom assessment task design for emergent bilingual learners. *Science Education, 104*(3), 393–420.

Fitchett, P.G., and Heafner, T.L. (2010). A national perspective on the effects of high-stakes testing and standardization on elementary social studies marginalization. *Theory and Research in Social Education, 38*(1), 114–130.

Fitzgerald, M.S. (2018). *Texts and Tasks in Elementary Project-Based Science*. Unpublished doctoral dissertation, University of Michigan, Ann Arbor.

Fitzgerald, M.S. (2020). Overlapping opportunities for social-emotional and literacy learning in elementary-grade project-based instruction. *American Journal of Education, 126*(4), 573–601.

Fleer, M., Gomes, J., and March, S. (2014). Science learning affordances in preschool environments. *Australasian Journal of Early Childhood, 39*(1), 38–48.

Flores, N., and Rosa, J. (2015). Undoing appropriateness: Raciolinguistic ideologies and language diversity in education. *Harvard Educational Review, 85*(2), 149–171.

Foglia, L., and Wilson, R.A. (2013). Embodied cognition. *Wiley Interdisciplinary Reviews: Cognitive Science, 4*(3), 319–325.

Forbes, C. (2011). Preservice elementary teachers' adaptation of science curriculum materials for inquiry-based elementary science. *Science Education, 95*, 927–955.

Forbes, C. (2013). Curriculum-dependent and curriculum-independent factors in preservice elementary teachers' adaptation of science curriculum materials for inquiry-based science. *Journal of Science Teacher Education, 24*, 179–197.

Forbes, C., and Davis, E.A. (2010). Curriculum design for inquiry: Preservice elementary teachers' mobilization and adaptation of science curriculum materials. *Journal of Research in Science Teaching, 47*(7), 820–839.

Ford, D. (2005). The challenges of observing geologically: Third graders' descriptions of rock and mineral properties. *Science Education, 89*, 276–295.

Ford, D.J. (2006). Representations of science within children's trade books. *Journal of Research in Science Teaching, 43*, 214–235.

Ford, D., Fifield, S., Madsen, J., and Qian, X. (2013). The science semester: Cross-disciplinary inquiry for prospective elementary teachers. *Journal of Science Teacher Education, 24*(6), 1049–1072.

Ford, M.J., and Forman, E.A. (2006). Redefining disciplinary learning in classroom contexts. *Review of Research in Education, 30*(1), 1–32.

Fox, D. (1983). Personal theories of teaching. *Studies in Higher Education, 8*(2), 151–163.

Fox, J.E., and Lee, J. (2013). When children draw vs when children don't: Exploring the effects of observational drawing in science. *Creative Education, 4*(7), 11–14.

French, L. (2004). Science at the center of a coherent, integrated early childhood curriculum. *Early Childhood Research Quarterly, 19*, 138–139.

Friedman-Krauss, A., and Barnett, S. (2020). *Access to High-Quality Early Education and Racial Equity.* National Institute for Early Education Research. Available: http://nieer.org/wp-content/uploads/2020/06/Special-Report-Access-to-High-Quality-Early-Education-and-Racial-Equity.pdf.

Frisch, J.K. (2018). Using a "hybrid" science notebook: Elementary teacher candidates' experiences. In E. Langran and J. Borup (Eds.), *Society for Information Technology & Teacher Education International Conference* (pp. 1882–1887). Waynesville, NC: Association for the Advancement of Computing in Education.

Fuller, C. (2020). Education innovation clusters: Supporting transformative teaching and learning. *Childhood Education, 96*(1), 34–47.

Furtak, E.M., and Alonzo, A.C. (2010). The role of content in inquiry-based elementary science lessons: An analysis of teacher beliefs and enactment. *Research in Science Education, 40*(3), 425–449.

Furtak, E.M., Seidel, T., Iverson, H., and Briggs, D.C. (2012). Experimental and quasi-experimental studies of inquiry-based science teaching: A meta-analysis. *Review of Educational Research, 82*(3), 300–329.

Fusaro, M., and Smith, M.C. (2018). Preschoolers' inquisitiveness and science-relevant problem solving. *Early Childhood Research Quarterly, 42*, 119–127.

Gallas, K. (1995). *Talking Their Way into Science: Hearing Children's Questions and Theories, Responding with Curricula.* New York: Teachers College Press.

Gamson, D.A., and Hodge, E.M. (2016). Education research and the shifting landscape of the American school district, 1816 to 2016. *Review of Research in Education, 40*(1), 216–249.

Gándara, P., and Hopkins, M. (Eds.). (2010). *Forbidden Language: English Learners and Restrictive Language Policies.* New York: Teachers College Press.

García, O., and Kleifgen, J.A. (2020). Translanguaging and literacies. *Reading Research Quarterly, 55*(4), 553–571.

Gee, J.P. (2000). Identity as an analytic lens for research in education. *Review of Research in Education, 25*(1), 99–125.

Gelman, R., and Brenneman, K. (2004). Science learning pathways for young children. *Early Childhood Research Quarterly, 19*(1), 150–158.

Gelman, R., Brenneman, K., Macdonald, G., and Roman, M. (2009). *Preschool Pathways to Science (PrePS): Facilitating Scientific Ways of Knowing, Thinking, Talking, and Doing.* Baltimore, MD: Paul H. Brookes.

Georgen, C. (2019). *"Can't Nobody Floss Like This!": Exploring Embodied Science Learning in the Third Space.* Available: https://45.55.127.102/bitstream/1/4415/1/280-287.pdf.

Georgen, C., and Manz, E. (2021). Interlocking models as sites of modeling practice and conceptual innovation. In E. de Vries, J. Ahn, and Y. Hod (Eds.), *15th International Conference of the Learning Sciences* (pp. 418–425). Bochum, Germany: International Society of the Learning Sciences.

Gerde, H.K., Schachter, R.E., and Wasik, B.A. (2013). Using the scientific method to guide learning: An integrated approach to early childhood curriculum. *Early Childhood Education Journal, 41,* 315–323.

Gergely, G., Bekkering, H., and Király, I. (2002). Rational imitation in preverbal infants. *Nature, 415*(6873), 755.

Giere, R.N. (1990). *Explaining Science: A Cognitive Approach.* Chicago, IL: University of Chicago Press.

Giroux, H.A., and Giroux, S.S. (2006). Challenging neoliberalism's new world order: The promise of critical pedagogy. *Cultural Studies—Critical Methodologies, 6*(1), 21–32.

Golinkoff, R.M., and Hirsch-Pasek, K. (2008). Why play = learning. In R.E. Tremblay, M. Boivin, and R. DeV. Peters (Eds.), *Encyclopedia on Early Childhood Development* (pp. 1–5). Montreal, Quebec: Encyclopedia on Early Childhood Development.

Goller, M., Ursin, J., Vähäsantanen, K., Festner, D., and Harteis, C. (2019). Finnish and German student teachers' motivations for choosing teaching as a career. The first application of the FIT-Choice scale in Finland. *Teaching and Teacher Education, 85,* 235–248.

Gotwals, A.W., and Songer, N.B. (2013). Validity evidence for learning progression based assessment items that fuse core disciplinary ideas and science practices. *Journal of Research in Science Teaching, 50*(5), 597–626.

Gould, S.J. (1996). *The Mismeasure of Man.* New York: W.W. Norton.

Gouvea, J., and Passmore, C. (2017). "Models of" versus "models for." *Science & Education, 26*(1), 49–63.

Gouvea, J.S., and Simon, M.R. (2018). Challenging cognitive construals: A dynamic alternative to stable misconceptions. *CBE—Life Sciences Education, 17*(2), ar34.

Grapin, S. (2019). Multimodality in the new content standards era: Implications for English learners. *Tesol Quarterly, 53*(1), 30–55.

Gray, R., McDonald, S., and Stroupe, D. (2021). What you find depends on how you see: Examining asset and deficit perspectives of preservice science teachers' knowledge and learning. *Studies in Science Education,* 1–32.

Greenfield, D.B. (2015). Assessment in early childhood science education. In K. Trundle and M. Saçkes (Eds.), *Research in Early Childhood Science Education* (pp. 353–380). New York: Springer.

Greenfield, D.B., Alexander, A., and Frechette, E. (2017). Unleashing the power of science in early childhood: A foundation for high-quality interactions and learning. *Zero to Three, 37*(5), 13–21.

Greenfield, D. B., Jirout, J., Dominguez, X., Greenberg, A., Maier, M., & Fuccillo, J. (2009). Science in the preschool classroom: A programmatic research agenda to Improve science readiness. *Early Education and Development, 20*(2), 238–264.

Grindal, T., Silander, M., Gerard, S., Maxon, T., Garcia, E., Hupert, N., Vahey, P., and Pasnik, S. (2019). *Early Science & Engineering: The Impact of "The Cat in the Hat Knows a Lot about That!" on Learning.* Waltham, MA: Education Development Center.

Gropen, J., Kook, J.F., Hoisington, C., and Clark-Chiarelli, N. (2017). Foundations of science literacy: Efficacy of a preschool professional development program in science on classroom instruction, teachers' pedagogical content knowledge, and children's observations and predictions. *Early Education and Development, 28*(5), 607–631.

Gross, C.M. (2012). Science concepts young children learn through water play. *Dimensions of Early Childhood, 40*(2), 3–11.

Grotzer, T.A. (2003). Learning to understand the forms of causality implicit in scientifically accepted explanations. *Studies in Science Education, 39*, 1–74.

Grover, S., and Pea, R. (2013). Computational thinking in K–12: A review of the state of the field. *Educational Researcher, 42*(1), 38–43.

Gruenewald, D.A. (2003). Foundations of place: A multidisciplinary framework for place-conscious education. *American Educational Research Journal, 40*(3), 619–654.

Gullberg, A., Andersson, K., Danielsson, A., Scantlebury, K., and Hussénius, A. (2018). Preservice teachers' views of the child—reproducing or challenging gender stereotypes in science in preschool. *Research in Science Education, 48*, 691–715.

Gunckel, K. (2011). Mediators of a preservice teacher's use of the inquiry-application instructional model. *Journal of Science Teacher Education, 22*(1), 79–100.

Gunckel, K. (2013). Fulfilling multiple obligations: Preservice elementary teachers' use of an instructional model while learning to plan and teach science. *Science Education, 97*, 139–162.

Gunckel, K.L., and Tolbert, S. (2018). The imperative to move toward a dimension of care in engineering education. *Journal of Research in Science Teaching, 55*, 938–961.

Gunckel, K., and Wood, M. (2016). The principle–practical discourse edge: Elementary preservice and mentor teachers working together on colearning tasks. *Science Education, 100*, 96–121.

Gunning, A., and Mensah, F.M. (2011). Preservice elementary teachers' development of self-efficacy and confidence to teach science: A case study. *Journal of Science Teacher Education, 22*(2), 171–185.

Guthrie, J.T., Wigfield, A., Barbosa, P., Perencevich, K.C., Taboada, A., Davis, M.H., Scafiddi, N.T., and Tonks, S. (2004). Increasing reading comprehension and engagement through concept-oriented reading instruction. *Journal of Educational Psychology, 96*(3), 403–424.

Gutiérrez, K.D. (2008). Developing a sociocritical literacy in the third space. *Reading Research Quarterly, 43*(2), 148–164.

Gutiérrez, K.D., and Rogoff, B. (2003). Cultural ways of learning: Individual traits or repertoires of practice. *Educational Researcher, 32*(5), 19–25.

Gutwill, J.P., and Allen, S. (2017). *Group Inquiry at Science Museum Exhibits: Getting Visitors to Ask Juicy Questions.* New York and Abingdon, UK: Routledge.

Guzey, S.S., Tank, K., Wang, H.H., Roehrig, G., and Moore, T. (2014). A high-quality professional development for teachers of grades 3–6 for implementing engineering into classrooms. *School Science and Mathematics, 114*(3), 139–149.

Haas, A., Januszyk, R., Grapin, S., Goggiins, M., Llosa, L., and Lee, O. (2021). Developing instructional materials aligned to the Next Generation Science Standards for all students, including English learners. *Journal of Science Teacher Education, 32*(7), 735–756.

Hall, R., and Jurow, A.S. (2015). Changing concepts in activity: Descriptive and design studies of consequential learning in conceptual practices. *Educational Psychologist, 50*(3), 173–189.

Hallinger, P. (2005). Instructional leadership and the school principal: A passing fancy that refuses to fade away. *Leadership and Policy in Schools, 4*(3), 221–239.

Hallinger, P., and Heck, R.H. (2011). Collaborative leadership and school improvement: Understanding the impact on school capacity and student learning. In T. Townsend and J. MacBeath (Eds.), *International Handbook of Leadership for Learning* (pp. 5–27). Dordrecht, The Netherlands: Springer.

Hallinger, P., Bickman, L., and Davis, K. (1996). School context, principal leadership, and student reading achievement. *Elementary School Journal, 96*(5), 527–549.

Halverson, R., Feinstein, N., and Meshoulam, D. (2011). School leadership for science education. In G. DeBoer (Ed.), *The Role of Public Policy in K–12 Science Education* (pp. 397–430). Charlotte, NC: Information Age.

Halvorsen, A.L., Duke, N.K., Brugar, K.A., Block, M.K., Strachan, S.L., Berka, M.B., and Brown, J.M. (2012). Narrowing the achievement gap in second-grade social studies and content area literacy: The promise of a project-based approach. *Theory and Research in Social Education, 40*(3), 198–229.

Hambrusch, S., Hoffmann, C., Korb, J.T., Haugan, M., and Hosking, A.L. (2009). A multidisciplinary approach towards computational thinking for science majors. *ACM SIGCSE Bulletin, 41*(1), 183–187.

Hammer, D., and Elby, A. (2002). On the form of a personal epistemology. In B.K. Hofer and P.R. Pintrich (Eds.), *Personal Epistemology: The Psychology of Beliefs about Knowledge and Knowing* (pp. 169–190). Mahwah, NJ: Lawrence Erlbaum Associates.

Hammer, D., Elby, A., Scherr, R.E., and Redish, E.F. (2005). Resources, framing, and transfer. In J.P. Mestre (Ed.), *Transfer of Learning from a Modern Multidisciplinary Perspective* (pp. 89–120). Greenwich, CT: Information Age.

Hand, V., and Gresalfi, M. (2015). The joint accomplishment of identity. *Educational Psychologist, 50*(3), 190–203.

Hansen, M., Levesque, E., Valant, J., and Quintero, D. (2018). *The 2018 Brown Center Report on American Education: How Well Are American Students Learning.* Washington, DC: Brookings Institution.

Hanuscin, D. (2013). Critical incidents in the development of pedagogical content knowledge for teaching the nature of science: A prospective elementary teacher's journey. *Journal of Science Teacher Education, 24*(6), 933–956.

Hanuscin, D., and Zangori, L. (2016). Developing practical knowledge of the next generation science standards in elementary science teacher education. *Journal of Science Teacher Education, 27*(8), 799–818.

Hapgood, S., Magnusson, S.J., and Palincsar, A.S. (2004). A very science-like kind of thinking: How young children make meaning from first- and second-hand investigations. *Journal of the Learning Sciences, 13*(4), 455–506.

Harlow, D. (2012). The excitement and wonder of teaching science: What pre-service teachers learn from facilitating family science night centers. *Journal of Science Teacher Education, 23*(2), 199–220.

Harraway, D. (1984). Teddy bear patriarchy: Taxidermy in the garden of Eden, New York City, 1908–1936. *Social Text*, (11), 20–64.

Hart, J.E., and Lee, O. (2003). Teacher professional development to improve the science and literacy achievement of English language learners. *Bilingual Research Journal, 27*(3), 475–501.

Hassinger-Das, B., Bustamante, A.S., Hirsh-Pasek, K., and Golinkoff, R.M. (2018). Learning landscapes: Playing the way to learning and engagement in public spaces. *Journal of Education Sciences, 8*(2), 74–95.

Hatt, B. (2012). Smartness as a cultural practice in schools. *American Educational Research Journal, 49*(3), 438–460.

Haverly, C., Calabrese Barton, A., Schwarz, C.V., and Braaten, M. (2020). "Making space": How novice teachers create opportunities for equitable sense-making in elementary science. *Journal of Teacher Education, 71*(1), 63–79.

Hawkins, S., and Park Rogers, M. (2016). Tools for reflection: Video-based reflection within a preservice community of practice. *Journal of Science Teacher Education, 27*(4), 415–437.

Heller, J., Daehler, K., Wong, N., Shinohara, M., and Miratrix, L. (2012). Differential effects of three professional development models on teacher knowledge and student achievement in elementary science. *Journal of Research in Science Teaching, 49*(3), 333–362.

Henderson, L., Klemes, J., and Eshet, Y. (2000). Just playing a game? Educational simulation software and cognitive outcomes. *Journal of Educational Computing Research*, 22(1), 105–129.

Henderson, P.B., Cortina, T.J., and Wing, J.M. (2007). Computational thinking. *ACM SIGCSE Bulletin*, 39, 195–196.

Hernandez, C., and Shroyer, M.G. (2017). The use of culturally responsive teaching strategies among Latina/o student teaching interns during science and mathematics instruction of CLD students. *Journal of Science Teacher Education*, 28(4), 367–387.

Herrenkohl, L.R., and Cornelius, L. (2013). Investigating elementary students' scientific and historical argumentation. *Journal of the Learning Sciences*, 22(3), 413–461.

Herrenkohl, L.R., and Guerra, M. (1998). Participant structures, scientific discourse, and student engagement in fourth grade. *Cognition and Instruction*, 16(4), 431–473.

Herrenkohl, L.R., and Mertl, V. (2010). *How Students Come to Be, Know, and Do: A Case for a Broad View of Learning*. Cambridge, UK: Cambridge University Press.

Herrenkohl, L.R., Tasker, T., and White, B. (2011). Pedagogical practices to support classroom cultures of scientific inquiry. *Cognition and Instruction*, 29(1), 1–44.

Herrenkohl, L., Palinscar, A., DeWater, L., and Kawasaki, K. (1999). Developing scientific communities in classrooms: A sociocognitive approach. *Journal of the Learning Sciences*, 8(3&4), 451–493.

Hertel, J.D., Cunningham, C.M., and Kelly, G.J. (2017). The roles of engineering notebooks in shaping elementary engineering student discourse and practice. *International Journal of Science Education*, 39(9), 1194–1217.

Hesse, M. (1966). *Models and Analogies in Science*. South Bend, IN: University of Notre Dame Press.

Hiebert, J., Carpenter, T.P., Fennema, E., Fuson, K., Human, P., Murray, H., Olivier, A., and Wearne, D. (1996). Problem solving as a basis for reform in curriculum and instruction: The case of mathematics. *Educational Researcher*, 25(4), 12–21.

Hmelo-Silver, C.E., Duncan, R.G., and Chinn, C.A. (2007). Scaffolding and achievement in problem-based and inquiry learning: A response to Kirschner, Sweller, and Clark (2006). *Educational Psychologist*, 42, 99–107.

Hollingsworth, H.L., and Vandermaas-Peeler, M. (2017). "Almost everything we do includes inquiry": Fostering inquiry-based teaching and learning with preschool teachers. *Early Child Development and Care*, 187(1), 152–167.

Honey, M., and Kanter, D.E. (Eds.). (2013). *Design, Make, Play: Growing the Next Generation of STEM Innovators*. New York: Routledge.

Honig, M., and Hatch, T.C. (2004). Crafting coherence: How schools strategically manage multiple, external demands. *Education Researcher*, 33(8), 16–30.

Honig, M.I., Venkateswaran, N., and McNeil, P. (2017). Research use as learning: The case of fundamental change in school district central offices. *American Educational Research Journal*, 54(5), 938–971.

Hooper, L., and Zembal-Saul, C. (2020). Portrait of a first-grade teacher: Using science practices to leverage young children's sensemaking in science. In E.A. Davis, C. Zembal-Saul, and S.M. Kademian (Eds.), *Sensemaking in Elementary Science: Supporting Teacher Learning* (pp. 31–45). New York: Routledge.

Hopkins, M., Ozimek, D., and Sweet, T.M. (2017). Mathematics coaching and instructional reform: Individual and collective change. *Journal of Mathematical Behavior*, 46, 215–230.

Horn, M.S. (2018). Tangible interaction and cultural forms: Supporting learning in informal environments. *Journal of the Learning Sciences*, 27(4), 632–665.

Housman, G., Tsurusaki, B., Tzou, C.T., Bang, M., and Reiser, B.J. (Eds.). (2021). *How Can We Make Decisions to Care for Ourselves, Our Families, and Our Communities?* [COVID-19 & Health Equity Unit, Grades 3–5]. Learning in Places, NextGen Science Storylines, and OpenSciEd. Available: https://www.openscied.org/instructional-materials/covid-3-5/.

Hsu, M.C., Purzer, S., and Cardella, M.E. (2011). Elementary teachers' views about teaching design, engineering, and technology. *Journal of Pre-College Engineering Education Research (J-PEER), 1*(2), 5.

Hudicourt-Barnes, J. (2003). The use of argumentation in Haitian Creole science classrooms. *Harvard Educational Review, 73*(1), 73–93.

Hussein, M.H., Ow, S.H., Cheong, L.S., Thong, M.K., and Ebrahim, N.A. (2019). Effects of digital game-based learning on elementary science learning: A systematic review. *IEEE Access, 7*, 62465–62478.

Hwang, J., and Duke, N.K. (2020). Content counts and motivation matters: Reading comprehension in third-grade students who are English learners. *AERA Open, 6*(1), 1–17.

Hynes, M., and Swenson, J. (2013). The humanistic side of engineering: Considering social science and humanities dimensions of engineering in education and research. *Journal of Pre-College Engineering Education Research (J-PEER), 3*(2).

Institute of Medicine and National Research Council. (2012). *The Early Childhood Care and Education Workforce: Challenges and Opportunities: A Workshop Report.* Washington, DC: The National Academies Press.

———. (2015). *Transforming the Workforce for Children Birth Through Age 8: A Unifying Foundation.* Washington, DC: The National Academies Press.

Ishimaru, A.M. (2019). From family engagement to equitable collaboration. *Educational Policy, 33*(2), 350–385.

Israel, M., Jeong, G., Ray, M., and Lash, T. (2020). Teaching elementary computer science through universal design for learning. In *Proceedings of the 51st ACM Technical Symposium on Computer Science Education* (pp. 1220–1226). New York: Association for Computing Machinery.

Iveland, A., Tyler, B., Britton, T., Nguyen, K., and Schneider, S. (2017). *Administrators Matter in NGSS Implementation: How School and District Leaders Are Making Science Happen.* WestEd.

Jaber, L.Z., and Hammer, D. (2016). Learning to feel like a scientist. *Science Education, 100*(2), 189–220.

James, A., Stears, M., and Moolman, C. (2012). Learning and teaching natural science in the early years: A case study of three different contexts. *South African Journal of Childhood Education, 2*(1), 82–99.

Jeong, J., Gaffney, J.S., and Choi, J.O. (2010). Availability and use of informational texts in second-, third-, and fourth-grade classrooms. *Research in the Teaching of English*, 435–456.

Jian, Y.C. (2016). Fourth graders' cognitive processes and learning strategies for reading illustrated biology texts: Eye movement measurements. *Reading Research Quarterly, 51*(1), 93–109.

Jin, H., Delgado, C., Bauer, M.I., Wylie, E.C., Cisterna, D., and Llort, K.F. (2019). A hypothetical learning progression for quantifying phenomena in science. *Science & Education, 28*, 1181–1208.

Johnson, H., and Cotterman, M. (2015). Developing preservice teachers' knowledge of science teaching through video clubs. *Journal of Science Teacher Education, 26*(4), 393–417.

Jones, G., Robertson, L., Gardner, G., Dotger, S., and Blanchard, M. (2012). Differential use of elementary science kits. *International Journal of Science Education, 34*(15), 2371–2391.

Jones, M.G., Corin, E.N., Andre, T., Childers, G.M., and Stevens, V. (2017). Factors contributing to lifelong science learning: Amateur astronomers and birders. *Journal of Research in Science Teaching, 54*(3), 412–433.

Jordan, M.E., and McDaniel, R.R., Jr. (2014). Managing uncertainty during collaborative problem solving in elementary school teams: The role of peer influence in robotics engineering activity. *Journal of the Learning Sciences, 23*(4), 490–536.

Joseph, N.M., Hailu, M.F., and Matthews, J.S. (2019). Normalizing Black girls' humanity in mathematics classrooms. *Harvard Educational Review, 89*(1), 132–173.

Judson, E. (2013). The relationship between time allocated for science in elementary schools and state accountability policies. *Science Education, 97*(4), 621–636.

Kademian, S., and Davis, E.A. (2018). Supporting beginning teacher planning of investigation-based science discussions. *Journal of Science Teacher Education, 29*(8), 712–740.

Kanari, Z, and Millar, R. (2004). Reasoning from data: How students collect and interpret data in science investigations. *Journal of Research in Science Teaching, 41*(7), 748–769.

Kane, J.M. (2012). Young African American children constructing academic and disciplinary identities in an urban science classroom. *Science Education, 96*(3), 457–487.

Kane, J.M. (2015). The structure-agency dialectic in contested science spaces: "Do earthworms eat apples?" *Journal of Research Science Teaching, 52*, 461–473.

Kane, J.M. (2016). Young African American boys narrating identities in science. *Journal of Research Science Teaching, 53*, 95–118.

Kanter, D., and Konstantopoulos, S. (2010). The impact of a project-based science curriculum on minority student achievement, attitudes, and careers: The effects of teacher content and pedagogical content knowledge and inquiry-based practices. *Science Education, 94*, 855–887.

Kapur, M., and Bielaczyc, K. (2012). Designing for productive failure. *Journal of the Learning Sciences, 21*(1), 45–83.

Karmiloff-Smith, A., and Inhelder, B. (1974). If you want to get ahead, get a theory. *Cognition, 3*(3), 195–212.

Katz, L.G. (2010). STEM in the early years. *Early Childhood Research and Practice, 12*(2), 11–19.

Kawagley, A.O., Norris-Tull, D., and Norris-Tull, R.A. (1998). The indigenous worldview of Yupiaq culture: Its scientific nature and relevance to the practice and teaching of science. *Journal of Research in Science Teaching 35*(2), 133–144.

Kaya, E. (2013). Argumentation practices in classroom: Pre-service teachers' conceptual understanding of chemical equilibrium. *International Journal of Science Education, 35*(7), 1139–1158.

Kazempour, M. (2018). Elementary preservice teachers' authentic inquiry experiences and reflections: A multicase study. *Journal of Science Teacher Education, 29*(7), 644–663.

Keeley, P. (2018). Using formative assessment probes to develop elementary learning stations. *Science and Children, 55*(9), 28–31.

Keifert, D., and Stevens, R. (2019). Inquiry as a members' phenomenon: Young children as competent inquirers. *Journal of the Learning Sciences, 28*(2), 240–278.

Keifert, D., Wang, X.C., Sacks, D.P., Levy, S.T., Tu, X., Danish, J., Humburg, M., and Enyedy, N. (2020). *Broadening Learning Sciences Theoretical Lenses to Understand Young Children's Sensemaking.* Available: https://45.55.127.102/bitstream/1/6663/1/390-397.pdf.

Kelemen, D. (2004). Are children "intuitive theists"? Reasoning about purpose and design in nature. *Psychological Science, 15*(5), 295–301.

Kelly, G.J. (2014). Discourse practices in science learning and teaching. In N.G. Lederman and S.K. Abell (Eds.), *Handbook of Research on Science Education* (vol. 2, 2nd ed., pp. 321–336). Mahwah, NJ: Lawrence Erlbaum Associates.

Kelly, G.J. (2017). Learning science: Discourse practices. In S. Wortham, D. Kim, and S. May (Eds.), *Discourse and Education. Encyclopedia of Language and Education* (3rd ed., pp. 223–237). Cham, Switzerland: Springer.

Kelly, G.J., and Cunningham, C.M. (2019). Epistemic tools in engineering design for K–12 education. *Science Education, 103*(4), 1080–1111.

Kelly, G.J., and Green, J. (Eds.). (2019). *Theory and Methods for Sociocultural Research in Science and Engineering Education.* New York: Routledge.

Kelly, G.J., Brown, C., and Crawford, T. (2000). Experiments, contingencies, and curriculum: Providing opportunities for learning through improvisation in science teaching. *Science Education, 84*(5), 624–657.

Kelly, L.B. (2018). An analysis of award-winning science trade books for children: Who are the scientists, and what is science? *Journal of Research in Science Teaching, 55*(8), 1188–1210.

Kelly, M., and Staver, J. (2005). A case study of one school system's adoption and implementation of an elementary science program. *Journal of Research in Science Teaching, 42,* 25–52.

Kenyon, L., Schwarz, C., and Hug, B. (2008). The benefits of scientific modeling. *Science and Children, 46*(2), 40.

Kesidou, S., and Roseman, J.E. (2002). How well do middle school science programs measure up? Findings from Project 2061's curriculum review. *Journal of Research in Science Teaching, 39*(6), 522–549.

Ketelhut, D.J., and Cabrera, L. (2020). *The Integration of Computational Thinking in Early Childhood and Elementary Science and Engineering Education.* Washington, DC: The National Academies Press. Available: https://www.nationalacademies.org/our-work/enhancing-science-in-prekindergarten-through-fifth-grade.

Ketelhut, D.J., Mills, K., Hestness, E., Cabrera, L., Plane, J., and McGinnis, J.R. (2019). Teacher change following a professional development experience in integrating computational thinking into elementary science. *Journal of Science Education and Technology, Computational Thinking from a Disciplinary Perspective,* 1–15.

Keune, A., and Peppler, K. (2019). Materials-to-develop-with: The making of a makerspace. *British Journal of Educational Technology, 50*(1), 280–293.

Kim, M., Anthony, R., and Blades, D. (2014). Decision making through dialogue: A case study of analyzing preservice teachers' argumentation on socioscientific issues. *Research in Science Education, 44,* 903–926.

Kimmerer, R.W. (2003). *Gathering Moss: A Natural and Cultural History of Mosses.* Corvallis, OR: Oregon State University Press.

Kimmerer, R.W. (2013). *Braiding Sweetgrass: Indigenous Wisdom, Scientific Knowledge and the Teachings of Plants.* Minneapolis, MN: Milkweed Editions.

King, D., and English, L.D. (2016). Engineering design in the primary school: Applying STEM concepts to build an optical instrument. *International Journal of Science Education, 38*(18), 2762–2794.

King, N.S., and Pringle, R.M. (2019). Black girls speak STEM: Counterstories of informal and formal learning experiences. *Journal of Research in Science Teaching, 56,* 539–569.

Kintsch, W. (2013). Revisiting the Construction-Integration Model of text comprehension and its implications for instruction. In D.E. Alvermann, N.J. Unrau, and R.B. Ruddell (Eds.), *Theoretical Models and Processes of Reading* (6th ed., pp. 807–839). Newark, Delaware: International Reading Association.

Kinzie, M.B., Whittaker, J.V., Williford, A.P., DeCoster, J., McGuire, P., Lee, Y., and Kilday, C.R. (2014). MyTeachingPartner-Math/Science pre-kindergarten curricula and teacher supports: Associations with children's mathematics and science learning. *Early Childhood Research Quarterly, 29*(4), 586–599.

Kirschner, P.A., Sweller, J., and Clark, R.E. (2006). Why minimal guidance during instruction does not work: An analysis of the failure of constructivist, discovery, problem-based, experiential, and inquiry-based teaching. *Educational Psychologist, 41*(2), 75–86.

Klahr, D., Zimmerman, C., and Jirout, J. (2011). Educational interventions to advance children's scientific thinking. *Science, 333*(6045), 971–975.

Klein, A. (2018). "Continuous improvement" model woven into state ESSA plans. *Education Week.*

Klein, E.J., Taylor, M., Munakata, M., Trabona, K., Rahman, Z., and McManus, J. (2018). Navigating teacher leaders' complex relationships using a distributed leadership framework. *Teacher Education Quarterly, 45*(2), 89–112.

Kloser, M. (2014). Identifying a core set of science teaching practices: A Delphi expert panel approach. *Journal of Research in Science Teaching, 51*(9), 1185–1217.

Knoester, M., and Au, W. (2017). Standardized testing and school segregation: Like tinder for fire? *Race Ethnicity and Education, 20*(1), 1–14.

Knorr Cetina, K. (2001). Objectual practice. In T. Schatzki, K. Knorr Cetina, and E. von Savigny (Eds.), *The Practice Turn in Contemporary Theory* (pp. 175–188). New York: Routledge.

Kober, N., and Usher, A. (2012). *A Public Education Primer: Basic (and Sometimes Surprising) Facts about the US Educational System.* Center on Education Policy.

Koerber, S., Mayer, D., Osterhaus, C., Schwippert, K., and Sodian, B. (2015). The development of scientific thinking in elementary school: A comprehensive inventory. *Child Development, 86*(1), 327–336.

Köksal, Ö., Sodian, B., and Legare, C.H. (2021). Young children's metacognitive awareness of confounded evidence. *Journal of Experimental Child Psychology, 205,* 105080.

Kotler, R.T. (2020). *Embodying Science: Latinx Children's Knowledge and Identity Construction While Studying Water.* Unpublished doctoral thesis. University of Illinois at Chicago.

Kozol, J. (2005). *The Shame of the Nation: The Restoration of Apartheid Schooling in America.* New York: Crown.

Krajcik, J., Schneider, B., Miller, E., Chen, I.-C., Bradford, L., Bartz, K., Barker, Q., Palinscar, A., Peek-Brown, D., and Codere, S. (2021). *Assessing the Effect of Project-Based Learning on Science Learning in Elementary Schools* (Technical Report). Michigan State University. Available: https://mlpbl.open3d.science/sites/default/files/MLPBL-technical-report.pdf.

Krishnamurthi, A., Alliance, A., Ballard, M., and Noam, G.G. (2014). *Examining the Impact of Afterschool STEM Programs: A Paper Commissioned by the Noyce Foundation.* Available: https://files.eric.ed.gov/fulltext/ED546628.pdf.

Krist, C., and Suárez, E. (2018). Doing science with fidelity to persons: Instantiations of caring participation in science practices. In J. Kay and R. Luckin (Eds.), *13th International Conference of the Learning Sciences* (vol. 1, pp. 424–431). London, UK: International Society of the Learning Sciences.

Küçükaydın, M., and Gökbulut, Y. (2020). Beliefs of teacher candidates toward science teaching. *Journal of Science Teacher Education, 31*(2), 134–150.

Kuhl, P.K., Lim, S.S., Guerriero, S., and Van Damme, D. (2019). *Developing Minds in the Digital Age.* Paris: OECD.

Kuhn, D., and Dean, D., Jr.. (2004). Connecting scientific reasoning and causal inference. *Journal of Cognition and Development, 5*(2), 261–288.

Kuhn, D., and Dean, D., Jr. (2005). Is developing scientific thinking all about learning to control variables? *Psychological Science, 16*(11), 866–870.

Kumpulainen, K., Burke, A., and Ntelioglou, B.Y. (2020). Young children, maker literacies and social change. *Education Sciences, 10*(10), 265.

Ladson-Billings, G. (2006). From the achievement gap to the education debt: Understanding achievement in U.S. Schools. *Educational Researcher, 35*(7), 3–12.

Ladson-Billings, G. (2009). *The Dreamkeepers: Successful Teachers of African American Children*. San Francisco: John Wiley & Sons.

Lampert, M. (2010). Learning teaching in, from, and for practice: What do we mean? *Journal of Teacher Education, 61*(1–2), 21–34.

LaParo, K., Pianta, R., and Hamre, B. (2008). *The Classroom Assessment Scoring System: Manual Pre-K*. Baltimore, MD: Brookes.

Larimore, R.A. (2020). Preschool science education: A vision for the future. *Early Childhood Education Journal, 48*, 703–714.

Lave, J., and Wenger, E. (1991). *Situated Learning: Legitimate Peripheral Participation*. Cambridge, UK: Cambridge University Press.

Learning in Places Collaborative. (2020). *Framework: Socio-Ecological Histories of Places Framework: Supporting Sense-Making and Decision-Making*. Bothell, Seattle, WA and Evanston, IL: Learning in Places.

Lederman, N.G., and Niess, M.L. (1997). Integrated, interdisciplinary, or thematic instruction? Is this a question or is it questionable semantics? *School Science and Mathematics, 97*(2), 57–58.

Lee, C.D., Meltzoff, A.N., and Kuhl, P. K. (2020). The braid of human learning and development: Neuro-physiological processes and participation in cultural practices. In N.S. Nasir, C.D. Lee, R. Pea, and M.M. de Royston (Eds.), *Handbook of the Cultural Foundations of Learning* (pp. 24–43). New York: Routledge.

Lee, I., Grover, S., Martin, F., Pillai, S., and Malyn-Smith, J. (2020). Computational thinking from a disciplinary perspective: Integrating computational thinking in K–12 science, technology, engineering, and mathematics education. *Journal of Science Education and Technology, 29*(1), 1–8.

Lee, O. (2017). Common Core State Standards for ELA/Literacy and Next Generation Science Standards: Convergences and discrepancies using argument as an example. *Educational Researcher, 46*(2), 90–102.

Lee, O., and Luykx, A. (2005). Dilemmas in scaling up innovations in elementary science instruction with nonmainstream students. *American Educational Research Journal, 42*(3), 411–438.

Lee, O., and Maerten-Rivera, J. (2012). Teacher change in elementary science instruction with English language learners: Results of a multiyear professional development intervention across multiple grades. *Teachers College Record, 114*(8), 1–42.

Lee, O., and Stephens, A. (2020). English learners in STEM subjects: Contemporary views on STEM subjects and language with English learners. *Educational Researcher, 49*(6), 426–432.

Lee, O., Penfield, R., and Maerten-Rivera, J. (2009). Effects of fidelity of implementation on science achievement gains among English language learners. *Journal of Research in Science Teaching, 46*, 836–859.

Lee, O., Deaktor, R., Enders, C., and Lambert, J. (2008). Impact of a multiyear professional development intervention on science achievement of culturally and linguistically diverse elementary students. *Journal of Research in Science Teaching, 45*(6), 726–747.

Lee, O., Llosa, L., Jiang, F., Haas, A., O'Connor, C., and Van Booven, C. (2016). Elementary teachers' science knowledge and instructional practices: Impact of an intervention focused on English language learners. *Journal of Research in Science Teaching, 53*(4), 579–597.

Legare, C.H. (2012). Exploring explanation: Explaining inconsistent evidence informs exploratory, hypothesis testing behavior in young children. *Child Development, 83*(1), 173–185.

Legare, C.H. (2014). The contributions of explanation and exploration to children's scientific reasoning. *Child Development Perspectives, 8*(2), 101–106.
Legare, C.H. (2019). The development of cumulative cultural learning. *Annual Review of Developmental Psychology, 1,* 119–147.
Lehrer, R., and Schauble, L. (2000). Inventing data structures for representational purposes: Elementary grade students' classification models. *Mathematical Thinking and Learning, 2*(1–2), 51–74.
Lehrer, R., and Schauble, L. (2004). Modeling natural variation through distribution. *American Educational Research Journal, 41*(3), 635–680.
Lehrer, R., and Schauble, L. (2006). Cultivating model-based reasoning in science education. In R.K. Sawyer (Ed.), *Cambridge Handbook of the Learning Sciences* (pp. 371–388). Cambridge, UK: Cambridge University Press.
Lehrer, R., and Schauble, L. (2012). Seeding evolutionary thinking by engaging children in modeling its foundations. *Science Education, 96*(4), 701–724.
Lehrer, R., and Schauble, L. (2015). The development of scientific thinking. In L.S. Liben, U. Müller, and R.M. Lerner (Eds.), *Handbook of Child Psychology and Developmental Science* (pp. 1–44). Hoboken, NJ: John Wiley & Sons.
Lehrer, R., Giles, N., and Schauble, L. (2002). Data modeling. In R. Lehrer and L. Schauble (Eds.), *Investigating Real Data in the Classroom: Expanding Children's Understanding of Mathematics and Science* (pp. 1–26). New York: Teachers College Press.
Lehrer, R., Schauble, L., and Petrosino, A.J. (2001). Reconsidering the role of experiment in science education. *Designing for Science: Implications from Everyday, Classroom, and Professional Settings* (pp. 251–278). New York: Routledge.
Lehrer, R., Schauble, L., Strom, D., and Pligge, M. (2001). Similarity of form and substance: Modeling material kind. In S.M. Carver and D. Klahr (Eds.), *Cognition and Instruction: Twenty-five Years of Progress* (pp. 39–74). Mahwah, NJ: Lawrence Erlbaum Associates.
Leithwood, K., and Mascall, B. (2008). Collective leadership effects on student achievement. *Educational Administration Quarterly, 44*(4), 529–561.
Leithwood, K., Louis, K.S., Wahlstrom, K., Anderson, S., Mascall, B., and Gordon, M. (2009). How successful leadership influences student learning: The second installment of a longer story. In A. Hargreaves, A. Lieberman, M. Fullan, and D. Hopkins. (Eds.), *Second International Handbook of Educational Change* (pp. 611–629). New York: Springer.
Lemke, J.L. (1998). Metamedia literacy: Transforming meanings and media. In D. Reinking, L. Labbo, M. McKenna, and R. Kiefer (Eds.), *Handbook of Literacy and Technology: Transformations in a Post-Typographic World* (pp. 283–301). Mahwah, NJ: Lawrence Erlbaum Associates.
Lemke, J.L. (2004). The literacies of science. In W. Saul (Ed.), *Crossing Borders in Literacy and Science Instruction: Perspectives on Theory and Practice* (pp. 33–47). Arlington, VA: NSTA Press.
Lesaux, N.K. (2012). Reading and reading instruction for children from low-income and non-English-speaking households. *Future Child, 22*(2), 73–88.
Lesaux, N.K., and Harris, J.R. (2015). *Cultivating Knowledge, Building Language: Literacy Instruction for English Learners in Elementary School.* Portsmouth, NH: Heinemann.
Levy, A.J., Jia, Y., Marco-Bujosa, L., Gess-Newsome, J., and Pasquale, M. (2016). Science specialists or classroom teachers: Who should teach elementary science? *Science Educator, 25*(1), 10–21.
Lewis, A. (2019). Practice what you teach: How experiencing elementary school science teaching practices helps prepare teacher candidates. *Teaching and Teacher Education, 86,* 1–10.

Lewthwaite, B. (2006). "I want to enable teachers in their change": Exploring the role of a superintendent on science curriculum delivery. *Canadian Journal of Educational Administration and Policy, 52*, 1–24.

Li, Y., Wang, K., Xiao, Y., Froyd, J.E., and Nite, S.B. (2020). Research and trends in STEM education: A systematic analysis of publicly funded projects. *International Journal of STEM Education, 7*(17).

Lim, M., and Calabrese Barton, A. (2006). Science learning and a sense of place in an urban middle school. *Cultural Studies of Science Education, 1*(1), 107–142.

Lim, M., and Calabrese Barton, A.C. (2010). Exploring insideness in urban children's sense of place. *Journal of Environmental Psychology, 30*(3), 328–337.

Lin, P.Y., and Schunn, C.D. (2016). The dimensions and impact of informal science learning experiences on middle schoolers' attitudes and abilities in science. *International Journal of Science Education, 38*(17), 2551–2572.

Lin, S.-F., Lieu, S.-C., Chen, S., Huang, M.-T., and Chang, W.-H. (2012). Affording explicit-reflective science teaching by using an educative teachers' guide. *International Journal of Science Education, 34*, 999–1026.

Lindgren, R., and Johnson-Glenberg, M. (2013). Emboldened by embodiment: Six precepts for research on embodied learning and mixed reality. *Educational Researcher, 42*(8), 445–452.

Liston, D.P. (2008). Critical pedagogy and attentive love. *Studies in Philosophy and Education, 27*(5), 387–392.

Liu, Y., and Boyd, W. (2018) Comparing career identities and choices of pre-service early childhood teachers between Australia and China. *International Journal of Early Years Education, 28*(4), 336–350.

López, F.A. (2017). Altering the trajectory of the self-fulfilling prophecy: Asset-based pedagogy and classroom dynamics. *Journal of Teacher Education, 68*(2), 193–212.

Lottero-Perdue, P.S., and Parry, E.A. (2017). Elementary teachers' reflections on design failures and use of fail words after teaching engineering for two years. *Journal of Pre-College Engineering Education Research (J-PEER), 7*(1), 1.

Louca, L., Elby, A., Hammer, D., and Kagey, T. (2004). Epistemological resources: Applying a new epistemological framework to science instruction. *Educational Psychologist, 39*(1), 57–68.

Loucks-Horsley, S., Stiles, K.E., Mundry, S., Love, N., and Hewson, P.W. (2009). *Designing Professional Development for Teachers of Science and Mathematics*. Thousand Oaks, CA: Corwin Press.

Lowenhaupt, K., and McNeill, K.L. (2019). Subject-specific instructional leadership in K-8 schools: The supervision of science in an era of reform. *Leadership and Policy in Schools, 18*(3), 460–484.

Lowenhaupt, R. (2014). School access and participation: Family engagement practices in the new Latino diaspora. *Education and Urban Society, 46*(5), 522–547.

Luke, A., Green, J., and Kelly, G.J. (2010). What counts as evidence and equity? *Review of Research in Education, 34*(1), vii–xvi.

Luna, M.J., Selmer, S.J., and Rye, J.A. (2018). Teachers' noticing of students' thinking in science through classroom artifacts: In what ways are science and engineering practices evident? *Journal of Science Teacher Education, 29*(2), 148–172.

Ma, J.Y. (2017). Multi-party, whole-body interactions in mathematical activity. *Cognition and Instruction, 35*(2), 141–164.

Madden, L., Wiebe, E.N., Bedward, J., Minogue, J., and Carter, M.C. (2009). *Elementary Science Teacher Identity through Science Notebooks: A Case Study of Three Exemplar Teachers*. Paper presented at the Annual Meeting of the National Association for Research in Science Teaching (NARST), Philadelphia, PA.

Malone, K. (2018). *Children in the Anthropocene: Rethinking Sustainability and Child Friendliness in Cities.* London, UK: Palgrave Macmillan.

Mangin, M.M., and Dunsmore, K. (2015). How the framing of instructional coaching as a lever for systemic or individual reform influences the enactment of coaching. *Educational Administration Quarterly, 51*(2), 179–213.

Manz, E. (2012). Understanding the codevelopment of modeling practice and ecological knowledge. *Science Education, 96*(6), 1071–1105.

Manz, E. (2015). Resistance and the development of scientific practice: Designing the mangle into science instruction. *Cognition and Instruction, 33*(2), 89–124.

Manz, E. (2016). Examining evidence construction as the transformation of the material world into community knowledge. *Journal of Research in Science Teaching, 53*(7), 1113–1140.

Manz, E. (2018). Designing for and analyzing productive uncertainty in science investigations. In J. Kay and R. Luckin (Eds.), *13th International Conference of the Learning Sciences* (vol. 1, pp. 288–295). London, UK: International Society of the Learning Sciences.

Manz, E., and Renga, I.P. (2017). Understanding how teachers guide evidence construction conversations. *Science Education, 101*(4), 584–615.

Manz, E., and Suárez, E. (2018). Supporting teachers to negotiate uncertainty for science, students, and teaching. *Science Education, 102*(4), 771–795.

Manz, E., Lehrer, R., and Schauble, L. (2020). Rethinking the classroom science investigation. *Journal of Research in Science Teaching, 57*(7), 1148–1174.

Mapp, K.L., and Kuttner, P.J. (2013). *Partners in Education: A Dual Capacity-Building Framework for Family-School Partnerships.* SEDL.

Marco-Bujosa, L.M., and Levy, A.J. (2016) Caught in the balance: An organizational analysis of science teaching in schools with elementary science specialists. *Science Education, 100,* 983–1008.

Marin, A., and Bang, M. (2015). Designing pedagogies for Indigenous science education: Finding our way to storywork. *Journal of American Indian Education, 54*(2), 29–51.

Marin, A., and Bang, M. (2018). "Look it, this is how you know": Family forest walks as a context for knowledge-building about the natural world. *Cognition and Instruction, 36*(2), 89–118.

Marino, J.-C. (2019). *Elementary Students' Coordination of Claims and Evidence in Science and History.* Unpublished doctoral dissertation, University of Michigan, Ann Arbor.

Martin, L. (2015). The promise of the maker movement for education. *Journal of Pre-College Engineering Education Research (J-PEER), 5*(1), 4.

Marx, R., and Harris, C. (2006). No Child Left Behind and science education: Opportunities, challenges, and risks. *Elementary School Journal, 106*(5), 467–477.

Mashburn, A.J., Pianta, R.C., Hamre, B.K., Downer, J.T., Barbarin, O.A., Bryant, D., Burchinal, M., Early, D.M., and Howes, C. (2008). Measures of classroom quality in prekindergarten and children's development of academic, language, and social skills. *Child Development, 79*(3), 732–749.

Masnick, A.M., and Klahr, D. (2003). Error matters: An initial exploration of elementary school children's understanding of experimental error. *Journal of Cognition and Development, 4*(1), 67–98.

May, L., Crisp, T., Bingham, G.E., Schwartz, R.S., Pickens, M.T., and Woodbridge, K. (2020). The durable, dynamic nature of genre and science: A purpose-driven typology of science trade books. *Reading Research Quarterly, 55*(3), 399–418.

Mayer, A., Woulfin, S., and Warhol, L. (2015). Moving the center of expertise: Applying a communities of practice framework to understand coaching in urban school reform. *Journal of Educational Change, 16*(1), 101–123.

McClure, E.R., Guernsey, L., Clements, D.H., Bales, S.N., Nichols, J., Kendall-Taylor, N., and Levine, M.H. (2017). *STEM Starts Early: Grounding Science, Technology, Engineering, and Math Education in Early Childhood*. The Joan Ganz Cooney Center at Sesame Workshop. Available: www.joanganzcooneycenter.org/publication/stem-starts-early.

McGill, T.A.W., Housman, G., and Reiser, B.J. (2021). Supporting elementary students' three-dimensional learning about waves with a storyline unit. *Science and Children*.

McGinnis, J.R., Hestness, E., Mills, K., Ketelhut, D.J., Cabrera, L., and Jeong, H. (2020). Preservice science teachers' beliefs about computational thinking following a curricular module within an elementary science methods course. *Contemporary Issues in Technology and Teacher Education, 20*(1), 85–107.

McGowan, V.C., and Bell, P. (2020). Engineering education as the development of critical sociotechnical literacy. *Science & Education, 29*, 981–1005.

McGuire, M.E. (2007). What happened to social studies? The disappearing curriculum. *Phi Delta Kappan, 88*(8), 620–624.

McLaughlin, D., and Calabrese Barton, A. (2013). Preservice teachers' uptake and understanding of funds of knowledge in elementary science. *Journal of Science Teacher Education, 24*(1), 13–36.

McMurrer, J. (2008). *Instructional Time in Elementary Schools: A Closer Look at Changes for Specific Subjects*. Center on Education Policy.

McNeill, K.L. (2011). Elementary students' views of explanation, argumentation, and evidence, and their abilities to construct arguments over the school year. *Journal of Research in Science Teaching, 48*(7), 793–823.

McNeill, K.L., and Berland, L. (2017). What is (or should be) scientific evidence use in K–12 classrooms? *Journal of Research in Science Teaching, 54*(5), 672–689.

McNeill, K.L., and Knight, A.M. (2013). Teachers' pedagogical content knowledge of scientific argumentation: The impact of professional development on K–12 teachers. *Science Education, 97*(6), 936–972.

McNeill, K.L., Lowenhaupt, R.J., and Katsch-Singer, R. (2018). Instructional leadership in the era of the NGSS: Principals' understandings of science practices. *Science Education, 102*, 452–473.

McNeill, K.L., Marco-Bujosa, L.M., González-Howard, M., and Loper, S. (2018) Teachers' enactments of curriculum: *Fidelity to Procedure* versus *Fidelity to Goal* for scientific argumentation. *International Journal of Science Education, 40*(12), 1455–1475.

McWayne, C.M., Mistry, J., Brenneman, K., Zan, B., and Greenfield, D. (2018). Supporting family engagement in science, technology, and engineering (STE) curriculum among low-income immigrant families with preschool children. In M. Caspe, T. Wood, and J.L. Kennedy (Eds.), *Promising Practices for Engaging Families in STEM Learning* (pp. 81–97). Charlotte, NC: Information Age.

McWayne, C.M., Mistry, J., Brenneman, K., Zan, B., and Greenfield, D. (2020). A model of co-construction for curriculum and professional development in Head Start: The Readiness through Integrative Science and Engineering (RISE) approach. *Teachers College Record, 122*(11).

McWayne, C. M., Greenfield, D., Zan, B., Mistry, J., and Ochoa, W. (2021). A comprehensive professional development approach for supporting science, technology, and engineering curriculum in preschool: Connecting contexts for dual language learners. In S.J. Vorkapi and J. LoCasale-Crouch (Eds.), *Supporting Children's Well-Being During Early Childhood Transition to School* (pp. 222–253). Hershey, PA: IGI Global.

Meier, L.T. (2012). The effect of school culture on science education at an ideologically innovative elementary magnet school: An ethnographic case study. *Journal of Science Teacher Education, 23*, 805–822.

Mejía-Arauz, R., Rogoff, B., and Paradise, R. (2005). Cultural variation in children's observation during a demonstration. *International Journal of Behavioral Development*, 29(4), 282–291.

Menon, D., and Sadler, T. (2016). Preservice elementary teachers' science self-efficacy beliefs and science content knowledge. *Journal of Science Teacher Education*, 27(6), 649–673.

Menon, D., Chandrasekhar, M., Kosztin, D., and Steinhoff, D. (2020). Impact of mobile technology-based physics curriculum on preservice elementary teachers' technology self-efficacy. *Science Education*, 104, 252–289.

Mensah, F.M. (2009). Confronting assumptions, biases, and stereotypes in preservice teachers' conceptualizations of science teaching through the use of book club. *Journal of Research in Science Teaching*, 46(9), 1041–1066.

Mensah, F.M., and Jackson, I. (2018). Whiteness as property in science teacher education. *Teachers College Record*, 120, 1–38.

Mensah, F.M., Brown, J., Titu, P., Rozowa, P., Sivaraj, R., and Heydari, R. (2018). Preservice and inservice teachers' ideas of multiculturalism: Explorations across two science methods courses in two different contexts. *Journal of Science Teacher Education*, 29(2), 128–147.

Mercer, N., Dawes, L., and Staarman, J.K. (2009). Dialogic teaching in the primary science classroom. *Language and Education*, 23(4), 353–369.

Metcalf, S.J., Reilly, J.M., Jeon, S., Wang, A., Pyers, A., Brennan, K., and Dede, C. (2021). Assessing computational thinking through the lenses of functionality and computational fluency. *Computer Science Education*, 31(2), 199–223.

Metz, K.E. (1993). Preschoolers' developing knowledge of the pan balance: From new representation to transformed problem solving. *Cognition and Instruction*, 11(1), 31–93.

Metz, K.E. (1995). Reassessment of developmental constraints on children's science instruction. *Review of Educational Research*, 65(2), 93–127.

Metz, K.E. (2004). Children's understanding of scientific inquiry: Their conceptualization of uncertainty in investigations of their own design. *Cognition and Instruction*, 22(2), 219–290.

Metz, K.E. (2008). Narrowing the gulf between the practices of science and the elementary school science classroom. *Elementary School Journal*, 109(2), 138–161.

Metz, K.E. (2009). Elementary school teachers as "targets and agents of change": Teachers' learning in interaction with reform science curriculum. *Science Education*, 93, 915–954.

Metz, K.E. (2011). Disentangling robust developmental constraints from the instructionally mutable: Young children's epistemic reasoning about a study of their own design. *Journal of the Learning Sciences*, 20(1), 50–110.

Michaels, S., and O'Connor, C. (2012). *Talk Science Primer*. Cambridge, MA: TERC.

Michaels, S., O'Connor, C., and Resnick, L.B. (2008). Deliberative discourse idealized and realized: Accountable talk in the classroom and in civic life. *Studies in Philosophy and Education*, 27(4), 283–297.

Miller, C.L. (2010). District leadership for science education: Using K–12 departments to support elementary science education under NCLB. *Science Educator*, 19(2), 22–30.

Miller, E., Severance, S., and Krajcik, J. (2021). Motivating teaching, sustaining change in practice: Design principles for teacher learning in project-based learning contexts. *Journal of Science Teacher Education*, 32(7), 757–779.

Mills, C.M., and Keil, F.C. (2004). Knowing the limits of one's understanding: The development of an awareness of an illusion of explanatory depth. *Journal of Experimental Child Psychology*, 87(1), 1–32.

Milner, A.R., Sondergeld, T.A., Demir, A., Johnson, C.C., and Czerniak, C.M. (2012). Elementary teachers' beliefs about teaching science and classroom practice: An examination of pre/post NCLB testing in science. *Journal of Science Teacher Education*, 23(2), 111–132.

Milner, H.R. (2020). Disrupting punitive practices and policies: Rac(e)ing back to teaching, teacher preparation, and *Brown*. *Educational Researcher, 49*(3), 147–160.

Moll, L.C., Amanti, C., Neff, D., and Gonzalez, N. (1992). Funds of knowledge for teaching: Using a qualitative approach to connect homes and classrooms. *Theory into Practice, 31*(2), 132–141.

Monteira, S.F., and Jiménez-Aleixandre, M.P. (2016). The practice of using evidence in kindergarten: The role of purposeful observation. *Journal of Research in Science Teaching, 53*(8), 1232–1258.

Monteira, S.F., Jiménez-Aleixandre, M.P., and Siry, C. (2020). Scaffolding children's production of representations along the three years of ECE: A longitudinal study. *Research in Science Education*, 1–32.

Moore, T.J., and Ottenbreit-Leftwich, A.T. (2020). *The Integration of Computational Thinking in Early Childhood and Elementary Education*. Washington, DC: The National Academies Press.

Moore, T.J., Johnston, A.C., and Glancy, A.W. (2020). STEM integration: A synthesis of conceptual frameworks and definitions. In C.C. Johnson, M.J. Mohr-Schroeder, T.J. Moore, and L.D. English (Eds.), *Handbook of Research on STEM Education* (pp. 3–16). New York: Routledge.

Morales-Doyle, D. (2017). Justice-centered science pedagogy: A catalyst for academic achievement and social transformation. *Science Education, 101*, 1034–1060.

Morgan, I., and Amerikaner, A. (2018). *Funding Gaps 2018: An Analysis of School Funding Equity Across the US and Within Each State*. Education Trust.

Mouw, J., Saab, N., Gijlers, H., Hickendorff, M., van Paridon, Y., and Van Den Broek, P. (2020). The differential effect of perspective-taking ability on profiles of cooperative behaviours and learning outcomes. *Frontline Learning Research, 8*(6), 88–113.

Murchison, L., and Banay, E. (2019). How one nonprofit combined established teaching strategies in new ways for a transformative approach to STEM education. *Connected Science Learning, 1*(10).

Murnane, R.J., and Raizen, S.A. (1988). *Improving Indicators of the Quality of Science and Mathematics Education in Grades K–12*. Washington, DC: National Academy Press.

Naidoo, K. (2017). Capturing the transformation and dynamic nature of an elementary teacher candidate's identity development as a teacher of science. *Research in Science Education, 47*, 1331–1355.

Nasir, N.I.S., and Cooks, J. (2009). Becoming a hurdler: How learning settings afford identities. *Anthropology & Education Quarterly, 40*(1), 41–61.

Nasir, N.S., Snyder, C.R., Shah, N., and Ross, K.M. (2012). Racial storylines and implications for learning. *Human Development, 55*(5–6), 285–301.

Nasir, N.S., Rosebery, A.S., Warren, B., and Lee, C.D. (2014). Learning as a cultural process: Achieving equity through diversity. In R.K. Sawyer, *The Cambridge Handbook of the Learning Sciences* (2nd ed., pp. 686–706). Cambridge, UK: Cambridge University Press.

Nasir, N.S., McKinney de Royston, M., Barron, B., Bell, P., Pea, R., Stevens, R., and Goldman, S. (2020). Learning pathways: How learning is culturally organized. In N.S. Nasir, C.D. Lee, R. Pea, and M. McKinney de Royston (Eds.), *Handbook of Cultural Foundations of Learning* (pp. 195–211). New York: Routledge.

National Academies of Sciences, Engineering, and Medicine. (2015). *Science Teachers' Learning: Enhancing Opportunities, Creating Supportive Contexts*. Washington, DC: The National Academies Press.

———(2017). *Seeing Students Learn Science: Integrating Assessment and Instruction in the Classroom*. Washington, DC: The National Academies Press.

———(2018a). *English Learners in STEM Subjects: Transforming Classrooms, Schools, and Lives*. Washington, DC: The National Academies Press.

——— (2018b). *How People Learn II: Learners, Contexts, and Cultures.* Washington, DC: The National Academies Press.

——— (2019a). *Monitoring Educational Equity.* Washington, DC: The National Academies Press.

——— (2019b). *Science and Engineering for Grades 6–12: Investigation and Design at the Center.* Washington, DC: The National Academies Press.

——— (2020). *Changing Expectations for the K–12 Teacher Workforce: Policies, Preservice Education, Professional Development, and the Workplace.* Washington, DC: The National Academies Press.

——— (2021). *Cultivating Interest and Competencies in Computing: Authentic Experiences and Design Factors.* Washington, DC: The National Academies Press.

National Academy of Engineering. (2008). *Changing the Conversation: Messages for Improving Public Understanding of Engineering.* Washington, DC: The National Academies Press.

National Academy of Engineering and National Research Council. (2009). *Engineering in K–12 Education: Understanding the Status and Improving the Prospects.* Washington, DC: The National Academies Press.

National Governors Association Center for Best Practices, Council of Chief State School Officers. (2010). *Common Core State Standards for English Language Arts.* Available: http://www.corestandards.org/ELA-Literacy/.

National Research Council. (1996). *National Science Education Standards.* Washington DC: National Academy Press.

——— (1999). *How People Learn: Brain, Mind, Experience, and School.* Washington, DC: National Academy Press.

——— (2002). *Scientific Research in Education.* Washington, DC: The National Academies Press.

——— (2007). *Taking Science to School: Learning and Teaching Science in Grades K–8.* Washington, DC: The National Academies Press.

——— (2008). *Ready, Set, SCIENCE! Putting Research to Work in K–8 Science Classrooms.* Washington, DC: The National Academies Press.

——— (2009). *Learning Science in Informal Environments: People, Places, and Pursuits.* Washington, DC: The National Academies Press.

——— (2012). *A Framework for K–12 Education: Practices, Crosscutting Concepts, and Core Ideas.* Washington, DC: The National Academies Press.

——— (2014a). *Developing Assessments for the Next Generation of Science Standards.* Washington, DC: The National Academies Press.

——— (2014b). *STEM Integration in K–12 Education: Status, Prospects, and an Agenda for Research.* Washington, DC: The National Academies Press.

——— (2015a). *Guide to Implementing the Next Generation Science Standards.* Washington DC: National Academies Press.

——— (2015b). *Science Teachers' Learning: Enhancing Opportunities, Creating Supportive Contexts.* Washington, DC: The National Academies Press.

Nayfeld, I., Brenneman, K., and Gelman, R. (2011). Science in the classroom: Finding a balance between autonomous exploration and teacher-led instruction in preschool settings. *Early Education & Development, 22*(6), 970–988.

Nelson, G.D., and Landel, C.C. (2007). A collaborative approach for elementary science: Lessons about using teacher expertise, learned from reforms in science, can improve science learning in every subject. *Educational Leadership, 64*(4), 72–75.

Nersessian, N.J. (2005). Interpreting scientific and engineering practices: Integrating the cognitive, social, and cultural dimensions. *Scientific and Technological Thinking,* 17–56.

Nersessian, N.J. (2008). *Creating Scientific Concepts.* Cambridge, MA: MIT Press.

NGSS Lead States. (2013). *Next Generation Science Standards: For States, by States.* Washington, DC: The National Academies Press.

Nieto, S., and Bode, P. (2007). *Affirming Diversity: The Sociopolitical Context of Multicultural Education* (5th ed.). Boston, MA: Allyn & Bacon.

Nixon, R., Smith, L., and Sudweeks, R. (2019). Elementary teachers' science subject matter knowledge across the teacher career cycle. *Journal of Research in Science Teaching, 56,* 707–731.

Novak, M., McGill, T.A.W., Fattaleh, K., Farkash, L., Michael, N., and Purdie-Dyer, R. (Eds.). (2019). *Why is Our Corn Changing? [v2.1]* [Curriculum Materials, Grade 2]. NextGen Science Storylines. Available: https://www.nextgenstorylines.org/why-is-our-corn-changing.

Nowicki, B., Sullivan-Watts, B., Shim, M., Young, B., and Pockalny, R. (2013). Factors influencing science content accuracy in elementary inquiry science lessons. *Research in Science Education, 43,* 1135–1154.

Nxumalo, F. (2019). Presencing: Decolonial attunements to children's place relations. In D. Hodgins (Ed.), *Feminist Research for 21st-Century Childhoods: Common Worlds Methods* (pp. 159–168). London: Bloomsbury.

O'Donnell, C. (2008). Defining, conceptualizing, and measuring fidelity of implementation and its relationship to outcomes in K–12 curriculum intervention research. *Review of Educational Research, 78,* 33–84.

Oakes, J. (2005). *Keeping Track: How Schools Structure Inequality* (2nd ed.). New Haven, CT: Yale University Press.

Office of Special Education and Rehabilitative Services (ED). (2018). *40th Annual Report to Congress on the Implementation of the Individuals with Disabilities Education Act.* ERIC Clearinghouse.

Olson, J., Bruxvoort, C., and Vande Haar, A. (2016). The impact of video case content on preservice elementary teachers' decision-making and conceptions of effective science teaching. *Journal of Research in Science Teaching, 53*(10), 1500–1523.

Osborne, J., Rafanelli, S., and Kind, P. (2018). Toward a more coherent model for science education than the crosscutting concepts of the next generation science standards: The affordances of styles of reasoning. *Journal of Research in Science Teaching, 55*(7), 962–981.

Osher, D., Cantor, P., Berg, J., Steyer, L., and Rose, T. (2020). Drivers of human development: How relationships and context shape learning and development. *Applied Developmental Science, 24*(1), 6–36.

Ottenbreit-Leftwich, A.T., and Biggers, M. (2017). *Status of K–14 Computer Science Education in Indiana: Landscape Report.* Submitted to the NSF's ECEP Alliance, the Indiana Department of Education, Governor of Indiana, Code.org, and Indiana legislators. Available: http://bit.ly/CSforINFinalReport.

Ozturk, Z., Dooley, C.M., and Welch, M. (2018). Finding the hook: Computer science education in elementary contexts. *Journal of Research on Technology in Education, 50*(2), 149–163.

Pace, J.L. (2011). The complex and unequal impact of high stakes accountability on untested social studies. *Theory & Research in Social Education, 39*(1), 32–60.

Pajares, M.F. (1992). Teachers' beliefs and educational research: Cleaning up a messy construct. *Review of Educational Research, 62*(3), 307–332.

Palincsar, A.S., and Magnusson, S.J. (2001). The interplay of first-hand and text-based investigations to model and support the development of scientific knowledge and reasoning. In S. Carver and D. Klahr (Eds.), *Cognition and Instruction: Twenty-Five Years of Progress* (pp. 151–194). Mahwah, NJ: Lawrence Erlbaum Associates.

Palincsar, A.S., Fitzgerald, M.S., DellaVecchia, G.P., and Easley, K.M. (2020). *The Integration of Literacy, Science, and Engineering in Prekindergarten through Fifth Grade.* Washington, DC: The National Academies Press.

Palmberg, I., Hermans, M., Jeronen, E., Kärkkäinen, S., Persson, C., and Yli-Panula, E. (2018). Nordic student teachers' views on the importance of species and species identification. *Journal of Science Teacher Education, 29*(5), 397–419.

Palmer, D. (2011). The discourse of transition: Teachers' language ideologies within transitional bilingual education programs. *International Multilingual Research Journal, 5*(2), 103–122.

Papert, S. (1980). *Mindstorms: Children, Computers and Powerful Ideas.* New York: Basic Books.

Paprzycki, P., Tuttle, N., Czerniak, C.M., Molitor, S., Kadervaek, J., and Mendenhall, R. (2017). The impact of a Framework-aligned science professional development program on literacy and mathematics achievement of K–3 students. *Journal of Research in Science Teaching, 54*(9), 1174–1196.

Parker, J., and Heywood, D. (2013). Exploring how engaging with reflection on learning generates pedagogical insight in science teacher education. *Science Education, 97,* 410–441.

Pattison, S.A., and Dierking, L.D. (2018). Early childhood science interest development: Variation in interest patterns and parent-child interactions among low-income families. *Science Education, 103*(2), 362–388.

Pattison, S.A., Gontan, I., Ramos-Montañez, S., and Moreno, L. (2018). Identity negotiation within peer groups during an informal engineering education program: The central role of leadership-oriented youth. *Science Education, 102,* 978–1006.

Pattison, S.A., Gontan, I., Ramos Montanez, S., Shagott, T., Francisco, M., and Dierking, L.D. (2020). The Identity-Frame Model: A framework to describe situated identity negotiation for adolescent girls participating in an informal engineering education program. *Journal of the Learning Sciences, 29*(4–5), 550–597.

Paugh, P., Wendell, K., and Wright, C. (2018). Elementary engineering as a synergistic site for disciplinary and linguistic learning in an urban classroom. *Literacy Research: Theory, Method, and Practice, 67*(1), 261–278.

Pearson, P.D., Moje, E., and Greenleaf, C. (2010). Literacy and science: Each in the service of the other. *Science, 328*(5977), 459–463.

Pedretti, E., and Iannini, A.M.N. (2020). *Controversy in Science Museums: Re-imagining Exhibition Spaces and Practice.* New York: Routledge.

Penfield, R.D., and Lee, O. (2010). Test based accountability: Potential benefits and pitfalls of science assessment with student diversity. *Journal of Research in Science Teaching, 47*(1), 6–24.

Penner, D., Giles, N., Lehrer, R., and Schauble, L. (1997). Building functional models: Designing an elbow. *Journal of Research in Science Teaching, 34*(2), 125–143.

Penuel, W.R. (2019). Infrastructuring as a practice of design-based research for supporting and studying equitable implementation and sustainability of innovations. *Journal of the Learning Sciences, 28*(4–5), 659–677.

Penuel, W.R., and Reiser, B.J. (2018). *Designing NGSS-Aligned Curriculum Materials.* National Academies of Sciences, Engineering, and Medicine. Available: https://sites.nationalacademies.org/cs/groups/dbassesite/documents/webpage/dbasse_189504.pdf.

Penuel, W.R., and Watkins, D.A. (2019). Assessment to promote equity and epistemic justice: A use-case of a research-practice partnership in science education. *The ANNALS of the American Academy of Political and Social Science, 683*(1), 201–216.

Penuel, W.R., and Wertsch, J.V. (1995). Vygotsky and identity formation: A sociocultural approach. *Educational Psychologist, 30*(2), 83–92.

Penuel, W., Bell, P., and Neill, T. (2020). Creating a system of professional learning that meets teachers' needs. *Phi Delta Kappan, 101*(8).

Penuel, W., Fishman, B.J., Gallagher, L.P., Korbak, C., and Lopez-Prado, B. (2008). The mediating role of coherence in curriculum implementation. In *Proceedings of the 8th International Conference of the Learning Sciences* (vol. 2, pp. 180–187). Utrecht, The Netherlands: International Society of the Learning Sciences.

Penuel, W.R., Bates, L., Pasnik, S., Townsend, E., Gallagher, L.P., Llorente, C., and Hupert, N. (2010). The impact of a media-rich science curriculum on low-income preschoolers' science talk at home. In K. Gomez, L. Lyons, and J. Radinsky (Eds.), *9th International Conference of the International Society of the Learning Sciences* (pp. 238–245). Chicago, IL: International Society of the Learning Sciences.

Peppler, K., Halverson, E., and Kafai, Y.B. (Eds.). (2016). *Makeology: Makerspaces as Learning Environments* (Vol. 1). New York: Routledge.

Peppler, K., Keune, A., and Dahn, M. (2020). *AISL New York Hall of Science Summative Evaluation Report*. New York Hall of Science.

Peppler, K., Wohlwend, K., Thompson, N., Tan, V., and Thomas, A. (2019). Squishing circuits: Circuitry learning with electronics and playdough in early childhood. *Journal of Science Education and Technology, 28*(2), 118–132.

Perkins, D.N., and Grotzer, T.A. (2005). Dimensions of causal understanding: The role of complex causal models in students' understanding of science. *Studies in Science Education, 41*, 117–166.

Perkins Coppola, M. (2019). Preparing preservice elementary teachers to teach engineering: Impact on self-efficacy and outcome expectancy. *School Science and Mathematics, 119*(3), 161–170.

Peters-Burton, E.E., House, A., Peters, V., and Remond, J. (2019). Understanding STEM-focused elementary schools: Case study of Walter Bracken STEAM Academy. *School Science and Mathematics, 119*, 446–456.

Peterson, S.M., and French, L. (2008). Supporting young children's explanations through inquiry science in preschool. *Early Childhood Research Quarterly, 23*, 395–408.

Philip, T.M., and Azevedo, F.S. (2017). Everyday science learning and equity: Mapping the contested terrain. *Science Education, 101*(4), 526–532.

Phillips, A.M., Watkins, J., and Hammer, D. (2017). Problematizing as a scientific endeavor. *Physical Review Physics Education Research, 13*(2), 020107.

Phillips, A.M., Watkins, J., and Hammer, D. (2018). Beyond "asking questions": Problematizing as a disciplinary activity. *Journal of Research in Science Teaching, 55*(7), 982–998.

Piasta, S.B., Pelatti, C.Y., and Miller, H.L. (2014). Mathematics and science learning opportunities in preschool classrooms. *Early Education and Development, 25*(4), 445–468.

Picha, G. (2020). STEM education has a math anxiety problem. *Education Week*.

Piekny, J., Grube, D., and Maehler, C. (2014). The development of experimentation and evidence evaluation skills at preschool age. *International Journal of Science Education, 36*(2), 334–354.

Pila, S., Aladé, F., Sheehan, K.J., Lauricella, A.R., and Wartella, E.A. (2019). Learning to code via tablet applications: An evaluation of Daisy the Dinosaur and Kodable as learning tools for young children. *Computers & Education, 128*, 52–62.

Pinar, W.F., Reynolds, W.M., Slattery, P., and Taubman, P.M. (1995). *Understanding Curriculum: An Introduction to the Study of Historical and Contemporary Curriculum Discourses*. Bern, Switzerland: Peter Lang.

Plonczak, I. (2010). Videoconferencing in math and science preservice elementary teachers' field placements. *Journal of Science Teacher Education, 21*(2), 241–254.

Plumley, C.L. (2019). *2018 NSSME+: Status of Elementary School Science*. Chapel Hill, NC: Horizon Research, Inc.

Plummer, J., and Ozcelik, A. (2015). Preservice teachers developing coherent inquiry investigations in elementary astronomy. *Science Education, 99*, 932–957.

Portsmore, M., Watkins, J., and McCormick, M. (2012). *Planning, Drawing and Elementary Students in an Integrated Engineering Design and Literacy Activity*. Paper presented at the 2nd P–12 Engineering and Design Education Research Summit, Washington, DC.

Powietrzyńska, M., and Gangji, A. (2016). "I understand why people need to ease their emotions": Exploring mindfulness and emotions in a conceptual physics classroom of an elementary teacher education program. *Cultural Studies of Science Education, 11*, 693–712.

Poza, L.E. (2016). The language of ciencia: Translanguaging and learning in a bilingual science classroom. *International Journal of Bilingual Education and Bilingualism, 21*(1), 1–19.

Prain, V., and Waldrip, B. (2006). An exploratory study of teachers' and students' use of multimodal representations of concepts in primary science. *International Journal of Science Education, 28*(15), 1843–1866.

Presser, A.L., Kamdar, D., Vidiksis, R., Goldstein, M., Domínguez, X., and Orr, J. (2017). Growing plants and minds. *Science and Children, 55*(2), 41.

Presser, A.L., Domínguez, X., Goldstein, M., Vidiksis, R., and Kamdar, D. (2019). Ramp It UP! *Science and Children, 56*(7), 30–37.

Quinn, D.M., and Cooc, N. (2015). Science achievement gaps by gender and race/ethnicity in elementary and middle school: Trends and predictors. *Educational Researcher, 44*(6), 336–346.

Radoff, J. (2017). *Dynamics Contributing to the Emergence and Stability of Students' Scientific Engagement over Multiple Timescales*. Medford, MA: Tufts University.

Rammer, R., Hayes, J., and Woods, B. (2017). Supporting and enhancing NGSS implementation: A tale of two principals' efforts. *California Classroom Science*.

Ray, M.J., Israel, M., Lee, C., and Do, V. (2018). A cross-case analysis of instructional strategies to support participation of K–8 students with disabilities in CS for All. In *Proceedings of the 49th ACM Technical Symposium on Computer Science Education* (pp. 900–905). New York: Association for Computing Machinery.

Rebello, C.M., Asunda, P.A., and Wang, H.-H. (2020). Infusing evidence-based reasoning in integrated STEM. In C.C. Johnson, M.J. Mohr-Schroeder, T.J. Moore, and L.D. English (Eds.), *Handbook of Research on STEM Education* (pp. 101–127). New York: Routledge.

Reiser, B. (2004). Scaffolding complex learning: The mechanisms of structuring and problematizing student work. *Journal of the Learning Sciences, 13*(3), 273–304.

Reiser, B., Novak, M., McGill, T., and Penuel, W. (2021). Storyline units: An instructional model to support coherence from the students' perspective. *Journal of Science Teacher Education, 32*(7), 805–829.

Reiser, B.J., Michaels, S., Moon, J., Bell, T., Dyer, E., Edwards, K.D., McGill, T.A.W., Novak, M., and Park, A. (2017). Scaling up three-dimensional science learning through teacher led study groups across a state. *Journal of Teacher Education, 68*(3), 280–298.

Remold, J., Rosier, S., Sauerteig, D., Podkul, T., Bhanot, R., and Michalchik, V. (2014). *BaySci: A Partnership for Bay Area Science Education, August 2014 Evaluation Report*. Menlo Park, CA: SRI Education.

Rennie, L., Wallace, J., and Venville, G. (2012). Exploring curriculum integration: Why integrate? In L. Rennie, J. Wallace, and G. Venville (Eds.), *Integrating Science, Technology, Engineering, and Mathematics: Issues, Reflections, and Ways Forward* (pp. 1–11). New York: Routledge.

Reyes, L.V., and Torres, M.N. (2007). Decolonizing family literacy in a culture circle: Reinventing the family literacy educator's role. *Journal of Early Childhood Literacy, 7*(1), 73–94.

Rice, D., and Kaya, S. (2012). Exploring relations among preservice elementary teachers' ideas about evolution, understanding of relevant science concepts, and college science coursework. *Research in Science Education, 42*, 165–179.

Rich, K.M., Spaepen, E., Strickland, C., and Moran, C. (2020). Synergies and differences in mathematical and computational thinking: Implications for integrated instruction. *Interactive Learning Environments, 28*(3), 272–283.

Rich, P.J., Jones, B.L., Belikov, O., Yoshikawa, E., and Perkins, M. (2017). Computing and engineering in elementary school: The effect of yearlong training on elementary teacher self-efficacy and beliefs about teaching computing and engineering. *International Journal of Computer Science Education in Schools, 1*(1), n1.

Richards, J., Johnson, A., and Nyeggen, C.G. (2015). Inquiry-based science and the Next Generation Science Standards: A magnetic attraction. *Science and Children, 52*(6), 54.

Riegle-Crumb, C., Morton, K., Moore, C., Chimonidou, A., Labrake, C., and Kopp, S. (2015). Do inquiring minds have positive attitudes? The science education of preservice elementary teachers. *Science Education, 99*, 819–836.

Rivera, S., and Oliveira, A. (2021). "Why would Benjamin Franklin want to know if lightning was electricity?" Elementary teachers and students making sense of the nature of science during interactive read-alouds. *Cultural Studies of Science Education, 16*, 47–69.

Rivera Maulucci, M.S. (2010). Revisiting the marginalization of science in an urban school: Coactivating social, cultural, material, and strategic resources. *Journal of Research in Science Teaching, 47*(7), 840–860.

Rivera Maulucci, M. (2011). Language experience narratives and the role of autobiographical reasoning in becoming an urban science teacher. *Cultural Studies of Science Education, 6*, 413–434.

Robertson, A.D., Scherr, R., and Hammer, D. (Eds.). (2015). *Responsive Teaching in Science and Mathematics*. New York: Routledge.

Rodriguez, A.J. (2015). What about a dimension of engagement, equity, and diversity practices? A critique of the next generation science standards. *Journal of Research in Science Teaching, 52*(7), 1031–1051.

Rodriguez, A.J., and Shim, S.W. (2020). Addressing critical cross-cultural issues in elementary STEM education research and practice: A critical review essay of Engineering in Elementary STEM Education. *Cultural Studies of Science Education*, 1–17.

Rogoff, B. (2003). *The Cultural Nature of Human Development*. New York: Oxford University Press.

Romance, N.R., and Vitale, M.R. (2001). Implementing an in-depth expanded science model in elementary schools: Multi-year findings, research issues, and policy implications. *International Journal of Science Education, 23*(4), 373–404.

Rosebery, A.S., Warren, B., and Tucker Raymond, E. (2016). Developing interpretive power in science teaching. *Journal of Research in Science Teaching, 53*(10), 1571–1600.

Rosebery, A.S., Ogonowski, M., DiSchino, M., and Warren, B. (2010). "The coat traps all your body heat": Heterogeneity as fundamental to learning. *Journal of the Learning Sciences, 19*(3), 322–357.

Roth, K., Garnier, H., Chen, C., Lemmens, M., Schwille, K., and Wickler, N. (2011). Video-based lesson analysis: Effective science PD for teacher and student learning. *Journal of Research in Science Teaching, 48*(2), 117–148.

Rouse, A.G., and Rouse, R. (2019). Third graders' use of writing to facilitate learning of engineering concepts. *Journal of Research in Science Teaching, 56*(10), 1406–1430.

Rowe, D.W., and Neitzel, C. (2010). Interest and agency in 2- and 3-year-olds' participation in emergent writing. *Reading Research Quarterly, 45*(2), 169–195.

Ruiz-Primo M., Solano-Flores G., and Li, M. (2014) Formative assessment as a process of interaction through language. In C. Wyatt-Smith, V. Klenowski, and P. Colbert (Eds.), *Designing Assessment for Quality Learning. The Enabling Power of Assessment* (vol. 1, pp. 265–284). Dordrecht, The Netherlands: Springer.

Russ, R.S., and Berland, L.K. (2019). Invented science: A framework for discussing a persistent problem of practice. *Journal of the Learning Sciences, 28*(3), 279–301.

Russ, R.S., and Sherin, M.G. (2013). Using interviews to explore student ideas in science. *Science Scope, 36*(5), 19.

Russ, R.S., Scherr, R.E., Hammer, D., and Mikeska, J. (2008). Recognizing mechanistic reasoning in student scientific inquiry: A framework for discourse analysis developed from philosophy of science. *Science Education, 92*(3), 499–525.

Russ, R.S., Coffey, J.E., Hammer, D., and Hutchison, P. (2009). Making classroom assessment more accountable to scientific reasoning: A case for attending to mechanistic thinking. *Science Education, 93*(5), 875–891.

Ryu, S., and Sandoval, W.A. (2012). Improvements to elementary children's epistemic understanding from sustained argumentation. *Science Education, 96*(3), 488–526.

Sabel, J., Forbes, C., and Zangori, L. (2015). Promoting prospective elementary teachers' learning to use formative assessment for life science instruction. *Journal of Science Teacher Education, 26*(4), 419–445.

Saçkes, M., and Trundle, K. (2014). Preservice early childhood teachers' learning of science in a methods course: Examining the predictive ability of an intentional learning model. *Journal of Science Teacher Education, 25*(4), 413–444.

Saçkes, M., Flevares, L.M., Gonya, J. and Cabe Trundle, K. (2012). Preservice early childhood teachers' sense of efficacy for integrating mathematics and science: Impact of a methods course. *Journal of Early Childhood Teacher Education, 33*(4), 349–364.

Salazar Pérez, M., and Saavedra, C.M. (2017). A call for onto-epistemological diversity in early childhood education and care: Centering global south conceptualizations of childhood/s. *Review of Research in Education, 41*, 1–29.

Salgado, M., and Salgado, N. (2019). *NGSS Stories: A Second Grade Classroom Explores the Flooding of the Town of Moncton.* Paper presented at the meeting of La Cosecha Dual Language Conferences, Albuquerque, NM.

Samarapungavan, A., Bryan, L., and Wills, J. (2017). Second graders' emerging particle models of matter in the context of learning through model based inquiry. *Journal of Research in Science Teaching, 54*(8), 988–1023.

Samarapungavan, A.L.A., Mantzicopoulos, P., and Patrick, H. (2008). Learning science through inquiry in kindergarten. *Science Education, 92*(5), 868–908.

Samarapungavan, A., Patrick, H., and Mantzicopoulos, P. (2011). What kindergarten students learn in inquiry-based science classrooms. *Cognition and Instruction, 29*(4), 416–470.

Sandoval, C., van Es, E., Campbell, S., and Santagata, R. (2020). Creating coherence in teacher preparation: Examining teacher candidates' conceptualizations and practices for equity. *Teacher Education Quarterly, 47*(4), 8–32.

Sandoval, W.A., and Çam, A. (2011). Elementary children's judgments of the epistemic status of sources of justification. *Science Education, 95*(3), 383–408.

Sandoval, W.A., Sodian, B., Koerber, S., and Wong, J. (2014). Developing children's early competencies to engage with science. *Educational Psychologist, 49*(2), 139–152.

Sandoval, W.A., Enyedy, N., Redman, E.H., and Xiao, S. (2019). Organising a culture of argumentation in elementary science. *International Journal of Science Education, 41*(13), 1848–1869.

Sarama, J., Brenneman, K., Clements, D.H., Duke, N.K., and Hemmeter, M.L. (2016). *Connect4Learning: The Pre-K Curriculum.* Connect4Learning.

Sarama, J., Brenneman, K., Clements, D.H., Duke, N.K., and Hemmeter, M.L. (2017). Interdisciplinary teaching across multiple domains: The C4L (Connect4Learning) Curriculum. In L.B. Bailey (Ed.), *Implementing a Standards-Based Curriculum in the Early Childhood Classroom* (pp. 1–53). New York: Routledge.

Sargianis, K., Yang, S., and Cunningham, C. (2012). Effective engineering professional development for elementary educators. In *Proceedings of the 119th ASEE Annual Conference and Exposition* (pp. 25.503.1–25.503.24). Washington, DC: American Society for Engineering Education.

Saribas, D., and Akdemir, Z. (2019). Using an innovative tool in science education: Examining pre-service elementary teachers' evaluation levels on the topic of wetlands. *International Journal of Science Education, 41*(1), 123–138.

Scardamalia, M. (2002). Collective cognitive responsibility for the advancement of knowledge. *Liberal Education in a Knowledge Society, 97*, 67–98.

Schauble, L. (1996). The development of scientific reasoning in knowledge-rich contexts. *Developmental Psychology, 32*(1), 102–119.

Schauble, L., Glaser, R., Duschl, R.A., Schulze, S., and John, J. (1995). Students' understanding of the objectives and procedures of experimentation in the science classroom. *Journal of the Learning Sciences, 4*(2), 131–166.

Schein, E.H. (1985). *Organizational Culture and Leadership* (3rd ed.). Hoboken, NJ: Jossey-Bass.

Schissel, J.L. (2019). *Social Consequences of Testing for Language-Minority Bilinguals in the United States.* Bristol, UK: Multilingual Matters.

Schlegel, R.J., Chu, S.L., Chen, K., Deuermeyer, E., Christy, A.G., and Quek, F. (2019). Making in the classroom: Longitudinal evidence of increases in self-efficacy and STEM possible selves over time. *Computers and Education, 142*, 103637.

Schmidt, W.H., Wang, H.C., and McKnight, C.C. (2005). Curriculum coherence: An examination of US mathematics and science content standards from an international perspective. *Journal of Curriculum Studies, 37*(5), 525–559.

Schulz, L.E., and Bonawitz, E.B. (2007). Serious fun: Preschoolers engage in more exploratory play when evidence is confounded. *Developmental Psychology, 43*(4), 1045.

Schwartz, R.S., and Gess-Newsome, J. (2008). Elementary science specialists: A pilot study of current models and a call for participation in the research. *Science Educator, 17*(2), 19–30.

Schwartz, R.S., Lederman, N.G., and Abd-El-Khalick, F. (2000). Achieving the reforms vision: The effectiveness of a specialists-led elementary science program. *School Science and Mathematics, 100*(4), 181–193.

Schwarz, C., Passmore, C., and Reiser, B. (Eds.). (2017). *Helping Students Make Sense of the World Using Next Generation Science and Engineering Practices.* Arlington, VA: NSTA Press.

Schwarz, C., Gunckel, K., Smith, E., Covitt, B., Bae, M., Enfield, M., and Tsurusaki, B. (2008). Helping elementary preservice teachers learn to use curriculum materials for effective science teaching. *Science Education, 92*, 345–377.

Schwarz, C.V., Reiser, B.J., Davis, E.A., Kenyon, L., Achér, A., Fortus, D., Shwartz, Y., Hug, B., and Krajcik, J. (2009). Developing a learning progression for scientific modeling: Making scientific modeling accessible and meaningful for learners. *Journal of Research in Science Teaching: The Official Journal of the National Association for Research in Science Teaching, 46*(6), 632–654.

Schwarz, C.V., Braaten, M., Haverly, C., and de los Santos, E.X. (2020). Using sense-making moments to understand how elementary teachers' interactions expand, maintain, or shut down sense-making in science. *Cognition and Instruction*, 1–36.

Seah, L.H. (2016). Understanding the conceptual and language challenges encountered by grade 4 students when writing scientific explanations. *Research in Science Education, 46*(3), 413–437.

Semken, S., and Freeman, C.B. (2008). Sense of place in the practice and assessment of place based science teaching. *Science Education, 92*(6), 1042–1057.

Seo, K.H., and Ginsburg, H.P. (2004). What is developmentally appropriate in early childhood mathematics education? Lessons from new research. In D.H. Clements and J. Sarama (Eds.), *Engaging Young Children in Mathematics: Standards for Early Childhood Mathematics Education* (pp. 91–104). Mahwah, NJ: Lawrence Erlbaum Associates.

Settlage, J. (2011). Counterstories from White mainstream preservice teachers: Resisting the master narrative of deficit by default. *Cultural Studies of Science Education, 6*, 803–836.

Sevian, H., and Dini, V. (2019). A design-based process in characterizing experienced teachers' formative assessment enactment in science classrooms. In E. McLoughlin, O.E. Finlayson, S. Erduran, and P.E. Childs (Eds.), *Bridging Research and Practice in Science Education* (pp. 325–337). Cham: Springer.

Shapiro, L. (2019). *Embodied Cognition*. New York: Routledge.

Shapiro, E.K., and Nager, N. (2000). The developmental-interaction approach to education: Retrospect and prospect. In N. Nager and E.K. Shapiro (Eds.), *Early Childhood Education. Revisiting a Progressive Pedagogy: The Developmental–Interaction Approach* (pp. 11–46). Albany, NY: State University of New York Press.

Shavelson, R.J., Young, D.B., Ayala, C.C., Brandon, P.R., Furtak, E.M., Ruiz-Primo, M.A., Tomita, M.K., and Yin, Y. (2008). On the impact of curriculum-embedded formative assessment on learning: A collaboration between curriculum and assessment developers. *Applied Measurement in Education, 21*(4), 295–314.

Sherin, M.G., Jacobs, V., and Philipp, R. (2011). Situating the study of teacher noticing. In M. Sherin, V. Jacobs, and R. Philipp (Eds.), *Mathematics Teacher Noticing: Seeing Through Teachers' Eyes* (pp. 3–15). New York: Routledge.

Shim, S.-Y., Thompson, J., Richards, J., and Vaa, K. (2018). Agree/Disagree T-charts. *Science and Children, 56*(1), 39–47.

Short, J., and Hirsh, S. (2020). *The Elements: Transforming Teaching Through Curriculum-based Professional Learning*. Carnegie Corporation of New York.

Shwe Hadani, H.S., and Rood, E. (2018). *The Roots of STEM Success: Center for Childhood Creativity*. Bay Area Discovery Museum.

Shymansky, J., Annetta, L., Yore, L.D., Wang, T-L., and Everett, S. (2013). The impact of a multiyear systemic reform effort on rural elementary school students' science achievement. *School Science and Mathematics, 113*(2), 69–79.

Shymansky, J.A., Yore, L.D., and Hand, B.M. (2000). Empowering families in hands-on science programs. *School Science and Mathematics, 100*(1), 48–58.

Siegel, M. (2006). Rereading the signs: Multimodal transformations in the field of literacy education. *Language Arts, 84*(1), 65–77.

Sikma, L., and Osborne, M. (2015). Conflicts in developing an elementary STEM magnet school. *Theory into Practice, 53*(1), 4–10.

Silander, M., Grindal, T., Hupert, N., Garcia, E., Anderson, K., Vahey, P., amd Pasnik, S. (2018). *What Parents Talk About When They Talk About Learning: A National Survey About Young Children and Science*. New York, NY, and Menlo Park, CA: Education Development Center, Inc., and SRI International.

Siry, C. (2013). Exploring the complexities of children's inquiries in science: Knowledge production through participatory practices. *Research in Science Education, 43*(6), 2407–2430.

Siry, C., and Gorges, A. (2020). Young students' diverse resources for making meaning in science: Learning from multilingual contexts. *International Journal of Science Education, 42*(14), 2364–2386.

Siry, C., and Lang, D. (2010). Creating participatory discourse for teaching and research in Early childhood science. *Journal of Science Teacher Education, 21*, 149–160.

Siry, C., and Lara, J. (2012). "I didn't know water could be so messy": Coteaching in elementary teacher education and the production of identity for a new teacher of science. *Cultural Studies of Science Education, 7*(1), 1–30.

Siry, C., Wilmes, S.E., and Haus, J.M. (2016). Examining children's agency within participatory structures in primary science investigations. *Learning, Culture and Social Interaction, 10*, 4–16.

Slavin, R., Lake, C., Hanley, P., and Thurston, A. (2014). Experimental evaluations of elementary science programs: A best-evidence synthesis. *Journal of Research in Science Teaching, 51*, 870–901.

Sleeter, C., and Owuor, J. (2011). Research on the impact of teacher preparation to teach diverse students: The research we have and the research we need. *Action in Teacher Education, 33*(5–6), 524–536.

Smetana, L.K., and Bell, R.L. (2012). Computer simulations to support science instruction and learning: A critical review of the literature. *International Journal of Science Education, 34*(9), 1337–1370.

Smith, C.L., Wiser, M., Anderson, C.W., and Krajcik, J. (2006). Implications of research on children's learning for standards and assessment: A proposed learning progression for matter and the atomic-molecular theory. *Measurement: Interdisciplinary Research & Perspective, 4*(1–2), 1–98.

Smith, D., and Jang, S. (2011). Pathways in learning to teach elementary science: Navigating contexts, roles, affordances and constraints. *Journal of Science Teacher Education, 22*(8), 745–768.

Smith, J., and Nadelson, L. (2017). Finding alignment: The perceptions and integration of the Next Generation Science Standards Practices by elementary teachers. *School Science and Mathematics, 117*(5), 194–203.

Smith, P.S. (2020). *2108 NSSME+: Trends in U.S. science education from 2012 to 2018*. Horizon Research, Inc. Available: https://files.eric.ed.gov/fulltext/ED611301.pdf.

Snyder, T.D., de Brey, C., and Dillow, S.A. (2019). *Digest of Education Statistics 2018* (NCES 2020-009). Washington, DC: National Center for Education Statistics, Institute of Education Sciences, U.S. Department of Education.

Snyder, T.D., Dillow, S.A., and Hoffman, C.M. (2009). *Digest of Education Statistics 2008* (NCES 2009-020). Washington, DC: National Center for Education Statistics, Institute of Education Sciences, U.S. Department of Education.

Sobel, D. (2004). *Place-Based Education: Connecting Classrooms and Communities*. Great Barrington, MA: Orion Society.

Sodian, B., Zaitchik, D., and Carey, S. (1991). Young children's differentiation of hypothetical beliefs from evidence. *Child Development, 62*(4), 753–766.

Solano Flores, G. (2016). *Assessing English Language Learners: Theory and Practice*. New York: Routledge.

Songer, N.B., and Gotwals, A.W. (2012). Guiding explanation construction by children at the entry points of learning progressions. *Journal of Research in Science Teaching, 49*(2), 141–165.

Spencer, M.B., Offidani-Bertrand, C., Harris, K., and Velez, G. (2020). Examining links between culture, identity, and learning. In N.S. Nasir, C.D. Lee, R. Pea, and M. McKinney deRoysten (Eds.), *Handbook of the Cultural Foundations of Learning* (pp. 44–61). New York: Routledge.

Spillane, J.P. (2001). Challenging instruction for "all students": Policy, practitioners, and practice. *Yearbook of the National Society for the Study of Education, 100* (Part 2, chapter 11).

Spillane, J.P. (2004). *Standards Deviation: How Schools Misunderstand Education Policy*. Cambridge, MA: Harvard University Press.

Spillane, J.P. (2005). Primary school leadership practice: How the subject matters. *School Leadership and Management, 25*(4), 383–397.

Spillane, J.P., and Hopkins, M. (2013). Organizing for instruction in education systems and school organizations: How the subject matters. *Journal of Curriculum Studies, 45*(6), 721–747.

Spillane, J.P., and Hunt, B.R. (2010). Days of their lives: A mixed–methods, descriptive analysis of the men and women at work in the principal's office. *Journal of Curriculum Studies, 42*(3), 293–331.

Spillane, J.P., Parise, L.M., and Sherer, J.Z. (2011). Organizational routines as coupling mechanisms: Policy, school administration, and the technical core. *American Educational Research Journal, 48*(3), 586–619.

Spillane, J.P., Diamond, J.B., Walker, L.J., Halverson, R., and Jita, L. (2001). Urban school leadership for elementary science instruction: Identifying and activating resources in an undervalued school subject. *Journal of Research in Science Teaching, 38*(8), 918–940.

Steele, A., Brew, C., Rees, C., and Ibrahim-Khan, S. (2013). Our practice, their readiness: Teacher educators collaborate to explore and improve preservice teacher readiness for science and math instruction. *Journal of Science Teacher Education, 24*(1), 111–131.

Stein, M.K., Remillard, J.T., and Smith, M.S. (2007). How curriculum influences student learning. In F.K. Lester, Jr. (Ed.), *Second Handbook of Research on Mathematics Teaching and Learning* (vol. 1, pp. 319–369). Charlotte, NC: Information Age Publishing.

Stevens, R., Wineburg, S., Herrenkohl, L., and Bell, P. (2005). Comparative understanding of school subjects: Past, present, and future. *Review of Educational Research, 75*(2), 125–157.

Stoddart, T., Pinal, A., Latzke, M., and Canaday, D. (2020) Integrating inquiry science and language development for English language learners. *Journal of Research in Science Teaching, 39*(8), 664–687.

Strawhacker, A., and Bers, M.U. (2019). What they learn when they learn coding: Investigating cognitive domains and computer programming knowledge in young children. *Educational Technology Research and Development, 67*(3), 541–575.

Strickler-Eppard, L., Czerniak, C.M., and Kaderavek, J. (2019). Families' capacity to engage in science inquiry at home through structured activities. *Early Childhood Education Journal, 47*(6), 653–664.

Stromholt, S., and Bell, P. (2017). Designing for expansive science learning and identification across settings. *Cultural Studies of Science Education, 13*, 1015–1047.

Stroupe, D. (2014). Examining classroom science practice communities: How teachers and students negotiate epistemic agency and learn science as practice. *Science Education, 98*(3), 487–516.

Suárez, E. (2020). "Estoy Explorando Science": Emergent bilingual students problematizing electrical phenomena through translanguaging. *Science Education, 104*(5), 791–826.

Subramaniam, K. (2013). Examining the content of preservice teachers' reflections of early field experiences. *Research in Science Education, 43*, 1851–1872.

Sullivan-Watts, B., Nowicki, B., Shim, M., and Young, B. (2013). Sustaining reform-based science teaching of preservice and inservice elementary school teachers. *Journal of Science Teacher Education, 24*(5), 879–905.

Sun, M., Wilhelm, A.G., Larson, C.J., and Frank, K.A. (2014). Exploring colleagues' professional influence on mathematics teachers' learning. *Teachers College Record, 116*(6), 305–335.

Sun, Y., and Strobel, J. (2013). Elementary engineering education (EEE) adoption and expertise development framework: An inductive and deductive study. *Journal of Pre-College Engineering Education Research (J-PEER), 3*(1), Article 4.

Taffe, M.A., and Gilpin, N.W. (2021). Equity, diversity and inclusion: Racial inequity in grant funding from the US National Institutes of Health. *eLife, 10*, e65697.

Tai, R.H., Liu, C.Q., Maltese, A.V., and Fan, X. (2006). Planning early for careers in science. *Science, 312*, 1143–1145.
Tate, W. (2001). Science education as a civil right: Urban schools and opportunity-to-learn considerations. *Journal of Research in Science Teaching, 38*(9), 1015–1028.
Thompson, J., Mawyer, K., Johnson, H., Scipio, D., and Luehmann, A. (2020). Culturally and linguistically sustaining approaches to ambitious science teaching pedagogies. In D. Stroupe, K. Hammerness, and S. McDonald (Eds.), *Preparing Science Teachers Through Practice-Based Teacher Education* (pp. 45–62). Cambridge, MA: Harvard Education Press.
Todorova, M., Sunder, C., Steffensky, M., and Moller, K. (2017). Pre-service teachers' professional vision of instructional support in primary science classes: How content-specific is this skill and which learning opportunities in initial teacher education are relevant for its acquisition? *Teaching and Teacher Education, 68*, 275–288.
Trumbull, D.J., Bonney, R., and Grudens Schuck, N. (2005). Developing materials to promote inquiry: Lessons learned. *Science Education, 89*(6), 879–900.
Trygstad, P.J., Malzahn, K.A., Banilower, E.R., Plumley, C.L., and Bruce, A.D. (2020). *Are All Students Getting Equal Access to High-quality Science Education? Data from the 2108 NSSME+*. Horizon Research, Inc.
Tu, T. (2006). Preschool science environment: What is available in a preschool classroom? *Early Childhood Education Journal, 33*(4), 245–251.
Tuck, E., and Yang, K.W. (2012). Decolonization is not a metaphor. *Decolonization: Indigeneity, Education & Society, 1*(1).
Tucker-Raymond, E., Varelas, M., Pappas, C.C., Korzh, A., and Wentland, A. (2007). "They probably aren't named Rachel": Young children's scientist identities as emergent multimodal narratives. *Cultural Studies of Science Education, 1*(3), 559–592.
Turpen, C.A., Radoff, J., Gupta, A., Sabo, H., and Elby, A. (2019). *Examining how Engineering Educators Produce, Reproduce or Challenge Meritocracy and Technocracy in Pedagogical Reasoning*. Paper presented at American Society for Engineering Education Annual Conference & Exposition, Tampa, FL.
Tyack, D., and Cuban, L. (1997). *Tinkering Toward Utopia: A Century of Public School Reform*. Cambridge, MA: Harvard University Press.
Tyler, B., and DiRanna, K. (2018) *Next Generation Science Standards in Practice: Tools and Processes Used By the California NGSS Early Implementers*. WestEd.
Tyler, B., Britton, T., Nilsen, K., Iveland, A., and Nguyen, K. (2019). *Investing in Science Teacher Leadership: Strategies and Impacts in the NGSS Early Implementers Initiative*. WestEd.
Tyler, B., Britton, T., Nguyen, K., Estrella, D., and Arnett, E. (2020). *Six Years of Scaling Up Districtwide Implementations of the Next Generation Science Standards*. WestEd.
Tyler, R.W. (1949). *Basic Principles of Curriculum and Instruction*. Chicago: University of Chicago Press.
Tytler, R., Prain, V., Hubber, P., and Waldrip, B. (Eds.). (2013). *Constructing Representations to Learn in Science*. Rotterdam: Sense Publishers.
Tzou, C., and Bell, P. (2010). *Micros and Me*: Leveraging home and community practices in formal science instruction. In K. Gomez, L. Lyons, and J. Radinsky (Eds.), *9th International Conference of the Learning Sciences* (vol. 1, pp. 1135–1142). Chicago: International Society of the Learning Sciences.
Tzou, C., and Bell, P. (2012). The role of borders in environmental education: Positioning, power, and the paradox of categories. *Ethnography and Education, 7*(2), 265–282.
Tzou, C., Suárez, E., Bell, P., LaBonte, D., Starks, E., and Bang, M. (2019). Storywork in STEM-Art: Making, materiality and robotics within everyday acts of Indigenous presence and resurgence. *Cognitive and Instruction, 37*(3), 306–326.

Upadhyay, B. (2009). Teaching science for empowerment in an urban classroom: A case study of a Hmong teacher. *Equity & Excellence in Education, 42*(2), 217–232.

U.S. Department of Education. (2020). *Fiscal Year 2021 Budget Summary*. Available: https://www2.ed.gov/about/overview/budget/budget21/summary/21summary.pdf.

U.S. Department of Health and Human Services. (2020). *Head Start Early Learning Outcomes Framework*. Available: https://eclkc.ohs.acf.hhs.gov/school-readiness/article/head-start-early-learning-outcomes-framework.

VanFossen, P.J. (2005). "Reading and math take so much of the time…": An overview of social studies instruction in elementary classrooms in Indiana. *Theory & Research in Social Education, 33*(3), 376–403.

Varelas, M., and Pappas, C.C. (2006). Intertextuality in read-alouds of integrated science-literacy units in urban primary classrooms: Opportunities for the development of thought and language. *Cognition and Instruction, 42*, 211–259.

Varelas, M., and Pappas, C.C. (Eds.). (2013). *Children's Ways with Science and Literacy: Integrated Multimodal Enactments in Urban Elementary Classrooms*. Routledge.

Varelas, M., Kane, J.M., and Wylie, C.D. (2011). Young African American children's representations of self, science, and school: Making sense of difference. *Science Education, 95*, 824–851.

Varelas, M., Pappas, C.C., Kane, J.M., Arsenault, A., Hankes, J., and Cowan, B.M. (2008). Urban primary-grade children think and talk science: Curricular and instructional practices that nurture participation and argumentation. *Science Education, 92*(1), 65–95.

Varelas, M., Pappas, C.C., Tucker-Raymond, E., Kane, J., Hankes, J., Ortiz, I., Keblawe-Shamah, N. (2010). Drama activities as ideational resources for primary-grade children in urban science classrooms. *Journal of Research in Science Teaching, 47*(3), 302–325.

Varelas, M., Kane, J.M., Tucker-Raymond, E., and Pappas, C.C. (2012). Science learning in urban elementary school classrooms: Liberatory education and issues of access, participation, and achievement. In B.J. Fraser, K. Tobin, and C. McRobbie (Eds.), *Second International Handbook of Science Education* (pp. 91–103). Dordrecht, The Netherlands: Springer Kluwer.

Varelas, M., Pieper, L., Arsenault, A., Pappas, C.C., and Keblawe-Shamah, N. (2014). How science texts and hands-on explorations facilitate meaning making: Learning from Latina/o third graders. *Journal of Research in Science Teaching, 51*(10), 1246–1274.

Veiga, G., Neto, C., and Rieffe, C. (2016). Preschoolers' free play: Connections with emotional and social functioning. *International Journal of Emotional Education, 8*(1), 48–62.

Verwayne, K.C.D. (2018). Becoming upended: Teaching and learning about race and racism with young children and their families. *Young Children, 73*(2).

Vinner, S., and Hershkowitz, R. (1980). Concept images and common cognitive paths in the development of some simple geometrical concepts. In R. Karplus (Ed.), *Proceedings of the Fourth International Conference for the Psychology of Mathematics Education* (pp. 177–184).

Vo, T., Forbes, C.T., Zangori, L., and Schwarz, C.V. (2015). Fostering third-grade students' use of scientific models with the water cycle: Elementary teachers' conceptions and practices. *International Journal of Science Education, 37*(15), 2411–2432.

Vogler, K.E., Lintner, T., Lipscomb, G.B., Knopf, H., Heafner, T.L., and Rock, T.C. (2007). Getting off the back burner: Impact of testing elementary social studies as part of a state-mandated accountability program. *Journal of Social Studies Research, 31*(2), 20.

Vossoughi, S., and Gutiérrez, K. (2014). Studying movement, hybridity, and change: Toward a multi-sited sensibility for research on learning across contexts and borders. *National Society for the Study of Education, 113*(2), 603–632.

Vygotsky, L.S. (1962). *Thought and Language*. Cambridge, MA: MIT Press.

Vygotsky, L.S. (1980). *Mind in Society: The Development of Higher Psychological Processes*. Cambridge, MA: Harvard University Press.

Wagler, R. (2010). Using science teaching case narratives to evaluate the level of acceptance of scientific inquiry teaching in preservice elementary teachers. *Journal of Science Teacher Education, 21*(2), 215–226.

Wahlstrom, K.L., and Louis, K.S. (2008). How teachers experience principal leadership: The roles of professional community, trust, efficacy, and shared responsibility. *Educational Administration Quarterly, 44*(4), 458–495.

Wallace, C., and Brooks, L. (2015). Learning to teach elementary science in an experiential, informal context: Culture, learning, and identity. *Science Education, 99*, 174–198.

Wallace, C., and Coffey, D. (2019). Investigating elementary preservice teachers' designs for integrated science/literacy instruction highlighting similar cognitive processes. *Journal of Science Teacher Education, 30*(5), 507–527.

Walther, J., Miller, S.E., and Sochacka, N.W. (2017). A model of empathy in engineering as a core skill, practice orientation, and professional way of being. *Journal of Engineering Education, 106*(1), 123–148.

Wang, J., and Sneed, S. (2019). Exploring the design of scaffolding pedagogical instruction for elementary preservice teacher education. *Journal of Science Teacher Education, 30*(5), 483–506.

Warren, B., and Rosebery, A.S. (2011). Navigating interculturality: African American male students and the science classroom. *Journal of African American Males in Education (JAAME), 2*(1), 98–115.

Warren, B., Ballenger, C., Ogonowski, M., Rosebery, A.S., and Hudicourt-Barnes, J. (2001). Rethinking diversity in learning science: The logic of everyday sense-making. *Journal of Research in Science Teaching, 38*(5), 529–552.

Warren, B., Vossoughi, S., Rosebery, A., Bang, M., and Taylor, E. (2020). Multiple ways of knowing: Re-imagining disciplinary learning. In N.S. Nasir, C.D. Lee, R. Pea, and M. McKinney de Royston (Eds.), *Handbook of the Cultural Foundations of Learning* (pp. 277–294). New York: Routledge.

Washinawatok, K., Rasmussen, C., Bang, M., Medin, D., Woodring, J., Waxman, S., Marin, A., Gurneau, J., and Faber, L. (2017). Children's play with a forest diorama as a window into ecological cognition. *Journal of Cognition and Development, 18*(5), 617–632.

Watkins, J., Spencer, K., and Hammer, D. (2014). Examining young students' problem scoping in engineering design. *Journal of Pre-College Engineering Education Research (J-PEER), 4*(1), 5.

Watkins, J., Coffey, J.E., Maskiewicz, A.C., and Hammer, D. (2017). An account of progress in teachers' epistemological framing of science inquiry. In G. Schraw, J. Brownlee, L. Olafson, and M. Vandervelt (Eds.), *Teachers' Personal Epistemologies: Evolving Models for Transforming Practice* (pp. 87–112). Charlotte, NC: Information Age.

Watkins, J., McCormick, M., Wendell, K.B., Spencer, K., Milto, E., Portsmore, M., and Hammer, D. (2018). Data-based conjectures for supporting responsive teaching in engineering design with elementary teachers. *Science Education, 102*(3), 548–570.

Webb, D.L., and LoFaro, K.P. (2020). Sources of engineering teaching self-efficacy in a STEAM methods course for elementary preservice teachers. *School Science & Mathematics, 120*, 209–219.

Weintrop, D., Beheshti, E., Horn, M., Orton, K., Jona, K., Trouille, L., and Wilensky, U. (2016). Defining computational thinking for mathematics and science classrooms. *Journal of Science Education and Technology, 25*(1), 127–147.

Weisberg, D.S., Kittredge, A.K., Hirsh-Pasek, K., Golinkoff, R.M., and Klahr, D. (2015). Making play work for education. *Phi Delta Kappan, 96*(8), 8–13.

Weisberg, D.S., Hirsh-Pasek, K., Golinkoff, R.M., Kittredge, A.K., and Klahr, D. (2016). Guided play: Principles and practices. *Current Directions in Psychological Science, 25*(3), 177–182.

Weiss, I., Pasley, J., Smith, P.S., Banilower, E., and Heck, D. (2003). *Looking Inside the Classroom: A Study of K–12 Mathematics and Science Education in the United States*. Chapel Hill, NC: Horizon Research.

Weller, J. (2019). Primary science preservice teacher (PST) online publishing: Is it recognized as valuable? *Journal of Science Teacher Education, 30*(7), 716–736.

Wendell, K.B., Wright, C.G., and Paugh, P. (2017). Reflective decision-making in elementary students' engineering design. *Journal of Engineering Education, 106*(3), 356–397.

Wendell, K.B., Andrews, C.J., and Paugh, P. (2019). Supporting knowledge construction in elementary engineering design. *Science Education, 103*(4), 952–978.

Wenner, J.A. (2017). Urban elementary science teacher leaders: Responsibilities, supports, and needs. *Science Educator, 25*(2), 117–125.

Wenner, J., and Kittleson, J. (2018). Focused video reflections in concert with practice-based structures to support elementary teacher candidates in learning to teach science. *Journal of Science Teacher Education, 29*(8), 741–759.

Wenner, J.A., and Settlage, J. (2015). School leader enactments of the structure/agency dialectic via buffering. *Journal of Research in Science Teaching, 52*(4), 503–515.

Wertsch, J.V. (1985). *Vygotsky and the Social Formation of Mind*. Cambridge, MA: Harvard University Press.

Wertsch, J.V. (1998). *Mind as Action*. Oxford, UK: Oxford University Press.

Whitehurst, G.J. (2009). *Don't Forget Curriculum*. Brookings Institute. Available: https://www.brookings.edu/wp-content/uploads/2016/06/1014_curriculum_whitehurst.pdf.

Whittaker, J.V., Kinzie, M.B., Williford, A., and DeCoster, J. (2016). Effects of MyTeachingPartner—Math/Science on teacher-child interactions in prekindergarten classrooms. *Early Education and Development, 27*(1), 110–127.

Whittaker, J.V., Kinzie, M.B., Vitiello, V., DeCoster, J., Mulcahy, C., and Barton, E.A. (2020). Impacts of an early childhood mathematics and science intervention on teaching practices and child outcomes. *Journal of Research on Educational Effectiveness, 13*(2), 177–212.

Whitworth, B.A., and Chiu, J.L. (2015). Professional development and teacher change: The missing leadership link. *Journal of Science Teacher Education, 26*(2), 121–137.

Whitworth, B.A., Bell, R.L., Maeng, J.L., and Gonczi, A.L. (2017a). Supporting the supporters: Professional development for science coordinators. *Journal of Science Teacher Education, 28*(8), 699–723.

Whitworth, B.A., Maeng, J.L., Wheeler, L.B., and Chiu, J.L. (2017b). Investigating the role of a district science coordinator. *Journal of Research in Science Teaching, 54*(7), 914–937.

Willard, A.K., Busch, J.T., Cullum, K.A., Letourneau, S.M., Sobel, D.M., Callanan, M., and Legare, C.H. (2019). Explain this, explore that: A study of parent–child interaction in a children's museum. *Child Development, 90*(5), e598–e617.

Wilson, R.E., and Bradbury, L.U. (2016). The pedagogical potential of drawing and writing in a primary science multimodal unit. *International Journal of Science Education, 38*(17), 2621–2641.

Wilson, R., and Kittleson, J. (2012). The role of struggle in pre-service elementary teachers' experiences as students and approaches to facilitating science learning. *Research in Science Education, 42*, 709–728.

Windschitl, M., Thompson, J., and Braaten, M. (2008). Beyond the scientific method: Model-based inquiry as a new paradigm of preference for school science investigations. *Science Education, 92*(5), 941–967.

Windschitl, M., Thompson, J., and Braaten, M. (2018). *Ambitious Science Teaching*. Boston, MA: Harvard Education Press.

Windschitl, M., Thompson, J., Braaten, M., and Stroupe., D. (2012). Proposing a core set of instructional practices and tools for teachers of science. *Science Education*, *96*(5), 878–903.

Wing, J.M. (2006). Computational thinking. *Communications of the ACM*, *49*(3), 33–35.

Winokur, J., and Worth, K. (2006). Talk in the science classroom: Looking at what students and teachers need to know and be able to do. In R. Douglas, M.P. Klentschy, K. Worth, and W. Binder (Eds.), *Linking Science & Literacy in the K–8 Classroom* (pp. 43–58). Arlington, VA: NSTA Press.

Wiser, M., and Smith, C.L. (2009). Learning and teaching about matter in grades K–8: When should the atomic-molecular theory be introduced? In S. Vosniadou (Ed.), *International Handbook of Research on Conceptual Change* (pp. 233–267). New York: Routledge.

Wohlwend, K.E., Peppler, K.A., Keune, A., and Thompson, N. (2017). Making sense and nonsense: Comparing mediated discourse and agential realist approaches to materiality in a preschool makerspace. *Journal of Early Childhood Literacy*, *17*(3), 444–462.

Wonch Hill, P., McQuillan, J., Hebets, E.A., Spiegel, A.N., and Diamond, J. (2020). Informal science experiences among urban and rural youth: Exploring differences at the intersections of socioeconomic status, gender and ethnicity. *Journal of STEM Outreach*, *1*(1), 10.

Worth, K. (2010). Science in early childhood classrooms: Content and process. *Early Childhood Research and Practice (ECRP)*, *12*(2), 2184–1489.

Wortham, S., Kim, D., and May, S. (Eds.) (2017). *Discourse and Education*. New York: Springer.

Wright, C.G. (2019). Constructing a collaborative critique-learning environment for exploring science through improvisational performance. *Urban Education*, *54*(9), 1319–1348.

Wright, C.G., Wendell, K.B., and Paugh, P.P. (2018). "Just put it together to make no commotion:" Re-imagining urban elementary students' participation in engineering design practices. *International Journal of Education in Mathematics, Science and Technology (IJEMST)*, *6*(3), 285–301.

Wright, T.S., and Gotwals, A.W. (2017). Supporting kindergartners' science talk in the context of an integrated science and disciplinary literacy curriculum. *Elementary School Journal*, *117*(3), 513–537.

Xu, Y., and Warschauer, M. (2020). "Elinor Is Talking to Me on the Screen!" Integrating conversational agents into children's television programming. In *Extended Abstracts of the 2020 CHI Conference on Human Factors in Computing Systems* (pp. 1–8).

Yang, H.T., and Wang, K.H. (2014). A teaching model for scaffolding 4th grade students' scientific explanation writing. *Research in Science Education*, *44*(4), 531–548.

Yin, R.K. (2008). The Math and Science Partnership program evaluation: Overview of the first two years. *Peabody Journal of Education*, *83*(4), 486–508.

Yüce, K., Şahin, E.Y., Koçer, Ö., and Kana, F. (2013). Motivations for choosing teaching as a career: A perspective of pre-service teachers from a Turkish context. *Asia Pacific Education Review*, *14*, 295–306.

Zangori, L., and Forbes, C.T. (2014). Scientific practices in elementary classrooms: Third-grade students' scientific explanations for seed structure and function. *Science Education*, *98*(4), 614–639.

Zangori, L., and Pinnow, R.J. (2020). Positioning participation in the NGSS era: What counts as success? *Journal of Research in Science Teaching*, *57*(4), 623–648.

Zangori, L., Forbes, C., and Biggers, M. (2013). Fostering student sense making in elementary science learning environments: Elementary teachers' use of science curriculum materials to promote explanation construction. *Journal of Research in Science Teaching*, *50*(8), 989–1017.

Zangori, L., Forbes, C.T., and Schwarz, C.V. (2015). Exploring the effect of embedded scaffolding within curricular tasks on third-grade students' model-based explanations about hydrologic cycling. *Science & Education, 24*(7), 957–981.

Zangori, L., Friedrichsen, P., Wulff, E., and Womack, A. (2017a). Using the practice of modeling to support preservice teachers' reflection on the process of teaching and learning. *Journal of Science Teacher Education, 28*(7), 590–608.

Zangori, L., Vo, T., Forbes, C.T., and Schwarz, C.V. (2017b). Supporting 3rd-grade students' model-based explanations about groundwater: A quasi-experimental study of a curricular intervention. *International Journal of Science Education, 39*(11), 1421–1442.

Zangori, L., Ke, L., Sadler, T., and Peel, A. (2020). *Supporting Elementary Learners to Explore Causal Interaction Patterns*. ISLS. Available: https://repository.isls.org/bitstream/1/6690/1/541-544.pdf.

Zembal-Saul, C. (2009). Learning to teach elementary school science as argument. *Science Education, 93*(4), 687–719.

Zembal-Saul, C., and Hershberger, K. (2020). Positioning students at the center of sensemaking: Productive grappling with data. In E.A. Davis, C. Zembal-Saul, and S. M. Kademian (Eds.), *Sensemaking in Elementary Science: Supporting Teacher Learning* (pp. 15–30). New York: Routledge.

Zembal-Saul, C., Carlone, H., and Brown, M. (2020). A possibility-centric vision of elementary teachers and ambitious science teaching. In D. Stroupe, K. Hammerness, and S. McDonald (Eds), *Preparing Science Teachers through Practice-based Teacher Education* (pp. 117–132). Cambridge, MA: Harvard University Press.

Zembal-Saul, C., McNeill, K., and Hershberger, K. (2013). *What's your evidence?: Engaging K–5 students in constructing explanations in science*. Boston: Pearson Education.

Zembal-Saul, C., Badiali, B., Mueller, B., and McDyre, A. (2020). Learning to teach science in an elementary professional development school partnership. In E.A. Davis, C. Zembal-Saul, and S. M. Kademian (Eds.), *Sensemaking in Elementary Science: Supporting Teacher Learning*. New York: Routledge.

Zembal-Saul, C., Siry, C., Monteira, S. and Bose, F.N. (in press). Preparing early childhood teachers to support young children's equitable science sensemaking.

Zhang, J., Scardamalia, M., Reeve, R., and Messina, R. (2009). Designs for collective cognitive responsibility in knowledge-building communities. *Journal of the Learning Sciences, 18*(1), 7–44.

Zimmerman, C., and Klahr, D. (2018). Development of scientific thinking. In J.T. Wixted (Ed.), *Stevens' Handbook of Experimental Psychology and Cognitive Neuroscience* (Vol. 4, pp. 1–25). New York: John Wiley & Sons, Inc.

Zoltowski, C.B., Oakes, W.C., and Cardella, M.E. (2012). Students' ways of experiencing human-centered design. *Journal of Engineering Education, 101*(1), 28–59.

Appendix

Biosketches of Committee Members and Staff

ELIZABETH A. (BETSY) DAVIS (*Chair*) is a professor at the University of Michigan's School of Education. Her research focuses on beginning and experienced elementary teachers, teachers learning to engage in rigorous and consequential science teaching, and the roles of curriculum materials and practice-based teacher education in promoting teacher learning. She was the chair for the Elementary Teacher Education Program at the University of Michigan for 4 years and helped lead the reshaping and redesign of this practice-based program. Davis received the Presidential Early Career Award for Scientists and Engineers at the White House in 2002 and the Jan Hawkins Early Career Award in 2004. She was a member of the National Academies of Sciences, Engineering, and Medicine Committee on Strengthening Science Education through a Teacher Learning Continuum and the Workshop Planning Committee on Design, Selection, and Implementation of Instructional Materials for the Next Generation Science Standards. Davis earned a B.S.E. in engineering and management systems at Princeton University and an M.A. and Ph.D. in education in mathematics, science, and technology from the University of California, Berkeley.

HEIDI CARLONE is the Katherine Johnson Chair of Science Education in the Peabody College at Vanderbilt University. She was previously the Hooks Distinguished Professor of STEM Education in the Department of Teacher Education and Higher Education at The University of North Carolina at Greensboro. She is a teacher educator and educational researcher who works to make science and engineering pathways more accessible and equitable for historically underserved and under-represented populations.

Her work leverages insights from research and practice. Her current work focuses on three primary questions: (1) How can innovative K–8 science and engineering instruction cultivate more meaningful and expansive learning outcomes (e.g., STEM identities) for diverse youth? (2) How can we enrich K–8 diverse youths' science and engineering learning ecologies in sustainable ways? (3) How can we design professional learning networks to support, nurture, and celebrate rigorous and equitable science and engineering teaching and retain excellent teachers in high needs schools? She has received a number of awards in her academic career, including the UNCG Alumni Teaching Excellence Award; the Early Career Research Award from the National Association for Research in Science Teaching; and the Early Career Development Award (CAREER) from the National Science Foundation. Carlone received her Ph.D. in instruction and curriculum from the University of Colorado Boulder.

JEANANE CHARARA is a professional development provider and K–2 science coach with the SOLID Start research project at Michigan State University. She also is currently a peer reviewer on WestEd's NextGenScience Peer Review Panel and is an EQuIP Science Leader. She evaluates science curriculum and determines their alignment to the Next Generation Science Standards (NGSS), as well as provides professional development on how to use the EQuIP rubric. She also works as an NGSX elementary pathway designer. Chahara was previously an elementary STEAM coach for Dearborn, Michigan, Public Schools, where she provided professional development to K–5 teachers and helped guide teacher pedagogies to more equitable science teaching practices and NGSS-aligned instruction. She also coached K–5 teachers by providing them with support in the science classroom and allowing them opportunities to demonstrate effective science instruction. She has formerly taught as an elementary teacher and was the distance learning coordinator at the Michigan Science Center. Charara has a B.S. in elementary education with a focus in integrated sciences from Wayne State University and an M.Ed. in education with an emphasis on teaching English as a second or foreign language from Spring Arbor University.

DOUGLAS H. CLEMENTS is distinguished university professor, Kenney endowed chair in early childhood learning, and co-executive director of the Marsico Institute at University of Denver's Morgridge College of Education. Previously, he worked as a kindergarten teacher for 5 years and a preschool teacher for 1 year and has since conducted research and published widely in the areas of (1) the learning and teaching of early mathematics and STEM; (2) computer applications in mathematics education; (3) creating, using, and evaluating research-based curricula in STEM and in taking successful curricula to scale using technologies and learning trajectories;

(4) development and evaluation of innovative assessments of mathematics achievement, as well as mathematics teaching; and (5) interdisciplinary and inclusive approaches to STEM subjects. Prior to his appointment at the University of Denver, he was a State University of New York (SUNY) distinguished professor at the University of Buffalo. Clements received his Ph.D. in elementary education from SUNY at Buffalo.

KATIE MCMILLAN CULP is the chief learning officer at the New York Hall of Science (NYSCI). In this role, she oversees the design, development, and implementation of NYSCI's exhibits, programs, and youth development initiatives. She also leads NYSCI's research and development team, which studies STEM learning among highly diverse populations in complex informal learning environments. Culp has also served as the director of research for the U.S. Department of Education-funded Regional Educational Laboratory for the Northeast and Islands, and directed many program evaluations focused on technology-rich STEM learning while working as a research scientist at Education Development Center, Inc. Her research has been funded by the National Science Foundation, the Bill & Melinda Gates Foundation, the U.S. Department of Education, and the Intel Foundation. Culp is a Phi Beta Kappa graduate of Amherst College and holds a Ph.D. in developmental psychology from Teachers College, Columbia University.

XIMENA DOMÍNGUEZ is the director of early STEM research at Digital Promise. Her research focuses on young children's science, technology, engineering, and mathematics (STEM) learning across home and school and involves partnerships with public preschool educators, curriculum developers, media designers and families from historically underserved communities to co-design equitable learning experiences for young children. In addition to studying how science and mathematics can be promoted early in childhood, her current work investigates how engineering and computational thinking can be introduced to support play and early learning and explores how STEM domains can be feasibly and meaningfully integrated in preschool classrooms. Her work also involves developing resources for multilingual learners and explores the affordances of technology and media for supporting early STEM teaching and learning. Her work has been funded by the National Science Foundation, the Institute of Education Sciences, and philanthropic foundations. Domínguez earned an M.S.Ed. in education from the University of Pennsylvania and a Ph.D. in applied developmental psychology from the University of Miami.

DARYL GREENFIELD is a professor of psychology and pediatrics at the University of Miami. He served as a member of the Expert Panel for the Canadian Institutes of Health Research's Networks of Centers of Excellence in Early Childhood Development and Society; an advisor for the Pan American Health Organization; a technical adviser for early science for each of the three funded statewide KEA Consortia (led by Maryland, North Carolina, and Texas) to create greater continuity between early childhood and the early elementary grades; and an adviser to the Office of Head Start for the new Head Start Early Learning Outcomes Framework (Birth to Five). He is currently a principal investigator on federally and privately funded research grants to develop and evaluate early childhood STE programs and with prior federal funding developed and evaluated equated touch screen computer adaptive preschool science assessments, for both English and Spanish speaking young children. He currently serves as the early childhood STE advisor for the Head Start National Center on Early Child Development, Teaching and Learning, the National Center on Parent, Family and Community Engagement, and the National STEM Innovation for Inclusion in Early Education Center. Greenfield received his Ph.D. in developmental psychology from the University of Connecticut.

MEGAN HOPKINS is an associate professor of education studies at the University of California, San Diego (UCSD). Before joining UCSD, she held faculty appointments at the Pennsylvania State University and University of Illinois at Chicago. In studies funded by the U.S. Department of Education's Office of English Language Acquisition, the Spencer Foundation, and the W.T. Grant Foundation, she has investigated the implementation of language policies and English language development course placement policies, as well as content-specific curricular reforms. She has also engaged in context-embedded teacher professional development focused on fostering science learning opportunities for multilingual learners in the early elementary grades. Her scholarship has appeared in several top-tier journals, including *American Educational Research Journal*, *Educational Researcher*, and *Journal of Teacher Education*, and she is coeditor of the volumes *Forbidden Language: English Learners and Restrictive Language Policies* and *School Integration Matters: Research-Based Strategies to Advance Equity*. In 2012, she received the Dissertation of the Year Award from the Bilingual Education Research Special Interest Group of the American Educational Research Association. In 2016, she was selected as a National Academy of Education/Spencer Foundation Postdoctoral Fellow. She served on the National Academies of Sciences, Engineering, and Medicine consensus committee that authored the report *English Learners in STEM Subjects: Transforming Classrooms, Schools, and Lives* (2018). Hopkins received her Ph.D. in education at the University of California, Los Angeles.

MARGARET KELLY is a senior program assistant for the National Academies of Sciences, Engineering, and Medicine Board on Science Education.

Margaret has more than 20 years of experience working in the administrative field. She has worked for the private sector, federal government and non-profit organizations, including American University, Catholic University, the Census Bureau, International Franchise Association, the Department of Defense and the University of the District of Columbia. Kelly has received numerous professional honors and awards throughout her career, including a Citizenship/Spirit Award; a Teamwork/Collaboration Award; a Superior Performance of Customer Service Award; Sustained Superior Performance Cash Awards; and Air Force Organizational Excellence Awards and Certificates of Appreciations.

EVE MANZ is assistant professor of science education at the Boston University Wheelock College of Education & Human Development. Her research focuses on understanding how to design and orchestrate learning environments that apprentice young students into science practices, such as modeling, argumentation, and explanation. She works closely with elementary teachers and instructional leaders to develop approaches to science teaching and learning that center student and teacher sensemaking, which includes understanding elementary teaching and learning as part of a multicontent area system to better support classroom instruction within and across the content areas of science, English language arts, and mathematics. Her work has been funded by the James S. McDonnell Foundation, the George Lucas Educational Foundation, and a CAREER grant from the National Science Foundation. She is the recipient of the 2019 Early Career Research Award from the National Association for Research in Science Teaching. Manz received her Ph.D. in mathematics and science education from Vanderbilt University.

TIFFANY NEILL is the deputy superintendent of curriculum and instruction for the Oklahoma State Board of Education and the past president for the Council of State Science Supervisors. She is a member of the National Science Foundation STEM Advisory Panel, an active advisory board member for Carnegie's OpenSciEd Project and EdReports for Science. She also serves as co-principal investigator for Advancing Coherent and Equitable Systems of Science. Prior to her current role, Neill served as the executive director of curriculum and instruction for 3 years and as the director of science and engineering education for 5 years at the Oklahoma State Department of Education. She began her career in education as a middle and high school teacher. She served on the National Academies of Sciences, Engineering, and Medicine consensus committee that authored the report *Changing Expectations for the K–12 Teacher Workforce: Policies, Preservice Education, Professional Development, and the Workplace* (2020). Neill is completing a Ph.D. in instructional leadership and academic curriculum in science education at the University of Oklahoma.

K. RENAE PULLEN is an elementary science specialist for Caddo Parish Public Schools in Shreveport, Louisiana. Besides being a dedicated science educator, she has served on several local, state, and national committees as well as presented at numerous workshops and conferences. Pullen was a consulting expert for the National Academies of Sciences, Engineering, and Medicine's practitioner's guide, *Seeing Students Learn Science: Integrating Assessment and Instruction in the Classroom,* and served on the National Academies' committee that produced *English Learners in STEM Subjects: Transforming Classrooms, Schools, and Lives.* She is currently a member of the National Academies' Board on Science Education, serves on the National Science Foundation's STEM Education Advisory Panel, and is a National STEM Ambassador for the National Science Teaching Association/National Council of Teachers of Mathematics. Pullen received an M.Ed. in education leadership from Louisiana State University in Shreveport and is certified as a teacher leader by the state of Louisiana.

WILLIAM SANDOVAL is a professor in the Division of Urban Schooling in the Graduate School of Education & Information Studies at the University of California, Los Angeles, and is also the faculty director of the school's Educational Leadership Program. His primary research interest is in how children understand the nature of scientific knowledge and its production and how to promote their understanding through epistemically rich teaching. He is particularly focused on how school can improve public understanding and engagement with science. He has published widely in the learning sciences, science education, and educational psychology on epistemic cognition and student and teacher learning. He has served as an associate editor of *Journal of the Learning Sciences* and is on their editorial board as well as the boards of *Cognition & Instruction, Educational Psychologist,* and *Science Education* and *Journal for Research in Science Teaching.* He is a fellow and past president of the International Society of the Learning Sciences, a fellow of the International Society for Design & Development in Education, and a member of the American Educational Research Association, National Association for Research in Science Teaching, National Science Teaching Association, and the American Psychological Association. Sandoval received his Ph.D. in learning sciences from Northwestern University.

HEIDI SCHWEINGRUBER is the director of the Board on Science Education at the National Academies of Sciences, Engineering, and Medicine. She has served as study director or co-study director for a wide range of studies, including those on revising national standards for K–12 science education, learning and teaching science in grades K–8, and mathematics learning in early childhood. She also coauthored two award-winning books for practitioners that translate findings of National Academies' reports for a broader audience, on using research in K–8 science classrooms and on informal science education. Prior to joining the National Academies, she worked as a senior research associate at the Institute of Education Sciences in the U.S. Department of Education. She also previously served on the faculty of Rice University and as the director of research for the Rice University School Mathematics Project, an outreach program in K–12 mathematics education. Schweingruber has a Ph.D. in psychology (developmental) and anthropology and a certificate in culture and cognition, both from the University of Michigan.

AMY STEPHENS (*Study Director*) is a senior program officer for the Board on Science Education of the National Academies of Sciences, Engineering, and Medicine. She is an adjunct professor for the Southern New Hampshire University Psychology Department, teaching graduate-level online courses in cognitive psychology and statistics. She has an extensive background in behavioral and functional neuroimaging techniques and has examined a variety of different populations spanning childhood through adulthood. She was the study director for the workshop on *Graduate Training in the Social and Behavioral Sciences* and recently released consensus reports *English Learners in STEM Subjects: Transforming Classrooms, Schools, and Lives* (2018), *Changing Expectations for the K–12 Workforce: Policies, Preservice Education, Professional Development, and the Workplace* (2020), and *Cultivating Interest and Competencies in Computing: Authentic Experiences and Design Factors* (2021). Stephens holds a Ph.D. in cognitive neuroscience from Johns Hopkins University and was a postdoctoral research fellow at the Center for Talented Youth and the university's School of Education.

ENRIQUE SUÁREZ is an assistant professor of science education at University of Massachusetts, Amherst. He is committed to making science learning equitable for students and teachers, emphasizing the importance of knowing about the natural world through investigation. Drawing on a range of learning theories, Suárez works in partnership with K–12 schools and communities to make science learning more equitable for learners from historically underserved communities. Specifically, his research focuses on designing learning environments that create opportunities for elementary-age emerging multilingual students to leverage their conceptual resources and translanguaging practices for learning science. He has extensive experience teaching elementary science methods courses, co-designing and co-facilitating professional development for K–12 science teachers, and developing physics-based K–12 curriculum. He is an astrophysicist who did cosmology research for 5 years before choosing a career in K–5 science education. Suárez holds a B.S. in astrophysics from the University of Oklahoma, an M.S. in science education from Tufts University, and a Ph.D. on curriculum and instruction–science education from the University of Colorado Boulder.

TIFFANY E. TAYLOR is currently a program officer for the Board on Science Education at the National Academies of Sciences, Engineering, and Medicine. In this role, she provides research, planning, and management support for several ongoing projects including the Standing Committee on Advancing Science Communication and the Symposium on the Future of Undergraduate STEM Education. Additionally, she is co-leading an expert study requested by NASA on Increasing Diversity and Inclusion in the Leadership of Competed Space Missions, in collaboration with the Space Studies Board. She is extremely passionate about the inclusion of persons of diverse background in science and aspires to leverage her Ph.D. training and science policy experience to address education equity within society, in both domestic and global settings. She came to the National Academies as a Christine Mirzayan Science and Technology Policy fellow in 2017. Taylor received her bachelor's degree in biology from Howard University and her Ph.D. in biomedical sciences from the University of California, San Diego.

CARRIE TZOU is a professor in science education in the School of Educational Studies and the director of the Goodlad Institute for Educational Renewal at the University of Washington Bothell. Her work applies sociocultural theories of learning and identity formation and methods from anthropology, psychology, and design-based research to understand how best to support learners' STEM-linked identities and center their cultural and linguistic resources within the context of science and environmental science learning. She focuses on desettling normative Western views and epistemologies of science, emphasizing the need to invite a heterogeneity of knowledge systems into all learning settings. This entails co-designing learning settings with multiple stakeholders (formal and informal educators, community organizations, families, and youth) that seek to make visible and center this heterogeneity, connecting learners' identities and cultural practices to STEAM learning. Tzou holds an M.S. in teaching and learning with a concentration in science education from Vanderbilt University and a Ph.D. in learning sciences from Northwestern University.

PETER J. WINZER joined Bell Labs (Holmdel, NJ, USA) in 2000 and from 2010 to 2019 headed Bell Labs' Optical Transmission Systems Research, first locally in NJ and then globally. His work has focused on all aspects of high-speed fiber-optic communications and networking, from opto-electronic devices and transmission systems to network architectures and network security. His research has significantly shaped the optical networking industry, including the optical portfolio of Lucent Technologies, Alcatel-Lucent, and Nokia, as well as the high-end test and measurement instrument market. In 2020, Winzer founded the VC-backed integrated optical communications start-up company Nubis Communications. He received multiple awards for his work, most notably the 2018 John Tyndall Award. He is a Clarivate Highly-Cited Researcher, a Bell Labs fellow, a fellow of Optical Society of America and of Institute of Electrical and Electronics Engineers, an elected member of the U.S. National Academy of Engineering, and holds an honorary doctorate from the Technical University of Eindhoven, The Netherlands. Winzer received his Ph.D. from the Vienna University of Technology, Austria.

CARLA ZEMBAL-SAUL holds the Kahn endowed professorship in STEM education at Pennsylvania State University. She is an educational researcher, science teacher educator, and biologist. Her work is situated in school–university–community partnerships in the United States and abroad. Her research investigates how preservice and practicing elementary teachers learn to engage children's equitable sensemaking in science through participation in disciplinary discourses and practices. Zembal-Saul's most recent work is situated in a semi-urban community undergoing rapid demographic shifts with teachers and other education professionals who work with emergent bilingual students and their families. She has been recognized for her scholarship in a number of ways: National Science Teaching Association fellow, Penn State College of Education Outstanding Faculty Member Award, Penn State Provost's Award for Collaboration, and National Science Foundation Early Career Development Award. She served on the National Academies of Sciences, Engineering, and Medicine's Board on Science Education consensus committee that authored the report, *Science Teachers' Learning: Enhancing Opportunities, Creating Supporting Contexts* (2015). Zembal-Saul received her Ph.D. in science education from the University of Michigan.